The Page Fence Giants

D1220658

The Page Fence Giants

A History of Black Baseball's Pioneering Champions

MITCH LUTZKE

McFarland & Company, Inc., Publishers

Jefferson, North Carolina

LIBRARY OF CONGRESS CATALOGUING-IN-PUBLICATION DATA

Names: Lutzke, Mitch, author.
Title: The Page Fence Giants : a history of Black baseball's
pioneering champions / Mitch Lutzke.
Description: Jefferson, North Carolina : McFarland & Company, Inc.,
Publishers, 2018. | Includes bibliographical references and index.
Identifiers: LCCN 2018011633 | ISBN 9781476671659
(softcover : acid free paper) ∞
Subjects: LCSH: Page Fence Giants (Baseball team)—History. |
White, Sol, 1868– | African American baseball players—Biography. |
African American baseball players—Michigan—History. |
Baseball—United States—History.
Classification: LCC GV875.P35 L87 2018 | DDC 796.357092 [B]—dc23
LC record available at https://lccn.loc.gov/2018011633

BRITISH LIBRARY CATALOGUING DATA ARE AVAILABLE

ISBN (print) 978-1-4766-7165-9
ISBN (ebook) 978-1-4766-3273-5

© 2018 Mitch Lutzke. All rights reserved

No part of this book may be reproduced or transmitted in any form
or by any means, electronic or mechanical, including photocopying
or recording, or by any information storage and retrieval system,
without permission in writing from the publisher.

Front cover: Cabinet card photograph
of the 1896 Page Fence Giants baseball team (C.A. Buss)

Printed in the United States of America

McFarland & Company, Inc., Publishers
Box 611, Jefferson, North Carolina 28640
www.mcfarlandpub.com

To my wonderful family
and to all of those involved
in putting the Page Fence Giants
on the baseball diamond,
including the players, team management
and the wonderful Adrian baseball cranks

Table of Contents

Acknowledgments

There are so many people who helped me finish this project, which I initially stumbled into while working on a local history book. First, my wife, Karen, and daughter, Laura, who left me to my own devices at home in researching and writing this book, and my sons, Matt and Greg, who live across town, also supported dad on this third book, and my mom, who offered her input during the entire process.

Next, I would like to thank all of the lovers of this sport and particularly "colored" baseball enthusiasts. It seemed as if every time I mentioned I was writing a book on the Page Fence Giants, they offered both resources and joy that this team was finally going to be the focus of their own book. On this list were Larry Lester, Leslie Heaphy, James Brunson, Jeremy Krock, Ryan Whirty, Todd Peterson, Ray Doswell, Jacob Pomrenke, Gary Ashwill, Gary Gillette and Peter Morris.

Those in the research departments of the libraries and historical societies I contacted saved me a lot of time and money in running down some of my leads. First, Jan Richardi and Jim Path at the Lenawee County Historical Society and Shirley Ennis, Heidi Neil and Cathy Chesher at the Adrian District Library found things for me and went out of their way to do extra research on this project. In the same category was Mike Roys at the Hudson (Michigan) Museum, Claudette Scrafford at the National Baseball Hall of Fame, John Timothy Fiest at Central Michigan University Clarke Historical Library, Justin Crawfis at the Hancock County-Findlay Branch Library, Debbie Ruth at the Grant County Public Library in Marion, Indiana, Mark Bowden at the Burton Historical Library in Ann Arbor, Joy Bennett of the Hancock County (Ohio) Historical Museum, Matt Pacer of the Library of Michigan, Sarah McLusky at the Bentley Historical Library, Nichole Manlove at the Charles H. Wright Museum of African American History in Detroit, David McCracken, Gratiot County historian, and Mike Johnson, a big PFC fan. I also spent many hours at the State of Michigan Library, and I want to thank that staff for a neat and organized place to do research. I hope I didn't miss anyone along the way, but if I did, you are included in my thanks.

My tour of the Negro League Baseball Museum in Kansas City in the summer of 2016 as part of the Society of American Baseball Research (SABR) and the Jerry Malloy Negro Baseball Conference was a wonderfully enjoyable and learning experience for both this book and me, personally. A tip of the hat goes to the conference organizers and everyone who supports SABR and the NLBM.

Along the way, I met Adrian College professor Michael Neal, whose movie project on Bud Fowler and his role with organizing the Page Fence Giants led to me appearing in the movie and spreading my knowledge of this wonderful team. It was a fun time and now we're linked for life.

The feedback from reading portions of the manuscript or just hearing me think aloud made my book better, and for that I thank high school colleagues Ray Herek and Tom Hampton, retired Lenawee County Historical Society curator Dr. Charles Lindquist for reviewing the Adrian chapter, and national baseball historians Peter Morris and Leslie Heaphy. I also want to thank all my Williamston friends, co-workers and students, who throughout this book project lent me a friendly ear.

Preface

For those seeking a way to place the Page Fence Giants on the black baseball continuum, the task is a difficult one. Figuring out why no one has ever written a book on this championship baseball team may be a bit easier to discern. Here are my thoughts as to why this team has been ignored throughout baseball history.

Playing in Adrian, Michigan, a small Midwestern town, they were stuck between the big city teams from Chicago and the Eastern powerhouse Cuban Giants and Cuban X Giants. While baseball had been played in Michigan since the time of the Civil War, the state's most influential city, Detroit, mostly ignored the team for the first two years of the Giants' existence. Unlike today, where about 90 percent of Detroit consists of black residents, during the 1890s that population demographic numbered only a few thousand. So news coverage from the state's most prominent city was left to a white-owned newspaper in a still mostly white town.

Adrian may seem to have been an odd choice for this powerhouse all-star black baseball squad. Michigan wasn't exactly a bastion of black baseball. As Peter Morris noted in his book *Baseball Fever: Early Baseball in Michigan*, Detroit, Battle Creek, Niles and Jackson all fielded black teams, briefly, at one time or another. Morris discovered a game featuring an all-black club as early as 1867 in Detroit. However, black baseball didn't then suddenly explode in Michigan, as Morris was able to locate only five games which involved an all-black team during the next decade.

An article written a few years ago by Keith Howard for the Kalamazoo Public Library noted that that city had fielded a few all-black teams on and off beginning in the late 1880s to about 1901. One team was known as the Kalamazoo Browns, but they were more known for travelling around the countryside and beating pick-up teams of amateurs. They were not traveling far distances to slug it out with professional ball clubs. Simply put, a Michigan-based black baseball team was a rare occurrence.

At the time of the Page Fence Giants' formalization in 1894, integrated baseball was still being played around the country. The year before the Giants, Adrian fielded an integrated team (the Light Guard) and played against at least one other such club. While many draw the end of the baseball segregation line with Jackie Robinson's entrance in 1947 with the Brooklyn Dodgers, that is historically inaccurate. Close followers of baseball know the names of Bud Fowler, George Stovey, Sol White, and the brothers Weldy and Moses Fleetwood Walker, just to name a few, as black men who played on professional white baseball clubs in the 1880s and 1890s.

There was even a failed attempt at making money off the burgeoning sport of baseball and fielding an all-black league in the late 1880s. The League of Colored Baseball Clubs was launched for a few weeks in 1887. It was an ambitious goal toward capitalizing on the country's growing love of baseball and to cater to rabid black spectators. The league lasted less than a month before financial issues doomed this progressive business model.

When Bud Fowler's grandiose and latest baseball scheme was revealed in the summer of 1894, the Page Fence Giants emerged. This club wouldn't be confined to playing the adjacent villages of Lenawee County for their competition. Instead, they would venture across a dozen Midwestern states and Ontario, Canada, all while traveling in an expensively and palatially furnished train car. A pre-game bike parade and singing and clowning on the ball field became part of the Page Fence Giants show, similar to the Harlem Globetrotters of later basketball fame. While this all-star contingent of black men would play against town clubs, they also spent a sizable portion of their schedule facing major league, minor league and semi-professional teams, some armed with hired ringers to attempt to defeat the mighty Giants.

The two main players, both literally and figuratively, in creating the Page Fence Giants were Fowler and Grant Johnson, both black men playing on the integrated Findlay (Ohio) Sluggers baseball club. Their selection of Adrian, Michigan, came following a pair of games in August of 1894, in which the southeastern Michigan community was regaling in their self-crowned designation as the baseball capital of the state. Fowler had been involved in many baseball-playing schemes in his two-plus decades of traveling the country. He looked for ball clubs that could promise fair pay and an opportunity to compete against the best players, both black and white. The idea was embraced by a few prominent business and political officials in Adrian, and the Page Fence Giants were born. The team name combined reference to sponsor J. Wallace Page's fence company, with "The Giants," the go-to team name for many black ball teams in the late 19th century.

A key to the team, and uncommon for the time, was the solid financial backing of the club, courtesy of farmer turned business mogul J. Wallace Page. The Civil War veteran had spent years developing a woven wire fence designed to compete with the much sharper barbed wire. His money made the Giants a unique company marketing tool to be showcased in towns, along with samples, from the local fence sales agents, of the Page Fence product. In his movie, "Bud Fowler and the Page Fence Giants," director Michael Neal of Adrian College spoke with Dr. Raymond Doswell, Vide-President of Curatorial Services at the Negro League Baseball Museum in Kansas City, Missouri. Dr. Doswell stated that J. Wallace Page's steady financial backing was key to allowing the team to compete and travel. Those finances allowed the Page Fence club to complete their four seasons without running out of money, which, as the movie notes, was not the case for the two major, East Coast rivals— the Cuban Giants and the Cuban X Giants. Not to be ignored, the Page Fence Giants' lavishly outfitted and staffed Monarch train car certainly added to the team's ballplaying mystique.

Despite the fact that these Giants established a wonderful win/loss record and included National Baseball Hall of Famer King Soloman "Sol" White on its 1895 club, along with some of the biggest baseball stars at the time—namely Bud Fowler, Grant "Home Run" Johnson and George Wilson—there has never been a book written about the Page Fence Giants. Interestingly, White may have contributed to the ignoring of the colored baseball champions.

In his seminal book, *Sol White's Official Base Ball Guide*, published in 1907 about black baseball, he devoted only about a page to his 1895 season on the Page Fence Giants. The next season, White changed clubs and played for the rival Cuban X Giants, whom his former Page Fence teammates soundly trounced in the 1896 black baseball championship series. White, while not dismissive of the Adrian ball club's talent, chalked up the opponent's win due to the youth and overall health of the Page Fence Giants and placed much blame on the out-of-shape and older Cuban X Giants. Even though White believed four of the championship club Page Fence Giants—George Wilson, Billy Holland, Charlie Grant and Grant "Home Run" Johnson—would have made their way to the major leagues, he didn't mention the Page Fence team as a great team. White also noted infielder James Patterson and catcher George "Chappie" Johnson, two other Page Fence players who were not on the 1896 championship team, as possessing major league talent. When White compared the two great teams from this era, he chose the 1891 New York Gorhams and the 1905 Philadelphia Giants. He also listed several great black ball teams which spanned that era, but omitted the Page Fence Giants.

White's book is undoubtedly considered the era's Bible of black baseball, and his personal litmus test ignored the Adrian team. White, the future Hall of Famer, giving little credence to the Page Fence Giants led what few black baseball researchers there were away from examining this mighty team. Another note, which may have played in White's perception, is that he was not one of the big stars of the 1895 Page Fence club. Ray Nemec's yeoman research on minor league baseball did manage to locate nine box scores of White playing against Michigan State League clubs and posting a healthy .357 average with the Page Fence Giants. However, in my research, White was more often noted for turning double plays rather than for his prowess at the bat and was rarely mentioned in 1895 game stories. Whether ego played a part in his Page Fence Giants slight is left for one to guess. What is a fact is that White was replaced in 1896 by slick-fielding second baseman Charlie Grant.

My reading clearly showed that the two team organizers, Fowler and Grant Johnson, were the two highest profile players on the 1895 squad. Then, in terms of mentions during that season, George Taylor and hurlers Joe Miller, George Wilson and Billy Holland, along with catchers Vasco Graham and Pete Burns, were all ahead of Sol White as stars of the team. White was well down the list on the Page Fence Giants' talent pool. To support this contention, when the Adrian Demons of the Michigan State League needed players, they signed six Page Fence Giants. Despite their having injury issues at second base, I could find not one morsel of information which indicated White was ever considered for the position, even though he had played there on Fort Wayne, Indiana's "white" minor league team earlier in the season.

However, laying too much blame on White is unfair, to say the least. Reading five years of *The Sporting News* and *Sporting Life* usually led to only a morsel of information—a sentence here or there—about the Page Fence Giants. The blurb was usually early in the baseball season, when they were playing the minor and major league clubs. The remaining few mentions, once the regular season started, were embedded in stories about other white minor league teams. Both national publications could go weeks or a few months without any mention of the Page Fence Giants. Searches of newspapers south of the Mason-Dixon line indicated non-existent coverage on the Giants. Black ballplayers defeating white teams was not what most Southerners wanted to read in their Jim Crow-era newspapers.

In Robert Peterson's classic book, *Only the Ball Was White*, he admittedly left out star player biographies from the late 1800s, justifying that because practically no one was alive who had seen them play. Even with that caveat, Grant "Home Run" Johnson and George "Chappie" Johnson were profiled (but Chappie Johnson's years with the Page Fence Giants were not mentioned), as their careers into the early 1900s managed to jog some oldsters' memories. Peterson gave a share of publicity to pioneer Bud Fowler, but other Page Fence stars, such as George Wilson, Joe Miller, Billy Holland, James Patterson, Bill Binga and Vasco Graham, were ignored. When one looks at the beginning stages of researching black baseball, the Peterson book joins Sol White's book as the foundation. When Peterson devotes only a scant mention (two paragraphs) of the Adrian club, it adds another reason why the Page Fence nine have been relegated to the dust bin of baseball history.

My observations of White's and Peterson's epic work should be viewed as not an overall criticism of their efforts, but rather a critical examination of why the Page Fence Giants have been ignored for over 120 years. Any number of people could have examined this fascinating collection of ball players who won the coveted world black baseball championship in 1896. They didn't. White and Peterson opened the door for research on black baseball—albeit nearly seven decades apart—and their work is why there is interest in old-time black baseball today.

I think another factor which played into ignoring this era of black baseball was the formation of the Negro National League in 1920. When Rube Foster led the group to establish a counterpart to the "organized" and all-white American and National Leagues, the barnstorming teams from black baseball's past were no longer as important. The "organized" Negro League, with a new generation of emerging stars, wanted to become the black counterpart of the whites-only leagues. These new teams and players quickly took the place of the old-timers in the hearts and minds of black baseball fans. Just as the integration of the major leagues slowly pushed the Negro Leagues to the back burner, this same process played itself out on the Adrian team a few decades earlier.

So compiling bits and pieces of information, as I had to do when creating this book, you take a small city, scant contemporary press coverage in the state's largest community (and after the first year, much less coverage in Adrian's daily papers), and only a brief mention in the two epic black baseball books and the emergence of the Negro Leagues, as reasons why the Page Fence Giants are not more readily known today.

Two years or so ago, I had no intention of writing a book on black baseball. I stumbled upon this team while researching and writing my history book on Williamston, Michigan, where I now reside. When I attempted to find out more about the Page Fence Giants, there was little information and most just repeated what was already out in public. I found people who were interested in the Giants' history, but there was little in the way of previously published material. People would say, "Someone needs to write a book on these guys." This is that book.

However, the book's scope is more than the outcome of four years of baseball games. In my other life, I am a history and sociology teacher, and I wanted to incorporate as much of the American experience in the 1890s into this work. While I did create a master roster, a won/lost pitching record, located the official 1895 Michigan State League statistics, used some of David Nemec's data, and compiled the tricky game-by-game scores of the 1896 championship series with the Cuban X Giants, this book is more than numbers. I purposely omitted creating a master list of game scores during the four years the Giants played on the ball diamond. My motive was twofold in this area. First, trying to track down each game, especially the last two years of the Giants' existence, would be next to impossible, as I lay out those reasons in the book. The detective work needed to confirm reports from different newspapers, in different towns, with different deadlines and in many cases conflicting final scores, was the most troublesome aspect of writing this book, by far. It would have added another two years to the book and still would have been riddled with errors. It was common to find several newspaper accounts of the same game, each offering different final scores, some disagreeing on the game location and even the date. The Giants played into this situation, too, no doubt. The club often added contests along their travels, cancelled games with projected low turnouts and simply failed to send data on a consistent basis back to Adrian newspapers for publication. Other towns were so giddy on trying to book the Giants, they would publicize games that were never on any schedule I could ever locate and were simply cases of local promoters putting the cart before the horse.

Second, I didn't want someone to discover that there was a three-game weekend series between the Giants and some team, but I only could find two scores, and that would lead them to think the narrative was riddled with similar errors. Once I decided that game-by-game scores were not going to be the focus of the book (even though there are many scores included in the text), I switched my emphasis to the Giants team members and their life in the 1890s, as best I could with the limited information available. The constant complaints of unfair umpires over this team's tenure impacts the overall statistical output of each player on the mound and at the plate. The racist nature of some of these umpires and opposing players skews statistical analysis in ways no one is able to measure. Simply put, games scores and statistics don't tell what you need to know about this team, these men and the country. This book is the story of Adrian's Page Fence Giants and not a book only geared toward stat heads and baseball nerds.

Once I began the research process, I quickly became enthused, enthralled, enchanted, and enamored with these black baseball pioneers, who played in a rapidly closed Jim Crow society. These Giants were the best black baseball team from 1895 to 1898, and several of their players would have, no doubt, played and starred in the white major leagues, given that opportunity. One made it into the National Baseball Hall of Fame, and a few others should be in there, too. They were the best financed, the most travelled and arguably black baseball's highest profile team during their brief four-year existence. Now, for the first time there is a book devoted to the Page Fence Giants.

A Baseball Crazy Town

In front of one of Adrian's banks, scratched on a piece of paper and plastered on the sidewalk: "Wanted—A pitcher. Address, Lotus base ball club, Monroe, Mich."[1]

Baseball crazy Adrian, Michigan, left that one last jab as the visitors sulked out of town. The Monroe contingent boarded the train back home and was headed by their mayor, E. G. J. Lauer, a "hopeless (baseball) crank." Earlier on August 7, 1894, 90 Monroe citizens had descended upon Adrian, filled with an air of optimism. Their pockets were stuffed with wads of cash, and a lotus flower adorned their overcoat button holes. Stepping off the morning train, they sauntered over to the Emery Hotel and awaited the base ball game at Lawrence Park. The visitors were anticipating a thrashing of the Adrian nine and hoped to make some quick coin by winning bets.[2]

Adrian's Lawrence Park's upscale grandstand seating was jammed with people, as others filled the less desired reserved section, while the remaining patrons simply stood on the grass, with their horses tied to the large shed on the grounds. Some spectators decided they didn't want to pay and peeked at the players under a large, makeshift canvas wall which organizers had draped across a portion of the outfield boundary in an effort to block the freeloaders' gaze. The ball game netted boosters a tidy profit of $108.60, even with the freeloaders eluding organizers. A local paper initially said that maybe Monroe's backers had good reason to anticipate a victory that day, as they had defeated the Adrian team the previous week in the first of a planned three-game series. But, the paper quickly noted, Monroe was "deluded" as that win was "attributed to luck, rather than superior play."[3]

Monroe's optimism on August 7 was for naught, as the Adrian Light Guard ball team pummeled the Lotus boys by a score of 15–7. A pair of Monroe pitchers allowed 17 hits, including five doubles and a home run. "It wasn't much of a game to brag about either way. The Monroe's [sic] were no match for their opponents, and as a rule played raggedly," the *Adrian Daily Times and Expositor* reporter noted. One could argue that the spectators fared much better than the winning Light Guard team, as a betting haul of $300 from Lotus City fans was now jingling in the pockets of various Adrian citizens.[4]

The Light Guard initially tried to hire a Detroit high schooler to pitch for them that day, but Monroe beat them to the punch.[5] As a result, Adrian instead started a local teenager, George Wilson, to face the mighty Lotus boys.[6] Wilson had pitched five solid innings in relief the previous week, when Monroe had claimed a 10–9 victory. One paper said that even though the Adrian starter, Cole, gave up five first-inning runs and "was hit badly, and the team generally is said to have played badly … the umpire is also said to have been partial to the home team."[7] Today's game was different for Adrian, as Wilson started, finished and won for the Light Guard club.[8]

Top: Lawrence Park as it appeared in 2016, behind the Adrian Public Works Department. This is a view from the center field bluff along Springbrook Avenue, looking toward where the diamond would have been located (author's collection). *Bottom:* View of a likely position on the infield facing center field toward Springbrook Avenue. The small creek, present in the 1890s, still runs along the base of the bluff in center and left field (author's collection).

Wilson was a strong, wiry, handsome fellow who grew up a half-dozen miles to the east of Adrian, in the hamlet of Palmyra, Michigan. He was a left-handed pitcher who was "an earnest student of the science of curves and drops." While growing up, Wilson had spent hours at his house, tossing a baseball against the family barn. Carefully drawing circles on the barn's siding, Wilson practiced firing left-handed missiles at the building, working on both speed and control. Jerry Wilson would stand in the home's doorway and yell at George, voicing his thoughts that his son was crazy for spending all his free time chucking a ball.[9]

Decades earlier, Jerry Wilson had followed the two DeGraff brothers off a Civil War battlefield and made the long trek to Michigan and to tiny Palmyra. He quickly earned a reputation as a hard worker. Wilson later married a local gal, Mary Lambert, and the couple had several children and became proud property owners in their new hometown. The same steely determination Jerry Wilson demonstrated in venturing to a state far away from his native Virginia, and his wife traveling even farther, coming from Mississippi, was likely passed onto their ballplaying son. After all, surviving Southern slavery was a much harder ordeal than their teenage son's job of facing the Monroe nine on a sweltering August day.[10]

◆ 2 ◆

Browne Out

The summer of 1894 had been very hot and very dry. The town of Adrian had been experiencing so little rainfall that what was a once-promising harvest forecast earlier in the year had long been forgotten. "Now there is scarcely anything growing that is not literally baked and blasted."[1] Not since before the Civil War had the month of August in Adrian had such little rainfall.

What also was burning up in Adrian was the business wheelings and dealings of its baseball lovers. The same August day it was announced that Bud Fowler had a fondness for Adrian and floated out his idea of relocating the Findlay Colored Western Giants there, a drastic change came to organized baseball in town. Some of the town's most prominent baseball boosters called a meeting and ousted Adrian Light Guard manager L. A. "Louis" Browne, a 26-year-old travelling salesman for the Chemical Ice Construction Company of Chicago, who doubled as the Light Guard ball team business manager. He had recently married 24-year-old Louisa "Fay" Beach in her parents' home one evening on South Main Street in April in a quaint, private ceremony.[2] Now, four months later, this New York native lost his baseball credibility in his new home town. He was being forced out, even though a local paper noted a much smoother transition when "the resignation of Manager Browne was accepted."[3] Browne had seen this power play coming, as he had been embroiled for two months in what seemed at the time to be a minor money controversy.

Throughout the summer, the patrons at Lawrence Park had been numerous. In early summer, a series of six games between the YMCA and Adrian College had drawn unexpectedly well, including several with more women than men in attendance. One news report noted that large crowds of females made for more orderly games and "jeers and cat-calls were unheard."[4] But after splitting the six games, a seventh contest was held between the Y and the college men. The usual boisterous crowd of men reappeared, and when the college boys fell apart in the tenth inning to lose the game, 15–11, an unruly and near riotous crowd emerged and heaped large amounts of blame on the umpire.[5] In early July, a contest between local lawyers and doctors had drawn the largest crowd of the season, with a grandstand jammed full of paying customers and over 200 people standing while ringing the playing field.[6] Other games pitted the Main Street clerks versus the Maumee Street clerks and the local YMCA challenging makeshift teams. Browne and the Adrian Light Guard seemed to have a great ability to grab talented players, but money issues and some high-profile defeats peeved the rabid boosters.

Another problem facing Adrian was the lack of ball diamonds. The YMCA had planned accordingly and reserved Lawrence Park for its exclusive use that summer and would not rent it out to other clubs. This action made the field-less Light Guard team mad, and they drafted a three-person committee who met one June night at the Emery Hotel. The trio consisted of H. C. Smith, Len Hoch and Howard Taylor, and their goal was "to wait upon the board of the directors of the YMCA and see if they would rent Lawrence Park."[7] If not, any designs for a new and improved crack ball team for Adrian was not possible.

A few days after the meeting, both Hoch and Taylor were involved in a hotly contested baseball game, pitting east side and west side men against each other, drawing a very large crowd. The game's highlight was a "grand stand catch" of a hot liner by third baseman Taylor, while Hoch was said to have "nearly knocked a hole in a base runner's back" during a tag play near second base.[8] As usual, the umpire heard a lot of "kicking," the slang of the day for loud complaining about calls. But Ump Muldary seemed perfectly fine as it was said "he was protected to the extent of having a large 44 Colt revolver and a dangerous dirk strapped around his waist," which apparently was very effective and stopped any serious escalation of tensions.[9]

Using their recent ball field exploits, Hoch, who was a former mayor and Adrian's current postmaster, and Taylor, who owned a successful hardware store in town with his brother, Rolla, along with Smith, managed to get the YMCA to rent the Lawrence Park diamond. It took only a little over a week to successfully "wait" on the YMCA Board.[10] The YMCA team continued to use the site, as a game in mid–July saw them nip Blissfield, 17–14. The contest featured a black gentleman by the name of Hancock who manned third base for the YMCA club. He was a porter for Adrian's Lawrence House hotel, had recently relocated from Florida, and claimed to have played a few years earlier for the famed Cuban Giants black team. Hancock's activity on the field quickly had the packed grandstand dub him the "Black Diamond in honor of his unmistakable color."[11] The *Adrian Daily Times and Expositor* used nearly two paragraphs of game coverage detailing Hancock's actions. It said he yelled a lot, was "active as a jumping jack," and when YMCA teammates crossed home plate, did single and double somersaults. However, Hancock's actions were twice compared to animals, yelling like a "loon" and "monkeying" during play. But the paper noted Hancock's popularity and stated, "at one time he was obliged to doff his cap to the applauding grand stand." The paper was more critical of a YMCA white player named Miller, who struggled with the boisterous crowd which razzed him for striking out three times. Umpire Pearl Southland even instructed the crowd to lay off Miller or the game would be forfeited to the visiting Blissfield team. However, Miller's poor batting attempts were not compared to an animal, as was Hancock's for his athletic and entertainment skills.[12]

During the summer, the Light Guard team held more meetings to discuss improving the team's talent. After dropping a game on a botched play at first base to neighboring Clinton and then storming off the field and forfeiting to the YMCA boys due to a dispute with the umpire, their rabid boosters desired a major improvement.[13] By the third week of July, it was announced that Adrian boosters, in order to put a better product on the field, would attempt to "organize a crack baseball team." They even went so far as to say that they would secure outside players for an upcoming contest with Kalamazoo.[14]

On Thursday, July 19, the day it was publicly announced that Adrian would upgrade its talent pool, a small crowd of 200 people witnessed teenager George Wilson pitch in Palmyra's 3–2 loss to the Adrian YMCA team. The game was halted after seven innings because some of the Wilson's Palmyra boys had to go home to do their chores, ending any chance for a comeback victory. Palmyra was handicapped by playing with three substitutes, not normally in their line-up. While the *Daily Times and Expositor* surmised that the small crowd was anticipating a poor contest, they were shockingly surprised at the quality of ball, as it "was the best of the season." Nearly one half of the newspaper's game coverage was centered on the visitors' young Wilson and his exploits in the pitcher's box.[15]

"The YMCA's ran up against a left-handed pitcher yesterday afternoon, who was as puzzling as the score…. He was a slender little darkey—a mere boy—and he looked like an easy mark. But he wasn't. No, siree. There was a sneaky wriggle to his lightening [sic]-like-ball that effectively disconcerted the batters as a rule."[16] The *Expositor* continued its glowing praise of the teenaged Wilson for another two lengthy paragraphs. "As soon as the home team began to think they had got on to his rail fence zig-zag, he would change his tactics and give them an undertwist they had never been introduced to before, and when they batter heard it land kerplunk into the catcher's glove, he softly confided his surprise to himself. His name is Wilson and to Mr. Wilson's honor be it said that he is the foxiest pitcher that has been in the box here this season."[17]

Wilson gave up only three hits on the day, all doubles, walked two, hit one batter and struck out eight YMCA boys. Clapp, the YMCA pitcher, allowed only one hit in the seven-inning contest, so Wilson lost the decision, but gained an Adrian fan club. A few days later, the reorganized and improved Adrian Light Guard team signed Wilson, "the clever pitcher of the Palmyra club."[18]

The neighboring hamlet of Palmyra was always in the spotlight's glare of the much larger and more cultured Adrian, but now they had their own star. A young black kid in an era of growing segregation was standing on his own, following the controversial success (*or failure*) of the nation's Reconstruction after the Civil War. Union General William "Tecumseh" Sherman had promised, though he had no authority from President Abraham Lincoln to do so, the famous plan to issue freed Southern slaves a grant of 40 acres and a mule. Sherman believed that what the black people needed was land and a way to grow food and make a living, without relying on receiving assistance from former white Confederate soldiers, ex-plantation owners and Southern bushwhackers. George Wilson's father, Jerry, probably figured this out much before the rest of the country, when two decades earlier he followed the DeGraff boys to a farm in Palmyra. Now, his 17-year-old son was the shining light of his tiny Michigan community. "That one little pitcher was capable of winning as much respect for his town as a real city with an electric street car line might expect," and batters "resolved to never again make sport of Palmyra by calling it 'Palmis-ery.'"[19]

The day following Wilson's celebrated loss, local baseball boosters met on Friday night at the Light Guard armory to satisfy their public announcement for a strong baseball team in town. The men agreed to strengthen the Light Guard club and use "some paid professionals." A vote elected Wheaton Crittenden as president, Seymour Howell as treasurer, John J. Morris as secretary, L. A. Brown as manager and Rolla Taylor as assistant manager. Howell and Taylor, along with two other men, were placed on a committee to raise additional start-up funds, with a goal of eventually making the team self-supporting. Word on the street was that so many businessmen had expressed interest in backing the new team, it might take just a single day to meet their subscriber goal. A board of directors was named, which included Crittenden, Morris, Taylor and James Holloway. However, it was announced that "the entire business of engaging paid players is in the hands of Manager Brown(e)." In order to secure a field, the Light Guard team would somehow arrange to join the YMCA and gain access to the coveted ball diamond at Lawrence Park.[20]

The *Adrian Times and Expositor* was a baseball supporter, devoting many paragraphs of coverage to each ball game in the city. "The attendance at base ball games here for the past two months demonstrates very clearly that it would pay to have a first-class club to meet such teams as Battle Creek, Kalamazoo, Toledo and Detroit, in which case the present liberal patronage will no doubt be doubly increased." While obviously the Adrian College and YMCA teams would be impacted by this upgraded Light Guard nine, the paper said not to worry. "It will in no way conflict with other city clubs, but on the contrary, will create more of an interest in the sport."[21]

Teenager George Wilson was back in town and playing for his new Light Guard nine against the Hudson Chaffs. About a dozen miles west along the rail line, Hudson and Adrian were baseball enemies. Hudson was a vibrant and growing community and already had two railroad lines through town, but had nowhere near the status of Adrian. Despite that, Hudson more than held their own in ball games against larger towns and tougher opponents. Before signing Wilson, the Adrian men had eked out a narrow victory about a week earlier over the Chaffs. Now with Wilson pitching and former major leaguer Henry Yaik catching, Hudson only managed five hits and two runs, losing 12–2. An Adrian newspaper headlined the rout "Active Gladiators of the Adrian Light Guard, Whisk Away the Hudson Chaffs." Wilson struck out 11 that day, even though his white pitching counterpart notched 13 strikeouts, Wilson was again the star in Adrian's eyes. The Light Guard management was congratulated on signing Wilson and declared, "considering his age and the limited experience he has had, he may correctly be styled a phenomenon. Not only was he virtually invincible in the box, but he batted splendidly."[22]

In a time where in some sections of the United States the social and economic advancement of those categorized as colored or Negro was questioned, stymied or violently blocked, Adrian looked upon Wilson with glowing admiration. "He was repeatedly cheered by the appreciative spectators, but he accepted his honours [*sic*] modestly, and respectively declined numerous invitations to take off his hat to the grand stand. He devoted his entire attention to playing ball, and wisely avoided doing anything that might cause him to be characterized as a 'grand stand player.'" The *Expositor* article said he pitched "cannon balls," praised his slick fielding, daring and clever base running, and highlighted a neat whirling pickoff throw of a runner attempting to swipe home during a double steal. The last paragraph of the game story was another positive note of a black man. The Adrian squad used an "ebony-hued little lad," clad in an attractive yellow costume, as a mascot for the winning Light Guard team.[23] Manager L. A. Browne continued to upgrade the roster, signing infielder Paul J. Kraft from Detroit to join pros Wilson and Yaik. Unlike the slim and trim Wilson, both Kraft and Yaik were full-grown men and were characterized as the heavyweights of the new Light Guard team. "Kraft strained the scales to 199½ (pounds) and Yaik scored 193. There appears to be no danger of either of them wasting away just at present."[24] The added costs of the new professional team required an adjustment to the Lawrence Park's admission fee. As July was nearing an end, gentlemen would now be charged 25 cents, and the ladies, previously admitted for free, would now be assessed 10 cents. The receipts for the Hudson Chaffs game netted organizers $48.50, but much more money would be needed to field a competitive professional team that would bring pride and joy to Adrian.[25]

The revamped lineup helped the Light Guard team destroy a Jackson club, featuring the three famous ballplaying Tray brothers, 30–4. The Adrian club slugged 31 hits in the lopsided victory. Lefty Wilson pitched brilliantly, scattered a few hits, walked none and struck out 12. The *Adrian Evening Telegram* said his most effective pitch was the "up-shoot" and dubbed the teenager "The Cyclone"—a nickname which never took hold for the

Palmyra teen.[26] To add insult to Jackson's defeat, over $100 was bet and lost by their boosters, including two high rollers who plunked down $15 each, according to Joe Emery of the Emery Hotel, the scene of the wagering.[27]

While the talent upgrade and the boosting of admission fees would seem to have solved the Light Guard and manager Browne's problems, they were not enough for the rabid baseball boosters. The revamped team dropped the first of three scheduled contests to Monroe, Michigan, on Thursday, August 2, by the narrow margin of 10–9.[28]

A relatively short, 32-mile morning train ride allowed the players and boosters to arrive early enough to wander around downtown Monroe and spend some time out on a local lake. At the ballpark, newly hired Monroe manager A. A. Jack was preparing his Lotus club for battle. The *Monroe Democrat* said that Adrian had brought with them a "husky looking lot of men," along with a young black mascot clad in a bright yellow outfit. The mascot "pranced around to the delight of the crowd," which was numbered at between 300 and 400 spectators.[29]

The Adrian Light Guard boys were behind from the start, giving up five two-out runs to the Monroe Lotus Club. Wilson relieved Cole and was effective, but the teen was later pulled to save him for a Saturday game with Britton. The *Daily Times and Expositor* of August 3 said their team had an "uphill" battle due to poor umpiring, which went along nicely with the Light Guard's generally all-around poor play that day. But the *Monroe Democrat* said, "excitement ran high," and several fans proclaimed it the best game ever played in their city. The Adrian Light Guard consisted of more experienced men, while the younger Monroe team was still learning how to play the sport. In this case, youth beat experience, and the home squad won the contest.[30]

A few days later, a passenger car load of boosters, attached to the rear of a morning Wabash freight train, followed the Light Guard out of Adrian to Britton for a six-inning game. The local farmers were actually ahead after three innings before the Light Guard tied it in the fifth, finally winning, 9–6. Britton natives cried foul, as the shortened game was due to the Light Guard squad having to catch the return train to Adrian. However, Britton boosters claimed manager Browne ordered his team off the ball diamond 45 minutes ahead of the next train. Britton backers offered free transportation back to Adrian if they stayed and played a full nine innings. Browne refused and claimed victory, while Britton declared they won the contest on a forfeit.[31] The lefty Wilson was not particularly effective, and the Brittonites spent much of their time yelling from the stands that his fancy pitching delivery (which alternated between overhand and a submarine style) was really a balk.[32]

Losing to arch-rival Monroe and then struggling against a bunch of farmers in Britton brought another crisis to the Adrian baseball community. The *Times and Expositor* publicly revealed a second issue—finances—as a cause of another problem between Browne and the boosters. Len Hoch, banker Seymour Howell and the Taylor Brothers, Rolla and Howard, who operated a popular hardware and sporting goods store, seemed to be the most vocal of the group. "There's a big row on in the Light Guard base ball association, and the air is full of 'foul tips' on each side of the question." The young Browne claimed that the reorganized professional ball club was a new entity and refused to pay a $60 debt from the old Light Guard squad. The investors correctly argued that the new Light Guard team did, in fact, use the club's recently purchased uniforms and their bats and balls. A meeting on August 6, 1894, was scheduled at the armory building, and the four key investors would do their best to replace Browne. Manager Browne, a young newlywed but no one's fool, announced a counter-meeting for the same evening. Browne instructed his supporters and new investors to meet at the Hotel Emery with the intention of going "over the heads of the Light Guard board of directors, by entirely wiping out the present organization and forming the Adrian base ball club." Browne told the paper that "every member" of the newly reorganized ball team, apparently including the young pitching phenom George Wilson, was in favor of his proposal.[33]

Whether they were invited or crashed Browne's meeting, everyone ended up at the Hotel Emery that Monday evening. Rumors of a "threatened riot" among the two baseball parties initially surfaced as the beginning of the discussion was characterized as a "hot meeting." Boosters jammed into the parlor and spilled into the hotel hallway as discussion ensued as to how to best handle Adrian's baseball fever.[34]

The old Light Guard group felt "Brown's [*sic*] work unsatisfactory and intimated that he talked too much on the outside."[35] "Considerable hard feelings" opened the "hot meeting," but once the initial complaints were heard, the business of the $60 debt was the focus. Soon good news was reported at the contentious gathering and "harmony" was created.[36] A temporary, two-person board of directors was elected, with Major Seymour Howell and Rolla Taylor being named, along with a yet-to-be-decided third person.[37] Taylor was to represent the new association's stockholders, and his baseball reputation was such that he was chosen while out of town and missed the meeting that evening.[38] Major Howell would represent the soldier boys on the team.[39] The pair, along with the third person, would go about hiring a manager and other baseball officers. In a final conciliatory gesture toward Browne's

The site of the former Hotel Emery, where Gus Parsons worked as a clerk and where many Adrian baseball meetings were held. The dining room, office and guest rooms were in the first two sections on the left of this now-closed furniture store on South Main Street (author's collection).

recently re-organized team, the $60 baseball debt was forgiven.[40] Browne's fate was still a bit up in the air. One paper reported that he would "be taken care of," and despite his indiscrete comments "it cannot be said against him that he lacks nerve and push." That same newspaper also noted that Browne was filling a hard role, as "there's nothing in it for him but glory and curses." For the time being, Browne would manage this new Adrian juggernaut.[41]

The day after "harmony" was reached, the rematch with Monroe was played. On a hot, August 7, 1894, afternoon, the teenager Wilson was very good, as he led the Light Guard to a 15–7 victory over the Monroe Lotus team. The visitors had arrived in town with "each man wearing an Egyptian lotus, from the beds of the Monroe marsh."[42] The *Times and Expositor* was less than congenial toward the visitors, referring to them as "patrons" of "Cemetery City," cheering a third-ranked team who "were no match for their opponents." To be fair, the newspaper said both teams were less than stellar and "it wasn't much of a game to brag about either way." The liveliest event the paper mentioned was when Adrian second baseman Paul Craft had to scamper under a barbed wire fence to retrieve a live ball, ripped his shirt and finished the game in a sweater. The Lawrence Park grandstand was packed, and a large crowd also watched from a nearby grove of trees west of the field. As usual, the freeloaders peered around and under the large canvas tarp stretched along a section of the outfield and managed to witness the game without paying. The paper said those people should be "ashamed" of their behavior.[43]

However, those being ashamed should actually have been everyone in Adrian who attended the game, cried the *Monroe Democrat* daily newspaper. "The visit was seriously marred by the ungentlemanly treatment received from the hands of those heretofore had supposed to be gentlemen." They said the playing ground was unsuitable, calling it "a small gully with a marsh on one side and a barb wire fence on the other, with weeds and grass waist high." When the contest began, "the umpire settled the game in favor of Adrian … [and] he was palpably dishonest," as even some non-biased, non–Monroe residents allegedly told the newspaper. Following the 15–7 loss, a financial "outrage" was placed on the Monroe Lotus team, as they were charged five dollars for renting the diamond and another five for police protection. The Monroe paper crowed that this injustice was like inviting someone over for dinner and then charging them for the food and rent![44] The ranting continued as the paper claimed the Monroe players and their 87 fans, as they headed toward the train station, were verbally abused along the way. Apparently, this type of treatment was to be expected, according to the *Democrat*, as Adrian was famous for this type of rowdyism. The rubber game of the three was already scheduled to be held in Monroe, and the *Democrat* promised "the Adrian visitors will be used as much like gentlemen, as their conduct will warrant while here."[45]

Between Monroe game number two and number three, the newly reorganized Adrian Light Guard management team continued to develop. On Monday morning, August 13, former mayor and current postmaster Hoch was named as the third member of the board of directors. Hoch and Howell likely had discussed the appointment on Sunday, as the pair spent the day as part of a small Adrian contingent biking around Detroit before riding up and down Woodward and Jefferson Avenues and over to Belle Isle.[46] Hoch, who was also in the grocery business with his brother in town, was named the baseball association's secretary, while original board member Rolla Taylor was selected president and Howell was named as the treasurer. Browne was retained as team manager. The meeting was summarized as noting that "steps were taken to organize the association more perfectly than heretofore."[47] The group also retained the Adrian Light Guard Base Ball Association as its name.[48]

Since the reorganization, the Light Guard ball club had posted some big wins. They had defeated Bryan, Ohio, 37–8, in a game shortened to eight innings due to the lopsided score, and later defeated Milan either 24–8 or 23–11, depending on an Adrian newspaper's account or the one recorded by Milan's female scorekeeper. A team from Jackson went down by a 33–4 count.[49] Wilson was doing nearly all the pitching, and the new additions, Kraft and Yaik, were accounting for themselves quite nicely, too. During this string of blowout victories and the win at home over Monroe, the *Times and Expositor* questioned, "either the base ball clubs which come here are very weak or else the Light Guard team is exceptionally strong. Which is it?"[50] The Adrian squad would soon find out. A third match with the tough Lotus team had to be postponed for a week, due to some of the Monroe men being out of town and drilling for guard duty. While Browne's conflict with the board seemed to have become a thing of the past with the team's much-improved play, his trip to Monroe would unfortunately increase the pressure.

"Buncoed!" screamed the *Adrian Daily Times and Expositor* headline following the Light Guard's upset loss to Monroe by a lopsided tally of 16–6 on August 22, 1894. It wasn't just the loss, but the way in which the entire affair played out, which caused Browne and Adrian public humiliation. The multi-layered headline, as was the norm of the day, continued with "Roughly used by the muskrat element of Monroe; The Lotus Club reinforced by professional ringers; Aided and abetted by a complaisant umpire; Leave the Light Guard team out in the cold; Manager Jack Figures in an unfavorable light."[51] The *Evening Telegram* stated that the local boys "made a very successful showing" against highly ranked professionals and "a team made up of Detroit and Toledo players." The paper claimed that Frank Pears was a Detroit league pitcher paid $25 to be on the mound for Monroe. His teammate, Rutter, manned third base, while one of the Guthard brothers, well known to Adrianites as they had played for their team too, started in left field. The Detroit Athletic Club's Connors was behind the plate, while Smith and Pecord, from Toledo, played second and third base. The *Evening Telegram* story even divided the game's runs as Detroit scoring nine, Toledo with seven and Adrian with six, and zero for the real Monroe team. To finish their tirade, the *Telegram* published the box score "for the benefit of the Detroit, Toledo and Adrian gentlemen who took part in it" and labeled both the game's box and line scores as Detroit vs. Adrian![52]

The Adrian team's one-run loss earlier in the month in Monroe was blamed, in the press, on shoddy fielding and a biased umpire which created an "uphill" game.[53] Most of the *Times and Expositor* game coverage centered upon the treatment of fans and spectators before and after the event, with much less devoted to the actual playing of the contest.

From the minute the 88 rabid Adrian baseball boosters stepped off the morning train, things were looking shaky. First, the customary meet and greet at the train depot, with an escort to the Monroe ball grounds, failed to materialize. While Adrian's 88 fans were on the way to the ball field, the "lawless mob" of Monroe rooters spit tobacco juice at the visitors, hurled items in their direction and yelled insults. As the trek became more contentious, Adrian booster Henry C. Lards rapped one Monroe "assailant" on the head with his cane. The *Times and Expositor* reporter had to escape this mob scene by jumping into a carriage "to save himself from harm."[54]

The *Adrian Evening Telegram* printed that Monroe had "Blood in the eyes of the Frenchmen ever since they were trounced here [and] the Adrian boys are playing their own team, while it is suspected that Monroe is loaded." The paper also announced the Adrian fans would not be betting money that day on the outcome in favor of their own boys.[55]

When the Adrian team and its entourage finally made it to the ball field, Monroe manager A. A. Jack and half of the players were nowhere to be found. Smelling a rat, the collective betting pot of $115, raised on the train trip by the boosters, was quickly returned to their original holders. According to one report, Adrian jeweler J. Will Kirk, who was on the train, had been warned by an honest Monroe businessman that the "majority of the team were not only imported, but that an umpire from Toledo had been 'fixed' to give the game to the home team." The new Monroe roster for this third and deciding game in the series flew in the face of a written agreement between manager Jack and L. A. Browne. Still sore from losing "considerable money" in bets in game two in Adrian, the Lotus team decided to fix things and guarantee a victory.[56]

Browne supplied the letters between himself and Monroe's manager to a local paper, which printed excerpts and demonstrated Monroe's lack of good faith. Using such phrases as "a good crowd will welcome your club," you will find "no cause to complain, win or lose," and words such as "honorable," "courtesy" and "fun," manager Jack clearly indicated he had planned a lovely reception for the Adrian Light Guard team. It was anything but.[57]

When the Adrian nine arrived at the ball field, and manager Jack was finally located, he refused to speak to Browne. The Monroe manager also, at first, said Browne could not be involved in monitoring the gate and taking tickets. Eventually, Browne managed to take tickets as the business manager of the Adrian team. But Jack shot back, saying that he had "arranged the preliminaries of the game with Director [Rolla] Taylor" and questioned Browne's current role with the team.[58] Jack indicated he was upset with Browne's treatment of him since the previous game in Adrian. According to Browne, the reason for the one-week delay in this final game was not due to the Monroe boys being away at guard duty. Browne claimed that Jack had tried to enlist three players from the high-powered Findlay, Ohio, team to join Monroe temporarily, violating their roster agreement.[59] Browne said he was "on to" Monroe's scheme, which caused Jack to begin his remaining correspondence with Taylor.[60]

The whole circus atmosphere surrounding the game rattled the visiting Light Guard team, who managed to hold up well for only the first two innings. The stands were filled, at least according to Adrian fans, "by the lowest element" of Monroe's population. Manager Jack allegedly provided his rooters with musical instruments to "roast 'em alive," and they played loud and long during key moments of the contest. Adrian lawyer Harry L. Larwill said, "I never saw such a disorderly mob of hoodlums in my life. They were spoiling for trouble and the slightest provocation would have undoubtedly led to a serious assault on the Adrian people." Larwill said they were cursed at and taunted, but concluded by saying it obviously was not a reflection of the better class in Monroe, just their hoodlums.[61]

During the game, Adrian's rooters sarcastically claimed the umpire "carefully concealed" that fact as to whether he had any actual knowledge of calling a baseball game. They alleged that the umpire would rely on nods and shakes of the head of the Monroe first baseman before ruling on close plays. Monroe batters were allowed "four strikes" over a one-sided, shrunken home plate, while the Adrian team was allotted the normal three strikes.[62] "He [the umpire] would call a foul ball fair and a fair ball foul to suit the occasion and lose the game for Adrian."[63] Despite this overwhelming circus-like atmosphere, the teenaged "Wilson never lost his nerve," and he tossed a better game than did Monroe's ringer.[64]

As the game continued along in this fashion, the Adrian boosters complained and yelled long and loud, only to be shouted down and insulted by Monroe backers, presumably between blasts from the musical instruments. The Monroe fans packed most of the stands, and they were on their worst behavior. "The manager scraped up every muskrat web foot he could find in the marshes and armed him with a tin horn and club."[65] Manager Jack milked the crowd and taunted the visitors by being overly chummy with his ball players, and he closely grasped them as they strolled to the plate. He even allowed his nattily clad young son to add to the spectacle by making an appearance on the diamond.

At the end of the contest, Wilson had struck out eight Monroe men and Paul Craft had slugged a home run. But the hired Monroe bunch hit two home runs, turned two double plays and saw 13 Light Guards go down on strikes. The imported umpire, Burgess, was the target of barbs from Adrian's home run-hitting Craft. "No one knows better how to roast a fresh umpire than Kraft and he accomplished it to the queen's taste." When Adrian catcher Henry Yaik was hit in the ankle by a pitched ball, Monroe citizens allegedly yelled "kill him" and "now you've got him down, murder him."[66] Needless to say, the two hour and 30-minute, "buncoed" baseball event concluded with hard feelings, as Monroe won two of the three games that summer. Light Guard board director Taylor, who also made the trek to Monroe, said that in his 20 years of baseball experience he had never seen such a sight, and vowed that neither team would ever play each other again, under any circumstances.[67]

To add insult to injury, the box office incorporated a new accounting system. The normal home team's 60 percent split and visitor's 40 percent was reduced to 37 percent for Adrian. Manager Jack kept five cents for each Adrian visitor for a grandstand charge (though there was no grandstand in Monroe) to mirror the fee Monroe natives had paid when they got to sit in an actual grandstand at Adrian's Lawrence Park. The final blow came when another ten dollars was held back to pay for the field's rent, despite the claim that Monroe's mayor let them use it for free.[68]

The way back to the train station was no better than the arrival. Using the game victory as the basis of their banter, the verbal harassment by the Monroe "hoodlum population" followed the Adrian players and boosters to the depot. One paper estimated that between 1,500 and 2,000 people massed at the depot "and pelted the cars with stones and sticks."[69] Frank M. English said the whole event reminded him of a Chicago railroad strike, while Frank Freytag's thoughts concluded the *Times and Expositor*'s scathing article, saying he would like to express "his gratitude to the Monroe people for allowing him to escape with his life." Freytag, along with Charles Harrison and Herman and George Burger, were boisterous Adrian rooters, and for their personal safety were escorted off the ball grounds at the end of the game by the town marshal.[70]

The *Evening Telegram* continued its assault on the host town. "Such treatment as the Monroe people accorded Adrian Wednesday is enough to disgust the saints who write the chronicles of the ages," and "Monroe ought to go and hide her head forever."[71]

The *Monroe Democrat* contended the Adrian fans got what they deserved. The paper compared how they had gracefully treated Adrian's visitors in game one with how the Monroe residents were greeted in game two while traveling to Lenawee County. At the first contest, the *Democrat* claimed, the Light Guard was met and escorted from the Monroe train station. The visitors were given a carriage tour of the city and a lake cruise aboard the steamship *Sterling*. They were "taken to and from the ball grounds in carriages and entertained 'til they left for home in the evening." While they admitted that the 10–9 Monroe victory didn't sit well with the Light Guard, the paper claimed there was no reason for what later occurred at game two in the Lenawee County community. Monroe had been gracious hosts in game one and expected the same in Adrian. It was not what they received.[72]

The *Monroe Democrat* stated that fans received "hostile treatment" from the minute no one met the Lotus club at the Adrian train station on August 7 for the second game of the series. There was no escort or any hospitality offered that day, and about 100 Monroe residents were "shamefully mistreated" by being called "muskrats, Frenchmen, dudes, etc." They also added that the surprise fees at the end of the third game in Monroe compared nicely with what the Light Guard's Louis Browne subtracted from them in grounds rental and police protection in Adrian. As the Monroe backers were heading away from the diamond and toward the Emery Hotel, the harassment continued. A group of Monroe citizens had to duck into a store to escape the mob. Finally safe at the Emery, they ate dinner and then experienced more verbal assaults as they awaited a special train car back to Monroe.[73]

As for the game three treatment, the *Monroe Democrat* used the Bible to justify their fans' actions. "With what measure ye mete, it shall be measured unto you again." They also claimed that the Adrian baseball cranks were no angels on August 22. The *Democrat* claimed that some long-haired Adrian boys, drunk on fresh whiskey, spent their time before the game acting rowdy and insulting the fine ladies on the streets of Monroe. The town marshal ordered them off the streets. They entered stores and continued their rowdy ways. Some Adrian boosters managed to damage furniture and fixtures in one store and simply blamed their behavior on their drunken state. After the game, some of the "Monroe boys" met the long-haired troublemakers and a fight would have ensued, but local "officers interfered." The Monroe paper claimed this incident was the only threatened violence that August day.[74]

The paper did admit to the tin horns, wild screams and yelling at the game. They also claimed that it was only just a bunch of kids who gathered at the public square "and hooted and tooted the visitors out of town." They denied that any Monroe women spit in the faces of Adrian's boosters and complained that the baseball game betting was poor. "Monroe was never so disgraced by a visiting crowd before or lied about afterwards through the papers. But we are not surprised as the above is characteristic of Adrian." The *Democrat* continued its harangue and said Adrian people were basically pigs, and composed a 16-line poem called "Adrian, My Adrian." Taunting the Light Guard and their fans, the poem included such wonderful stanzas as "How you boasted when you started for the 'Pretty Lotus Town'; Said you 'had the game right in your pocket'—so did Manager Browne; But we're glad to have you home again, along with Captain Kraft; And let me warn you once again—Adrian, it surely must be so; You must always play second fiddle, to your brother, old Monroe."[75]

And if that wasn't enough, over a week later, someone in Monroe was going around spitting tobacco juice into the corner mailboxes. The *Monroe Democrat* had an easy explanation for this crime: "someone, probably a part of the Adrian contingent left over from the ball game," was responsible.[76]

No to sit idly by, one Adrian newspaper published an account that Monroe manager Jack was forced to resign by the good businessmen of their town, as they held him "principally to blame for the disgraceful treatment accorded to Adrian visitors."[77] However, nothing could be further from the truth. In fact, about ten days after that erroneous story, Jack did try to resign to accept a full-time job offer with the Northern Pacific Railway Company. The *Monroe Democrat* claimed, "the club promptly declined to accept," and Jack remained on the job, scheduling two games with the Findlay Sluggers and mulling over 27 additional ball game requests.[78]

Needless to say, the past two weeks of controversy between Adrian and Monroe would not be good for future business. Who would want to take his wife or kids to a riotous and potentially dangerous baseball game? What Rolla Taylor, Howell and Hoch thought of Browne's behavior at Monroe and his issue with manager Jack is anybody's guess. With Taylor communicating behind Browne's back, he could, if devious enough, just sit back, watch the young man get abused by the Monroe baseball establishment, and use that for fodder to replace him as manager. Browne knew the pressure was on, but the Light Guard's recent lopsided victories, save for this Monroe debacle, probably allowed him some breathing room in his eyes.

Fresh off Adrian's embarrassment in Monroe, a few days later the powerful Detroit Crescents came to town. There was a "faint shadow of a doubt" by some as to exactly how good this new Light Guard team was. Some regulars characterized some of the latest victories as "snap games." A cloudy morning filled with a much-needed light rain gave way to a clear afternoon, which ushered in a large crowd totaling around 500 at Lawrence Park. The power struggle between Browne and Taylor's group was likely well known to those attending, as the "stand was filled with an unusual number of economically inclined men and women," along with the regular group of cheapskates and youngsters taking in the game, on the outfield creek bank, for free. While some in the stands that day may have been there for the ball game, some were looking for an investment option. As a jab to Monroe, the Adrian home crowd was described as of "model nature" and was "one of the features of the game."[79]

The Crescents had long been one of Detroit's top amateur teams, but they were no match for Wilson and the professional Light Guards. Wilson scattered a few hits and struck out five Crescents, and the Light Guard ran wild on the bases. The game took a little over two hours, and the locals notched a 23–5 victory. Even the freeloaders got involved in the game; when slugging first baseman Jim Tracy slammed a ball to the creek bank, they dug it out and returned it to play. The outcome was a nice tune-up for the impending invasion of the Findlay Sluggers, next week. The *Daily Times and Expositor* used their printing presses to create large advertising "hangers" announcing the Sluggers' appearance on August 29 and 30.[80] The *Evening Telegram* announced "come and witness the Adrians fool the champions. The 29–30."[81]

This follow-up win over the Detroit Crescents after the Monroe debacle was not enough to hold off Browne's opponents. He would last exactly one more week on the job. After the games with Findlay (both losses), the local and wealthier baseball investors decided to accept Browne's obviously forced resignation. They turned to an Emery Hotel clerk, Augustus S. "Gus" Parsons, to fill their newly created vacancy. The *Evening Telegram* stated that Parsons was "reluctant" to accept the position but offered their praise, saying he knew the country's base ball history "better than any other man in the city."[82] The *Times and Expositor*, which had appeared to be such a strong supporter of Browne, proudly announced on August 31 that the selection of Parsons "displayed excellent judgment," as "he is not only gentlemanly and conservative, but better posted on base ball matters than anyone in the city." Whether that observation of being a gentleman and conservative was a knock on Browne is anyone's guess over a century later. But the newlywed Browne would be back on the road as a travelling salesman, and Parsons was now in charge of finding talent for the Light Guard team.

Parsons' efforts were quickly appreciated by the Adrian baseball community. During a final fund-raising game in early October, Parsons was the acting umpire between the YMCA and the Adrian Light Guard squad. Sometime during the game, Willard Stearns appeared out of the crowd holding a silk umbrella and, after some lofty words about Parsons and the baseball community's work together, presented the gift to Parsons as a token of appreciation. The crowd roared its approval.[83]

The baseball game was a close contest all the way, but was stopped in the eighth inning, when George Wilson stabbed at a hot comebacker to the pitcher's box. The ball split open the middle finger of his right and, thankfully, non-pitching hand. However, the wound was bad enough that he had to retire from the game, and that promptly ended the contest. The Adrian players were given $7.50 each and the baseball season concluded for 1894.[84]

The Adrian and Monroe verbal war continued as summer turned to autumn. When the *Evening Telegram* claimed that the Findlay ball club had been abused while playing in Monroe, the *Democrat* struck back. It printed an alleged response by Charley Strobel, Findlay's manager, denying the charge, saying they were "treated … just as fine as we ever were treated in any city," and even requested a game next year with Monroe.[85] The *Democrat* added a scathing view of Adrian. "This is characteristic of Adrian not only in play but in business and social affairs, and is the principal reason why it has no social or business standing. It is the reason why every self-respecting man, except ministers, and missionarys [*sic*], want to get out of it."[86]

Team business manager Gus Parsons (left) and the two Taylor Brothers (Howard and Rolla) on the rear platform of the Page Fence Giants Monarch train car (courtesy Adrian District Library).

   This is the atmosphere that newly named business manager Parsons, Hoch, Howell and the two Taylor Brothers were confronting in late September 1894. But despite this zoo-like home game atmosphere, they decided to think big. With the aid of a local fence manufacturing company, the group would add another partner, Bud Fowler, a 36-year-old baseball veteran and black gentleman, and together attempt to create the greatest black baseball team the world had ever seen.

◆ 3 ◆

Two Dreamers

Baseball's itinerant vagabond, John W. Jackson, better known as Bud Fowler, stepped onto the train in Findlay, Ohio, one morning in late August 1894. Fowler was headed north to the burgeoning baseball metropolis of Adrian, Michigan. His Findlay Sluggers in the previous two days had defeated the Detroit Western League professional ball team and had lost only a few games all summer. The Ohio nine looked to add more victories upon their arrival in the southeastern Michigan town, about 60 miles from Detroit. Fowler led his paid baseball stars to play in the Michigan city which had put in a claim as being the Wolverine state's hotbed of baseball that summer.[1]

Jackson, somewhere along the way, changed his name for a reason long lost to history and became Bud Fowler, famed black ballplayer. As luck would have it, Fowler was born in 1858 to John and Mary Jackson near Cooperstown, New York.[2] Cooperstown long boosted itself as baseball's birthplace, the reason that the Hall of Fame was established there. Cooperstown took some literary license as to where the game began, which it did not in that village. Fowler, along with Adrian Constantine "Cap" Anson, whose father once lived in Adrian and included the town in his son's name, battled in the national media over who had played ball longer.[3] Anson held the claim, being six years older than Fowler, and began playing professional ball when Fowler would have been 13 years old. But Fowler was known for changing his birth date so he could "age" and, as a result, be older than Anson, and it also fit nicely with his hometown Cooperstown's trick.[4]

Today, Fowler was a 36-year-old ballplayer and manager of the Findlay club. His nearly two decades of playing had led him to teams around his home state, along with such far-off stops as Keokuk, Iowa, a couple of towns in the middle of Nebraska, far out west in New Mexico, and in Canada. At most of his stops, Fowler played and stayed in a place only briefly. Likely moving on to a better place, when offered more money or confronted with unaccepting and hostile white crowds, Fowler was a tumbleweed across the country's baseball diamonds.[5]

Riding on that same morning train bound for Adrian was a 21-year-old Findlay native, Grant Johnson. Like Fowler, he was a black ball player.[6] Unlike Fowler, whose career was well established around the country, Johnson's was just getting started. On his way to slugging 60 home runs during this summer of 1894, he joined Fowler as the undisputed stars of the integrated Findlay Sluggers. By the end of the season, Johnson too would have a different name—"Home Run."

The Lake Shore and Michigan Southern train number 15 was a bit delayed as it chugged into Adrian shortly before 11 o'clock in the morning on Wednesday, August 29, 1894.[7] The Findlay team disembarked from the train, with Fowler likely limping, as a rumor out of

24

The 1894 Findlay (Ohio) Sluggers baseball team. Bud Fowler is pictured far right in the second row. Grant "Home Run" Johnson is on the far left second row. The remaining Sluggers: (Front row) Fred Swartz and Kid Ogden; (Second row) Johnson, George Derby, manager Charles J. Strobel, Bobby Woods, and Fowler; (Back Row) Harvey Pastorius, Fred Cooke, Howard Brandenburg and Bill Reidy (Hancock Historical Museum).

Ohio said that he had broken his leg in a game earlier that week. However, the rumor proved unfounded, as he hit a double and stole a base in the first game with Detroit, and apparently did not have a broken leg.[8]

Adrian was all abuzz as it prepared for a pair of titanic matches between the Light Guard and Findlay. The *Findlay Daily Courier* proudly exclaimed that their Sluggers were the "best semi-professional team in the country."[9] One game would be played that afternoon and one the next day. The Michigan town would be represented by the recently improved Adrian Light Guard team, comprised of men serving in the National Guard unit, local hired stars, and players imported from Detroit. The Light Guard would be clad in their brand new, spiffy, maroon-and-white uniforms, purchased from the Spalding Athletic Company in Chicago, which would be unveiled for the first time in the battles with Findlay.[10] Local jewelers vied for some free publicity over the next two days, as they promised prizes to local ball players. J. Will Kirk offered a gold stick pin to the first batter who slugged a home run against Findlay. George M. Tripp donated a silver match box for the Adrian man who bashed out the most doubles over both games, while William Sheldon offered a pair of cuff links to the first Adrian man to hit a triple.[11]

The 1894 Adrian Light Guard team wearing their new uniforms following the ouster of L.A. Browne. New business manager Augustus "Gus" Parsons is standing in the middle, back row. The team's star hurler is teenager and Palmyra, Michigan, native George Wilson, who is holding a ball in his left pitching hand. Paul Craft is on the far right in the middle row (courtesy Adrian District Library)

Findlay left Ohio, where a couple of thousand people had seen them twice defeat Detroit, 8–7 and 9–5. The latter game featured $2,000 wagered by local bettors. The Findlay victory had been a raucous affair and featured a 20-minute delay to search for a stolen bat and a hotly contested balk call. The pitching infraction led to a threat against the umpire, who promptly summoned a policeman, who grabbed the mouthy Frank Pears by the head and legs and dragged him off the diamond. Not to be deterred, Pears climbed onto a roof adjacent to the ball field and yelled at the players and umpire for the duration of the game.[12]

There was no reason to believe that baseball-crazed Adrian would be any different. A large crowd was expected, and Adrian organizers wanted to recoup their costs. The *Adrian Times and Expositor* offered its support and proposed a threat to those who wanted to view the ball game for free by taking in the game from afar. "It is suggested that the crowd which views games from the northern banks of Lawrence Park be broken up by having a Kodak snapped on them, and having the photograph exhibited in store windows."[13] Instead the paper promoted the fact that "those coming to the games in carriages ... will have ample room to come inside of left field and witness the games with safety. So, come every body."[14]

There was even hope that a great ringer would be inserted into the Adrian Light Guard lineup: a major league player from Philadelphia named Bob Allen. Considered the best-fielding shortstop in the majors, he was friends with local baseball enthusiasts Howard and Rolla Taylor. Since breaking his jaw two months earlier when hit in the face by a pitch in a game against Cincinnati, Allen had gone home to Paulding, Ohio, to recuperate. He was expected to arrive before the first game with Findlay, and rumors were that he had healed enough to help the local boys.[15]

A Findlay-Light Guard game preview illustrated Fowler's masterful marketing ability. The *Times and Expositor* proclaimed that Fowler "has the reputation of being an exceedingly lively and skillful hitter, despite the fact that he is 47 years old. He has been playing ball for 25 years and has been a member of nearly every league that has existed in that time. He is the man that Anson kicked on because of his color when he was playing with the Bostons in '87."[16] This story made him 11 years older than he was—a typical Fowler marketing move. Another news blurb again made Fowler much older than Anson, as a Cincinnati paper said, "the colored veteran who was playing ball when Anson was making mud pies and riding a hobby horse in Marshalltown, Iowa, is in the old man stakes, but he is a hustler."[17] However, in a much less flattering description of Fowler, the *Times and Expositor* said his look was of an "emaciated, consumptive looking individual."[18]

The headline in the next day's *Adrian Times and Expositor* said it all: "Flayed by Findlay." Fowler, Johnson and the rest of the Ohio professionals racked up 19 runs versus only two for the Light Guard team. While the paper admitted the Light Guard was likely to go

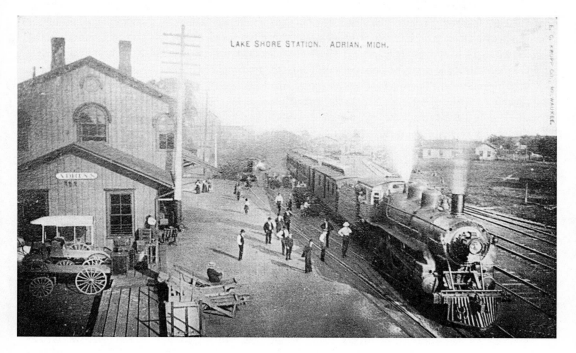

A postcard of Adrian's Lake Shore and Michigan Southern Railroad Depot, where many baseball teams stopped through the years (courtesy Lenawee County Historical Society).

down to defeat, "it was not anticipated that they were so completely outclassed. The trouble was, they went to pieces and were unable to keep their feet." Findlay had come into the game with a record of 62 wins and only 12 losses, and just watching them practice before the game gave the Adrian squad the "rattles" and left them "scared out of their wits." The saving grace was the performance by the Detroit imports, Charles and Henry Guthard, along with Jim Tracy. The entire Light Guard team was the target of Findlay's "joshing" and "incessant chattering," which apparently befuddled both the local nine and the umpire. Findlay was a very aggressive team, as the visitors "played ball every minute as if their lives depended upon the struggle."[19]

The Light Guard, clad in their shiny new uniforms, managed two walks in the opening inning before being retired without scoring. Fowler led off for Findlay, was promptly hit by the pitch, and later scored on a sacrifice fly. Johnson blooped a hit over second base and into center field and later scored on an error, and the Light Guard escaped the first inning only down, 2–0.[20] After a walk and an error, Adrian's second promising inning left them scoreless. Findlay tallied three more runs in their half of the second inning. Fowler knocked in the first run and later scored on Johnson's homer into the weeds as he "pounded" the ball to "the north bank for a home run, making the longest hit seen on the grounds this year."[21]

One exciting play came in the third inning when both Fowler and Johnson, following the latter's blooper over shortstop, became caught in a rundown. Fowler tried to score, but stopped between third base and home. Attempting to return to third, Fowler looked up to see Johnson trying to advance to third, too. A fumbled toss allowed both runners to scamper back to their previous bases. A groundout ended the Light Guard agony for that inning after three runs. However, after four innings Findlay had 14 runs and never looked back. When Adrian did eventually score, the success was tamped down a bit when a second runner was nailed on a head-first slide at home plate in a close play.[22] The day ended in the lopsided 19–2 score, with Johnson and three teammates recording three hits and Fowler two, including a double. Bets were placed all morning, including by at least a few of the visiting players, that the Findlay Sluggers would score more runs in one inning than the local boys would in the entire game. And they were right.[23]

"The attendance at the game was unusually large," reported a paper and likely making the organizers quite happy and rich. "The grand stand being filled to overflowing, while a great many carriages were standing in the field."[24]

The following day, the crowd was again anticipating a good game. The teenaged George Wilson, from little Palmyra, was on the mound for the Light Guard team, while the ace of Findlay, Harry Pastorius, was pitching for the visitors. Over 800 people jammed Lawrence Park "and when Umpire Skip Mullaly tossed the new ball into the diamond and called play, the enthusiasm was at a fever heat. All occupying the grand stand were anxious to learn the outcome of young Wilson's ability against such sluggers."[25] Major leaguer Bob Allen made an appearance, but not as a hired ringer for the Light Guard squad. Instead, Allen was a special, one-day sports correspondent for the *Times and Expositor* to add credibility to the game's story.[26]

Game two was a much closer and cleaner affair than the first. Wilson held Findlay mostly in check, giving up only three runs through seven innings. Unfortunately, Findlay's Pastorius was handling the locals much better and shutting them out, 6–0. Wilson struck out three but walked four and gave up ten hits. The previous day's nine Adrian fielding errors were cut to just four miscues, thanks largely to better play at shortstop by Ernie

Sorter. For the home team, Wilson was the star of the afternoon. He picked off his counterpart Pastorius, who "was caught napping off first base" and was tagged out in a rundown. Later, when Wilson came off the field in the fifth inning after holding the Sluggers to two runs, "the audience cheered long and loud [and] he was made to doff his cap." In the eighth inning, "much to Wilson's delight," he struck out "Home Run" Johnson, and again the young lad was loudly applauded. In the ninth, Wilson was the Light Guard's last batter, and when he grounded out to Fowler at second base, "the greatest game of the season came to an end." Findlay had swept the two-game series.[27]

Local jeweler George Tripp was good to his word, and Paul Kraft won the silver match box, thanks to a pair of doubles he slugged in the second game. Due to the Light Guard's lack of success, both Sheldon and Kirk's prizes were safely returned to their jewelry store. Another problem was that there were still, according to one paper, "entirely too many people occupying the free seats on the north bank." This issue would have to be resolved for Adrian's claim to be the state's baseball hotbed to be turned into a profitable venture. Findlay's business manager, William H. Drake, said his club "has had the nicest kind of treatment and is desirous of again returning to Adrian soon." The feeling was mutual, as the *Adrian Times and Expositor*, despite seeing the visitors outscore the locals, 25–2, declared, "we shall always welcome any club that may be under Mr. Drake's management."[28]

The wheels of profit were not only just spinning in the heads of Adrian boosters. After seeing the crowds in Adrian, Bud Fowler had let it be known that he was signing black ball players for the next year, and they would be called Findlay's Colored Western Giants. The *Evening Telegram* claimed that Fowler would relocate the club in Adrian in 1895 if the town could "guarantee him $500 and fix up good grounds." Fowler was also concerned about the freeloaders on the creek bank. Adrian resident Doug Underwood had met Fowler years ago, while Fowler pitched on a team out west and Underwood was an official scorer. So Fowler had at least one Adrian connection. To add to this local tug, Fowler apparently told people his proposed team needed a pitcher and he liked George Wilson.[29]

Following their victories and before he boarded the train to head out of town Friday morning, Fowler told more people he thought Adrian was a good baseball town "and would make the club's headquarters here, if enough support was given him by business men." Acting upon the hint, Len Hoch floated an idea that he would stake one-half or $250 of the Fowler requirement and work on improving the Lawrence Park grounds. Someone came up with the idea of a specially outfitted train car, with a cooking area and living compartments large enough for 15 to 18 people, to serve as the team's travelling hotel, if dining rooms and hotels for black men could not secured in a town. It was even hinted that the profits would be split. Fowler claimed his roster would rival the present-day, East Coast–based all-star black team, the Cuban Giants. The *Evening Telegram* was excited for the city and bragged, "Nothing would advertise as that, and we could soon become the ball center of the state, if not the west."[30]

The progressive town of Adrian had just the man to lure the baseball stars to the Lenawee County community. He was a modern businessman who was putting Adrian on the map with his fence-making factory. While Fowler would be the baseball brains in the operation, a middle-aged white gentleman would provide the money and marketing for this crack team.

John Wallace Page, who was normally referred to as simply J. Wallace, was dubbed the laughingstock of his Rollins Township farming neighborhood. In the 1880s, he began to tinker around with wire, which led to him creating a large, wooden weaving loom contraption. Couple that with the fact that J. Wallace, a married man with three young children, spent much of his time in his barn with a teenaged assistant, Charles Lamb, who doubled as his cousin, made him the butt of jokes. But Page greeted the cynics with a broad grin and unbridled optimism and kept plugging away with a goal to build a better fence.[31]

His father, John Olson Page, died when little J. Wallace was about three years old. It left his mother, Martha Hannah Lamb Page, a young widow, to raise him and his younger brother, Henry, on their Rollin Township farm. Within a few years, Martha married Gilbert Sackett, another farmer and native New Yorker. Martha then gave birth to a son, Charlie. Unfortunately, Martha died in 1852, leaving Sackett with three young boys to raise, all under the age of eight. By the time the Civil War broke out, J. Wallace and Henry had been pawned off to their paternal grandmother, Evalina, and step-grandfather, Samuel Bachelor. In the 1860 census, both boys were incorrectly listed with the last name of Bachelor. Living and farming nearby was his mother's brother, uncle Roswell Sylvetus Lamb, who was Charles Lamb's dad, and J. Wallace's future trusty and inventive assistant.[32]

Page initially joined the war in the fall of 1862 as an under-aged enlistee in the 17th Michigan Volunteer Infantry Regiment. Persuaded by friends and relatives to reveal his true age and back out of his service commitment, Page did so, much to the relief of his neighbors. Eventually, John Wallace Page got his wish, and in the fall of 1863 signed up with Company F, 1st Michigan Light Artillery. Within a year, Page was promoted from private to corporal and served under one of the war's most famous men, General William Tecumseh Sherman. As part of the artillery battery, Wallace was a member of the 23rd Army Corps, which spent time with Sherman conquering Atlanta and then burning and destroying Southerners' property through the Carolinas. Wallace was also able to see up-close what happens to wooden fences when someone or something is determined to wreck them.[33]

Unlike one of his Lamb ancestors, a famous Revolutionary War Minuteman, who joined the fight the day following Paul Revere's famous ride, Page's military experience wasn't as notable.[34] There was no record of him ever being injured, wounded or taken prisoner, and his promotion was just one level—private to corporal. Page was officially mustered out in July 1865 in Jackson, Michigan, took the train home to Adrian, and walked a few miles north to Rollins Township. Wallace later told how he immediately returned to farm life by mowing his grandparent's Bachelor front yard the afternoon he arrived home from the war.[35]

With the thought of inventing a non-wooden fence seared into this mind, J. Wallace resumed civilian life. His full-time farming operation apparently meant that designing fence was not his main occupation. Two years later, he married Alice Morehouse, from Albion, Michigan, and the couple settled into the Page farm in Rollins Township, adjacent to the Bachelors. Living with the newlyweds was Alice's father, Aaron Morehouse, and sister, Helen, a school teacher. In 1869, Charles Page was born and was the first of the couple's three children. By 1880, J. Wallace and Alice had added two other children, Bertha and Homer.[36]

Leaving the raising of the children to Alice in the early 1880s allowed fence creating to become a major factor in Page's life. Using the relatively new Joseph Glidden invention of barbed wire as a starting point, J. Wallace quickly hit a roadblock and discarded that metal fence design. Page believed barbed wire was too sharp and unsuitable for livestock, who could brush against it and become injured. He explored an alternative to the sharp, twisted metal fence.[37] Tinkering in his barn with his cousin, Charles Lamb, who was just in his early teens, and with supportive assistance by fellow Rollins farmers Austin Fitts and Frank E. Harvey, Page spent several years bending and shaping metal wire. He first bent them by hand, but soon invented his own tools to work the metal. He also spent much time with a rickety wooden loom, originally designed to weave cloth. While seen as a "crank" by neighbors, J. Wallace's personality did not let those doubters affect his spirit or work ethic. After finishing his daily farming chores, he was back to his metal fence and loom. Visitors to his work shed, greeted with a broad grin, would laugh and poke jokes, and some suggested he should have his head examined for spending so much time with these "wheels, and levers and pulleys."[38] Ignoring the naysayers, he continued working and in 1884, with the help of some of his more supportive neighbors, strung a section of the woven wire fence on his Rollins Township farm. He had eliminated the barbs and single twisted wire concept that Glidden had adapted. This new Page fence invention consisted of a series of single strands of "wire woven into a square mesh fabric, with cross wires and horizontal wires wrapped and knotted," creating a stronger and safer alternative to wooden fence posts or barbed wire.[39]

Page sold what he could weave in his shed and briefly in 1888 opened a shop in nearby Hudson, Michigan. About a year later, he moved his metal weaving loom to an old brick building on the east end of Adrian, along the north side of Michigan Avenue, adjacent to the Lake Shore and Michigan Southern Railroad tracks. A newspaper article later described the first Page Fence office as pretty barren and rustic. J. Wallace Page was quoted as saying,

J. Wallace Page's famous wire loom in use at the Page Woven Wire Fence Company factory in Adrian (courtesy Lenawee County Historical Museum).

A spool of fence awaiting shipping, produced by J. Wallace Page's unique weaving machine in Adrian (courtesy Lenawee County Historical Museum).

"The office desk was an inverted flour barrel, with an old door thrown across it, and the office chair, instead of being a revolving affair, was a nail keg with a board top. The bookkeeping was done in an ordinary grocer's order book."[40] The year of the move to Adrian, 1889, this farmer turned fence designer incorporated his idea into the Page Woven Wire Fence Company.

Within a few years, the company would employ hundreds of people and ship his woven fence all over the world. By the beginning of the next century, in 11 short years, the Page Fence Company would be the largest employer in Adrian. Long known as a railroad town, with the Lake Shore and Michigan Southern car repair shops located here, Adrian was now the fence capital of the world, as others tapped into Page's idea. His sprawling factory complex, along Michigan Avenue and McVicar Street, sat right across the street from the L. S.

& M. S. railroad shops, a reminder of the new dominant business in town. Page's success was not only due to his novel and inventive cross-mesh fencing design, but wonderfully creative and unique marketing strategies.

The *Daily Times and Expositor* story was entitled, "Fertile Fancies, Of the Page Wire Fence Promoters, Evolve an Excellent Advertising Idea." The three-paragraph article told how the company had just constructed an 80-foot-long fence of "coiled wire, with a slat floor for a footway." Engineers calculated it would hold 240 people, each weighing 200 pounds, for a total of 24 tons of humans. Now stretching across the back-factory lot, this portable bridge would be shipped, along with caged wild animals, to county fairs back east, as a testament to the strength of the Page's wire designs. Definitely an excellent advertising idea, as the article noted.[41]

Adjacent to this Page Fence article was a preview story promoting the Findlay baseball team coming to Adrian. In the story, Bud Fowler unveiled to Adrianites for the first time his plan for creating his

A portrait of J. Wallace Page, founder and President of the Page Woven Wire Fence Company (courtesy Lenawee County Historical Museum).

"Findlay Colored Baseball Giants."[42] Fowler's squad would travel around the country the following summer and play high-caliber baseball. As an added benefit to the nation's culture, these gentlemen would promote black excellence to a still largely segregated America.

It is not known if J. Wallace Page read the two articles that day. But a white farmer from southern Michigan, turned business tycoon, and a black ballplayer from upstate New York both knew how to promote their product. And in 1895, that is what they did.

◆ 4 ◆

The Boys Are Back in Town

Fowler had returned to Adrian in mid–September following a game against Monroe, but without his Findlay Sluggers. An Adrian paper claimed that the rival Monroe team tried to steal a game from Findlay using "an unscrupulous umpire" and manager Jack's (who obviously had not been fired last month as one Adrian paper had gleefully reported) "unmanly tactics."[1] How truthful the latest report was is pure conjecture, but Monroe did defeat Adrian two games out of three to claim the 1894 Michigan amateur championship. Both Adrian and Monroe used paid players to improve their team's chances. Monroe, as the crowned champions, would have been a ripe spot for Fowler's new black all-star team. But maybe the Lotus city's unscrupulous baseball management and the town's rabid boosters' antics were indeed critical factors in Fowler considering Adrian over Monroe.

On Wednesday, September 19, 1894, Grant Johnson joined Fowler in Adrian "for the purpose of booming the scheme of making this city the headquarters of the 'Cuban Giants,' the colored team." There were rumors that both men would play for Adrian's Light Guard team that afternoon against Delphos, Ohio, but they were quickly quashed when it was said there were no infield openings and Gus Parsons "had too much tact" to make room for the Findlayites. Fowler apparently made no bones about it, saying that this was a strictly business trip and he wanted to see what could be arranged in baseball-crazed Adrian. However, Johnson decided to play, so Parsons put him in the outfield against Delphos and kept the Light Guard infield intact. On Tuesday, Adrian had beaten Delphos, but today Delphos earned its revenge, defeating the Light Guard, 13–6. Wilson was not particularly effective on this chilly day on the mound, but Johnson lived up to his star billing. The shortstop turned right fielder slugged his 58th home run, which plopped into the creek past right field, making the "splash as of a drowning horse," while a phalanx of kids dug the ball out of the muddy water. Johnson skipped his way around the bases, jumped on home plate and bowed to the appreciative crowd. In the field, Johnson played the outfield "like a circus canvas covering a 40-acre lot."[2] While the Adrian team's play was not stellar that day, local rooters were optimistic about the proposed team for next season. "Local base ball enthusiasts are much interested in the enterprise and it is not improbable that Fowler's scheme may succeed."[3]

The *Adrian Evening Telegram* purported to scoop the decision, saying that Len Hoch and Fowler had a long meeting Wednesday morning to settle the proposal. Local businessman Rolla Taylor would invest in the other 50 percent of the team, matching Hoch's original pledge. The paper's scoop said the location of the ball diamond was still a question mark and that Adrian needed to "push, push hard" for the team. The rumored name of the team would be the Western Colored Giants, and both Fowler and Grant Johnson would be on the roster.[4]

Two days later, on September 21, the *Adrian Daily Times and Expositor* blared that the team's name would be the Page Fence Giants and it would be "a crack colored base ball team." The same day, the competing *Adrian Evening Telegram* said Fowler's proposed team would consist of "the finest aggregation of colored professional ball players ever brought together in this country." In addition, "the name of one of the best institutions in this city will become a household word from one end of the country to another," referring to the Page Woven Wire Fence Company. The *Daily Times and Expositor* also outlined some of the business arrangements between Fowler and the Page Fence Company. The company would not share in any of the game receipts and would generate profits by using the team as an advertising vehicle for both their firm and the town of Adrian. This arrangement was characterized as a "novel and effective medium," and the Page Fence Company paid a "nice little amount" for this sponsorship privilege.[5] As part of the advertising campaign, whenever the Giants appeared in a community, a locally based Page Fence Company sales agent would display fence samples down at the ball field, hoping the baseball tie-in promotion would lead to increased sales.[6]

Fowler had told the papers on the day of the announcement that his black ball players would be of high character, which was "extremely gratifying to the Adrian gentlemen having the matter at heart [likely Hoch and the Taylors]."[7] As the 1894 baseball season still had about two weeks remaining, Fowler's contact with currently employed ball players was likely problematic, as team owners wondered about their next season's roster. However, Fowler used his immense nationwide baseball contacts to offer black players a new team option for the 1895 season.

The paper backed off its story from two days earlier that Hoch and Taylor would lead the company themselves. However, it would also not be led by Fowler or Johnson, as the issue of race began to creep into the new business arrangement. "The club will be accompanied on this tour by some capable and energetic white man as general business manager, representing the financial end of the association. The plan is that this should also be an Adrian man."[8] While Hoch and Taylor were prominent, now that the Page Fence Company was involved, someone from that firm needed to make decisions for the ball club too. There were hints that additional business partners could be added to the Giants management group.

The other issue to be resolved was where the Giants would play in Adrian. Hoch noted that the local Lawrence Park, in its present state, was not suitable for hosting the team, but if "put in proper shape and can be secured at a reasonable rate," it was the likeliest local option. However, Fowler's goal was to play many games in other cities and promote the Page Woven Wire Fence Company. The possibility of playing six to eight games a month in Adrian against strong teams was still likely, giving the locals the chance to see the team. Team management was busy drawing up their 1895 schedule, already had games with Cincinnati, Cleveland, Toledo and Milwaukee, and was awaiting word from other national and Western professional leagues.[9]

On the management side, Len Hoch and Rolla Taylor would be involved with the Giants in a yet-to-be-defined role. The recently appointed Light Guard business manager, Gus Parsons, following the August coup against L.A. Browne, would assume that same role with the Giants. But the actual managing of game strategy would be left to baseball legend Bud Fowler, who would also play second base. His Findlay teammate and shortstop phenomenon, Grant Johnson, now dubbed "Home Run" after slugging 60 round trippers that year, would be the Page Fence Giants' captain.[10]

Fowler's plan was to sign 13 black ball players from across the country, and Palmyra's George Wilson was one who would be approached. The experienced baseball man felt that Wilson, with strong support from this all-star squad, would develop into a fine hurler.[11] This Page Fence Giants was a new and novel idea for Adrian and the state of Michigan. But there were other black teams in the United States, such as the eastern-based Cuban Giants and the Chicago Unions, who also traveled to play amateur and professional squads. Adrian's attempt would just add one more team to this unique and competitive entertainment market.

Another feature of the Page Fence Giants would be the pre-game promotional entertainment. Every Giants player would be given a bicycle, from a yet unsecured manufacturer, and "drilled in various maneuvers" to create a parade to the ball park.[12] Clad in firemen's helmets and brightly colored red outfits, the players would lead baseball fans to the diamond, a la the Pied Piper. Eventually, the Massachusetts-based Monarch Bike Company was selected as the supplier, and Adrian's Taylor Brothers quickly added that brand for sale at their hardware store on South Main Street.

Like baseball, bicycle riding was becoming a new rage for Americans in the 1890s. This mode of transportation was easy to use and offered the burgeoning middle class a new travel contraption. Horses could be bothersome to feed and water and were also hard to control when spooked. Bicycles were much easier to control than a team of horses pulling a buggy. This new contraption was even a symbol for the women's rights movement. The movement championed the bicycle as a way for modern young ladies to visit friends, go to work, or tour the countryside without a male chaperone. It signified freedom and with its price tag became a status symbol for those able to afford this new fad. Those people who were physically too small or too weak to control a horse could certainly ride a bike. Baseball and bikes seemed to be a perfect meshing of where modern America was heading as it neared the end of the century.

One especially innovative aspect of the new baseball team had nothing to do with modern conveniences, at least as its underlying reason. The team planned to travel and live in "a special combination dining and sleeping car," manned by a resident chef and a combination railroad porter and barber. While on the surface this plan sounds like the modern charter jets of today's professional teams, in reality, this arrangement was due to necessity.

The famed attempt at Civil War Reconstruction faded quickly following the disputed 1876 Presidential election. As part of the day's political wheeling and dealing, the Republicans would be given the White House and Rutherford B. Hayes made President, if the remaining soldiers, who the South still saw as those damn Yankees, would be withdrawn from the old Confederacy. The troops were stationed in the South to ensure that black rights were accorded, following the passage of the 13th (ending slavery), 14th (granting civil rights) and 15th (granting voting rights to black men) Amendments to the U.S. Constitution. Also, the Ku Klux Klan, which outgoing President U. S. Grant had done his best to thwart by authorizing aggressive action against these purveyors of terror, would no longer be a federal government target with him out of office.

Several contested governor's races involved in the national political shenanigans would be given to the Democrats, as part of the quid pro quo presidential agreement. Basically, the Republicans traded a seat in the White House for control over the South. The political deal resulted in many Republicans turning their back on black people and the idea of Reconstruction. It gave the entire South back to the Democrats, who still harbored resent-

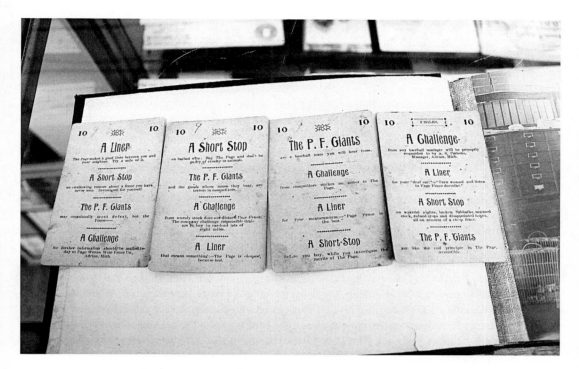

An advertising deck of playing cards distributed by the Page Fence Company. The four number-10 cards of the 52-card deck featured the Giants baseball team (courtesy Hudson Museum).

ment against the long-dead Abraham Lincoln, the Yankee military, and the North in general. By 1894 this earlier political wheeling and dealing had seeped across the country, and now the rights of "colored" people were being diminished in many places, both in the North and South.

First, there was no possibility a train car of young, athletic and mostly Northern-born and raised black ballplayers was going to ride into some Southern town to play the local white team. Allowing high school and college educated black gentleman to beat the locals was not going to happen. Many white towns in the North were now struggling with racial animosity, a generation after the end of Reconstruction. Acts of intimidation and violence were commonplace in parts of the United States. Newspapers noted the activity of the Ku Klux Klan or "white caps," as they were often referred to now. It became very clear when one read a news story whether the paper supported these self-proclaimed defenders of American Christianity and whiteness, or thought they were troublesome activists and conduits of unlawful, vigilante justice. During this KKK reincarnation, they branched out and targeted white citizens who committed heinous crimes, were abject drunkards, violated the vows of marriage or just simply supported black rights. While the majority of "white cap" attacks were aimed at black citizens, including carrying out the horrifying crime of lynching, whites were targeted in communities without a black population.

Second, a well-equipped and staffed train car would save Gus Parsons time, effort and the stress of trying to locate hotels and restaurants that would accommodate the black men. The Giants would simply hitch their fancy car to the rear of a passenger or freight train, arrive in town, uncouple, and sit on a side track to await their daily parade and ball game.

If the local business establishment wanted to feed or house the Giants, they would. If not, lounging, eating and sleeping could be done safely in the train car. As an added safety measure, the very athletic black men would also be kept away from curious white women, often the greatest fear white Americans, both North and South, had about integration.

Postmaster Hoch greatly assisted Fowler's effort to sign the right type of ballplayer. The *Daily Times and Expositor* noted, "the organization of this remarkable team, and the establishment of its headquarters here, are largely due to the energetic efforts of Mr. Hoch." It is likely Hoch was aware, and Fowler absolutely was aware, of what type of ball player would draw white crowds, even in the North. "It may be of interest to the public to know, however, that none of the men drink intoxicants and that only two of them use tobacco. Five of them are college graduates, and one a high school graduate," bragged the *Expositor*. At the time, the "white caps" included temperance (forbidding the drinking of alcohol) in their platform, which added Roman Catholics and many other European immigrants onto their updated enemies list. However, it is hard to verify the education and vice level of the Page Fence Giants at the time of the team's formal unveiling. Hoch, putting feelers out to black players currently under contract on both integrated and segregated professional baseball teams, didn't want tampering accusations to sully Adrian's grand idea. The paper noted that Hoch would not be releasing any future Giants' player's names yet.[13]

Adrian newspapers highlighted Fowler's baseball acumen, and whatever negative racial undercurrents were present across the country, they appeared to be non-existent, or at least not widely publicized, in the Lenawee County community. The *Daily Times and Expositor* wrote of Fowler's many years of ball playing and "extensive knowledge" of the game. They added his "familiarity with followers of the game enabled him to select his men with a perfect understanding of their ability." They bragged that in addition to the slugging Grant Johnson, one prospective player even had a higher batting average than the young star shortstop.[14] The following day, the *Detroit Free Press* picked up the story, announced "Adrian's New Colored Team" in a headline, and stated that it would likely be an "invincible" squad and "fifteen of whom are already signed." The *Free Press* said the goal was to provide a "first-class" roster and noted the prominent enterprising interests of Roe (Rolla) Taylor and Hoch. Despite Hoch's wish to keep the names under wraps, except for the previously announced Fowler and Johnson, the *Free Press* said George Wilson was one of the 15 players in the fold. Again, bragging of the character of the players, the paper described them as of "superior intelligence," with five college graduates and others completing "academies or high schools," while "not a member uses liquor in any form."[15] The team's message was loud and clear to both the white caps and to the general public: these were the good black men you could trust around your wife and children.

The following week, Fowler's business scheme was detailed by the leading sports magazine in the country, *The Sporting News*, based in St. Louis, Missouri. Their September 29, 1894, edition confused one of the current black teams with Fowler's new nine. The national paper wrongly called the new Page Fence Giants by the name Cuban Giants. They correctly noted that the club would travel in a special train car and open their season with an exhibition game with the Cincinnati Reds. During the late 1800s, often the code names for black teams were Cubans or Giants. Presumably, the Cuban island natives were not like the United States' negatively stereotyped lazy black people. The Giants name, for some reason, was also often attached to teams comprised of black athletes.

When Bud Fowler, baseball's tumbleweed, returned to Adrian on Wednesday night, October 10, 1894, much work had already been completed in compiling the all-star travelling team for the 1895 season. His usual winter job as a barber had secured him a position at Reid and Craig's shop in Adrian. His arrival was much anticipated, as baseball-crazy Adrian and the local ball cranks were already excited for the next season.

Around the time Fowler arrived in town, the companion paper to the *Adrian Daily Times and Expositor*, the *Weekly Times and Expositor*, unveiled the names of the 1895 Page Fence Giants prospects. Reprinting an article from the *Findlay Ohio Times*, where Fowler or Grant was their likely source, the first Page Fence Giants roster listed 12 names. Palmyra's lefty hurler, Wilson, was offered a contract, but had not yet responded to Fowler and Hoch's letter. Of the 12, two had not yet returned a signed contract, but the story didn't indicate which two. According to the report, the catchers would be Vasco Graham of the Dubuque, Iowa, Whites and a man named Barner from the Texas Colored League. On the mound, Joe Miller, also of the Dubuque Whites, was approached, as was veteran George Hopkins of the Chicago Unions black team, along with a Chattanooga native named Dewheny. At first base would be George H. Taylor, with Fowler at second, Grant "Home Run" Johnson at shortstop, and J. W. Patterson of the Cuban Giants at third. The outfield was to consist of John Nelson of Oberlin College in Ohio in center, flanked by Gus Brooks of the Chicago Unions in right and a man named Howard of Ohio's Wilberforce University in left field. Fowler said about his recruits, "this team will be the strongest colored aggregation ever organized."[16]

While the 1894 baseball season had concluded, Hoch had no problem contacting highly regarded and morally straight black men for the 1895 campaign. Unfortunately, the other clubs didn't see it that way and did not like the competition for their squad's best players. Thus, for the next four years public sniping took place, as players and management tried to portray their respective team as the best black nine in the country. The upstart Page Fence Giants were making no friends in going after players from the Cuban Giants and Chicago Unions, the reputed top dogs in this narrow, but lucrative entertainment field.

Hoch was also busy wiring established teams around the country to meet his all-star group for games beginning in April of 1895. He and his wife traveled to Chicago in mid–November and met with Western League representatives to secure games.[17] The Findlay paper claimed that agreements had been made with big city professional teams in Cincinnati, Cleveland, Toledo and Milwaukee, as previously publicized. In addition, Grand Rapids, Detroit and Indianapolis were now on the list, as were the Findlay Sluggers, minus Fowler and Johnson, along with northern Ohio clubs in Lima, Delaware, Kenton, and Mansfield.[18]

National publicity continued for Adrian, the Page Woven Wire Fence Company and baseball great Bud Fowler. Another national magazine, *Sporting Life*, based in Philadelphia, printed a release in early December 1894, from an unnamed someone in Adrian, likely Hoch, touting the talent of the Giants. The Philadelphia magazine screamed "Some More Giants" and "Michigan has a Colored Rival for the Eastern Cuban Giants." The old Light Guard upper management of Rolla Taylor, Seymour Howell, Len Hoch and Gus Parsons were bombarded with requests to field the best team possible, proving that "base ball fever is still holding the attention of the people of Adrian."[19] The release falsely claimed that "Adrian holds the amateur championship of the state, and we have something to defend," and ignored the two losses against Monroe a few months earlier. The *Sporting Life* article reiterated the use of a special passenger train car and a bicycle parade before each game and said Fowler would be the team's manager. An added note was that Hoch had been successful in securing many games, as the Giants were booked up to June 1 and would travel to at least ten states. Showing the old orientation of the United States, Michigan was referred to as the Northwest, which had recently "gained prominence" from baseball enthusiasts and ensured "undoubtedly one of the strongest teams in the country."[20]

Later that month, *The Sporting News* printed a release signed by an H. Emery, who was either J. H. Emery, the proprietor of the Hotel Emery, or Gus Parsons, desk clerk of the Hotel Emery. The headline claimed the "Page Fence Colored Team Will Create a Sensation Next Year." Emery's note stated that the Giants would be "the strongest colored team ever organized." An updated roster unveiled some new players over the previously published October list. Eight players—Fowler, Johnson, Patterson, Miller, Brooks, Hopkins, Howard and Taylor—were holdovers. Billy Holland, William Malone and Fred Van Dyke were new names, along with a player only referred to as Maupin (Frank), were added to "the pick of a hundred colored players." The young hurler, George Wilson, was not mentioned. Game dates were also revealed, and April 9 and 10, 1895, against Indianapolis would be the first official contests for the Page Fence Giants. The schedule followed with games against the Cincinnati Reds, April 11 and 12, in Toledo on April 13, in Grand Rapids, Michigan, on April 14, 15 and 16, in Chicago, April 17, in Milwaukee on April 18 and 19, followed by an additional stop in two new towns—St. Paul and Minneapolis, Minnesota.[21] The Giants were planning on traveling far and wide in their inaugural season and playing top-level minor league squads, not to mention the major league Reds.

Locally, Bud Fowler and his reputation were good for business in Adrian. "Play Ball" screamed the advertisement in the *Evening Telegram* of the Oriental Barber Shop, operated by Craig and Reid, the "live, young, energetic business men, whose Tonsorial manipulating works is done in first-class style." The pair's ad featured Fowler's efforts at organizing the Page Fence Giants, as Craig and Reid never mentioned Fowler's hair cutting abilities. Claiming the new team would be the "greatest colored club ever" and that the fence company never did "business by halves," they invited friends to stop by their store and visit with Fowler.[22]

To further publicize the fence company and the team, the new Monarch bicycles would be delivered to Adrian in January. The Giants were also reportedly going to arrive in town sometime during the winter, to be outfitted in their baseball uniforms and photographed for a promotional calendar. The 1895 calendars would then be sent to baseball managers and fence company agents across the Midwest to help spread the word about the modern and safe fence product and the greatest group of black ball players ever assembled.[23]

◆ 5 ◆

It Had to Be You

Adrian wasn't the original name for the community. It was first dubbed Logan, after a Native America chief, and for about a decade was referred to by that name.[1] By 1829, Logan had established its first grist mill, school and post office, and a year later the 1830 census counted 500 people living in the River Raisin community.[2] Logan (Adrian) experienced additional growth with the arrival of the Erie and Kalamazoo Railroad from Toledo, Ohio, in 1836.[3] The railroad allowed farmers and businessmen to ship products, while travelers arrived with new ideas to spread, as the town featured the most modern transportation system known to man at the time. A few months before the train's arrival, political wrangling in March 1836 saw Tecumseh lose its county seat status to Logan. The Michigan legislature voted to transfer the headquarters of county government, but the effective date wasn't until the fall of 1838, the same year Logan became Adrian.[4]

When Michigan conducted it first state census in 1837, the town of Logan and surrounding townships had 1,962 people, which was a three-fold increase from just seven years earlier.[5] During Michigan's territorial phase, the bulk of the populace consisted of white settlers from the east, living among a smattering of Native Americans traversing the region. The Logan area had recorded just a single black person (male) in 1830 but increased to 11 black people in 1840. The black population in Adrian remained sparse for the next decade, as only two mulatto families were living in Adrian in 1850, with four of the children enrolled in school.[6]

About two decades earlier, the area became familiar with some black people as a stop on the Underground Railroad. Beginning sometime in the 1830s, famed abolitionist Laura Haviland and husband, Charles, placed Adrian as the state's first Underground Railroad station. Living a few miles northeast of Adrian on their Raisin Township homestead, the Havilands did their part to smuggle runaway slaves out of the South and into Canada.[7] Laura's journeys from Cincinnati, Ohio, to Windsor, Canada, chaperoning runaway slaves caused irate plantation owners to place a $3,000 bounty on her head, which masters would pay, dead or alive. "Aunt Laura," as she was popularly known, had a zest for black freedom that soon made her a household name around the country. She and her husband also opened the Raisin Institute in the 1830s. Light years ahead of its time, "it was to be a school for all people of good moral character regardless of sex or color." It was Michigan's first coeducational school, which was also open to black students, with a focus on training new teachers. When the Institute closed after 11 years of operation in 1849, it allowed the now-widowed Laura time to focus all her efforts on ending slavery. While her home was in nearby Raisin Township, Haviland's presence was felt in Adrian. Later, when she finally relocated her Raisin Asylum to Adrian, she became a full-fledged member of the town's society.[8]

When the Republican Party was formed in 1854 under the famed oaks in nearby Jackson, Michigan, the town of Adrian was well represented. A group of white men from Adrian traveled the 40 miles north to Jackson and created the new political party whose main goal was, at the very least, to stop the expansion of slavery. A more radical wing of the newly created Republican Party manifested itself in the Michigan Anti-Slavery Party and believed in the complete abolition of slavery. About a dozen Adrian residents, including three African Americans, were involved in this fledgling political organization.[9]

A few years later, in 1858, Adrian's black population held the town's first Colored People's Festival, which continued for many years and was centered on the British West Indies' abolition of slavery. The event also drew neighboring black people to Adrian to participate in the festivities. In that same year, Adrian's black citizens founded the town's Bethel African Methodist Episcopal Church.[10]

The following year, in 1859, the Wesleyan Methodists opened Adrian College. Nestled on a 20-acre spread on the west end of town, it began with four buildings.[11] The Methodists were one of the long-time groups advocating the ending of slavery, and that idea meshed nicely with the local Republicans and with the reinvigorated Michigan Anti-Slavery Party. Controversial preacher Asa Mahan led Adrian College, bringing from the ultra-liberal Oberlin College in Ohio a strident zeal for equality. While Oberlin's President, Mahan presided over the country's first coeducational school that awarded both men and women college diplomas. Mahan's vision carried over to his long stay in Adrian. However, his fiery anti-slavery speeches were said to have driven as many people away from the college as it attracted.[12] While Mahan may have irritated some of the people in Adrian, there were enough whites and blacks who embraced his message. During the 1861–1862 academic year, two black students, William and Elizabeth Fitzbutler, a brother and sister, were enrolled at Adrian College.[13]

The struggle to end slavery was not solved in the halls of Congress, and as a result, in the spring of 1861 the country split over the issue. During the Civil War, Michigan sent more people per capita to battle than any other Northern state. They also lost many men in the four-year struggle, both black and white. As the war was winding down in January 1865, a group of black men organized the St. John's Lodge of the Masonic Order in Adrian. Unlike the other half-dozen Mason groups in town, they were unable to meet in the whites-only, elegant Lodge Hall. As a result, these black Masons gathered above a store on East Maumee Street.[14]

As the war ended in the spring of 1865, leisure activities replaced fights on the battlefields. In June, the Adrian Anchora Base Ball Club challenged the Monroe Star Club and won, 14–10. Afterward, there was a dinner at the Lawrence House in honor of both teams. A rematch a week later in Monroe saw Anchora again victorious. That summer the Anchora team split two games with the Detroit Baseball Club. The game's excitement carried over as Adrian baseball boosters organized a tournament in conjunction with hosting the state fair in September. The four-team event saw Detroit defeat the Anchora squad once again. The local squad played three more games that season, both in and out of town.[15] An 1866 map shows the baseball field on a slab of land adjacent to the mill race on the city's west side of town and on what would later be known as Lawrence Park.[16] These early baseball games were evidence that this Midwestern town had an early and longtime association with what would become America's pastime.

Following the war, as men trickled back home or to new and exciting places to resume their lives, the town grew. Adrian's black population also continued to play a key role in the community. In 1866, the college-educated, Louisiana-born gentleman, W. J. Clanton, was hired to a "responsible position" at Adrian's Oakwood Cemetery. Eventually his three decades of work made him a well-known man about town. An active black Republican, Clanton never ran for office, but often advised those seeking votes. He was described as "modest ... and unassuming," with the "worthy traits of integrity and reliability."[17]

Near the end of the decade, the black community found the need for another similar church in town. In 1869 the Second Baptist Church was organized and met on North Broad Street, in what was called the Wells block, near East Maumee Street. One of its founding members and its first preacher was a Mr. Jackson, who remained there for about four years. A member of the original organizing body was Champ Carter, who became a Reverend and later led the congregation. The Carter family would remain in Adrian well into the 20th century.[18]

In 1870 Adrian was the sixth-largest city in the state, trailing only Detroit, Grand Rapids, Jackson, Kalamazoo and East Saginaw. The Lenawee County community boasted a population of around 12,000 with its borders spanning two and a half miles east to west and a little over a mile north and south. The ever-growing railroad freight traffic saw Adrian produce and sell many diverse items which provided the towns with jobs and money. Everything from wool to apples, wheat, oats, flour, potatoes, lumber, bricks, ales and beers flowed out of the town.[19]

The black community also continued to grow along with the town. It's possible the reputation of Haviland, Mahan, Adrian College and two black churches was a guiding light to black people looking for a new beginning. An 1870 city directory has more than 60 black households and 160 residents within Adrian, a great jump from the 11 in 1850. While the bulk of the black residents were hired laborers, or lived as servants with some of the wealthier white families, a fair number ran businesses on their own. There were about a dozen African American barbers in town. A pair of 30-somethings, L. W. Burton and James Smith, ran the O.K. Barber Shop, William M. Jones and Joseph Lowery operated another as Jones and Lowery, while W. Riley Robinson and George W. Lewis managed their own places. The Lewis brothers, John and William, operated a saloon in town. There were a half-dozen men involved in mason and brick work. Dr. James Fields and wife and nurse, Mary Ann Fields, conducted a medical practice together. Their son, 23-year-old James A. Fields, secured the prestigious position as a clerk at the Lenawee County courthouse. Darius Roberts, a mulatto, was a horse dealer and a native of North Carolina. His family consisted of wife, Mary, and three kids, all enrolled in school. An elderly woman, possibly Darius' mother, resided with them. James Johnson, another mulatto, was a tailor and operated a store at 111 South Main Street.[20]

The entrepreneurship wasn't just left for Adrian's black men. As with white women at the time, some of Adrian's black ladies operated businesses. Elizabeth Jones, the barber's wife, ran a store offering "all styles" of hairdressing and was located over the *Times and Expositor* newspaper office at 63 East Maumee Street. A competitor, Bell Lowery and Luzerne Scott, were the "fashionable hair dressers," who advertised stylish hair for "all seasons" and operated at the entrance of the Opera House at 80½ East Maumee Street.[21]

There was even one mixed race-owned business, as 58-year-old William Moreland (white) and 40-year-old Thomas Dale (black) operated a laundry under the name of Moreland and Dale. There was even at least one mixed race couple in town in 1870. William Jones, a 50-year-old mulatto from Maryland and laborer, was married to a native Irish woman named Mary, who was ten years his junior. The couple had three children, Albert, Mary and Elizabeth, who were all enrolled in Adrian schools.[22]

Unlike many towns, where new immigrants and blacks were segregated to one section of town, that was not the case in Adrian. The black families were spread all over town, with homes on Bristol, Broad, Budlong, Chestnut, Finch, Locust, Main, Merrick, Mulberry, and South Winter Streets, to name just a few. A review of the 1870 census showed that each of the town's four Wards had black residents and businesses.[23]

While many of the black school-aged children were born in Michigan, their parents came from many places. As with many of the white settlers, New York was a popular birthplace for many of the black citizens who moved to Adrian, but also common was neighboring Indiana, along with the former slave states of Virginia and Kentucky. One elderly woman in town was born in Africa nearly a century earlier, a reminder of the country's slave trade, even though any black person older than five years of age in 1870 could have been born into slavery.[24]

However, the separation by race in Adrian was evident in two places. First, despite upsetting people with his fiery anti-slavery language before the war, Adrian College President Mahan had no black students, either male or female, living in the dormitories on campus. This doesn't mean there were no black students enrolled, as they could have walked to class from their home in town or boarded with a family off-campus. However, if the college was instructing black students, they were not living on campus. While the lack of black students may seem normal for the era, Adrian wasn't your regular town. A clear majority of the black families in town had enrolled their children in the local public schools. Nearly all the parents in the 1870 census could read and write, and with the establishment of two black churches, one Masonic Lodge and a healthy number of businesses, there would have been no shortage of qualified black students for the college to enroll. In addition, with a small black middle class in town, recruiting or relocating educated black professors should not have been a hindrance either.[25]

The other segregated area was the railroad. When the Lake Shore Railroad absorbed the old Michigan Southern rail line, Adrian became their headquarters and was the town's largest employer for many years. The location of the car shops and the rail yard had Adrian also labeled as a railroad town. Over a dozen railroad jobs, from the popular train engineer and conductor to bridge builders, dispatchers, freight agents and telegraphers were filled only by white men. The more numerous and more dangerous switchman, brakeman and fireman positions were all filled by local white workers. Even maintenance jobs such as repairman and simple rail yard laborer were all filled by whites. The lowly job title of "train boy" was filled by a white teenager. Needless to say, the car repair shop foremen were all whites, too. While many of the railroad workers were native born, there was a sizable contingent from Europe, including many from the German provinces.[26] In the latter half of 19th century, the country's wealth creation was largely based on the railroad industry, and Adrian's black residents were shut out of these respected and well-paying jobs.

Segregation was not an issue in the publicly run Adrian schools, as they accepted and educated students of all races. Adrian High School even graduated black students as early as the 1880s. At a time when few of the country's adults held a high school diploma, this feat was a notable and honorable achievement for any American citizen. Horace E. Craig, the son of Peter and Margaret, was reportedly the first black male to graduate from Adrian High School, as a member of the class of 1881. This mixing of the races continued at progressive AHS, with two young black ladies, Jennie Harris and Lida Pate, graduating in the class of 1895.[27]

The explosion of small-town newspapers during the latter half of the 19th century was also having a positive impact on Adrian. In 1892 the *Adrian Daily Telegram* was founded and, unlike the norm of the times, was not either officially or unofficially the sounding horn for one political party. Trying to play it straight down the line, the *Telegram* followed a non-partisan reporting approach.[28] Not embracing that novel idea, the *Adrian Times and Expositor* was a non-apologetic Republican mouthpiece. It was the area's leading daily newspaper in the 1890s, under the tutelage of its late, long-time editor and publisher, Tom Applegate. A force in state Republican politics for many years, he died suddenly of a heart attack at the age of 53.[29] His widow, Harriet Applegate, in 1892 assumed the running of the paper for the next decade. So one of the state's leading towns had as its most powerful editor a woman.[30]

This use of the influential printed word was not limited to the white men and women of Adrian. The "Lenawee County, Michigan Afro-American Journal and Directory of 1895" was the brainchild of two black gentlemen, Dewise Barrett Wilson and William Wendell Gaskin. The pair, both Adrian residents, printed their noble goal for all to read. "We have given a few brief sketches of men and women who have been closely identified with the progress and elevation of the race in this community." The two wanted to provide "honest examples of encouragement to those who think they can accomplish nothing on account of their color. We wish to call the attention of those who have grown to regard their color as a barrier to success and honorable attainment, to the principles of honesty, energy and reliability which have characterized the lives of those who have worked their way to the front." Wilson and Gaskin also pledged to provide a free directory to the "home of every Afro-American" in Adrian.[31]

Dewise Barrett Wilson was the eldest of Thomas and Mary Wilson's four children. Thomas Wilson originally was a barber, but later changed his career to boot and shoemaking, an occupation he followed for at least the next three decades. For many years, the family resided on North Main Street, between Bristol and Chestnut. Dewise's entrepreneurship must have been well known in town, as at the young age of 20, he joined with Gaskin to print the directory.[32]

Gaskin was a Michigan native, although both of his parents were of Southern birth. John and Matilda Gaskin had previously lived in Lansing and Jackson with their two children. John Gaskin ran a very successful blacksmith business in those two southern Michigan communities. In 1880, William attended school in the state's capital city. When his father decided to leave Lansing, the family relocated to Adrian in the mid–1880s, as John Gaskin opened Foster and Gaskin at 66 West Maumee Street, specializing in "horse-shoeing, carriage ironing and general blacksmithing." The family joined Adrian's black middle class and allowed the 25-year-old William to start his business venture.[33]

The pair of motivated young men wanted to impact Adrian's black population in 1895. Gaskin had spent the previous two years working as a cook in Jackson and saw his family ties bring him back to town for this project. The booklet also included short biographies of Adrian's Albert C. Carter, Horace E. Craig, William Austin Henson, W. J. Clanton and Thomas Wilson, Dewise's father. Reaching out to cover the fairer sex, the pair authored equally impressive biographies about Miss Hattie Clanton-Reid, Miss Allie Lou DeHazen and Mrs. Mary Jacobs-Rogers, to name a few. Wilson and Gaskin also reproduced attractive portraits of their featured citizens and included a narrative about the town's two black churches. Wilson was the project's president and secretary, with Gaskin named as the editor and business manager, and both acted as co-publishers.[34]

The gentlemen made themselves quite clear when addressing Adrian's racial climate in 1895, which they mentioned in the beginning pages of the directory.

> Many of the business men of Adrian have taken this opportunity of showing their appreciation of our patronage, and also, their feeling toward race enterprises. The reason the Afro-American does not enter the commercial field and lay up dollars for himself like the white man, is because so many pretended friends of the race stand at the entrance way and refuse to let him enter, by withholding recognition and support.

The pair claimed that many motivated young black men and women were discouraged for reaching the top rung of society "because those we patronize refuse to recognize us and hold out that they can control our patronage and influence by an occasional nod or smile. Forbearance has ceased to be a virtue, and we should now take the weapon of reciprocity in our hands and go forth to demand recognition."[35]

This confrontational language was very uncommon for the day and likely roused some ill will between members of Adrian's black and white community. Wilson and Gaskin were also quite firm in asking the black community to patronize those in the white business world who supported the directory. While some business men were progressive and "willingly and cheerfully" advertised in the book, others in the white community felt this directory was not necessary.[36]

The two black men also poked holes at the mythical American dream as "the land of the free and the home of the brave; a fair field and no favor; and the best man gets the plum." Whites told blacks to educate themselves, be industrious and honest, "and we will take you in. It is needless to point out this deception.... Few are sincere and many versus," the pair continued, but emphasized that those local white businessman who advertised in the directory "see the value of our endeavor and industry" and "have manifested their appreciation in a substantial manner," therefore deserving to see black citizens at their stores. "Let us use them then for the advancement of the race by patronizing our friends who will patronize us."[37]

Gaskin and Wilson continued their written lecture with three paragraphs under the title "Afro-American Need of Cooperation," and urged their community to come together. They asked blacks to work in earnest to support positive and progressive projects, such as their directory. They were also quick to point out that while blacks in the North were living with full citizenship, "our brother in the south lives in constant denial of such rights," and with whites who felt they were superior to the black race.[38]

The two men concluded their view with a hopeful message that with unity and support, blacks could rise out of the everyday ranks, become leaders in business and politics, and become "illustrious men upon the tablets of fame."[39]

William Wendell Gaskin would be one such man. In the spring of 1895, before the directory was in print, the industrious young man was hired to work as the cook on the Page Fence Giants' train car. His job would be to feed the greatest collection of black ball players the world had ever seen.[40]

◆ 6 ◆

The Cracker Jack Team

"The Page Fence Giants will have a cracker jack team this coming season…. Managed by Bud Fowler, [it] will be the strongest colored club ever organized" is how 1894 ended.[1] A few weeks later, 1895 opened with a response from the Chicago Unions, one of the country's few black ball teams.

Frank Leland, the Unions' business manager, was not going to sit by and let the Page Fence Giants steal publicity and players from his business empire. In *The Sporting News*, in an article with the offensive headline, "Dem Sassy N——s; Dey'se Not Champions and Don't You Fergit It," Leland fired off a response to the Adrian club. He stated that his Chicago Unions had posted 229 wins, 48 losses and eight ties since 1886, while the newly organized Page Fence Giants had earned 0 wins and 0 losses. He claimed to have the black ball champions of the West, as Leland noted his Unions had defeated "all the leading colored organizations throughout the West and South during the past eight years." The Unions were only the champions of the West, as the Cuban Giants, from out East, had recently defeated them in the final game of the Colored World Championship. Leland added that the Page Fence Giants were using some of the Chicago Unions' players' names on booking requests to "deceive different managers." Leland went so far as to publicize his mighty roster for the upcoming 1895 season, not knowing that two of them would, instead, break camp with the Adrian club and not with the Unions. The player poaching added fuel to the battle between the established black teams and the upstart Giants. Leland closed the letter by noting that he was still scheduling games, and those who would like to "book the Chicago Unions, the only colored champions in the West" could contact him.[2]

Meanwhile, in Findlay, Ohio, they had moved on from the losses of two of their star players, Fowler and Grant "Home Run" Johnson. John J. Rafferty, who played with Poughkeepsie in the New York State League last season, and Findlay holdover Fred Cooke were tentatively plugged in to replace Fowler and Johnson and play second base and shortstop. Findlay Sluggers manager Charles J. Strobel planned for a new park, which was dubbed "The Wigwam," and would include new grandstands, outfield fences and a ticket booth. Strobel also announced that the Page Fence Giants would play the Sluggers at "The Wigwam," as part of Decoration Day (Memorial Day) ceremonies in late May.[3]

With baseball fever at its height, Adrian boosters were looking to capitalize on a second baseball opportunity. Following the raucous summer series between Monroe and Adrian, lively tilts between Monroe and the Detroit Athletic Club, clashes between Monroe and Findlay, and spirited contests apparently by everyone else and Monroe, there was intense statewide interest in the game of baseball. The winter months saw men looking for ways to make money off the growing sport. The activity led to the spawning of a reincarnated Michigan State League, and Adrian was looking to enter a team.

In November, Hoch, Parsons and Rolla Taylor organized a town meeting at the Hotel Emery to gauge the local interest in a minor league team. Even before the league entry became official, the trio was already looking to sign players, and the mere rumor also had men contacting Adrian. One member of the management trio announced that George Wilson would be signed for the minor league team and not to pitch for the Page Fence Giants. If the minor league club won league approval, it "will have a white and colored battery" and Vandalia's Fred D. Van Dyke, another black gentleman, would sign to catch the Palmyra Wonder. There was enough encouraging talk that the proposal was approved, pleasing the baseball cranks. A committee was formed, headed by Seymour Howell, to attempt to sell season tickets to each business in town. Howell's group was so successful that their goal of selling 75 season tickets was two-thirds to being met in just a few weeks.[4]

In late December, *The Sporting News* article authored by H. Emery officially announced that Adrian would have a "white club" and "will begin signing players in a short time and by the time the grass begins to grow look out for a winner."[5] For several months, rumors and meetings dogged the proceedings, until Corunna's Walter H. Mumby was tabbed the commissioner of the new Michigan State League. Mumby had played for and managed the Lansing Farmers minor league team in the first Michigan State League in 1889, so he was well known across the state's baseball circles. That 1889 minor league contained six cities: Jackson, Grand Rapids, Saginaw, Kalamazoo, Lansing and Greenville. On the Greenville team was a black infielder named Bud Fowler, now the current manager of the Page Fence Giants. The MSL sent 29 players to the major leagues, but despite being an excellent ballplayer, the black Fowler was not one of them.[6]

Both Taylor and Hoch spent time travelling around the state and meeting with league boosters. The pair also served on several schedule-making committees, as the organizers tried to streamline travel routes with a goal of saving money on train fares. Early plans called for an eight-team league, as Monroe grabbed the final spot and joined the Adrian Demons, Lansing Senators, Kalamazoo Celery Eaters, Owosso Colts, Jackson Jaxons, Battle Creek Adventists and Port Huron Marines.[7] Probably much to Adrian's delight, their Monroe rivals never secured enough stable financial backing and dropped out of the league before Opening Day. Port Huron was also a very late MSL addition and joined in May of 1895, when Adrian's small-town neighbor and baseball rival, Hudson, was rejected. The *Kalamazoo Daily Telegraph* reported, "Hudson has been voted out of the league and the franchise has been given to Port Huron."[8]

Other Michigan leagues were being formed and included one on the west side of the state. The Ottawa County League would have professional teams in Grand Haven, Spring Lake, Holland, Coopersville, Berlin and Nunica.[9] Another one on the west side of the state, but much farther north, would be called the Northern Michigan Resort League. Five towns—Petoskey, Bay View, Charlevoix, Harbor Point and Wequetonsing—would comprise this league, which would not begin play until the July 4 weekend and would run through early October.[10] These new teams would all be fighting to fill rosters with white players who might come in handy for Adrian's minor league team. For financial backers of the Page Fence Giants and the Adrian league team, Michigan's current baseball fever aligned quite nicely with their 1895 business plans.

Whether by design or accident, the Michigan State League took no position on banning black players. With Rolla Taylor and Len Hoch exerting major control of both teams, the pair would be faced with a moral, political and financial question: would Adrian's minor league team be allowed to field black players? It was already released to the public that two black players, Wilson and Van Dyke, would be on the white club's roster. Would the Page Fence Giants squad lose additional players to the Adrian team once the minor league season began in May? How would league criticism be navigated if another town rejected the progressive approach on race? How would the Page Fence players react to being stripped of presumably some of its best players to support the goals of the white club? How would the management split their time between the two clubs?

While the Chicago Unions were complaining and the Findlay team moving ahead, Adrian's Page Fence Giants were preparing for their first season. The plan was for the Giants to gather for pre-season practice in the central Indiana town of Marion on April 1, 1895. Initial plans called for all the players to meet in Adrian and travel en masse on their specially outfitted train car to Marion. The plan soon hit a snag as a rented train car, sent from Chicago, was deemed unfit and too expensive to refurbish.[11] That problem sent Gus Parsons and Rolla Taylor scurrying to find a replacement, and they hopped a train and headed east to shop for cars. The pair was successful at the Jersey Car and Storage Company and settled on a coach manufactured in New York by the Monarch Company.[12] In mid–March, Gus Parsons would return east and retrieve the Monarch train car the Page Fence Giants would use during the season.[13] The cost of the fancy travel car was never revealed, but when "Hi

The palatial Monarch train car, used to transport, feed and bed the Page Fence Giants for each of their four seasons. On the front and to the far left is business manager Augustus "Gus" Parsons, with Rolla Taylor to the far right. In the middle appears to be Howard Taylor (courtesy Adrian District Library).

Henry's Minstrel Show" appeared in Adrian in the fall of 1894, with a similar, but a bit larger train car, its value was listed at over $30,000.[14]

As planned in mid–March, Parsons quit his desk job at the Hotel Emery and the next day headed east. He was gone for a week. When he arrived in Adrian on Monday, March 25, with the new coach, it caused a stir. "It is a handsome combination dining and sleeping car the Monarchs make in perfect condition. The name of the team will be painted on its sides at the Lake Shore shop" said the *Adrian Daily Times and Expositor*.[15] The town's other daily newspaper noted that the car was painted dark brown "and ornamented in gilt [gold paint]" measured 60 feet in length, and would be coupled to a passing train and hauled from town to town. Two lines of advertising adorned the car. The top line was "Page Woven Wire Fence Co., Adrian, Mich.," and right below in gold was "Page Fence Giants Base Ball Club, Adrian, Mich." The train car was becoming as much of a star as the players. The *Evening Telegram* ran a lengthy story on the interior of the car, devoting much more time to that than to any player's biography.

> Passing in on one end of the car, at the right hand is a conveniently arranged lavatory, and just in front of you is a door opening into Manager Parsons' private office and state room. Here are two berths and a table, and along the side of the apartment are seats upholstered in leather. Passing along through a narrow passage way we come to a door that opens into the kitchen. Will Gaskin will be in charge of this room, which is fitted up with an Acorn steel range and all the modern conveniences in the way of cooking utensils. Everything has its place on the shelves or in the handy cupboard in the corner of the room. Going through another door opening off the passage way, we find ourselves in a much larger apartment which is the dining, sitting, and sleeping room combined. At the end toward the kitchen is a handsome sideboard in which the silverware and chinaware are kept. There are twelve upholstered chairs. The berths—20 in all—swing in toward the wall, so that they look like panels in the side of the cars. The floor of the dining room is covered with a pleasing design, and the sitting room is carpeted with brussels. Opening off the other end of the car are the closets, and in this part also is the heater. The fuel is carried in lockers under the car. Double windows prevent any dust from getting in and also keep out the cold and damp air more effectively. The name of the car is Louis XVI. Joining Parsons, Gaskin and the players, will be Albert Carter, an Adrian native and black man, who will serve as the team's porter and barber.[16]

On display at the Taylor Brothers store, at 27 South Main Street and adjacent to the Hotel Emery, was a "base ball window" arranged "in a tasteful manner," with the Giants' equipment for the season.[17] The team uniforms were very stylish and the best of quality and consisted of black shirt and pants, with maroon Page Fence Giants letters in simple block style, along with tan socks and a tan ball cap.[18] Around this time the 12 Monarch-brand bicycles were delivered. They were sold to the team by local bicycle dealer and jeweler William Sheldon. Word was that Sheldon would also display these in his downtown store window. The Monarch Company was also furnishing the players with fancy firemen-type caps, which would be worn during a bike parade preceding the ball game.[19]

An alternate site to old Lawrence Park could not be found, so work was begun on preparing the ball grounds for yet another season. Due to a mild winter, work continued to mid–December, when a "large and dangerous stump" was pulled up as part of a massive field plowing and grading project.[20] Lawrence Park would be rented for $400 and host all local games that year. Design plans specified a new high board wooden fence, with barbed wire attached at the top, on the north side of the park. The goal was to prevent the previous year's freeloaders from standing on the steep ridge located at the edge of the outfield and get them to come inside and pay for tickets. Boosters were hoping for "quite a difference in gate receipts" in 1895. James K. Wolverton, a 49-year-old Adrian resident, was hired to

Another look at the Monarch car as a group of children marvel at the train. In the front, in the white outfit is William Wendell Gaskin, the team cook and emergency substitute player for at least the first two years of the Giants' existence. Standing on the rear platform appear to be Gus Parsons and his wife, Minnie. Standing at the far right appears to be Rolla Taylor (courtesy Lenawee County Historical Society).

be in charge of improving the grounds and preparing the infield. On the morning of Wednesday, April 3, Wolverton laid out a new diamond, but finishing touches would have to wait until the ground thawed from the winter.[21]

While locally, Adrian was preparing for their new black team, nationally, Bud Fowler lashed back at Leland in a letter to *The Sporting News* in early March. "I notice in your valuable paper that several colored clubs have already won the colored championship.... Now the Page Fence Giants have never claimed any championship." Fowler invited the other teams to win the championship on the diamond and not through the paper. He purposed a series with each club paying its own expenses, but the winning team being awarded all the gate receipts. He quipped, "I hope this will meet the approval of some of the championship managers." He also downplayed that he had signed any players already under contract and listed his team as "Miller, Taylor, Maufin [*sic*], Lincoln, Malone, Van Dyke, Murphy, Johnson and myself." For some reason, Fowler didn't mention two previously signed Giants, Gus Brooks or George Hopkins.[22] A news blurb in the *Chicago Inter Ocean* paper in late February confirmed that Frank Leland was indeed going to lose them to the Page Fence Giants. "Hopkins, Brooks and Holland, three local colored players, will be members of the new aggregation," playing with Bud Fowler that year.[23]

"The Car Is Off" screamed the headline, as about 150 residents braved chilly, 38-degree weather to see the Page Fence Giants leave from the Lake Shore Depot on their way to Marion, Indiana. The depot was conveniently located across the street from the fence company's large brick buildings, which probably allowed Page Fence employees to witness the event. The crowd watched as Lake Shore engine number 43 chugged westward out of the depot around 12 noon, Monday, April 1.[24] The train, pulling the decorated special train car, would travel a few miles west to Hudson and then follow the tracks south on its way to Indiana. Railroad officials said the car should arrive in Marion around 11 a.m. Tuesday. When full, the fancy PFG car would hold 16 passengers, but on its maiden voyage only four made the trek. Parsons, cook William Wendell Gaskin (sometimes incorrectly referred to as Gaston), and barber and porter Albert Carter rode out that morning. The only player riding out of Adrian was William Malone, who came from his hometown of Detroit to catch the car. The remaining players would meet in Marion and begin practice there.[25] Fowler must have gone ahead and made arrangements, while investors Hoch and Taylor would meet and travel with the team "occasionally during the season."[26]

As far as the Giants playing in front of their hometown, two games in June and another set of contests in September were tentatively scheduled. The papers printed the Page Fence Giants' schedule for the first two months of the season, which was highlighted by games against the majors' Cincinnati Reds, several against minor teams of the Western League, and a two-week jaunt to Canada.[27]

To prepare for the season, the Giants' publicity machine repeatedly announced that the team's first game would be Tuesday, April 9, against Indianapolis, a team in the Western League. Gus Parsons sent eager fans back in Adrian practice updates and his assessment of the Giants' talent level. In a letter to postmaster Hoch, Parsons reported

Top: **William Wendell Gaskin was also nationally known as a possessor of exquisite handwriting and later as one of the publishers of the 1895** *Adrian African-American Journal. Bottom:* **Albert C. Carter in his later years, while residing in Adrian. He was the Page Fence Giants' first porter and barber and was a substitute pitcher in at least one victorious game in 1895 (both photographs courtesy Lenawee County Historical Society).**

that by Wednesday all but one of the players, catcher Frank Maupin, who was home ill, had reported to Indiana. The plan was for Maupin to be the team's starting catcher, but two others would temporarily hold down that position. They thought Maupin would return around April 17, when the team was playing in Chicago.[28] Parsons added that they were in the "pink of condition" and people could "put to rest any doubts which may have been entertained as to the ability of the Page Fence Giants to play ball."[29] Interjecting some humor into the situation, Parsons quipped that if the Giants played base ball as well as they ate, they would be world beaters![30]

Continuing with the assessment, Parsons wrote that he was getting a good look at the team during an unseasonably warm spring in Marion.[31] A second letter from Parsons to Hoch gushed about the team. The major investors of Hoch, Taylor and the Page Fence Company had not seen any of the players practice, so much trust was placed in Parsons. The *Evening Telegram* and *Daily Times and Expositor* both printed Parsons' latest note home: "The boys were all out yesterday and again today and they are a fast lot of fellows I can tell you. Miller and Holland [pitchers] were out this morning and they have speed to sell. Brooks, Howard and Hopkins are the fastest outfielders I have ever seen. They all hit the ball and if they don't make some of the league teams sick with a little more work than I am no judge."[32]

The excitement was so intense that the Giants were ready to move up their public unveiling. An early exhibition game was scheduled on Saturday, April 6, against a Marion team, and then another exhibition on Monday, before the regularly scheduled contest with Indianapolis on the ninth.[33] The *Marion Chronicle* said the Giants game would open the local baseball season and they would be in town for a few days "to gain a little practice." The paper predicted a good game and said manager A. S. "Gus" Parsons believed he had a good team with him.[34] In game notes that offered little detail back home in Adrian, the Page Fence Giants trounced the Gas City Cyclones, 21–1, not exactly a competitive game. The *Adrian Weekly Press* proudly exclaimed on April 12, "First blood for the Giants." Postmaster Hoch received the official Saturday game score from Bud Fowler, but it did not come until Tuesday morning![35] The Monday exhibition was cancelled due to heavy rain, but the hope was that the Tuesday tilt with a real professional team could be played.[36]

The Indianapolis team, known that year as both the Hoosiers and Indians, were in the competitive Western League. A few days earlier, they had lost a tough, 3–2 decision in 12 innings to the major league Cincinnati Reds.[37] The *Indianapolis News* promoted the Page Fence Giants and noted, "Besides playing ball they perform feats of tumbling, and there is a quartet among them that sings between innings."[38] There were two rates for game tickets, with 50 cents for what was called preferred seating and 25 cents for general admission. The games were slated for Tuesday and Wednesday at 3 o'clock at Indianapolis' League Park on East Ohio Street.[39]

Tuesday came and went with no word from Fowler, Parsons or anyone else in Indianapolis. The sign at the Indianapolis grandstand said the field was too wet for play, and the baseball pennant on the courthouse flagpole was missing, notifying everyone locally that the game had been cancelled.[40] However, neither of those displays helped the fans back in Adrian. Rumors flew that the Giants had been so badly beaten by the highly skillful minor leaguers that no one wanted to disappoint those back in Adrian by reporting the score. Other rooters gazed up toward the Adrian sky, saw the clouds, and felt that no game was played that day in far-off Indy. Finally, on Wednesday morning, Howard Taylor received a card from his brother Rolla, who had made the trek to Indiana, that Tuesday's game was not played due to wet grounds. However, that afternoon there would be a game, and there was a promise of a big crowd.[41]

The Page Fence Giants faced Indianapolis with a starting infield of George Taylor at first base, Fowler at second, Johnson at shortstop and William Malone at third. The outfield was Gus Brooks in centerfield, flanked by George Hopkins in left and a man named Howard in right field. Pete Burns was behind the plate, and Billy Holland was the pitcher.[42]

As good as the Giants looked Saturday against the over-matched Gas City team, they probably looked just as bad against Indianapolis that Wednesday, April 10. The pride of Adrian, Michigan, representing the town's largest employer, was drubbed, 26–1. The *Indianapolis News* printed one story focusing on the quality and variety of the Page Woven Wire product and noting the factory's ability to produce 45 miles of fence a day. "The Page Fence is adjustable to expansion and contraction, being the only wire fence, which has mastered these essentials. It is ornamental, as well as perfectly impregnable, against all intrusion." Their baseball story was headlined "Base Ball Massacres." The title, in this case, was unfortunately true. The Giants did very little at the plate or in the field. They chalked up only five hits (four singles and a double), earned only one base on balls, stole no bases and committed ten errors in the field.[43] Billy Holland started for the Giants, lasted only six innings and was relieved by Joe Miller, who finished the game. Holland was described as "wild," while Miller "lost heart" as the game wound down. Indianapolis pitcher Fisher was effective and tossed seven innings, giving up the Giants' only run. Harry Pastorius, a team-mate last season with Fowler and Johnson on the Findlay Sluggers, hurled the final two innings for the victors. The opening official contest for the much-ballyhooed Page Fence Giants lasted two hours and ten minutes.[44]

A reprinted story (possibly from the *Indianapolis Sentinel*) in the *Findlay Daily Courier* was not kind to their former baseball stars. "Old man Fowler at second was stiff and sore, and Johnson at short was limber and wild," with the two combining for five errors.[45] Rolla Taylor's note home to Adrian was much more consoling. He claimed the Indianapolis nine had been practicing for three weeks and was one of the strongest teams in the Western League.[46]

The Adrian team was undoubtedly nervous in the official season opener, as most had enough experience to know the Hoosiers were no Gas Light Cyclones. They were on a new team and, except for Johnson, playing for a new manager. To add to the pressure that day, a large contingent of Indianapolis' black citizenry had made their way to League Park. "The bleachers were very nearly peopled with blacks." Attendance was estimated at around 300 that afternoon, as patches of sunshine shone through the clouds and a brisk wind made conditions less than ideal for base ball.[47] The fans saw the game spiral out of control from the start, as Indy sent 14 men to the plate in the first inning and tallied eight runs. They came back for two more in the second inning and three runs in the third for a quick 14–0 lead. Johnson finally broke the scoring drought for the Giants, slugging a long double to center field and scoring on a wild throw.[48] Black partisans yelled for the Giants to "get into the game," and when the visitors finally scored in their half of the fourth inning, the black people in the crowd let out a mighty cheer.[49] But that was quickly answered when a white man suggested the Giants join the Separation Society. One of the fans yelled for the Giants to join a Separation Society. When one of the black gentlemen responded with, "What am dat Separation Society, moke?" it brought the retort of it being a "noble order" which separated a man from his money. Wagering on the game's outcome, as in many baseball contests in the 1890s, was rampant.[50]

From day one, the Page Fence Giants were facing not only the men on the ball field, but also the umpire behind home plate. In 1895, games were umpired by a single man, whose control over the outcome of a contest was vital. Wallace Andrews was the umpire that day, and he gave a great account of himself—if one had bet on Indianapolis, the home team, to win. The unfair umping of ball games was often noted in the newspaper accounts, and this one would be no different. Reporters were quick to praise the local players, but would add opinions and observations about the quality of the umpire. While no doubt allowing the minor leaguers to score eight runs to begin the game made it nearly impossible to recover and win, umpire Wallace must have played a key role in the lopsided 26–1 outcome. "It seemed evident that one more inning of slaughter like the first would precipitate a race riot, and President [Bill] Watkins diplomatically let up." This sounds gracious of Watkins, even with a comment that during the early innings he could have called the game due to "darkiness," a double meaning which alluded to when games were ended early due to the sun setting on lightless fields and an obvious jab at the black ball players.[51]

However, while Watkins may or may not have been a benevolent manager, the *Indianapolis News* noted the victory wasn't all due to the efforts of their own players. "The ease with which Indianapolis did everything it wanted to and the 'rough deal' the Giants received at the hands of Umpire Andrews conspired to make the score look like the original report of the Armenian massacre." So there it was, literally in black and white—race had played a part in the outcome of this baseball game. The fact that it was publicized indicated that this treatment was of no surprise to anyone, white or black, as to how things operated in some parts of America. The paper's final sentence, right above the line score and all of the wonderful statistics of the home team, summarized the 26–1 game in this manner: "The one-sided score, which misrepresents both teams, as far as figures are concerned."[52]

Fowler, with his over two decades of ball, and former members of the Chicago Unions such as Brooks and Hopkins were no strangers to this type of mistreatment. But one wonders what Gus Parsons and Rolla Taylor thought and felt about their investment being damaged by an unscrupulous white umpire. The black players knew this was the treatment they would receive for much of the season. The white men on the train probably hoped today's contest was just an aberration. To make matters worse, the team that just beat them, 26–1, had just lost to the Cincinnati Reds, the next opponent on the Page Fence Giants' calendar.

Reds and Gold Bugs

Aboard their special train car, the Page Fence Giants headed south to play a team even better than the Indianapolis club, namely the Cincinnati Reds. The city was host to the country's first all-professional baseball club nearly 30 years earlier, and the state of Ohio was a hotbed of talent and rabid fans.

The 1895 Reds squad was touted as one of the best in the National League that year. Coming off a tenth-place finish the previous season, "no expense has been spared in perfecting the team" for this campaign. Featuring future Hall of Fame catcher Buck Ewing, along with Dusty Miller, Dummy Hoy, Germany Smith, Arlie Latham, Billy Rhines and Frank Dwyer, hopes were high in Cincinnati. The Reds had been practicing for most of February and March and were in much better condition than the Giants, who were not even in their second week of official training.[1]

"There were many faint hearts among the 'fans' after the result in Indianapolis.... The Giants were greatly outclassed," and it may have been a mistake to begin the season with such strong competition, commented the *Adrian Evening Telegram*.[2] Couple this feeling with the fact that Cincinnati had defeated Indianapolis three times this exhibition season, and the ride down to the city on the Ohio River was probably a bit gloomy.

"But when the score came … there was almost as much rejoicing as could have been, had the game been won," crowed he *Adrian Evening Telegram*.[3] True, the Page Fence Giants lost, 11–7, to the Reds, but they had managed to out-hit the major leaguers. In addition, the Giants jumped out briefly to a 2–0 lead and scored in several innings.

The Giants started pitcher Joe Miller, whose support was improved from what Holland had received the day before, as the Page Fence squad fielded the ball much better. The right-handed Tom Parrott took the ball for the Reds and put the Giants down in order in the first two innings. To begin the third, George Hopkins singled and was followed by base hits by Pete Burns, Miller and George Taylor, which led to two runs and a Giants lead. The Reds responded in the fourth inning, when Dummy Hoy knocked in a run with a triple off Miller. Hoy tied the game after Germany Smith's ground ball to third put him in a pickle. Malone threw to the plate to get Hoy, but instead pegged the runner in the back, allowing the run. Smith, who had managed to race to third during the rundown, later scored on a single by George Hogriever, giving the Reds a 3–2 lead. In the fifth inning, a series of hits, walks and errors led to five Reds runs and saw the major leaguers increase their lead to 8–2.

Undaunted, the Giants came back and scored three runs in their half of the sixth inning; "two of them were gifts from Umpire Sheridan."[4] After one was out, Gus Brooks, William Malone and John Nelson (playing right field for Howard) all singled, plating a run. When a Hopkins come-backer resulted in an out at first, Harry Spies fired the ball across the diamond to cut down Malone at third base. Malone slid back safely, in a close play in which Umpire Sheridan ruled against the home team. Giants catcher Pete Burns then singled in both Malone and Nelson, cutting the margin to 8–5. The Reds notched two runs in their half of the sixth, increasing their lead to 10–5, only to see the Giants again respond. "Big" Bill Phillips was now pitching for the Reds, and doubles by Grant Johnson and Malone and an error by Reds shortstop Germany Smith helped the Giants score a pair of runs. The game's final tally came after the Reds' Arlie Latham singled in the seventh, stole second, went to third on a passed ball, and scored on Bid McPhee's double play to Johnson at short, who tossed it to Fowler at second, who completed it by throwing to Taylor at first. The final score was Reds 11, Giants 7.[5]

The *Adrian Evening Telegram* reprinted large sections of the *Cincinnati Enquirer*'s Thursday game story. Their commentary centered on both the game and the large throng of black spectators present in the stands. "Every colored barber, every palace car porter and every member of the local colored population of the male gender who could get off … was on the seats of the Cincinnati Park." Those fans were excited to see the Page Fence Giants, and despite the cold weather, the stands were hot. When the Giants grabbed the first lead, the local paper both insulted and praised black fans. The *Enquirer* claimed one "could have tossed a ripe Georgia watermelon or a fat possum" into the crowd and they would have kicked it aside and continued cheering for the visiting black team. The black section of the pavilion was the loudest anyone in Millcreek Valley had heard at a game in years. The Cincinnati paper also noted that the Reds "didn't have a picnic" and the Giants "fought nobly" and gave them a battle from the start of the game to the very end. After using derogatory stereotypes about the black rooters, the next paragraph heaped glowing praise on the Giants. "All jokes aside, it was a great game. Bud Fowler, the veteran, has got together a great team of players. They will win more games than they will loose [*sic*]." The newspaper noted that the Giants were well coached and "scrappy," singled out center fielder Gus Brooks for his "three wonderful catches," along with slick play at third by Malone, and said that Fowler played "like a young blood." The *Evening Telegram* also printed excerpts from the *Cincinnati Gazette*, which praised the visitors and believed that a large majority of the crowd had expected an easy victory, but "the Giants batted and fielded in a way that surprised and delighted everyone."[6]

The *Enquirer* was not done with its praise. While the Giants were in town, it published a lengthy history of Bud Fowler, which he gave during an interview at their Cincinnati office. They again pushed the story of Fowler being older than Cap Anson (not accurate) and Candy Nelson. They detailed how Fowler was spry and fast without any aches or pains to slow him down. They spoke of how Fowler had played all over the country and in nearly every organized league and had been paid with money, with trapper's furs, and bags of gold dust. The distinguished black ballplayer had played with "cowboys and the Indians" and, while he began his career as a pitcher and later moved to catcher, he could be placed anywhere on the diamond. Over the years, the story claimed, when the games became dull, Fowler would run the 100-yard dash in ten seconds to amuse the fans. On March 16, Fowler allegedly turned 48 years of age and credited his fitness to ignoring wine, women and song. The *Enquirer* ended the glowing article by encouraging area residents to go out to the ball park and see Fowler play.[7]

With the closeness of game one, the Giants' spirits were probably buoyed for the second game with those same Reds on Friday. Just as he had in the game with Indianapolis,

Giants pitcher Billy Holland got rocked in the first inning. A total of 11 Reds crossed the plate, and the major leaguers sailed to an easy 16–2 victory. The Giants scored once in the second inning and once in the last inning—the seventh—as the game was shortened for some reason. The Page Fence highlights were doubles by George Taylor and cleanup hitter Gus Brooks and the fact that Fred Van Dyke made his first appearance that season, relieving Holland, while getting a base hit in his only at-bat. Fred Foreman pitched a complete-game victory for the Reds.[8]

While umpire Sheridan was pointed out by one local paper for giving the Giants two runs in yesterday's game, it was balanced out in this contest. George Hogriever, a 26-year-old native Cincinnatian, who was coaching at third, caused a disruption leading to those two runs from the day before being given back to the Reds. With Germany Smith on first and Dummy Hoy on third, Hogriever distracted the Giants by pretending to be the base runner at third. When Smith broke for the bag to steal second base, Giants catcher Burns fired the ball to Fowler, covering second. Fowler, who saw Hogriever's big jump to home, rushed his toss to the plate because he thought Hoy was running, when he was not. Fowler's throw was off-target and the confused Burns then threw to Malone at third base, trying to catch a Red off the bag. That throw, too, was off its mark, and when Malone muffed the catch and scrambled for the ball, he again saw Hogriever running toward home. Malone "let go with might and main and threw over the catcher's head." When all was said and done, both Hoy and Smith managed to score two runs for the Reds. The *Enquirer* wrote that Hogriever's antics "caused a great deal of merriment," but "under a strict interpretation of the rules Hog was entirely out of order." Needless to say, the runs did not come off the board, and whatever hopes the Giants had of winning this game likely ended with the illegal scoring play. The *Cincinnati Enquirer* quipped, "The Reds played good ball, while the Giants … appeared to have put in a bad night."[9]

When the season ended, this 1895 Reds team finished two spots higher from the previous year and in eighth place. The team was known for its speed, as they led the NL in stolen bases and triples, were second in doubles, third in slugging percentage and fourth in team batting average. They were in the middle of the 12-team league in fielding, but were in the bottom half of the league in pitching. The two hurlers the Reds tossed against the Giants were in the starting rotation all year, but both finished with losing records against National League clubs, as Tom Parrott went 11–18 and Fred Foreman was an equally disappointing 11–14. Even the relief pitcher in game one against the Giants, Bill Philips, sported a losing record in 1895. Surprisingly, the Reds finished with a record over .500, with 66 wins and 64 losses, under player-manager Buck Ewing.[10]

The Page Fence Giants headed north from Cincinnati Friday night. The specially equipped Monarch coach would be pulled into Sturgis, Michigan, and pick up Len Hoch, who took a train Friday night from Adrian to meet the team there.[11] Hoch joined Gus Parsons and Rolla Taylor in the front section of the train and traveled with the Giants to Grand Rapids. Carter waited on the players and loaded their equipment, while Gaskin prepared everyone's meals. If the weather permitted, the next four games would be played in the Wolverine state.

The Gold Bugs were in the same Class A Western League as the Indianapolis Hoosiers, so the competition would again be very tough. The itinerary for Saturday was for the Giants to arrive in Grand Rapids, on Michigan's western half of the Lower Peninsula, at about 7:30 in the morning. Shortly after noon, the players, riding their shiny new Monarch bicycles, and clad in bright red jackets and fancy hats, would parade through the streets of Grand

The Page Fence Giants at John Ball Park in Grand Rapids, Michigan. The appearance of Sol White (second from left) places this in the 1896 season. *(Left to right)* Joe Miller, So. White, George Wilson, Bill Binga, Pete Burns, business manager Augustus "Gus" Parsons, unidentified player, Grant "Home Run" Johnson, George Taylor, Billy Holland and James W. Patterson. The unidentified seated player holding the ball could be right-handed pitcher James Chavous. In some descriptions of this photograph a man named "Walker" is labeled. I name him as Joe Miller. I have been unable to find any reference to a man named Walker who ever played on the Page Fence Giants (courtesy Adrian District Library).

Rapids on their way to Recreation Park for a 3 o'clock game.[12] As part of the parade promotion, the firm of Adams and Hart, at 12 West Bridge Street, told residents they were the exclusive "Monarch wheels" sales agents and sold the quality Page Woven Wire Fence, too. Representatives of Adams and Hart spent at least one of the games passing out free cigars on the ball grounds, to promote their wide range of products.[13]

Neither Adrian paper had eyewitness accounts of the game, as both reprinted the *Detroit Free Press* version of the affair. Fortunately, the big first-inning meltdown that had visited the Giants in two of their first three games was absent in this contest. Joe Miller earned the Giants' first win of the year against a professional team, as they bested the Gold Bugs, 8–7. The Giants trailed going into the ninth inning, 7–5. With one out, Burns and Holland singled and gave the Giants some hope. Miller helped his cause at the plate and doubled in a run to cut the Grand Rapids lead to one. Following walks to Taylor and Fowler, the bases were loaded when shortstop Grant Johnson "took the willow" and lined "a corker" to center for the winning two-run double.[14] Three Gold Bugs pitchers, Red Donahue, Mike Kilroy and John Stafford, kicked off their exhibition season by giving up 13 hits.[15] The *Free Press* commented, "The colored aggregation played hard, fast ball and will make all of the professional clubs hustle."[16] The game took two hours to play, with the Grand Rapids paper estimating the crowd at 500 and the *Free Press* doubling that figure to 1,000 fans.[17]

Sunday's game had to be moved outside of Grand Rapids as the city fathers and local ministers had deemed it sinful to play baseball on the Sabbath. So, the Gold Bugs "management has spent considerable money in putting the grounds in condition" at Alger Park at Reed's Lake, located outside of the Grand Rapids city limits.[18] The Easter Sunday crowd was estimated between 1,700 and 2,000 fans at Alger Park. Women dressed in their Sunday best, heads topped with Easter bonnets, hands clutching flowers, sat with their husbands as they filled the decorated grandstand. This spring day featured a chilly wind, but that didn't seem to dampen the spirits of the well-behaved crowd.[19]

Unfortunately, the festive and religious day was not honored by umpire Bobby Caruthers, a player on the Gold Bugs roster. Caruthers had logged nine years as a star pitcher in the highest professional leagues, twice winning 40 games. He was born in Memphis, Tennessee, during the Civil War and was trying to resurrect his career.[20] At his peak, he earned the princely sum of $4,500 a season.[21] With the Gold Bugs coming off a season-opening loss to the Giants, it probably did not sit well with the white players. This second game would be different.

Rolla Taylor wired a telegram home with a simple summary of the Easter Sunday game. Adrian resident and baseball fan Charles L. Robinson agreed to publicize the scores during the season. Taylor's message was this: "Wilson pitched.... Rapids team seven, umpire 10, total 17, Giants 13. Attendance 1,700."[22] The score of the Easter afternoon game was only close due to the final Gold Bugs pitcher, Doc Parker, being very wild, as a combination of walks and wild pitches allowed five runs in the ninth inning.[23] By that time, the game was out of reach. Billy Holland, maybe the only bright spot on the day for the Adrian club, slugged a home run after he relieved Wilson on the mound.[24]

In the first game of the season, the Giants had outclassed the Gas City boys and won the game. After their first contest with Indianapolis, umpire Wallace Andrews was called out publicly by the local newspapers for not being fair. The second game with Cincinnati had umpire Sheridan allowing a goofy and disruptive illegal play to score two runs for the Reds, as they cruised to a victory. After they recorded their first real victory of the season on Friday against Grand Rapids, an umpire on Saturday again made an impact on the outcome of the game.

The Gold Bugs were clad in uniforms of black and gold, very similar to the Page Fence Giants' black and maroon that day. The similarity was such that one young boy in the crowd wrongly cheered for the visiting black ball club, when the Giants ran onto the field to begin the game. There would be no such confusion by player turned temporary umpire Caruthers. The *Grand Rapids Democrat* downplayed the umpire situation and called out the Giants for their poor sportsmanship. "The Giants demonstrated ... that they can 'kick' as vigorously on the umpire's decision as can a regular league team. They were displeased with Caruthers' decision upon several occasions."[25] The *Adrian Evening Telegram* called Caruthers' decisions "rankly favorable to the home team," while the *Detroit Free Press* didn't mention any issues with the umpire. The *Evening Telegram* reprinted the *Detroit Tribune* story, which offered a much more detailed and upsetting game account. The *Tribune* claimed that Caruthers nearly started a riot by calling one of the Giants "an opprobrious epithet." His word or words triggered a firestorm as the Giants stormed toward Caruthers and demanded an apology. Several apologizes were offered by the Grand Rapids baseball management, and apparently possibly one from Caruthers, too, in an effort to get the game back on track.[26]

Caruthers' highly offensive comment was combined with the fact that young George Wilson was making his Giants debut and doing poorly. Wilson issued an unheard-of 11 (or 12) walks to Gold Bugs batters.

Len Hoch gave his view of the umpiring on that Easter Sunday and began by stating that Wilson's pitching was "splendid work." Hoch lamented Caruthers' negative influence on the game. The postmaster and investor said Wilson would throw the ball over the plate, the Grand Rapids batters couldn't hit it, and it quickly became a two-strike count. Then Caruthers just wouldn't call that third and final strike, even when Wilson threw it over the middle of the plate. The umpire basically fixed the game against the Giants. Hoch claimed the Giants had to "fight for everything" in that game, even though Caruthers decided they weren't going to win the contest. Hoch was not too optimistic about future dealings with hometown umpires, either. "The prejudice, however, that they are compelled to encounter, may lose them games just as it did at Grand Rapids," the *Evening Telegram* summarized Hoch's belief.[27]

On a more positive note, only a week into their season, Hoch, Taylor, Parsons and the Page Woven Wire Fence Company were very pleased with the fledging enterprise. Hoch stated that "management is fully satisfied with their team" and felt the Giants were hard workers, gentlemanly, and were leaving behind a good impression. In the all-important area of finances, it was reported that the team was, so far, a success and "far beyond the expectations of the management."[28]

The series with the Gold Bugs returned to inside the city limits of Grand Rapids for Monday's 3 o'clock game at Recreation Park. The Giants lost, 13–6, with their fielding described as "slovenly," as Malone made three errors at third base. It was the first poorly played game for the Giants during this trip. Caruthers was again behind the plate, and the game dragged on for a very long two hours and 20 minutes. About 800 people attended this game, a much smaller crowd than the Easter Sunday affair.[29]

The final game on Tuesday featured free admission for all ladies to Recreation Park. This was a very exciting contest, as after eight innings the local boys were ahead only 4–3. Despite being the home team, rules in 1895 allowed for either team to bat first, unlike today when the hosts always bat in the bottom of each inning. The Giants' Fred Van Dyke was cruising along on the mound entering the top of the ninth. He began to tire and gave up five unearned runs following a throwing error by second baseman Fowler. The result was a 9–3 Giants loss. The *Evening Telegram* called it "by far the snappiest game of the series," while the *Grand Rapids Democrat* noted, "the colored Giants demonstrated that they are good, clean ball players, under all circumstances." The Giants managed only seven hits, again led by Gus Brooks, who slugged two doubles. Van Dyke did not strike out any of the Gold Bugs, but he also didn't walk any. The smallest crowd of the four games, 300 people, attended the game, which only took an hour and 45 minutes to complete. Bobby Caruthers was again the umpire.[30]

The Giants boarded their special train car and headed south for a game in Illinois. The coveted catcher, Frank Maupin, was still not with the team. A reported illness left him out of spring training in Marion, Indiana. Reports were that he had recovered enough to join the team and play in Grand Rapids, but that was not the case. The new word was that he would join them in Rockford, Illinois. To make room for him on the roster, the plan was to release pitcher Fred Van Dyke, who had been shaky in the last game against the Gold Bugs.[31] The published current roster had Taylor, Fowler, Johnson and Malone around the infield, Nelson, Hopkins and Brooks in the outfield, and Holland and Van Dyke as the main pitchers, with Burns and Maupin as the catchers, for a total of 11 players. But Maupin had yet to appear, and George Wilson and James Lincoln were surprisingly not listed on the roster.[32]

Back in Adrian, interest in the black ball team was growing. In addition to Charles Robinson announcing that he would publicize the game scores, members of the black business community followed suit. The barbershop which had employed Bud Fowler over the winter, Craig and Reid on South Main Street, was doing their part to support the Giants. They told people they would post games scores and team information at their business and invited residents to stop in and take a look.[33] In the nearby community of Blissfield, groups of white school children thought that with some practice, they too could play on the Page Fence Giants.[34]

The 60-foot, elegantly painted Page Fence Giants train car pulled into Chicago on Tuesday evening. Their next scheduled contest was against one of the top amateur clubs in the country, the Chicago Edgars. Their claim to fame in 1894 was almost defeating the Chicago Unions, a strong professional black team. The Giants' Billy Holland had pitched for the Unions in that key game last year and now would face the Edgars with his new teammates.[35]

The game was scheduled for a field at 37th and Butler Streets in Chicago, called the Union Ball Park. One Chicago newspaper which promoted the game quoted Fowler as saying "his team was in excellent form," and even printed projected starting lineups for both the Edgars and the Giants.[36] By all accounts, it was a fine game, and each team started out strong with three runs in the opening frame. The teams ended the contest tied at 5–5 when darkness set in, before they could begin the tenth inning. The Giants were lucky to tie the game, as an error by the Edgars allowed the fifth run to score in the final inning. George Wilson started the game, struck out five Edgars and walked four. The fielding highlight was an unassisted double play by the Giants' George Taylor.[37]

As the Giants had pulled into Chicago earlier that morning prior to playing the Edgars, someone else pulled out of Grand Rapids. The now infamous Bobby Caruthers, former major league pitching star and now the highly criticized umpire, was released that day by the Grand Rapids Gold Bugs. In 1894, Caruthers had played first base and captained the team, but he was deemed expendable just a year later. The *Adrian Evening Telegram* wrote that Caruthers was "getting his deserts."[38]

The Giants original schedule had them playing two games in Milwaukee, Wisconsin, against a member of the same Western League that had fielded the Grand Rapids and Indianapolis teams. Instead, the Giants were in Illinois to play two games on April 18 and 19 against Rockford, a member of the ten-team, Class B Western Association. Also known as the Forest City Reds, they used heavy hitting, slugged four home runs and defeated the Giants, 7–2. The Rockford squad was led by former major leaguers Ed Pabst and Gus Alberts and 20-year-old rookie Johnny Kling, before he embarked on a 13-year major league career, mostly with the Chicago Cubs. Joe Miller pitched for the Giants, struck out four and walked only one. The Giants struggled at the plate and notched only five hits. The Giants tried a different batting order, dropping Taylor from his customary leadoff position and inserting Fowler into that spot. Fleet-footed center fielder Gus Brooks was moved up to the second spot from his normal cleanup position. Catcher Pete Burns, whom the club was still trying to replace with Frank Maupin, batted cleanup, with James Lincoln inserted at third base for the recently error-prone Billy Malone. It didn't really help, as Brooks, Johnson, Taylor and Lincoln were the only Giants to record hits.[39]

The second game had Page Fence winning the rematch, 12–11. It was Rockford's first loss of the baseball season. Both teams hit a bunch of singles, and the Giants rallied from being down 6–2 to grab the win. The Giants scored 11 of their runs in the last four innings off Rockford pitcher Fred Underwood, who had his major league debut in Brooklyn the year before and would post 29 wins in 1895. The home team's poor fielding was also seen as key to the Giants' victory. Later, after poor performances by two Rockford players, the loss was blamed on a "traveling hypnotist." The rumor was that the hypnotist had attended the game, rooted for the Giants, and apparently cast a bad spell on the Rockford pair.[40] Lincoln again replaced the struggling Giants third sacker, Billy Malone, who was placed in right field. Miller, who had pitched the day before and lost, earned this win after he relieved Billy Holland and the Giants rallied.[41]

Newspaper accounts of this team were uneven as the season went along. Billy Holland was listed as Howland in some box scores, and the yet-to-appear catcher, Frank Maupin, was referred to as Maupins and Maufin. Catcher Pete Burns was listed as Burn and Barnes on several occasions. It was also apparent than neither Gus Parsons nor Bud Fowler made it a priority to send game details back to the Adrian newspapers. When Len Hoch or Rolla Taylor travelled with the team, Adrian newspapers printed game articles. When the pair was back in Adrian, even simple game scores were hard to locate in the papers. To add to the confusion, the host towns often confused this new Page Fence Giants squad with other black teams. As the team left Rockford and headed north for Minnesota, the *St. Paul Daily Globe* newspaper said the Page Fence Giants was formerly the team called the Cuban Giants, which was obviously incorrect.[42]

Another issue was the ever-changing schedule. The stop in Rockford was not on the schedule that Fowler had sent to *Sporting Life* back in late March. However, on another page in that same issue, Rockford's organizers announced that they would play the Page Fence Giants in April.[43] These two game dates were supposed to be played against the Milwaukee club, but Rockford was later substituted when the Wisconsin town's diamond couldn't be prepared in time.[44] In another booking story, Rockford was scheduled to play the Giants later in April, but league games bumped those contests.[45]

One wonders about the community backlash when word leaked out that an all-black baseball team was coming to town. Some places likely back-tracked and cancelled the Page Fence Giants appearance, while others kept them on the schedule. Were towns afraid of violence or a threat of violence, such as what recently occurred in Grand Rapids with umpire Caruthers? What influence did the KKK or the White Caps have in controlling who appeared in a town? The possibility of an all-white club losing to an all-black team had to be on someone's list as problematic in some communities. Originally, the much-publicized game against the major league Cincinnati Reds was scheduled, cancelled and ultimately re-scheduled and played in April. The original cancellation was based on the claim that following a spring training trip to New Orleans, the Reds would have only two weeks to practice, which wasn't enough time to prepare for the Giants.[46]

The Giants had traveled through the night following their victory over Rockford, in order to arrive in Minneapolis around 11 o'clock Saturday morning, April 20. The schedule called for four straight games with the Minneapolis Millers and then five with the St. Paul Saints, both members of the Western League. However, as with the rest of the early-season bookings, what was printed on a piece of paper didn't always occur.

The Giants' parade was set for noon, and the game was to begin at 3 o'clock at Athletic Park. John Barnes was the well-known manager of the Minneapolis Millers, and a "hot game" was anticipated.[47] A large crowd estimated to be around 1,200 fans was on hand to see the Millers' tryout pitcher, Bob Martin, face George Wilson and the black team from Michigan.[48] Freshly painted advertising on the wooden fence surrounding the field made for a splendid site that day. Martin fired the first pitch of the game to the unidentified Giants leadoff batter. The ball was turned around quite quickly and sailed over the Second Avenue fence for a home run. The section of black spectators at Athletic Park cheered with approval, and the *St. Paul Daily Globe* said that blast resulted in "great joy in Blackville."[49] The same paper wrongly printed the final score as 17–1 in favor of the locals. Subsequent sources reported the final score at a much closer 7–1 margin. "For the first half, the game was hot enough to suit the most crack-brained fan," and the "crowd roared with joy at the quick play." After the sixth inning, the Millers pulled away and sealed the victory. The *Daily Globe* noted, "Applause was bestowed liberally, and the color line was not drawn to any appreciable extent."[50]

Sunday's game again saw the Millers win comfortably, 11–5, at Minnehaha Park, while the Monday afternoon businessmen's special was rained out.[51] The originally scheduled Tuesday game with Minneapolis was then given to St. Paul, where the Giants would also play on Thursday. The regularly scheduled Wednesday game with St. Paul was moved to Minneapolis, probably to make up for the loss at the gate with Monday's rainout.

Charles Comiskey's St. Paul Saints (also called the Apostles) would be the foe on Tuesday at the newly built League Park on University Avenue.[52] Ten Saints players would finish that season batting over the magic .300 mark, with Bill George hitting an incredible .403.[53] Comiskey was very confident in his team, and one local paper claimed the Saints "would in all probability wipe the Fence Giants off of the face of the diamond."[54] That prediction was close to accurate as the Saints won, 15–2. A sparse crowd witnessed the game, but those who did attend brought with them tin horns, which they blew at the appropriate time. Manager Comiskey was upset that the Giants did not do their usual pre-game bike parade and said the visitors needed to perform that stunt before Thursday's game. Whether by design or accident, Giants starter George Wilson drilled the first Saints batter, Ollie Smith, with the game's first delivery. Wilson later hit another batter, walked four, struck out four and chucked two wild pitches. Joe Miller came on and didn't fare much better than his teammate. At the plate, the Giants were held scoreless until Billy Holland drilled a long home run in the eighth inning. The next batter, Billy Malone, almost duplicated the feat, but the Saints' Bill Van Dyke ran the ball down in deep center field for an exciting and a long out. In the bottom of the ninth, Grant Johnson led off with a single and George Taylor singled him home for the Giants' second and final score.[55]

One humorous event took place midway through the game, following a single by Malone. Once he reached first, the Giants' Holland strolled out to the first base area to help coach the runner. His chatter was so distracting that when George Hopkins hit a liner to the Saints' Tony Mullane at first, Malone was caught paying attention to Holland's gibberish and was doubled off.[56]

The constant schedule changes also caused problems back in Adrian. The *Daily Times and Expositor* followed the original dates, wrongly stated that this game was against Minneapolis and reported the wrong score, too.[57] The *Adrian Evening Telegram* had the incorrect score, but did name the proper opponent. They also added, "The Giants seem to be outclassed when they tackle league teams."[58]

Wednesday was the make-up game for the Monday rainout and put the Giants back in Minneapolis. The Millers drubbed the Giants again, this time 18–7. The visitors were said to have performed much better than in the earlier games. One Adrian paper reported the score as 17–7.[59]

The Millers also announced a Friday game with the Giants with a promotion targeting the local black community. In addition to free admission for women that afternoon, the club was giving away a gift to "the most popular colored lady on the grounds." To win, all one had to do was drop a ticket in the box and await the drawing. The winner of the $25 tea set would be announced during the game.[60]

It was back to St. Paul to tackle Comiskey's Saints on Thursday afternoon at 3 o'clock. The Page Fence Giants management granted Comiskey's wish, as the *Saint Paul Daily Globe* notified the citizenry that at 1 o'clock "the colored contingent will parade the principal streets. Muscular arms and generously proportioned calves will be displayed by the Giants as they expertly manipulate the bicycles."[61]

The Giants lost again to the powerful St. Paul league team by a score of 9–2. A young phenom by the name of Messerly (he was released before the regular season) pitched the first six innings for the Saints and held the Adrian club to a single run. Things started off well when Bud Fowler stroked a "pretty single" to lead off the game, but it failed to lead to a run. Wilson, the Giants' starter, used his left-handed delivery to keep some batters off-balance, while others found success. "The colored artist's curves were quite deceptive and completely mystified such hard hitters as [Ollie] Smith, [Lew] Camp and [Tim] O'Rourke." Unfortunately, the rest of the Saints' lineup fared better and chalked up eight runs in the first three innings against Wilson. Wilson again drilled Smith with a pitch and later nailed the rookie pitcher Messerly for good measure. Wilson also walked three and gave up eight hits, half of them doubles, but struck out six Saints. The Giants notched tallies in the fourth inning off Messerly and in the seventh off reliever Harrison Pepper. Billy Malone had the lone extra-base hit, a ground rule double to right field that bounced over the fence and plated Pete Burns, who had singled. Despite the 9–2 setback, one paper declared that these Giants were "no novices," even though their fielding had yielded seven unearned runs for the Saints.[62]

The troublesome rain from earlier in the week returned, and Friday's tilt was canceled due to the wet weather, costing one lucky lady the chance to win the fancy tea set. However, on Thursday, Rolla Taylor had telegrammed Len Hoch back in Adrian that there was now a new Giants schedule.[63] The St. Paul and Minneapolis teams had recently agreed to face each other in a three-game exhibition series beginning Saturday. Minneapolis would host the first contest, Comiskey's St. Paul would host on Sunday, and then it was back to Minneapolis on Monday. Interesting to note was that Comiskey was currently battling St. Paul residents and preachers over the sinful act of playing baseball on the Sabbath. The April 28 game would be a challenge to that proposed ban.

So the last two games in the Twin Cities, which had been announced a month earlier, were no longer going to be played. Rolla Taylor worked with Western League President John Barnes, who also doubled as the manager of the Minneapolis Millers, and the Giants' new bookings were completed. Taylor said he would be home on Saturday with the new schedule.[64] In addition to the pair of games dropped in Minneapolis, Cedar Rapids, Iowa was also removed from the original Page Fence Giants schedule. In its place was a pair of games in La Crosse, Wisconsin, on Sunday and Monday. Beloit, Wisconsin, was a new stop, while Dubuque, Iowa, was pushed further down the schedule. The Mississippi River town of Galena, Illinois, remained as previously announced, a stop in Clinton, Iowa, was added, and Dubuque's games were moved to later in the month.[65]

In the same telegram to Hoch, Rolla Taylor said the Giants had signed a "Crack Jack for third base ... their third baseman being especially weak."[66] Taylor had "not lost faith" in the Giants but also admitted the being weak in both corner outfield spots. George Hopkins, the regular left fielder, and Jimmy Lincoln at third base, who had temporarily replaced Billy Malone, would be released. For some reason, neither player was being paid on the regular Page Fence Giants salary structure. Billy Holland, a starting pitcher, had been forced to play right field, and the plan was to get him to re-focus on pitching. Taylor claimed these moves would make the Giants a more competitive team.[67] The catching situation between Pete Burns and the still absent Frank Maupin was also solved. It is possible that the soon-to-be-signed third baseman was actually Vasco Graham, a catcher whose name first appeared in game stories right around this time. Graham, described as the Omaha catcher, would pair with George Wilson and form one of the Giants' stronger batteries. However, with the coming of the Michigan State League and Adrian's entry, the Giants' lineup would have some additional holes to plug. Both Graham and star twirler Wilson would be leaving the Giants in about two weeks and joining the Adrian Demons.[68]

Rolla Taylor's discussion with a local paper reiterated the issues the Giants were having with the umpires. He claimed that in every game, except for the one with the Cincinnati Reds, the Giants were on the wrong side of the calls. In the *Daily Times and Expositor* interview, Taylor contended that local umpires "are invariably home players, and hate to see a colored team beat a white one."[69] The *Evening Telegram* repeated that view and said, "prejudice against being beaten by a colored team has had its weight."[70]

The quality of the Giants' play began to improve as they spent more time together and became more comfortable with each other. The early-season games against the top-level minor league teams would soon be replaced by clubs with less experience or weaker skills. Also on the good side, despite the changed lineup and umpire woes, the attendance had been strong and the team was making money.

As Gus Parsons and the Giants were shuffling their itinerary and traveling on a day they were to play in the Twin Cities, the *St. Paul Daily Globe* morning edition was on the newsstands. This popular eight-page paper covered the news headlines of the day. On page five were three or four columns of sports, covering baseball, horse racing and target shooting. As one read from left to right across the eight-column paper, the sporting topics transitioned to hard news. Column four had a story entitled "Lynched the Black," where a "whitecap" mob in Jensenton, Kentucky, broke into the local jail and hung George Ray, described as a "disreputable Negro" who had been ordered out of the area. Ray was accused of "lawlessness" and had earlier been dragged from his home and whipped. When Ray went around town and accused "prominent men" of having a hand in his beating, he stirred up further trouble. Law officers had a hard time locating Ray, and when they did, they arrested him and placed him in jail. Somehow, the "prominent men" of white caps stole Ray out of jail and proceeded to hang him, a day before his scheduled trial on the criminal complaint.[71]

One column over was the screaming headline "Killed Her in Jail." A distraught Ohio spouse, upset that his wife was having an affair with a black man, entered the county jail and murdered her. Don Purkepile hid a newly purchased revolver in a shoe box and told the jailer his wife needed shoes. His wife, whose name was never even mentioned in her murder story, had been ordered to serve 15 days for "lewdness." When her husband asked his wife to come home, she refused, stating that she preferred the company of her new boyfriend. Purkepile promptly removed the hidden gun from the box and shot his wife in the head. She died one hour later. The shooter somehow managed to elude the jailer and ran into the street. A local search party was formed, but a day later, Purkepile was still on the loose.[72]

Scanning over to the final column on the right, "Legally Lynched" was yet another gruesome headline. In Abbeville, South Carolina, Stuart Burst, a black man, was hanged for the December shooting death of another man. Burst reportedly said right before his hanging "that he would be in heaven by dinner time." Whether this death sentence was a lynching or capital punishment was not stated.[73]

It was now on to La Crosse, Wisconsin, for games on Sunday, April 28 and Monday, April 29, followed by an off-day on Tuesday and then two games with college boys in Beloit, Wisconsin. With the train clicking rhythmically along the tracks and headed west to Wisconsin, and the headlines of violence swirling in their heads, bad umpires were not the worst thing that could happen to a Page Fence Giant.

♦ 8 ♦

Giants and Demons

"It would keep a stenographer and type writer pretty busy to keep up with the corre-spondence of the Giants and our local ball team."[1] It appeared that even before the Giants had played a single game, plans were in the works to use some of their players in the newly re-established Michigan State League and on the Adrian Demons.

Even though the league was supposed to have been all ready to go, financial issues were still dogging the proposed Lansing entry to the MSL.[2] Adrian had paid their league entry fee by mid–March, and word was that excitement was such that the proposed league would feature eight teams instead of six.[3] Battle Creek hosted a meeting March 28 with either Hoch or Taylor in attendance (the news story is unclear) as they considered additional entries to the league. The towns of Benton Harbor and Dowagiac, both in Michigan's far southwestern corner, were being examined for possible teams. The application from Port Huron, on the other side of the state, seemed to rest on shaky finances.[4] By mid–April, a six-team league was organized with teams from Adrian, Battle Creek, Jackson, Kalamazoo, Monroe and Owosso.[5] At the last minute, the financing in Lansing was shored up and they were added as the seventh team.[6] Monroe's finances then became in question, and Port Huron replaced them to keep it a seven-team league.

Despite the fact not all the team entries had been confirmed, the MSL created a sched-ule committee in mid–March, and President Mumby selected Rolla Taylor, who was the official head of the Adrian delegation, for the task, along with O. G. Hungerford from Kala-mazoo.[7] Later, an updated scheduling committee was joined by an R. E. Wicking and Adrian's Len Hoch, and it was finalized that the MSL would open on Tuesday, May 21. Hoch was given the greater portion of the credit for creating this schedule. The Adrian minor league team was to play the Page Fence Giants three times (June 3, 4 and 5), with one of those games moved to Monroe. But, as with everything dealing with base ball at the time, it was cautioned that these dates were still tentative. Eventually, Adrian would open the season in late May, hosting Port Huron as part of a 90-game league schedule which con-cluded in September.[8]

The MSL also approved their umpires as they hired James Grogan of Detroit, Lewis Burnett of Springfield, Ohio, and George Perrin of Toronto, Canada. In addition, each town was supposed to have one substitute umpire on hand, in case the trains were late and the regularly assigned man could not make the game.[9] Pearl Southland, an Adrian High School class of 1894 graduate, had applied for one of the regular league umpire positions, but was probably deemed too young for the full-time work. However, he was appointed the Adrian substitute umpire, with James Stevens tabbed as the home club's official scorer.[10] Business-men were snatching up season tickets to support the team, which promised to bring huge crowds and spendable cash into town. Adrian was charging only $10 for season tickets, while other cities set the price at $15. Adrian's tickets included both regular season and any exhibition games, such as those scheduled with the Page Fence Giants. So far, Adrian's boosters were happy with the ticket sales.[11] For individual games, the league ticket rate was 25 cents for general admission. In Adrian, their grounds included a wooden grandstand, and it was announced that those would cost 35 cents, but patrons would now be able to sit in the middle of the grandstand in a section dubbed reserved. To the left of the reserved section would be a lady's section, which apparently would cost only 25 cents. Both sections would be protected by wire fencing, so balls would not hit unsuspecting fans. The troublesome barbed wire fence from the area north of the foul line on the west side of the grounds would be removed before the first official game, as it was described as "a nuisance" to patrons.[12]

James Wolverton was still in the process of finishing Lawrence Park's grounds. Since the Giants were not to play in town until early June and the Adrian MSL entry not until late May at the earliest, he had time. Wolverton claimed he needed another $200 to get Lawrence Park's diamond in the best shape and looked for donors.[13] There were still some problems with the outfield fencing. During an April exhibition game, the fence on the west edge of the grounds inhibited a play, but the story was not specific. In a later game, a visiting player from Jackson was retrieving a long hit over the left field wall and tried to scramble over it, only to get snagged on the barbed wire, which was affixed to the top of the wooden fence boards. The left fielder was hooked, dangled on the barbed wire and had to be helped down by a group of schoolboys. The fence wasn't the only issue with left field, as an uneven section of low ground sloped into a nearby ditch![14]

To combat the freeloaders problem which plagued organizers in 1894, an elaborate plan was created prior to the first MSL game. "The high board fence will be continued to the northwest corner of the grounds and three hundred feet of canvas six feet high will be stretched on poles across the grounds east of the diamond. Taking another step, the club rented two adjacent parcels of land, apparently containing high ground and hired policemen to patrol the area and rid it of its nonpaying customers."[15]

Ball players were now writing to Adrian management, asking for a chance to play on the Class B–rated club, one step below the highest-ranked, Class A Western and Eastern Leagues. Local management was spreading the world that Adrian was a "base ball city of importance." In March, the legal structure of the players' paperwork made the news, and it was claimed they were "much more binding than the original independent contracts," such as with last year's Adrian Light Guard nine.[16] Within one week, the MSL Adrian club's business office had sent and received most of their player contracts. Club officials said they were just waiting on three or four more and expected those at any time. One player who returned his signed agreement was current Giants pitcher George Wilson. His minor league deal required a different contact from what he had signed with the Page Fence Giants. No terms of either contract were revealed.[17]

Wilson would not be the only black ball player on the Adrian Demons this season, as he would be joined by fellow Giants catcher Vasco Graham. There was no longer any mention of Fred Van Dyke joining the Demons and becoming the team's black catcher. The remaining Adrian Demons white players came from all over the Midwest. Elmer Smith from Jacksonville, Illinois, was another catching prospect. Litchfield's Fred Van Giessen joined the "Palmyra Wonder," George Wilson, and Jess T. Derrick of Indianapolis on the pitching staff. The infield candidates were Ed Mulhearn from Battle Creek at first, German-born and Detroit resident Paul J. Kraft at second, J. S. Schulte of Grand Rapids at shortstop, and Maurice Justice of Sugar Grove, Illinois, at third. The outfield candidates were Joe O'Rourke of Fort Wayne, Indiana, W. H. Miller of Flint, and Verne Cutting, a second Jacksonville native. Following two weeks of practice and exhibitions, two of the 12 players would be cut from the Opening Day roster.[18] By the first of May and well before the season began, League President Mumby approved each player's contract with Adrian, including the two black stars, Wilson and Graham. During the league meetings over the previous months, nothing was ever published about anyone submitting a formal motion forbidding black men to play in the Michigan State League.

More than a decade earlier, in 1883, Adrian Constantine "Cap" Anson had launched a public crusade to ban black ball players from playing on or against white professional teams. It began in Toledo in an August game between Anson's Chicago nine and the locals, featuring the college-educated black catcher Moses Fleetwood Walker. Anson at first refused to field a squad but relented after he was threatened with a loss of gate receipts was combined with the Toledos' unwavering support of Walker. Over the next few years, however, whenever Anson's Chicago team faced an integrated squad, the black player or players sat out that game for some strange reason. During the Toledo confrontation, Anson was quoted as using the derogatory "n" word and made his feelings about black people well known over the years. Anson, who obviously was not the only white person to help establish this black player ban, may have been the most influential.[19]

Anson was not just a regular white ballplayer; he was an excellent one, maybe the best in the game's first 50 years. His National Baseball Hall of Fame Plaque begins with "Adrian Constantine Anson 'Cap'; Greatest Hitter and Greatest National League Player-Manager of the 19th Century."[20] He towered over the other players at six-feet-tall and a hefty 227 pounds; he was one of the game's first great sluggers. He led the National League in RBI eight times, was a four-time batting champion, and spent two decades hitting above the magical .300 barrier. He was the first to amass 3,000 hits, won five pennants as a player/manager, and was one of the first inductees into the National Baseball Hall of Fame. The Iowa native had turned professional in his teens and used his vast experience, physical size and stellar statistics to help construct a segregated, whites-only ball diamond for the next 60 years.[21] Unfortunately, with his size and talent and his long list of accomplishments, the introduction of black players into the professional major leagues would have done little, if anything, to diminish Anson's contribution to the game. In fact, it would have raised Anson's qualifications, as he would be a star in a league which embraced all ball players, regardless of color. However, he decided to use his clout to become a baseball superstar and to ban others from doing so. His behavior was typical of many white people in the latter part of the 1800s and was detrimental to black citizens, baseball fans and American society in general.

This unwritten Anson rule later became known as the "Gentleman's Agreement" and was aimed at every black player in every major or minor league in the United States. Coming about ten years after the collapse of Reconstruction, it was up to league organizers to enforce this word of mouth agreement. Incidentally, Anson had a unique connection to Adrian, Michigan, and the home of the Page Fence Giants. His father had lived in both Adrian and Constantine, Michigan, in the 1840s, before making the trek farther west across the Mississippi River. When "Cap" was born in Marshalltown, Iowa, in 1852, his father used the two previous Michigan cities of residence, naming his son Adrian Constantine Anson.[22] Anson's anti-black player stance had worked, for the most part, up until this time. However, the new Michigan State League, with a team based in his namesake town, would not follow his lead.

President Nick Young of the National League (the only major league at the time) predicted that the 1895 season would be the greatest ever and that regardless of where one went, baseball was on the tongue.[23] Recent rule changes probably also lent a hand to the game's popularity. This year, for the first time, the infield fly rule was adopted, hopefully eliminating the intentional dropping of pop-ups, which caused chaos on the base paths and confusion among the fans. Also in 1895, a strike was called when a foul tip was caught by the catcher. Two years earlier, the distance from the pitcher's box to home plate had been increased from 50 feet to the odd distance of 60 feet and six inches. Along with that switch, the pitcher's box was eliminated and the slab/rubber was added for hurlers. Earlier rules changes making the game quicker and more enjoyable for spectators occurred in the late 1880s. Starting in 1887, batters could no longer request high or low balls from the pitchers. Second, in 1889 four balls were needed for a walk, a big reduction from the earlier days of nine, which dramatically sped up the pace of play and likely saved the arms of countless pitchers everywhere.[24]

In the area of equipment, all official bats were now rounded and replaced the earlier versions, where one side was flat and was used for hitting the pitched ball. The wooden bats were either store-bought or homemade and had a large, knobbed handle to balance the weight of the barrel. The ever-evolving use of the glove hit its stride in the mid–1890s. Large, padded catcher's mitts were common and joined the earlier use of the chest protector and face mask. First basemen now commonly sported mitts larger than their hand to catch the ball. Many players were using larger, specialized gloves, but not all. The previous mitt style included some sort of palm padding of your glove hand, which extended up and over the lower portion of your fingers, with the ends of your digits exposed. This partially gloved method was inaccurately referred to as playing bare-handed. The use of these new fielding mitts, which covered the entire hand, was sometimes referred to as the big glove movement.[25] Adrian's Page Fence Giants were apparently slow to make the jump to the new fielding style. "The big glove rule has no terrors for the Page Fence Giants. Every man on the team, except the catcher and first baseman plays bare-handed."[26]

While the Adrian minor league club was getting ready to launch their season, the Page Fence Giants, the other team in town, was just hitting their stride. In early May, Len Hoch sent a lengthy story to *The Sporting News*, detailing all the baseball doings in Adrian, both in the MSL and about the Page Fence Giants. He noted that the Demons had added Minneapolis native, slugger and noted hothead Mike Lynch at third base and C. E. Hicks (who had earlier defeated the Giants in their first game with the Minneapolis Millers) to the pitching staff, apparently cutting infielder Schulte and hurler Van Giessen. Lynch was named team captain, while T. J. Levine had been hired as manager (though Levine's name was never again mentioned).[27] Hoch's article crowed about the recent success of the Page Fence Giants. "They won their tenth successive game by defeating the Edgars in Chicago, 15–6. They won two games at La Crosse, two at Beloit, two at Galena, one at Clinton and two at Dubuque." The travelling show had played in eight states since the season began six weeks ago.[28]

As the Giants were now playing, for the most part, lower-level minor league teams, it would diminish their national media coverage. Playing the National League Cincinnati Reds and top Class A minor league squads was one thing, but taking on the Beloit College boys and clubs from the independent Eastern Iowa league was quite another. Details of the contests were hard to gather for residents back home in Adrian. Usually the newspapers printed a simple sentence that would accompany the game score. Often, towns and dates were incorrect due to both the lag in communication and the Giants' ever-changing schedule. Box scores were almost never printed for Giants' games by either of the major Adrian newspapers, the *Evening Telegram* or the *Daily Times and Expositor*. Even the basic line score, which included inning by inning tallies along with key game details, was not published for the Giants' games. That was not the case for the Adrian Demons minor league squad. Depending on the opponent and newsprint space, the papers nearly always printed line scores, on many occasions the more detailed box score, and often a paragraph or two about the contest. Even out-of-town MSL games were accompanied with line scores and brief summaries. While baseball excitement was still high in Adrian, the team of black ball players was now competing with their white (mostly) counterparts for media coverage. As American was in 1895, one could easily see that as the minor league team began their season, the Demons' news coverage would eclipse the Giants'.

As Rolla Taylor had left the Giants before they tangled with La Crosse, details of the remaining games of this stretch of the schedule were sparse. It was even hard to match up Hoch's *Sporting News* claim with what was printed back in Adrian. The Giants swept La Crosse, 13–5 and 9–3, with Miller and Wilson earning the wins. Wilson gave up just three hits in his victory.[29]

An off-day on April 30 preceded a game on the Beloit College campus on May 1. The Giants trounced the boys, 16–4, with the battery of Miller and Vasco Graham. Beloit was described as similar in talent to the college in Ann Arbor and provided a "choice" team, as the Giants were "not playing against striplings by any manner of means."[30] The second Beloit game was apparently not played (even though Hoch's *Sporting News* letter claimed they defeated them twice) and was instead moved to Galena, Illinois. Billy Malone was on the mound for what one Adrian paper called the Giants' fourth straight victory (which supported the idea that the second Beloit contest was indeed cancelled), a 9–1 thrashing of Galena. The Giants' batters were the leaders as they rapped out 15 base hits and were also slick in the field, committing just one error.[31] On Friday, Galena again fell to the Giants, 10–3. Pete Burns was behind the plate for the first time in about a week, and Holland earned the win.[32] The *Minneapolis Tribune*'s report of the game made it into an Adrian paper and glowed with its praise of the black players. They singled out a "brilliant running catch by Holland," and plays by Fowler and center fielder Gus Brooks, along with the daring base running of George Taylor.[33]

The big news on the trip from La Crosse to Beloit was that a special meeting had been held and a major shake-up had taken place within the Giants' operation. This meeting possibly took place on the off-day of April 30 or before the Beloit College game on May 1. The *Adrian Evening Telegram* called it a "reorganization of the club." Rolla Taylor had left the team in La Crosse the previous weekend and was already home in Adrian, but undoubtedly discussed the plan with Gus Parsons. The *Evening Telegram* continued, "the entire management, both of the business matter of the tour and the players was placed in the hands of A. S. Parsons." This action would mean that star black player, the iconic Bud Fowler, would no longer have a hand in the operation of his brainchild—the Page Fence Giants. For the time being, the baseball tumbleweed remained playing with the Giants. The article's final statement claimed, "everything is moving smoothly now, and the prospect is that the club will be winners."[34]

The changing of the guard did not slow down the Page Fence Giants baseball juggernaut. They had a series of games in three cities that had entries in the independent Eastern Iowa League. They scored in double digits in both victories against Dubuque, Iowa, as Wilson won the first game and Miller the second. Vasco Graham caught both contests. It was in the games in Dubuque, Iowa, that the derogatory and racially stereotyped phrase "watermelon battery" was used to describe stars George Wilson and Vasco Graham.[35]

Riding the rails and travelling south along the banks of the Mississippi River, the Giants chugged into Clinton, Iowa, for two scheduled games. On Monday, May 6, rain washed out the first one with Clinton. Word was that if the grounds could be improved, a Tuesday morning/afternoon doubleheader would be played. The weather cooperated for a short time as Tuesday morning the Giants shut out Clinton, 12–0, behind the pitching of Billy Malone.[36] However, the rain must have returned, as the afternoon contest was canceled, and the Giants boarded the train and headed across the river and into Illinois.

The ride was maybe 30 miles as their specially equipped coach rolled into Rock Island, Illinois. They arrived on the evening of May 7 and gave their customary bike parade before the game the next day.[37] In "this excellent exhibition," the highly regarded and professional Giants went down to defeat, 5–1. Rock Island's team was called the Twin Cities, and pitcher William Goodhart tossed a one-hitter and held the Giants off the board until the final inning, when they tallied their lone run. "He pitched a pretty good game, and the big black boys, one after another, meandered back to the bench, victims of his speed and crookedness."[38] In the parlance of the day, "crookedness" would mean the use of a curve ball. However, Gus Parsons, if he read the game story the next day in the *Rock Island Argus*, would take "crookedness" in another way.

The only known photograph of the Page Fence Giants in action, year and location unknown. Lacking the screened wooden grandstand, it does not fit the description of Adrian's Lawrence Park. It appears the Giants are batting and their team bench is in the middle of the photograph, along the first base line (courtesy Adrian District Library).

Despite Hoch claiming in a letter home that the Giants had won ten games in a row, they didn't. Parsons would later adjust winning streaks by using the rationale that some defeats were due to bad umpires and did not actually count as real losses. In this contest, Parsons claimed in another letter that the game was "ruled over by one of the rankest umpires the team has yet encountered." Parsons explained that one time a Giant had been struck out, but the Twin City catcher missed the ball, and the batter made a mad dash to first base. Despite the batter "getting there fully a rod ahead of the ball," the umpire declared him out on the third strike.[39] The Rock Island paper agreed it was a controversial play and said, "the Giants first refused to play after a decision by Umpire Baker in the eighth inning in calling a man out at first." However, either Parsons or Bud Fowler convinced the Giants to continue with the game, which they eventually lost.[40]

The Page Fence Giants train left Rock Island, crossed the northern half of the Prairie State, and arrived in Chicago for weekend games. The Adrian men were much superior to the Edgars and the Unions. On Saturday, May 11, the Giants rallied in the seventh inning and tallied 12 runs in that one frame to grab a 14–5 victory over the Edgars. The next morning, the Edgars again were defeated by the Adrian visitors, this time by either 12–4 or 12–6. The Giants delivered their runs on 15 hits and were helped along by five Edgars errors.[41]

That Sunday afternoon, the Giants were to face the always tough Chicago Unions. Billy Holland and Gus Brooks had been stars for the Unions the previous year, so player chatter and spirited coacher antics were likely displayed throughout this contest. The Giants scored their runs on 17 hits, while the Unions had more errors, nine, than hits, eight, as the Adrian contingent easily won, 16–8.[42] The *Adrian Daily Times and Expositor* commented, "The Giants are undoubtedly improving."[43]

The special Page Fence Giants train, while pulling out of Chicago and heading for Indiana, left two men behind. George Wilson and Vasco Graham, the "watermelon battery," would take another train and travel to Adrian to begin their stint with the minor league Adrian Demons. Left with just nine men, manager Parsons contacted the recently released Fred Van Dyke, who resided relatively close by in Vandalia, Michigan, and asked him to rejoin the team in time for the upcoming contests. The always talked-about, but forever missing, Frank Maupin again was publicly mentioned as a possible catching replacement, with Graham now gone with the Demons.[44]

The next games on the Page Fence Giants schedule were in Hammond, Indiana, on Monday and Tuesday, but both were rained out.[45] The train turned north and headed into western Michigan, to Kalamazoo for a series of games with their minor league team. Excitement was high in Kalamazoo as they were one of the proud entries in the upstart Michigan State League. Going by the creative names of the Celery Eaters and Zooloos, along with the blander Kazoos, this team wanted a piece of Adrian.[46] They figured to get one bite from Lenawee County and the Page Fence Giants now, and another one later, when they faced the Adrian Demons.

After playing before friendly black fans in Chicago over the weekend, the Giants returned to the diamond in front of potentially more hostile crowds. The reporter for the *Kalamazoo Daily Telegraph* wrote flowery and sarcastic descriptions of the three games the Giants and the local nine played that week. The stinging barbs were aimed at each ball club. The May 13 game was preceded by the usual parade to the ball grounds, with the Giants riding their Monarch bicycles. Game one was an easy, 10–5 victory for the Page Fence team. The *Daily Telegraph* was highly complimentary in their comments toward the visitors. Their story was headlined "Twas a Cloudy Day; And the Kazoo Sluggers Couldn't

See the Ball; Gentlemen of the Hueebony; Bring Their Bats into Intimate Acquantance [*sic*]." The article gave much credit to the Page Fence men and not much to the locals. The skin tone of the visitors was mentioned often, so readers had a clear idea that the ballgame was between black and white players.[47]

"Nine chocolate colored ball players" was how one paragraph began, describing the barnstorming team. It noted that teams around the country "had succumbed to African muscle and brains." Specifically noting the Wednesday loss, the scribe reported, "Kalamazoo's scalp was added to the already big stock of cappilaceous [*sic*] relics. In fact, these dusky-hued sons of Adrian rubbed the rich celery earth of the league grounds deep into the hides of the local players." The story characterized five Kalamazoo fielding errors as "traitorously" assisting the visitors. The Celery Eaters' pitching was poor that day too. "Bean Eater Plummer was put in to pitch, but his curves and the home plate were not on speaking terms and when one did get in the other's vicinity, some one of the opposing nine was ready to send it far out of the reach of any fielder." The Giants knocked around three pitchers that day, including Fred Van Giesen, who had recently been released by the Demons. Billy Malone was the Giants' starting pitcher and earned the win, but Joe Miller came on in relief and was effectively wild that day. Catcher Burns had a hard time handling Miller, who apparently uncorked a slew of wild pitches that careened off the backstop. It was said that Miller's tossing "threatened to raise havoc with the construction of the grand stand." Home Run Johnson lived up to his name and slugged a round-tripper, while Brooks and Fowler also shined at the plate.[48]

In a rare move, there were two umpires hired to work this game. What is unknown is whether this duo was something the locals decided or was a demand by the umpire-targeted Giants. Almost all the 1895 season games were umpired using just one man stationed behind the plate.[49]

This opening Kalamazoo game also marked the first appearance of Jim Chavous, a native of Marysville, Ohio. Apparently giving up on the rumored appearance of Frank Maupin, Chavous was signed instead and started in left field for the Giants. He would also replace George Wilson as one of the team's pitchers. As the Giants were trying to restock the club after the loss of Wilson and Graham, they saw another Page Fence team member leave. Following the Wednesday contest, Johnson hopped a train back to Adrian to deal with a family illness. Johnson's absence would place Billy Malone at shortstop, and Fred Van Dyke would be forced to pitch.[50]

The second game went much better for Kalamazoo, as they chalked up an 11–3 victory on Thursday. The game was not close, as the Giants had a hard time with the 17-year-old Kalamazoo pitcher, George Harris, who allowed just five hits. The Giants hit the ball hard, but the orb didn't evade many of the Kalamazoo fielders. Behind the plate for Kalamazoo was 23-year-old Lou Criger, who next summer would begin a 16-year major league catching career. Upon his retirement, largely due to his throwing ability Criger would even garner a few votes for the hallowed Baseball Hall of Fame. Malone struggled as Johnson's replacement at shortstop and committed three errors, while first baseman George Taylor had two miscues. A crowd of about 1,000 attended this contest. One newspaper reported that the Giants had to use a local man to fill out its roster, but never offered his name. It was possible that Fred Van Dyke was the local man.[51]

His reputation now growing as a great coacher, Billy Holland's full work was again on display during this series. As it is today, a first or third base coach's job is to aid the runners around the diamond. In 1895, the job also consisted of yelling, distracting opposing players, and in the case of the Page Fence Giants, entertaining the crowd. The goals in this endeavor were likely two-fold. First, the base running coaching was standard parlance of the day and fit right in with what white clubs would be doing. However, when the black Giants were whipping the local white team and tensions were likely rising in the grandstand, Holland and his teammates could calm things down. The Giants would soothe the fears and egos of the white players and spectators with clowning behavior, physical stunts and clever quips, to take an edge off the lopsided game. Holland also had a reputation as being an outstanding singer and thus added his melodic voice to his catcalls and jeers.

Holland's coacher act was very well received on Wednesday, when the Giants won the series opener, as he had "convulsed the spectators." Game two was much different, as the *Daily Telegraph* pointed out. Holland had begun with the same vim and vigor as yesterday, "but as the game progressed his voice grew husky, his face sad and great tears welled from his eyes, standing out by third base, he saw the Giants die in attempts to kill Harris' deceptive curves." A seasoned ball player such as Holland was likely not crying over the potential loss. The paper created the image of a black man's child-like response to a loss; again, not a flattering depiction. It is always possible that Holland was the target of verbal abuse and was upset. A rumor circulated that game number two was fixed so the locals could claim a victory over the powerful Page Fence Giants. Maybe that was the cause of Holland's reported teary eyes—if it even happened. To its credit, the *Daily Telegraph* strenuously denied the fixing accusation, saying it negatively reflected on both teams and their management, and stated that the rumor was repeated either in malice or out of stupidity.[52]

While the *Daily Telegraph* dished out colorful details of the second game, it was not equal in its content. While the local white team was praised or cursed for its play, their physical characteristics were never mentioned. This was not the case with the Page Fence Giants. For the game two Giants loss, the headline included the phrase "Nine Kinky Scalps" and was repeated in greater detail as "nine wooly, curly, kinky scalps, once the property of the Page Fence Giants, but now suspended from the belts of nine Zooloos."[53] One could argue that this writing was simply a very creative use of words and not offensive. However, if the paper had described the previous day's Kalamazoo loss as suffered by nine mangy, pig-haired ghosts, one could not reasonably argue that using similar terms was not offensive.

Bud Fowler apparently took great umbrage to the *Kalamazoo Daily Telegraph* story. He either cornered the reporter at the third and final game, or went downtown to the newspaper office to lodge his complaints. It is obvious that the paper heeded Fowler's call, as the game story for the Friday contest, a 4–2 Page Fence win, did not contain any poorly selected or racially charged adjectives. The game story gushed with praise of the Adrian club and ended with a lengthy apology to the Page Fence Giants and Bud Fowler. Joe Miller pitched a four-hitter "whose shoots hovered around the plate out of reach of the Zooloos," with a "cannon ball delivery" in what the paper called the "prettiest game of the season." The Giants were set down in order the first time through the lineup and trailed, 2–0, before rallying for the win. Those nine scalps Kalamazoo had claimed the day before were replaced by ones "fluttering on the rear platform of the Page Fence Giants private car, as it pulled away from the celery marshes of this city." Probably in an attempt to appease Fowler and also repairing Holland's reputation, the paper said the expert coacher (Holland) was "in the lead" as the Giants waved farewell to the Kalamazoo players.[54]

The article's conclusion apologized for its failed attempt at what was characterized as humor in describing the Kalamazoo victory. In what was likely rare in the 1890s, the white-owned paper publicly printed what appeared to be a heartfelt response to the grievance of a black gentleman.

> The *Telegraph* is genuinely sorry that Mr. Fowler should have taken to heart the account of Thursday's game as published in yesterday's *Telegraph* and regrets that the facetious attempts of the sporting editor should fall flat, and it would assure Mr. Fowler that no insinuation to hurt his or the feelings of any colored person was intended. The *Telegraph* appreciates the ability of the Giants to play ball, and splendid ball too, and has given them credit for the excellent game they have put up in this city.

They could have stopped there, but they didn't and added another layer to their apology. The *Telegraph* felt the "members of the Page Fence Giants are gentlemen and ball players on and off the field and should be treated as such." The paper continued that they had defended the Giants regarding the rumor that the second game was fixed and countered that "the morning papers" never attempted to debunk the gambling theory.[55] The original negative story was not just read in Kalamazoo. The *Adrian Evening Telegram* reprinted the racially insensitive excerpts about game two, but skimped when printing the praise of the Giants after game three. The Adrian reprinted story made no mention of the gambling conspiracy rumor, Fowler's complaint, or the subsequent mea culpa by the *Telegraph*.[56]

The Giants had earlier announced games in Battle Creek and Grand Rapids over the next week. However, apparently with the excitement of the Adrian league team, neither of Adrian's papers had any coverage or scores of these contests, or a mention that these games were even still on the schedule. There was much excitement in the local Adrian papers about the Demons (though they were usually referred to as "the league team") and the work progressing on Lawrence Park. The *Evening Telegram* crowed about the return of George Wilson to town and said he had gained 35 pounds since last year. The paper announced they would be "keenly disappointed" if Wilson wasn't the best pitcher in the league.[57] Following the Demons' exhibition trouncing of the Adrian College boys (20–3), the same day the Page Fence Giants were defeating Kalamazoo the first time, Wilson made a relief appearance on the mound. Using his now man-sized body, he threw faster than last year and with better control, too. Catcher Graham possessed "a quick, snappy, accurate" throwing arm, which fans believed would be difficult to steal on that season. The two rising stars were also again referred to in the newspaper as the "watermelon battery." The college boys were so overmatched by the minor league team, they never even managed to hit a fly ball to the outfield, though someone did knock a double off Wilson.[58]

Lawrence Park continued to take shape in anticipating the appearances of the Demons and later the Giants. J. C. Buck prepared to open a refreshment stand, and one local newspaper pushed for a large scoreboard to help the fans follow the game.[59] The week of the first game, the Adrian City Council, specifically Alderman A. M. Allen, brought forth a complaint which threatened some of the ball playing in town. Allen announced at the council meeting that some residents had approached him about the playing of ball games on the Sabbath at Lawrence Park. Allen also claimed that the owner of the ball park, Willis T. Lawrence, preferred a better class of citizens on his property and wanted a city ordinance prohibiting Sunday baseball. Lawrence's view of Sunday baseball as a sin was odd coming from a man who first came to town three decades earlier and operated a hotel with a liquor bar and billiard room.[60] The elderly Lawrence, now in his mid-'70s, was also small in stature and had recently confronted some young boys playing Sunday baseball at his park. When Lawrence approached them, they told him to "mind his own business" and to go to hell. (One paper printed the interaction as Lawrence being told by the boys "to seek a more tropical climate.")[61] When Mayor Clifford Kirkpatrick addressed the issue by saying Lawrence Park wasn't a city park and as such there wasn't much the council could do, Allen asked that the idea "be looked at."[62] And that was the end of that.

The Lawrence Park ball diamond was raked and smoothed and manicured, though late freezes and frosts that spring hampered Wolverton's efforts. A last-minute measurement from home plate to the newly erected outfield fences found it to be 12 feet farther than was needed to meet the league's regulation. The total distance was never published, and the management simply decided to keep everything where it was. There was also another round of public warnings that strategic fencing would eliminate the freeloaders from viewing any games this year.[63]

Local jeweler George Tripp printed Michigan State League folding pocket schedules.[64] Modern technology reached the ballpark as a telephone was installed on May 23, 1895.[65] Last, and certainly not least, the local management requested "courteous treatment" and hoped that Lawrence Park would be free from "jeers, criticism or derisive language toward the players or umpire." The management also wanted to "extend all over the state, Adrian's reputation for generous hospitality." The town of Monroe must have been amused.[66]

◆ 9 ◆

Umpires and June Bugs

While the Page Fence Giants had been on the road for nearly two months, there was still confusion about this black barnstorming ball team. The *Fort Wayne News* declared that the Giants were from Indianapolis, were supported by an Indianapolis company, and promoted the fence products.[1] The city was aware that the Giants consisted up of black players, as one headline simply stated, "White vs. Black."[2]

The Fort Wayne trip would be eventful for what occurred both on and off the field. The usual bike parade before the first game in town was on tap. The *Fort Wayne News* called the pregame act "attractive and unique" and said it resembled a circus, which also happened to be in town that week. The paper also promoted Bud Fowler "as the oldest and best colored player living" and said the Giants were "almost invincible." The *News* also said that the game time was pushed back to 4 o'clock so people could visit the circus first.[3]

The original Tuesday, May 21, game was not held for some reason, but the Giants still experienced some excitement nevertheless. While out in downtown Fort Wayne that evening, a horse-drawn carriage filled with some of the Giants was struck by a streetcar. Several of the players were tossed out of the carriage and dumped onto the road. It was reported that a few had suffered unspecified injuries, but apparently not bad enough to miss the next game.[4]

Another similar tragedy struck the team about this time, too. A Kalamazoo laundry hired to wash the Giants' uniforms botched the order. The cleaners ruined "all the Giants' sweaters by shrinking them to boy's sizes." Team management was none too pleased and vowed to file a damage claim against the business to cover the cost of replacing the three-dollar uniforms. The *Adrian Evening Telegram* eventually obtained Joe Miller's recently shrunken uniform. Miller, who was the largest man on the Giants, had a uniform that would now fit only a 12-year school boy.[5]

When the Giants returned to the ball diamond in Fort Wayne, things did not go well for the first two games of the series. The Adrian club dropped the first one at Lakeside Park on Wednesday, 12–6 and then lost, 8–7, on Thursday. The first tilt featured a racially integrated Fort Wayne team, as King Solomon "Sol" White, a black player, manned second base for the Hoosiers. He had starred in baseball for nearly the past decade and had spent the last two years barnstorming with the all-black Cuban Giants. His keystone partner was Art Bell, who had played a single game the previous year for the lowly major league St. Louis Browns. Bell would return to the majors in 1898 as a utility player with the Baltimore Orioles and bat nearly .300.[6] The Indiana stop also featured another umpire problem, where repeated blown calls, all neatly and clearly noted in the newspapers, contributed to the opening loss.[7]

Starting pitcher now turned emergency right fielder Joe Miller struggled mightily in his new temporary position. He dropped two fly balls which led to Hoosier runs and committed a third error. The Giants' fielding was dreadful. One paper categorized it as "hideous," and even the sure-handed center fielder, Gus Brooks, contributed to the carnage with an error. George Taylor replaced the still-absent Grant Johnson at shortstop and kicked in with three errors, and "coacher" extraordinaire, Billy Holland, at third base, added two of his own. Jim Chavous took the loss on the mound. Sol White, for Fort Wayne, knocked out a single and triple off Giants reliever Billy Malone. The *Fort Wayne Journal Gazette* reported that Malone yelled at White, "That guy's a bum batter." White promptly flashed a grin and belted the next pitch for a long triple, as Malone covered his face in shame, or laughter, or a little bit of both.[8]

The umpire's work, as poor as it was, greatly favored the home team. The Fort Wayne manager, named Belger, began the game as the umpire and was said to be "impartial and faithful," but still blew two calls at third base, one for each team, early in the game.[9]

Robert Walsh, a player on Fort Wayne's team, took over for the frazzled Belger. He was also said to be honest, but Walsh made even more mistakes. In the fifth inning, already victimized at third base by Belger's early bad call, Fowler hit another ball in the infield. The throw pulled Wallace Andrews off first base, as he "clearly left the bag to make the catch." Unfortunately, Fowler was wrongly called out again. In the next inning, the Giants' Billy Holland was batting with the bases loaded in what was still a close game. The Giants had already scored three runs that inning, courtesy of three walks from 20-year-old pitcher Jay Parker and four errors. On a two-strike pitch, the Fort Wayne righty sailed the ball "a foot above" Holland's head, but he was called out on strikes and ended a rally.[10] Incidentally, Parker would make the briefest of appearances in the major leagues in 1899 for the Pittsburgh Pirates. In a late-September game, Parker faced three batters; he walked two of them and hit another and was removed from the game, and that ended his major league career.[11]

The second loss to Fort Wayne came the next day and was a one-run affair, 8–7. The Giants jumped out to a quick 4–0 lead off Raymond Gregory after three innings at Lakeside Park. Fort Wayne pounded Miller throughout game and a ninth-inning, three-run Giants rally fell short by a single mark. Sol White was again Fort Wayne's hitting star and rapped out two singles and two triples. White also won a bet with the Page Fence club that Fort Wayne would record more than six base hits off Miller. They did, as Miller surrendered 15 safeties that afternoon. A new umpire, likely Fort Wayne player Joe O'Rourke, was behind the plate for this contest.[12] The *Adrian Times and Expositor* had few details of either losing contest, but did exclaim, "The umpire is said to have robbed them" in Thursday's game.[13]

The Fort Wayne umpiring problems and missed calls were something the black team faced all season long. The *Adrian Evening Telegram* announced that the black gentleman "have to knock the ball clear into the next township to get a safe hit."[14] How bad were the calls against the Page Fence Giants in Fort Wayne? An anonymous note to Gus Parsons seems to detail clearly what the Giants faced, day-in and day-out. An unsigned, handwritten letter on YMCA stationary, delivered before the final game, suggested that Parsons should be upset with the umpiring. "In the first game, you were outrageously robbed by the umpires, and yesterday, while not so bad you got all the worst of it." A group of local ball fans were so bothered by the crooked calls they suggested an experienced local businessman, who "was up to date," to ump the final game. The letter also claimed he was "honest and fair" and would work the game for free. The letter was signed "A few of the fans and lovers of fair play" and implored Parsons to contact the man. He did. The local businessman umpired the game and the Giants pounded out 24 hits to defeat Fort Wayne, 14–13.[15]

That weekend, the Giants traveled farther south and played a six-inning, rain-shortened affair with the team from Anderson, Indiana. The visitors were behind, 11–6, when the game was halted due to the wet weather. The Giants won a game the next day against Anderson. The two teams then traveled to Muncie, Indiana, where the Giants lost the finale in the three-day series.[16] The Giants headed for a return visit to the baseball hotbed of Cincinnati to play one of their top amateur clubs, the Shamrocks, on Decoration Day.

The Giants arrived in the Queen City during a summer heat wave and drought. The *Cincinnati Enquirer* promoted that game and announced that the Giants' morning bicycle parade would begin at 10 o'clock on Decoration Day. The paper touted the strength of the black team to get fans to attend the game. "Let it be understood that the Giants came here with scalps from the very best teams of the Northwest, having defeated some of the Western League clubs."[17]

The temperature was in the upper 80s on May 29, when the special 60-foot luxury train car rolled into town. The next day, the temperature broke the 90-degree barrier and mimicked the rising excitement throughout Cincinnati. "Every color [*sic*] barber, every wine boy, every palace car porter and every member of the local colored population of the male gender, who can get off today, will be holding down front row seats … this afternoon."[18] In front of 7,100 people at Cincinnati's League Park, the Page Fence nine dropped a 3–2 contest.[19] The Shamrocks scored their runs before the Giants crossed the plate for the first time in the ninth inning. The *Enquirer* called it a "splendid fielding game" and "one of the most exciting" at League Park that season.[20]

Fowler led off and played second base, and the rest of the lineup followed with Taylor, Johnson, Brooks hitting cleanup, then Burns, Holland, Chavous, and Malone, with pitcher Cyclone Joe Miller ninth. "Home Run" Johnson didn't live up to his moniker but did lead the Giants with a double and a triple as the Page Fence club was held to six hits. While this very large crowd added to the day's excitement, it would just prepare the team for their battle, in a little over a week, with the Adrian Demons.

To hype the epic affair, the *Adrian Times and Expositor* reprinted a lengthy story a week before the first contest, featuring ace hurler, "Palmyra's Phenomenon, George Wilson, the Demons' Dexterous Pitcher." Wilson's mound work combined finely tuned control with a fast and lively delivery. "(H)is long, lean arms can fire the ball over the pan like a streak of lubricated lightning." The story claimed that Wilson was a smart pitcher, as just when a batter thought he had him figured out, the Palmyra twirler would change his style. With the right coaching, Wilson was headed to the major leagues. The glowing article's writer was George Miller, like Wilson a Palmyra native, who was now a reporter for the *Detroit Evening News*. The story included a picture of Wilson in its Detroit edition. Miller even traced the pitcher's family heritage and claimed Wilson's parents followed the DeGraff boys from the Civil War battlefield to Palmyra. (This version conflicted with another that claimed Mary Lambert's family left her behind while on the Underground Railroad.) The paper's version said George Wilson's father, Jerry, was "a sturdy lad, well grown, straight as an arrow and a born athlete." Jerry's wife (Mary), who in the custom of the times, was never mentioned by name, was described as "a modest and pretty girl." The couple fell in love, got married and through hard work and "intelligent economy" were now "respected citizens of Palmyra and a man of some means."[21]

Not to be outdone, the *Evening Telegram* reprinted the same *Detroit News* story, but added a lengthy introductory paragraph and praised the work ethic of young Wilson. "Many people seem to think that all Wilson has to do is to get his hands on the ball and it goes where he wills, almost without effort. But that is all a mistake." The *Evening Telegram* informed readers of Wilson's target throwing for long hours at his house last winter. The paper acknowledged that Wilson was born with a great ability, but noted, "It is said that there is no excellence without labor."[22]

This public praising of a young black man and his parents was uncommon for this era. The three articles didn't include any negative black stereotyped portrayals and were without a hint of sarcasm either. Mary Wilson was called "pretty" and "intelligent," and her family were "respected citizens." These printed words to describe black Americans rarely appeared in the 1890s. It demonstrated both the quality of the Wilson family and that a segment of Adrian's white people accepted and apparently embraced this black family.

The Page Fence Giants remained in Ohio and played their next two games in the tiny farming hamlet of Cygnet. During the first weekend of June, they split the series, with Billy Malone losing, 15–8, on Saturday before the Giants rebounded behind Joe Miller and won, 20–9, on a Sunday afternoon.[23] The second game, which may actually have been played in Findlay, Ohio, featured Cygnet's atrocious fielding. The Giants managed only seven hits but were aided by 16 Cygnet errors, as the Ohio club out-hit the Giants, 14 to 7.[24]

The final tune-up before facing the Demons was Wednesday with a 9–8 victory in Findlay, as a large crowd paid to see their former Sluggers, Johnson and Fowler. The game went ten innings and ended on Fowler's winning run. Billy Holland pitched all ten innings and led the Giants at the plate with three hits. The contest was a back and forth affair which added to the day's excitement. A local physician named Beardsley was the umpire and was "roasted by both sides."[25] At the time, the Ohio club had a 16–9 record and was in third place in the Interstate League.[26] Another Giants game scheduled in Defiance, Ohio, was canceled to give the black gentlemen time to rest before the big game on Saturday.[27]

It was business manager Gus Parsons' decision to cancel the Defiance game and head back to Adrian. Parsons had the dual distinction, as did Rolla Taylor, of being financially involved with both the Page Fence Giants and the Adrian Demons. The duo was likely quite concerned at the quality of ball the town would witness that Saturday. While some observers may have felt that Parsons and Taylor were in a financial win-win situation with the upcoming Adrian battle, if one looked at it from a more personal perspective, that was not the case. Parsons would avoid being accused of favoring the mostly white minor league club over the black Giants. Outwardly favoring one team would eventually hurt the performance of the other and create difficulties when it came time to sign future players. After all, what ball player wanted to sign with a team that was the owner's second priority? In addition, if Parsons didn't give his best effort in making the Giants a viable and competitive team, his long train rides alone with his black players and employees Gaskin and Carter would become even longer. Added in was Adrian's goal of becoming Michigan's baseball capital, and any effort less than one's best would quash that idea. Everyone had to make sure both teams would be competitive that Saturday at Lawrence Park.

Working his magic, Parsons had heard that the Western Interstate League, where Fort Wayne was situated, was barely making ends meet. Since the Giants left town, three league teams had disbanded. League President Schmidt warned other clubs against tampering with players on the three remaining organizations, which included Sol White with the still operational Fort Wayne team.[28] Undeterred, it was announced on Tuesday, June 3, in both of the Adrian daily newspapers that Sol White, "the crack second baseman," was on his way to play for the Page Fence Giants.[29] In ten games with Fort Wayne, White went 20-for-52 at the plate for a .385 average and scored 15 runs.[30] White's pay would be about the same as he was receiving in Fort Wayne. His Indiana contract paid him $80 a month, while the Giants signed him for $75, plus expenses.[31]

Not stopping with that move, both papers revealed that Parsons continued to strengthen the Giants by inking James W. Patterson, "the great third baseman of the Cuban Giants."[32] White was to meet the team in Findlay and may have even played in the final tune-up game there, while Patterson wasn't scheduled to arrive until Friday or Saturday from Pennsylvania.[33] Patterson had been a member of the East Coast–based Cuban Giants.

There has been some confusion over the years about whether this Patterson was J. W. "Pat" Patterson or a George Patterson from Starkville, Mississippi. It appears they could be the same man. In a September 1894 news article in the *Findlay Times*, in which Fowler touted his future line-up, the paper noted that player Patterson (no first name) was on the 1894 Cuban Giants and hailed from Starkville, Mississippi. J. W. Patterson, in numerous sources, was born in 1872 in Omaha, Nebraska, and began his ballplaying career there in the early 1890s. His marriage license and death certificate validate this birth fact. A contemporary account of his baseball career stated that he joined the Page Fence Giants in 1895, as a player/manager.[34] In 1895, the Adrian papers confirmed he was with the Cuban Giants and printed his name as J. W. Patterson. A review of Cuban Giants box scores coincides with James Patterson leaving that club and joining the Page Fence Giants in June. Later in his life, two census reports confirmed Mississippi heritage for either one or both of his parents, adding some validity that his family could have been from Starkville. However, following the Civil War, it was common for former slaves and even black freemen to travel to Nebraska to begin a new life, as part of a group called the Exodusters. The best guess is that the paper later printed the name George for J. W. Patterson. To complicate matters, later in life, J. W. was referred to as Pat Patterson.[35]

With all of his wheeling and dealing, Parsons must have been more confident of the Giants' chances on Saturday. The special car, attached to the rear of the Lake Shore Railroad train, chugged into the depot near the Page Fence Woven Wire factory at 12:17 Thursday afternoon. The team had stayed overnight in Findlay, Ohio, before catching the train north into Michigan.[36] They were likely anxious for the chance to play in front of their Adrian friends and also to face former Giants Wilson and Graham. They were also hoping for good weather and the chance to play in the state of Michigan for much of the month of June.[37]

The Adrian Demons were also looking forward to the confrontation. They had started out with a winning record and destroyed the visiting Port Huron team in the season opener on May 21, 28–5, in front of about 800 paying customers. Adrian mayor Clifford Kirkpatrick welcomed the patrons with a lengthy speech and then threw out the first pitch. The fencing used to stop freeloaders was for the most part successful, except for a couple of people who were scattered across area rooftops taking in the game for free. The Lawrence Park grounds were in better shape, as the weather had apparently cooperated with groundskeeper Wolverton. "It was an enthusiastic, good natured crowd, impartial in its treatment of good plays" and even cheering so loudly for Port Huron's first run that a scribe surmised the fans could have been heard as far away as Tecumseh. George Wilson struck out the game's first batter and was the winning pitcher in the league opener. Likely a bit nervous, he also hit four Port Huron batters. Wilson was one of four Adrian men to rap out three base hits in the rout, while teammate Mike Lynch bashed a single, double and triple.[38]

The first three games at Lawrence Park drew 1,700 fans, which meant the 800 customers for the opener nearly dropped in half for the next two contests. Parsons, Taylor and the other local investors surmised that if the league could average 400 paying customers, they would survive the first season. Adrian and Port Huron then left town and headed north for a second slate of games.[39]

A little over a week into the season, the Lansing Senators were undefeated in all eight contests, with Adrian in second place, sporting six wins and just two losses. The Celery Eaters from Kalamazoo were 5–3, Port Huron and Owosso 2–6, and Battle Creek was a lowly 1–7.[40] The Jackson team never made it to opening day, and the MSL was reduced to six teams. In Port Huron on May 27, Wilson pitched another victory, with Graham as his battery mate, in a 10–6 win. The "Black Demon" was the key to the victory and pitched "fast and furious."[41] The *Evening Times and Expositor* had recently dubbed the Adrian club the Demons. This move caused a controversy, as the May 31, 1895, edition of *The* (Adrian) *Weekly Press* said their rival paper was "trying to inflict the name of 'The Demons' upon the Adrian" club, but declared it was "idiotic." However, the name stuck.

By the end of the first week, the *Evening Telegram* claimed that Wilson, Noel Babcock of Port Huron (whom Wilson had just defeated) and George Harris of Kalamazoo were the best pitchers in the league. If all three were placed on the same team, their club would win every game![42]

During the second week of league play, the giddy excitement in the six baseball communities across the state was replaced by the ugly race issue. Cap Anson's goal to ban all black players was now at the forefront of the Michigan State League.

A doubleheader in late May in Kalamazoo was the setting for the ideological showdown. First, the two games promised to be a circus, even before the race issue was made public, due to a controversial roster issue. George Harris, who had defeated the Page Fence Giants in mid–May, originally signed to play for Port Huron. He apparently reported to them, and when Kalamazoo offered a better contract, Harris bolted for the Zooloos. League President Mumby was aware of the Harris charade and ordered him immediately back on Port Huron's roster. Harris and Kalamazoo refused Mumby's edict and announced that the teenager would pitch in the afternoon contest against Adrian phenom George Wilson. In support of Mumby's ruling, umpire James Grogan threatened to boycott, which would nullify the contest as an official league game.[43] In Adrian, interest was so high in this doubleheader that the newly installed telegraph connection at Lawrence Park was ready to receive inning by inning updates.[44]

The morning game of the doubleheader saw the Celery Eaters jump out to a quick five- run, first-inning lead, as the Demons' Jess Derrick got rocked. The Adrian club roared back with eight runs of their own in the fourth inning to take the lead. Unfortunately, Derrick couldn't hold it and dropped a 13–10 decision. A crowd estimated at around 500 saw Vasco Graham, the Demons' other black player, catch and slug a double. Behind the plate, umpire Grogran did his work.[45]

By the time the afternoon contest began, the Kalamazoo crowd had swelled to between 1,100 and 1,300 patrons. How much of this was to see the Zooloos defy Mumby's directive and how much of it was to protest the use of black players? No one knows. It is likely rumors were in the wind during the morning game, and by the time the afternoon contest was scheduled to start, the two controversies were in full swing.[46]

Harris was instructed not to pitch, but he did, and umpire Grogan boycotted. Kalamazoo's regular substitute umpire, W. H. Doyal, along with W. H. Miller, an Adrian Demons player, were put in place and the game began. Word was that Adrian was protesting the game and would do so all the way up to National League President Nick Young. The excitement surrounding Harris' contract may have been a bit too much, as Adrian jumped all over him with three runs in the opening stanza and another five in the sixth inning to lead 8–4. But Wilson couldn't maintain the lead and Kalamazoo claimed an 11–10 victory, in 11 innings, as both starters went the distance. Wilson struck out a game-high 13 Zooloos, walked only one, and hit future major league catcher Lou Criger. Harris struck out five, also walked only one, and hit Paul Kraft. Both Criger and Vasco Graham had two passed balls, while the Adrian backstop added a triple at the plate.[47]

Adrian promptly ignored the second game loss and declared a victory by forfeit, due to Kalamazoo defying Mumby's league directive. About two weeks later, the 33-year-old Mumby ruled that Adrian didn't win by forfeit. Citing section 45 of the league constitution, which the Corunna, Michigan, man had written, the controversial contest was merely postponed and would have to be rescheduled.[48] The previous outcomes (Kalamazoo's win on the diamond, nor Adrian's declared forfeit victory) would not count in the league standings.[49]

Whether it was when Adrian was complaining about Harris' contract status, or possibly before the doubleheader began, Kalamazoo made it known they were not happy with the "watermelon battery" of Wilson and Graham. They brought up Cap Anson's "Gentlemen's Agreement" and the two players' skin color. Adrian club officials quickly retorted that Mumby had approved Wilson's and Graham's contracts, and added fuel to the Kalamazoo fans' dislike for the league President that day. Adrian argued that the league had no by-laws against non-white players and told Kalamazoo people their "kick" would amount to nothing.[50] For whatever reason, Kalamazoo dropped their protest and played the second game of the doubleheader.

Two days later, on June 1, the Demons were scheduled to play Lansing, and the rumor was going around that Anson's "Gentlemen's Agreement" was again going to be invoked. Adrian officials claimed not to care and were unconcerned about the legality of Graham's and Wilson's MSL contracts.[51] President Mumby was a successful businessman, three-time city alderman, and an efficient steward in carrying out his league duties. Exactly one month before the Michigan State League opened, the *Detroit Free Press* declared that Mumby "has the courage to carry out his convictions."[52] He probably also wasn't too worried about those contracts, either.

The Lansing league games were played, and no one was barred due to his skin color. As Lansing and Adrian were the top two teams in the league, the games were roughly played. The short-tempered Mike Lynch slugged one Senator in the neck during a steal attempt, which raised the ire of Lansing fans. The Demons also complained about the umpire's calls, which apparently rubbed off on the Senators, demoralized the bunch and gave them a case of "razzle-dazzle."[53] Apparently, Adrian was characterized as the main troublemaker in the series. The *Lansing Republican* newspaper noted, "The two colored men, Graham and Wilson, about whom many persons have been inclined to raise a howl, are both gentlemanly ball players, a thing which can not be said of any other player who has appeared in Adrian's infield except Justus [Maurice H. Justice]."[54]

As the hometown Giants-Demons clash was nearing, the tension was rising on both clubs. The *Times and Expositor* predicted a Page Fence Giants win and claimed that Joe Miller was a better pitcher than George Wilson. The paper quipped that "Wilson will try his twists on his old-time companions." Everyone was anticipating a great game.[55]

Saturday, June 8, 1895, had wild predictions and gossip filling the air. One such story was that the game was fixed and the outcome predetermined. The *Evening Telegram* squashed that idea as "nonsense" and claimed there was no reason why it could not be an honest game. They described the Giants as walking around town with "quiet determination," as they knew of the importance of this game, as did the Demons, who would enjoy clobbering the Page Fence club.[56] Although the city of Adrian was overwhelmingly white, there was a segment of town consisting of hard-working, educated black residents, who most likely would be pulling for the Giants.

In their relatively short time in existence, the Page Fence Giants were already so famous they were even used in local advertising. The Excelsior Laundry put an advertisement in the paper saying "The Page Fence Giants know how to play ball and know a good laundry too. A large amount of work was received from them this week." The Excelsior had even hired two additional employees that week just to meet the demand from the Giants and their regular patrons. The use of the Giants in advertising was unusual in that the Excelsior was not one of the many black-owned businesses in Adrian. The owner was Arthur Oram, a little white man with an oval face, straight nose, with blue eyes under a head of brown hair. A native of England, he had come to Adrian in the 1870s and eventually went into the laundry business. His wife and children also worked there, and later his son, William, operated the Excelsior on West Maumee Street for decades.[57] Using a black baseball team to advertise your white-owned family business indicated how mainstream and accepted the team had become around Adrian.[58] No one knows whether Gus Parsons selected the Excelsior or the black athletes felt comfortable and respected and made the decision themselves. Maybe the decision was left to Albert Carter, the porter for the Page Fence Giants, who felt the Oram family would give them a fair shake. What is interesting is that during this 1895 season, the Adrian Demons apparently were not used in any advertising. The Giants were featured by the Excelsior Laundry and, of course, by the Page Fence Woven Wire Company.

How popular the Page Fence Giants were that Saturday afternoon, after they drubbed the Demons, is anyone's guess. The black gentlemen scored 20 runs, while the (mostly) white gentlemen tallied ten runs. George Wilson was supposed to be one of the centers of attention, except he didn't pitch until the eighth inning when the suspense was long over. The anticipated duel of local phenom Wilson versus Joe Miller took place for one less than scintillating inning. When he did eventually pitch, Wilson sulked and lobbed the ball from the pitcher's box, and was subsequently heavily fined for his efforts, or lack thereof. The local press jumped all over his lackadaisical attitude. The *Evening Telegram*'s main game story was very vague in attacking Wilson. They told of men who should try and do their best no matter what position they are asked to play. (When Wilson refused to pitch seriously against his friends on the Giants, he was moved to right field, a rare field appearance for the hurler.) There was a lot of "kicking" amongst the Adrian Demons, who were short-handed, tired and watching their best pitcher not pitch that day.[59] Oh, and they were getting clobbered by a black club, in America, in the 1890s, in front of their home crowd. The *Evening Telegram*, at least in its main story, did pick on the Demons' hot-headed Mike Lynch, saying that despite being the team captain, he needed to clean up his act or baseball would be given a "black eye." What little praise could be dished out to the local minor league team was reserved for pitcher Hicks and player/manager Jess Derrick, who tried to deal with a difficult and combustible situation.[60]

However, in the *Times and Expositor* section entitled "Baseball Bat" the *Evening Tele-*

gram ramped up their criticism of pitcher Wilson and it was specific, this time. "It cost genial George $25 to play the baby act. He won't do it again." It called his behavior "booby ball" and said he had disappointed his friends. Another $3 fine was tacked on when Wilson wouldn't pinch-run for an injured Smith, which resulted in a grand total of $28 in fines.[61] The paper supported the hefty fine and suggested that Wilson "can only square himself by getting down to business and being himself again."[62]

The *Times and Expositor*, owned and operated by Harriet Applegate, printed a much more scathing attack on Wilson. Her paper claimed that most of the large crowd, estimated at between 1,800 and 1,900, had come to see Wilson pitch and the two teams play a "snappy game." Instead, they got neither. Ignoring crowd calls until the pivotal eighth inning, the *Times and Expositor* suggested it would have been better off if Wilson had just ignored the whole thing, "for he merely made a pretense of pitching." After Wilson lobbed deliveries to three Page Fence Giants, resulting in two hits and a long fly out, manager Derrick lifted him and returned him to right field. To be fair, this paper reported Wilson's claim of a bad arm, but the paper harped on his attitude, saying he appeared uninterested and "indifferent" to the outcome of the contest, and it supported the club fining him. "He evidently had no desire to become a target for the colored sluggers."[63]

The (Adrian) *Weekly Press* added a different twist to the Wilson saga that neither of the town's daily papers reported. Its June 14 edition stated that Wilson used "the technicalities" within his "contract" to justify his actions. Those contract terms were never spelled out to the public, but they apparently concerned Wilson pitching against the Page Fence Giants, or more likely NOT pitching against his former teammates. *The Weekly Press* assailed the young man and said the public paid for an honest game, and if a player "lets jealousy or big-head control his course" he "should be promptly released."

Who could have blamed him? While Mrs. Applegate's paper had believed the Giants would win the epic contest, most of the fans were said to be solidly in the camp of the Adrian Demons. After all, they had local pitching wizard George Wilson. The 20-year-old was, admittedly, in a tight spot. For about a month, he had endured catcalls, jeers, and hostile crowds as part of the Giants. Then he and Vasco Graham were transferred to the majority white ball club (whether they wanted to go or not). Wilson faced more mistreatment and added discrimination as the Kalamazoo and Lansing league clubs threatened his livelihood by trying to invoke the powerful, but unwritten "Gentlemen's Agreement." While one could be sure the all-black Page Fence Giants were solidly in his corner while on the field, in 1895 the league squad was not. Some Demons probably resented both Wilson and Graham taking a white man's spot on the club. Others, such as team captain Mike Lynch, didn't seem to get along with anyone. Who knows if the diving and running after batted balls changed from when Wilson was pitching if a white hurler was on the slab. With the Page Fence club, you could retreat to the safety and solidarity of your private train car and commiserate with your diamond brothers. How much was that likely to occur on a public train car, with the Demons, while staying in hostile towns, where even speaking to a white person was seen by many as problematic? So Wilson was asked to pitch against his friends while representing the Demons in front of many fans who wanted to see the black men lose. Wilson was 20 years old, playing in front of his family, friends, and the black community of Adrian. It was a no-win situation.

To his credit, Vasco Graham, the other Page Fence Giant turned Demon, shone in one stellar play, in which he tagged out Grant Johnson at home plate, and he drove a double in one at-bat. His attitude that day was never questioned by either newspaper. Wilson, though, wasn't the only player to be fined that day, as the Demons' starting pitcher, O. Hicks, was assessed a $2 penalty for yelling inappropriate comments from the bench.[64]

As for the fans, the crowd was the largest ever to attend a baseball game in Adrian, as they jammed into Lawrence Park well before starting time to secure the choice seats. The Adrian furniture factories and of course, the Page Fence Woven Wire Company, all closed shop to allow their workers to view the game. It's possible that the Michigan State League Kalamazoo Zooloos were in the crowd, as they had arrived on the 1:45 train. When the grandstand became full, the people lined around the edge of the field "five to ten deep."[65] While the *Evening Telegram* estimated the crowd at 1,800, Len Hoch said it was closer to 1,900.[66]

The Adrian Demons had arrived in town early that morning on a train from Battle Creek and were tired. They were also banged up and had three men playing out of position, including at the crucial shortstop spot. Maurice Justice was too hurt to play, so second baseman Paul Kraft was moved to that spot. Wilson was not pitching and occupied right field. On the opposite side, the Giants were all rested and ready to go, having last played on Wednesday, and had been waiting in town since about noon Thursday. They also added Sol White and James Patterson, the latter arriving Saturday morning in time for the mid-afternoon affair. White's signing pushed Bud Fowler out of his normal second base position and into right field, another blow to the proud old man. Whatever problem that lineup change may have caused in the dugout was not recorded that day. The Giants were also missing their best pitcher, George Wilson, and best catcher, Vasco Graham, who were on the other team's bench. Cyclone Joe Miller was quite public about the Giants missing Graham and settling for Pete Burns as their catcher. Miller told a reporter that he and Graham had played together last season and Vasco was the only person able to catch the talented hurler. Miller wanted Graham off the Demons and reassigned to the Page Fence Giants.[67]

Demons pitcher Hicks was batted around by the Giants, who tallied a pair of runs in the first inning, three in the second, six in the third, and one in the fourth. The Demons could only manage to counter with two runs in their half of the second inning. Before you knew it, the Page Fencers and the arm of Miller were up, 14–2, and were never threatened in the 20–10 victory. The final box score credited the Demons with three extra-base hits, with one being Graham's double. The Giants had five, including a triple by newcomer Patterson, straight off the train, along with a double and triple by Grant Johnson. Even the displaced Bud Fowler rapped out a triple for the winning squad.[68]

In the field, there were several splendid plays, including a Sol White fly out resulting in the Johnson and Graham play at the plate. Adrian's Paul Kraft made a nice running catch in the outfield grass from his infield position, ruining Patterson's debut at-bat for the Giants. The Page Fence infield defense, with the addition of Patterson at third and White at second, was said to be like a "high brick wall, without any holes." On the other side of the coin, Lynch was not good at third base, and the Giants apparently made him a target of a series of line shots and hot grounders. Witnessing this off-day, one paper said Lynch guessed his hands were made from an India rubber ball, which would explain his difficulty in handing the Giants' missiles.[69] *The Weekly Press* was even more biting with its comments about Lynch, calling him "the evil spirit that shadowed the game."[70]

Despite all the sad faces with the local team's loss, the *Times and Expositor* noted that their respect for the Giants had soared, and most fans believed that at least half of their losses had been the result of robbery.[71] There was also no doubt that Billy Holland was the "best coach" in existence and was another show all by himself that Saturday afternoon. The *Evening Telegram* crowed, "The Giants were Giants indeed."[72]

◆ 10 ◆

Till Death Do Us Part

Life was grand for the Page Fence Giants gentlemen. They had soundly defeated the Adrian Demons, the bulk of their upcoming games would be in Michigan, which eliminated long train rides, and they received a Sunday afternoon off from baseball.

The Giants' Fred Van Dyke took advantage of the Sabbath day of rest by biking around Adrian on his bright red Monarch cycle. While riding along East Railroad Street, he saw Charlie Severson's horse hitched to a buggy. The horse decided to leave the Severson property without a driver and trotted down the street. Van Dyke pursued the runaway horse and managed to pedal fast enough to get alongside the animal. However, the horse became startled by Van Dyke's presence and bolted, which caused the Giant to crash his bike. The horse dashed through the downtown area, through an alleyway, and crashed into open doors, which were then slammed shut. Someone managed to corral the horse eventually, while Van Dyke, not seriously hurt, had to turn his red Monarch into Gus Parsons for repair.[1]

Back on the ball diamond, the Giants won games that week from the Monroe club, the Michigan Central Railroad Team in Jackson, and a pick-up nine from Charlotte.[2] Gus Parsons was in a good mood as his wife, Minnie, accompanied the team on these short trips. Eleven players (Burns, Taylor, White, Johnson, Patterson, Brooks, Holland, Fowler, Miller, Malone and Van Dyke) were on the train, along with cook Will Gaskin. There was no mention of porter Albert Carter being on these short trips.[3] The Giants must have sized up the Charlotte team when they arrived, as a major change to the regular lineup occurred in the Eaton County game. Star shortstop Grant Johnson was in the pitcher's box, and the venerable Bud Fowler was behind the plate. Fowler had caught very early in his career, so it was a return to an old position. The Giants slugged out numerous hits and won, 29–12.[4] The *Adrian Telegram* surmised "It must have been a regular circus."[5]

The excitement surrounding the Giants' winning ways inspired members of Adrian's black community. A group of teenage boys, most of them between 16 and 18, formed their own ball team. The ten—Scott and Aldebert Green, Frank Waters, George Grassman, James Bird, Allie Johnson, Sumner Lewis, Fred Clayton, Walter Stone and Silvester "Silver" Butler—would don brand new uniforms and be sponsored by the Powers Clothing Company. The black teenagers wanted to play teams in neighboring towns and, hopefully, the mighty Page Fence Giants.[6] One would even get his chance to play for the hometown heroes.

On the other side of the spectrum, a comment in the *Adrian Telegram* about the Giants' victory over the Adrian Demons appeared in their Saturday "Factory News" section. Under the Page Fence Factory column, it was reported, "It seems that the principal trouble with the Giant ball game was that the score showed up on the wrong side." This is a revealing

A postcard from the turn of the 20th century of the Page Fence factory on the east end of Adrian (courtesy Lenawee County Historical Museum).

view, as a bulk of the white company workers apparently wanted to see the minor league Demons defeat the company's all-black promotional ball club![7]

While the racial animosity would be nothing that the Giants had not experienced before, either on the diamond or away from the field, they could not be prepared for what happened next. Center fielder extraordinaire Gus Brooks dropped dead. Brooks, who had played on 1894 Chicago Unions with current teammates Billy Holland and Pete Burns, collapsed after catching a fly ball during a game in Hastings, Michigan. A few hours later, they were planning his funeral.

The weekend had started out quite well for the Giants. They had defeated the Hastings all-star club, 21–3, on Friday, June 14. The *Hastings Banner*, a staunchly Republican newspaper, bragged that the town's reputation for poorly receiving black people was not evident. "Previous to their coming they had heard that Hastings had no respect for colored people and their good treatment came all the more as a pleasant surprise." The Giants reportedly even wanted to schedule additional games in Hastings later in the summer. The paper echoed the community's alleged reputation as it offered the Giants a back-handed compliment. The Giants "are all colored gentlemen and they were gentlemen too—at least their conduct while here would signify they were." The *Banner* added that the Giants' lack of "drunkenness" and "rowdyism" won them favor with the locals.[8]

The streets of the Barry County community were soon filled with spectators, once the Friday afternoon Page Fence Giants bike parade commenced. "Dressed in their black uniforms and old gold stockings and caps…. [The streets] in an incredibly short time were black with people—not black people either."[9] This example apparently indicated that Hastings' poor reputation for not liking black people was unfounded.

As the bike parade wound its way to the ball grounds west of South Market Street, near where Court Street ended, a crowd nearly as large as a July 4 celebration packed the grassy area surrounding the diamond. Tickets sales netted $170 over the two-day period, which was a tidy sum considering that all women and children were admitted for free. The *Banner* stated that everyone got double their money's worth.[10]

The Giants were expert at handling batted balls, and much coacher activity was undertaken by Holland and the others. The newspaper said the Giants were talking and yelling "expressions as darkies only can," and occasionally turned a cartwheel on the field. "The home team sat in opened eyed astonishment at the exhibition and had a bad case of razzle dazzle" on Friday. The Hastings men had played so badly in the 21–3 loss, the paper offered no box score, only a line score, and refused to name the local men "whose muffs, wild throws, passed balls, etc. went to swell the error column to an amazing figure." The paper noted the local team's pitcher, Damoth, was not particularly effective against the more powerful Giants. Adding yet another negative stereotype, the *Banner* said the Giants took "kindly to Damoth's straight swift balls as they would to the core of a nice juicy water melon."[11]

Saturday's game on June 15 was a much closer affair, as Hastings brought in some outside men to fortify their local squad.[12] Adding to the festivities, Hastings resident Charles B. "Lady" Baldwin, a six-year major league veteran and a hurler on the championship 1887 Detroit Wolverines team, was the umpire that day.[13] The second game was much more competitive, and the *Hastings Banner* gave a detailed, inning-by-inning account of the contest. Billy Malone started for the Giants and set down the first three Hastings men in order. Just as they had the day before, the Page Fence gentlemen scored in the first inning thanks to a hit and a series of throwing errors, which plated George Taylor and James Patterson. Unlike Friday, when they scored only a total of three runs, the Hastings boys recorded four scores in the fateful second inning.[14]

R. Green worked Malone for a base on balls, one of seven that day for Hastings, and Murphy's single placed runners on first and second with no outs. Third baseman Wooten was out on fly ball "skyscraper," which Brooks corralled after a long run in center field. Green tagged and went to third on the play, as Brooks staggered following the catch and clutched his head. The center fielder yelled to his teammate Grant Johnson to get someone to replace him in the field, as Brooks made his way, with some trouble, to a shaded area. A couple of the Giants had managed to reach Brooks by this time, as one escorted him to the ground, while another placed himself under Brooks' body as the young man collapsed into a state of unconsciousness. Doctors were summoned to the ball field, and Brooks was somehow revived. He was placed in a carriage and transported about four blocks to the Hastings House hotel on the northwest corner of State and Church Streets. Joe Miller replaced Brooks in center field and the game was resumed. It's unclear as to how serious the Giants felt Brooks' condition was at this time. The original thought was that he had suffered sunstroke. Another report was that Brooks reportedly had experienced similar symptoms before, but not to this extent.[15]

The Giants were rattled by Brooks' illness, and the Hastings men then tallied four runs on a pair of two-run singles, to take a 4–2 lead. The Giants and Hastings battled back and forth, and entering the sixth inning (Hastings batted first), the home team was leading, 7–6, a much more competitive game than the Friday blowout. Malone's curve ball had lost its bite, and manager Fowler pulled him and inserted reliever Billy Holland. The moved worked, and the home squad was held scoreless for the next two innings. Miller, the pitcher for the Hastings club who was rumored headed to the Grand Rapids Gold Bugs, responded by walking the first three Giants in their half of the sixth inning. James Patterson roped a bases-clearing triple and put the Giants up, 9–7. In the seventh, Fowler scored on a Pete Burns single, as the catcher was thrown out trying to reach second, which bumped the lead to 10–7. Hastings, on a combination of hits and walks, scored two runs in the top of the eighth inning to make it a one-run gap and had the bases loaded before Holland struck out Angie to end the threat.[16]

The Page Fence men failed to score in the bottom of the eighth inning and hung to a precarious 10–9 lead. Hastings would not go quietly in their half of the ninth as "Holland doubled himself up like a jackknife, set his teeth firmly together and shot his curves around the plate like a streak of lightning." The Hastings pitcher, Miller, who was also known for his strong bat, led off the ninth inning with a long and high fly ball. "The ball sailed up in the blue sky and held sweet communion with the larks, seemingly for about five minutes, but when it came down a smiling darky stood right under it with both paws wide open ready to take it in, which he did." A fine fielding play by an unnamed Giant notched the second out of the inning. Hastings' hope was extended a bit when Borrendame singled, but the next batter hit a "hot liner to third," which Patterson "fired to first," ending the game and recording a Giants victory.

After this game, the Giants players praised the team Hastings fielded on Saturday and declared that it would give Michigan State League teams some trouble and would win more times than not.[17]

Following the Saturday afternoon win, the Giants hurried to the Hastings House. Local physicians Lathrop and Timmerman were at Brooks' bedside when the players arrived to check on their teammate. While the game was being played, Brooks appeared to rally, but as the players filed into his hotel room, he began to drift into unconsciousness again. Despite the doctor's efforts, and his teammates crowded about his bed, Brooks died shortly thereafter. The Giants players and management were shocked beyond words by what had just occurred. Word of the death quickly spread back to Adrian, as business manager Parsons wired a telegram to Len Hoch saying Brooks had passed away around 6 o'clock from heart disease.[18] Brooks was said to be about 25 years of age. Other details surrounding his death and his family history are not known, as the Barry County Clerk's office never issued a death certificate. Parsons wired another telegram that Saturday evening to Gus Brooks' grandmother in St. Louis, Illinois. It apparently took some time to find the elderly woman, as first reports were that she could not be located. Parsons later claimed she was unable to assist in the burial, so the club took care of the funeral arrangements.[19]

The Rev. John Taylor of Adrian's Second Baptist Church hopped aboard a train and headed to Hastings to conduct the funeral service. He and his church had been praised in one local paper a few months earlier for holding an outstanding Easter Sunday service.[20] It is possible that Brooks worshipped at Second Baptist on North Broad Street, and from what was said, the deceased young man was a wonderful human being.

The *Evening Telegram* stated that Brooks "was one of the best players" and was a "man of exceptional qualities" who minded his own business and "was pleasant and honorable" to all of those around him.[21] The *Hastings Banner* managed to change its tone and offered a highly, even for them, favorable account of the young man's life. Speaking to the ball players, the *Banner* said Brooks was known as the "peacemaker" amongst the team, as all disputes on the squad came before this highly respected ball player. The *Banner* claimed Brooks was 26 years of age and was responsible with his money, having saved $100 of his salary so far this season.[22] On the diamond, in 53 games he hit for a .346 average, always batted in the top half of the lineup and committed only two errors as a steady and sure-handed center fielder.[23]

In the same hotel where he had died, the club organized a funeral the following day. Parsons, Hoch and Rolla Taylor paid for the funeral and decided, with Brooks being single and with his grandmother living three states away, the center fielder would be buried in Adrian. Sunday afternoon at the Hastings House Hotel, the Reverend Taylor presided over Brooks' funeral service "and made the most appropriate remarks," as many of the Page Fence Giants wept openly for their fallen comrade. The Hastings Methodist Episcopal Church choir sang at the service. Following the ceremony, Brooks' body remained at the hotel until the midnight train arrived and the special Page Fence palace car was attached.[24] Through the dark ride across southern Michigan, Billy Holland accompanied the body, and possibly the Reverend Taylor, too. As the body arrived in Adrian and was removed from the special palace car, a small group awaited it at the train station. Former Page Fence Giants George Wilson and Vasco Graham, along with 23-year-old local barber Amos Hill and 30-year-old Adrian native and shoemaker (Dewise) Deweeze B. Wilson, served as pallbearers and escorted the body from the depot to Oakwood Cemetery. The Reverend Taylor performed another service, this time at the graveside, which was adorned with "numerous and beautiful" floral arrangements. Despite announcing that Hoch, Taylor and Parsons would arrange for a "proper" burial, they never purchased a headstone.[25] Gus Brooks lay in an unmarked grave at B27–1, Row 2 in Oakwood Cemetery for 131 years, until a marker was purchased in 2016 by several baseball historians familiar with the Page Fence Giants and the circumstances surrounding Brooks' death.[26]

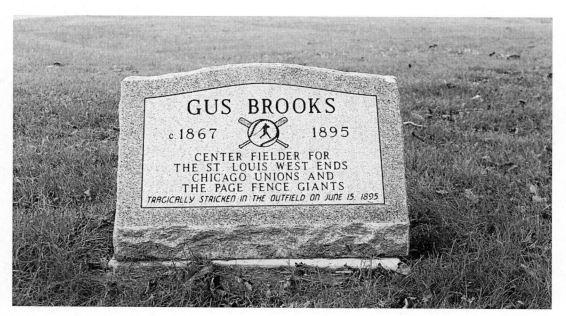

Photograph of the Gus Brooks gravesite at Oakwood Cemetery in Adrian, Michigan. It remained unmarked until SABR members paid for the headstone in 2016 (author's collection).

The day of the funeral, the ball club sent a letter to the *Banner*, addressed it "To the citizens of Hastings," and thanked them for their assistance in their time of grief.

> We desire to express our sincere thanks and gratitude for the hospitable manner in which you have received us and for the many favors you have shown us during the illness and death of our beloved comrade and friend, Mr. Augustus Brooks. We shall ever bear in mind and remember the many kindnesses shown us by your citizens and friends. Signed, The Page Fence Giants, Base Ball Club.[27]

The *Banner* devoted a lengthy story to Brooks' death, much longer than they did for Friday's lopsided loss to the Giants. Whatever negative feelings, whether real or imagined, the community of Hastings had toward black people in the 1890s was no longer evident in reporting Brooks' death. "The Page Fence Giants are a fine gentlemen lot of fellows, and carried themselves while here in a manner that won the respect of all," said the *Hastings Banner*.[28]

On a national level, the death of Brooks wasn't seen as a major event. *The Sporting News* devoted one sentence to the incident, under their potpourri column, "Caught on the Fly." "G. B. Brooks, of the Page Fence Giants, dropped dead of heart disease, on the field at Hastings, Mich., the other day."[29]

Gus Brooks' graveside service was Monday morning, as that afternoon the Page Fence Giants played in Owosso, Michigan. They had a three-game set with the MSL Owosso Colts, a team which had won fewer than one-third of their games so far this season and were only ahead of the woefully inept Port Huron club.[30]

The Giants were down to ten players with the death of Brooks, and nothing was in the local papers about Gus Parsons looking for a replacement. The situation would mean a lot more playing time for Fred Van Dyke and regular outfield appearances for pitchers William Malone and Billy Holland.

The Giants were probably looking forward to easy games against a seven-win Colts team. After all, they had defeated the Adrian Demons of the same league less than two weeks ago, and the game wasn't even close. Owosso knew all about the Page Fence Giants and their string of victories. The Colts were determined not to be another scalp on the belt of the visiting gentlemen.

Oh, and they weren't. Racking up victories of 13–12, 5–3, and 16–14, the Colts had better luck with the traveling superstar team than they did with the clubs in the Michigan State League.[31] The *Owosso Evening Argus* used phrases such as "The Giants Slain; well contested; splendid game" to describe the victory over the Giants, who they said (incorrectly) had lost only twice all year.[32] Owosso had imported a ringer named Ed Shields from the University of Michigan, who was promptly placed in the starting lineup and named team captain. He brought with him two other Wolverines as ringers, Charles F. Watkins, the starting pitcher in game one, and fielder John Bloomington.[33] Crowd totals were listed between 1,200 and 1,500 for the series opener, which saw the lefty Watkins battle Joe Miller. The Page Fence men were sloppy in the field, committing errors in double digits. Apparently shocked by their opening 13–12 victory, one Colts fan yelled out after the win, "What's the matter with the Colts?"[34]

With baseball fever spreading in Owosso, another decent crowd showed up the following day, even though the sky was overcast and rain was forecast. The ringers' good work in game one continued in game two, as Shields had the Colts "gingering up" and they defeated the mighty Giants, 5–3. Billy Holland was in the pitcher's box for the visitors and battled Owosso's Al Kern. The Colts were leading by that 5–3 score in the fifth inning and were threatening again, when Joe Miller came in to pitch for the Giants to quell the Owosso threat. The rain clouds opened in the seventh inning and, after a 30-minute delay, umpire Pfeifle called the game in favor of the Colts.[35]

Game three saw a larger crowd, as attendance was estimated around 1,800 at the Shiawassee community ball field.[36] For some reason, Billy Holland convinced the team to start him again in back-to-back games and that was a mistake. Holland surrendered ten runs in the first two innings before he gave way to Van Dyke. The *Owosso Evening Argus* said that both teams played a determined game of ball. The Giants managed to peck away at the Colts' lead, but even a five-run ninth inning couldn't close the gap. They dropped their third in a row to the Colts, 16–14. The *Argus* said, "the Giants were out played by the Colts in every instance and proved to be quite an easy mark for them."[37]

Even with the sweep of the traveling team, the *Evening Argus* printed a feature story on the Giants. They said the current Page Fence Giant record was 31 wins, ten losses and one tie. The paper described the history of the club, but spent a chunk of ink misspelling and misidentifying Giants players and management. They said "Bud Towley" had recently resigned as a member of the management team, but kept with the Bud Fowler spirit and claimed he was 52 years old and had played ball for 26 of those years. They said two players, "Montague and Vandike are from the old Cuban Giants team, playing with them for the previous seven years."[38] There has never been any record of Van Dyke playing for another professional team in his brief baseball career, and one can only guess that former Cuban Giant Billy Malone was the Montague mentioned in the article.

The *Evening Argus* feature also shed light as to the reason behind Fowler's ouster from his ownership position, something that was never discussed in the Adrian papers. "The general opinion is that the Page Fence Co. are running this team. They made a contract to play 50 games under the name of Page Fence Giants for a good sum. The games have been played and the team now stands dependent upon their success in the future. The proprietors are Parson & Hock [sic], Taylor, Fowler and Johnson."[39] If this version is true, it is anyone's guess as to how much input the Page Fence Company and owner J. Wallace Page had at this point.

The Adrian papers focused very little on this swing by the Giants through mid–Michigan. Unfair umpiring was a culprit, again, in the three Owosso losses. Colts captain Shields was asked about umpire John Pfeifle and his work over the course of the three games. The *Times and Expositor* gave Shields' response as "he admitted that the umpire who officiated was incompetent, but said that his decisions were as bad against the Owosso's as they were against the Giants."[40] Yes, and the Page Fence team which had destroyed the Adrian entry of the MSL now had just dropped three straight games to an Owosso nine near the bottom of the standings. Shields' comments about the work of umpire Pfeifle may have been only half-right.

After the Page Fence team faced Owosso, the Demons were soon slated to play a four-game set with the Colts. In the opener, George Wilson fanned 11 Colts to go along with his one-hitter, as he out-dueled Watkins in the 6–2 victory.[41] The University of Michigan trio, who had helped to stymie the Giants, made the Owosso club now one of the strongest in the league. The Demons were strengthened by the addition of Tim Nevins, a four-year minor league veteran, along with the arrival of future all-time great and Hall of Famer Honus Wagner. In their debut, both new players recorded a hit, as Wagner subbed for the still-injured second baseman, Paul Kraft. An intriguing side-note is that the Demons' baseball management had a long meeting the night before this game "and talked over matters."

What those matters were is anyone's guess, but the two black players on the Demons or the pay scale would be good ones.[42]

Meanwhile, over in Kalamazoo, the Page Fence gentlemen were doing their best to rebound from their sweep by Owosso. They eked out a 3–2 victory by scoring two runs in the eighth inning on a passed ball. Cyclone Miller won the game, and the other Giants run came on Patterson's solo homer. The Kalamazoo locals may have been excited for this rematch, as the Owosso team had just dusted the Giants. It was not so, as the *Kalamazoo Daily Telegraph* noted "beyond the pale of any reasonable doubt that they had lost none of their cunning or ability" as they entered "Zoolooland and wreaked their vengeance on the innocent masticator of celery."[43]

The second match-up was a "dull uninteresting game" before a very small Friday afternoon crowd. Fewer than 200 people saw the Giants post a 14–3 victory. The game's highlight was when Kalamazoo manager Ed Mayo sarcastically yelled at his right fielder, Colonel Shadrack McHoovetor, that he was playing really well. The catcall infuriated McHoovetor so much so that he stormed off the field and forfeited $25 in pay.[44]

The Saturday game was more of the same, as "fifteen times the yellow-legged, Page Fence Giants scampered across the plate." The Giants rapped out 16 hits and Holland took the win in another big victory, 15–5. The Kalamazoo men fumbled the ball for 12 errors, and Lou Criger did both the catching and later some pitching for the losing squad.[45]

Business manager Gus Parsons was still unhappy with the Giants' recent losses to Owosso. When the Adrian Demons took three of four from Owosso in MSL games, Parsons sent them a batch of good cigars as a thank you. Parsons also let it be known that in a "fair test" he would have the Giants spot the Colts three runs, and the Owosso club wouldn't take even one game from them. He also said if he had his chance, he wanted to ump a game between Owosso and either one of the Adrian clubs.[46]

Details of one of the four games between Owosso and the Demons could have had an impact on the Giants' earlier losses against the Colts. In the Friday, June 28, contest between the Colts and the Demons, there were allegations that umpire Pfeifle had placed a "two to one bet" on Owosso. This allegation was in a telegram from Demons pitcher Jess Derrick sent to someone in Adrian. Apparently, the regularly assigned league umpire, Burnett, resigned, and the local Pfeifle was a convenient replacement (MSL records note that Owosso's sub umpire was a John Fifly, which is how Pfeifle is pronounced). Pfeifle was also the name of the umpire in each of the three games the Colts had won over the Giants. To be fair, the Owosso club had greatly strengthened their minor league team in anticipation of the Giants' arrival. However, Pfeifle's calls were so bad on this day, Demons first baseman Ed Mulhearn was ejected in the first inning for threatening the umpire over his "rank decisions." Mulhearn was arrested, escorted off the ball grounds, and fined $25 plus court costs for his behavior. That move didn't calm things down, either. George Wilson, whom the *Evening Telegram* described as "always quiet and orderly," was also escorted off the diamond and ejected for complaining about Pfeifle's calls. Teammate Derrick said Wilson was removed for "coaching." Derrick also stated that Vasco Graham was heading toward home plate to score the winning run in the ninth inning when he was grabbed by the Colts catcher, hit by the thrown ball and declared out. Parsons, who was traveling with the Giants, heard of the Pfeifle issues and wired Len Hoch back in Adrian: "Heard you were robbed by Pfeifle yesterday. Protest the game." Six hundred people were in the stands and watched this debacle unfold.[47]

Parsons was also working the telegraph wires and looking to raise the profile of the

Page Fence Giants. Plans were under way to schedule a world black ball championship series sometime in September between the Page Fence Giants and the Cuban Giants. The idea was to bring the Eastern-based Cuban Giants to Adrian to play the best of three games, following the conclusion of the Michigan State League season. That schedule would ensure that George Wilson and Vasco Graham would be available to play for the Page Fence club. Cuban Giants owner and manager John Bright had claimed the 1894 black championship, and the club had been strong for ten seasons.[48] Parsons hoped that after the Cuban Giants finished their swing through Ohio, Pennsylvania, New York and New Jersey, they would make the trek much farther west to Michigan.[49]

The telegraph wires were also burning up between Adrian and Paulding, Ohio, the hometown of Rolla and Howard Taylor. Famed shortstop and Taylor family friend, Bob Allen, contacted Parsons and asked for the use of the "watermelon battery" of Wilson and Graham for a July 4 game with Toledo of the Class A Western League. Parsons had to reject the request, saying the Demons had two games at home on the Fourth.[50]

The Page Fence Giants continued their travels through western Michigan. The team returned to Barry County to play the tiny farming village of Nashville. The game was only about ten miles from Hastings, where Brooks had died less than two weeks earlier. Fred Van Dyke pitched the team to an uncompetitive, but exciting, 17–7 victory over the Nashville Cherubs. The home club scored the bulk of their runs in the final inning and made the score look a bit more respectable. Len Feighner, the publisher of the *Nashville News*, devoted a lengthy article to the contest. A story covering more than one column included the starting lineup, Feighner's game comments, an inning-by-inning play-by-play, and the line score. With that type of baseball coverage, it was no wonder the attendance was between 2,000 and 2,500, twice the size of the village, that day.[51]

According to the *News* article, the Nashville boys hadn't competed in a while, were missing a few guys, and had some "livid streaks of yellow in their playing." The Cherubs' play was "the color of a ripe pumpkin," and they were no match for the "brilliant" Giants, who dominated every step of the way. The Giants batted first and scored two runs, but Fowler got nabbed at third in a base running error to end that treat. Nashville hit Fred Van Dyke hard in their opening inning, the first single a comebacker which he couldn't handle. However, a caught stealing and a man gunned down between second and third ended the Cherubs threat. Following a hit by Ketcham in the second, Weber knocked him home and the score was 2–1, Giants. The game was still close after five innings, 3–1, as the Giants were victimized by bad base running in trying to stretch hits for extra bases and attempted steals. Both pitchers, Miller for Nashville and Van Dyke for the Giants, were effectively wild, but they did manage to strike out batters using their curve balls. However, one must wonder if the Giants were just toying with Nashville, as the Page Fence club exploded for 14 runs over the final four innings. The Giants' last out came when they were ahead, 17–1, when Bud Fowler singled and got caught in an exciting rundown, which required all nine Cherubs fielders to make a play before he was tagged out between second and third base. Probably as an act of kindness and to increase the day's entertainment value, the Giants let Nashville score six runs in the bottom of the ninth to close the gap to 17–7. Three of the Nashville runs scored with the bases loaded when the Page Fence men threw the ball around so much that all three Cherubs scored. The *Nashville News* article was fair and well-balanced and lacked any negative comments about the visiting team. Grant Johnson was once incorrectly referred to as "Fence Rail" Johnson, but that tag never stuck.[52]

The Giants then defeated Lowell and Greenville, towns outside of Grand Rapids, and split games with the tough Muskegon newspaper-sponsored team.[53] The first three days of July sent the Giants to mid–Michigan. In the unique and usual fluid scheduling of the 1890s, the first and third games were to be against the Lansing Senators MSL team and played in the capital city. The second game, on July 2, was scheduled about 15 miles east of Lansing, in the new and improved Riverside Park in Williamston.[54]

The first contest saw Lansing throw a third-line pitcher, and they dropped a 23–4 contest to the Giants. Nearly a thousand people crammed into Parshall Park to watch the Monday afternoon affair in a hastily erected structure a few blocks from the state's capital building. The highlight of the game, if it can be called that, was the 20 combined errors by these two professional teams. At one time, the game was close, only a 10–8 Giants lead, but the visitors eventually pulled away behind the pitching efforts of Billy Holland and Joe Miller. "Home Run" Johnson, Holland and Van Dyke all hit round-trippers.[55]

The Giants planned to take the Detroit, Lansing and Northern Railroad on a short trip east to Williamston. However, when game day arrived, Eaton Rapids had replaced Williamston on the schedule, and the Giants headed south on the Lake Shore Railroad to that Eaton County community. "Sweet Revenge" was the headline in the *Lansing Republican* as the Senators atoned for their previous day's loss to the Giants with a sloppy 21–10 victory. The 20 errors in Monday's game were easily eclipsed by the two clubs, who posted 27 fielding miscues, including five in left field by Charlie Ferguson, usually Lansing's ace pitcher. The attendance was very small, and the Eaton Rapids ball field was strewn with rocks and weeds, which the players largely blamed for the error-fest. The Senators slugged three homers, including one by future Cincinnati Reds second baseman Johnny Morrissey. Both sides decided that due to the small crowd and the poor playing surface, no more games would be played in Eaton Rapids, including a third game, originally scheduled in Lansing that had been moved to Eaton Rapids.[56]

As Independence Day approached, Parsons must have returned to Adrian to be with his wife, as the reports of the Giants' games became less frequent for the first half of July. Even stories of the Adrian Demons games were sporadic during this time. One thing Parsons was doing back in Adrian was trying to solve the Tecumseh question. The Demons' management had wanted to play one of every three MSL games scheduled for Adrian in nearby Tecumseh.[57] However, they announced that scheme after selling season tickets to Adrian residents, who then became upset at the loss of home dates. Len Hoch declared in the second week of July that the Tecumseh plan was off, due to the town not having an adequate ball diamond, saving the investors a headache with the Adrian ball cranks. In the same edition announcing the ending of the Tecumseh plan, Adrian Demon John "Honus" Wagner told the ball club he had to return home to be with his sick father.[58]

Adrian residents were giddy about their Demons. Despite the fact that they were beaten by the Page Fence Giants, the Demons were given new uniforms. However, the uniforms did not come from Parsons and team management, but from residents of the city. A local banker, Harry Waldby, rounded up donations and presented the new baseball suits, as they were called then, before the Demons' games with Port Huron on July 4. The ten-member Demons, including Wagner and former Giants Graham and Wilson, affixed their names to a letter of thanks in the newspaper, for the "nobby uniforms." Club secretary Hoch also sent a letter to the Detroit firm of Stanton and Morey for "their elegant and tasty ball shirts" the firm had sewn for the Demons. They say if you look good, you play good, and the Demons swept a doubleheader that day from Port Huron. A couple of days later and presumably clad in the nobby new tops, George Wilson struck out 12, held the Celery

The Adrian Demons, July 1895. This photograph shows the Demons wearing their new blue and white uniforms and features future Baseball Hall of Famer Honus Wagner, in the back row, second from the left. The player to Wagner's left is Paul Craft. In the front row is the famed "Watermelon Battery" of George Wilson (left front) and Vasco Graham (right front). In the middle is one of the team owners, Rolla L. Taylor, along with his eight-year-old son, Will Taylor. Based on the "Thank You" letter the club sent to the local papers for the new uniforms, the others in this photograph would be Jess Derrick, Michael Lynch, Maurice H. Justice, Elmer E. Smith, Tim Nevins and Ed Mulhern. The young man in black, to the far left, appears to be the local MSL substitute umpire and Adrian native, Pearl Southland (courtesy Lenawee County Historical Museum).

boys to four hits, and knocked in the winning run at Kalamazoo. The *Evening Telegram* bragged, "No such pitching record was made ... by any man in the state, national or western league. Wilson is undoubtedly a prodigy, and undoubtedly had speed to throw away."[59]

Praise also flowed in for the Giants. Coming off wins against Manistee, 21–1, and Traverse City, 14–10, Greenville then weighed in about the Giants. The Page Fence nine had recently defeated Greenville quite handily, and one of the town's newspapers published a glowing report, calling the Giants "gentlemen." The *Adrian Evening Telegram* printed excerpts, noting that "although they hitched up the farmers to their plows and drove them all over the field yet they did it in such a nice and pleasant manner, that nothing but good feelings exist among the home players as well as the audience."[60] Billy Holland's humorous "coaching" was likely on display that day, too, adding to the positive atmosphere.

Greenville's racially progressive sentiments were echoed by the Page Fence Woven Wire Company in the 1895 summer issue of the *Coiled Spring Hustler*. An excerpt of the company's paper was printed in the *Evening Telegram*. The firm's official mouthpiece declared its strong support for the black ball club and said the team "was not only winning nearly every game played, but are winning friends." The *Hustler* added that even when the umpire acted as the "best man" for the opponents, the Giants used their humor to deal with the situation. Answering some still lingering complaints that the June 8 game between the Demons and the Giants was a "put up job," quoting either Bud Fowler or Gus Parsons (it's unclear as the article said "team manager"), they said "a four-minute horse always seemed slow when trotting in a 2:20 race." The same manager declared that the behavior of the black ball club had been perfect and "not one of them had given him one minute's trouble. No drunk or disorderly, nor staying out late at night."[61]

The *Coiled Spring Hustler* was not just speaking to Adrian residents in this article, as the newspaper was sent to fence dealers across the country. Continuing to take a progressive stand on this first-year promotional ball team, the *Hustler* attacked a negative stereotype of the poor work habits of black men and women in the United States. Using the manager's quotes about the players' good behavior, the *Hustler* pointed out that "we call the attention of those Agricultural papers that have been discussing the Negro laborer questions to this statement, as some of their correspondents insist there is no such thing as a reliable colored man who 'growed up' since the war."[62] It was evident that the Page Fence ball club was being accepted by the company's management, and they were happy with the message it portrayed about their firm, the town of Adrian, and black people in general.

Nearby Hudson, Michigan, whose bid to join the Michigan State League that spring was awarded to the now-sagging Port Huron franchise, was excited to play the Giants in mid–July. The Hudson ball diamond was carved out of the flats adjacent and east of the Cincinnati, Jackson and Mackinaw Railroad depot, and they would do their best to bring in some ringers to help their cause.[63] This game would be a big event for the town. A new baseball grandstand had been erected earlier that season at a place now dubbed Recreation Park. Both the major newspapers, the *Hudson Post* and the *Hudson Gazette*, did their best to capture the baseball lover's fancy in the western Lenawee

---

VOL. IV.   ADRI

THE COILED SPRING HUSTLER.

PUBLISHED MONTHLY BY

The Page Woven Wire Fence Company.

The Page Fence Giants.

The special car was fitted out from Adrian, and is quite attractive in appearance, of the regular palace car color with "Page Woven Wire Fence Co.," Adrian, Mich.," in large gilt letters the whole length of the car, and "Page Fence Giants Base Ball Club, Adrian, Mich.," in scroll on each side. The interior is nicely arranged, fitted up with berths, easy chairs, dining room, and cook room with range and all conveniences for "light housekeeping," also a private state room for the Manager, and a colored cook and a porter complete the crew.

Unfortunately they had but a few days practice before meeting a strong League team at Indianapolis. This team had been in practice for a much longer time, and although they won with ease it was admitted that the Giants played a good game. The next day at Cincinnati they met a still stronger team, one of the best of the National League, and the Cincinnati papers speak of the audacity of the Page Fence Giants in tackling such a strong team, as being a matter of surprise, and an easy victory was expected. We quote from the Cincinnati Enquirer: "While the local team won the game they did not have a picnic doing it. The colored players gave them an argument right from the start. It was a great game. Bud Fowler has got together a great team of players. They will win more games than they will lose. Brooks, the center fielder, made three wonderful catches. Malone, the third baseman, played in good style, and Bud Fowler wears his 46 years like a young blood." The Enquirer also devotes a third of a column to Captain Bud

One
DEAR S₁
grave for s
sent to put
me to take
two towns
enough fo₁
two townsh
couldn't f₂
home and
done wond
arranged st
when I too
put up ele
double the
it only for
I have a
it any day,
just put in
etc., especi
Giants.
I am adv
local pape
discussing

Of cours
that catch
is cheap.
talking ma
"Elasticit]
Page.

GROVEL

Ho₁

DEAR S
that took]
gentlemen
any of yo
cates of 1
rods this €

Coiled Spring Hustler, the official factory newspaper of the Page Fence Woven Wire Company. The front page features a long story in the left column about the Giants. This paper must have been printed in late April 1895, as the game report complained of the poor umpire work (though Bob Carruthers is unnamed), but rejoiced in his recent release from the Grant Rapids team, in part due to his "obnoxious" work behind the plate (courtesy Lenawee County Historical Society).

County village, as both offered colorful game descriptions. Hudson's ballists had honed their skills by either defeating the Toledo Fats, 14–12, or losing 15–10 (the papers printed different scores and victors) and about a week before the Page Fence Giants' invasion, simply demolished a club from Addison, 53–6.[64]

Nobody in Hudson thought the local guys were going to defeat the Giants, and they said so publicly. The *Hudson Post* was quite blunt in its pre-game assessment. "The game will be well worth seeing, not because the Hudsons expect to win, but because they will be trying to get a few of the crumbs while the Giants are walking away with the loaf." The *Post* maintained that if luck went their way and the Hudson nine managed to score just a couple of runs, "their friends will be pleased."[65] Both papers played up the prowess of the travelling group of ball stars and said the Giants had no plans to show up in Hudson and be "ignominiously beaten" by the local nine.[66]

The Giants had covered a lot of miles over the past week before arriving in Hudson. They had dropped a game to Traverse City, 13–10, on Wednesday, July 10, but rebounded for wins at Midland, Howell, Milan and Monroe.[67] They had stayed overnight on their train following their win at Monroe and didn't head west for Hudson until mid-morning. This route allowed the elegant train car and stop for about an hour around noon Monday in Adrian, for a short visit before they resumed their trip to Hudson.[68] Likely traveling on that same string of rail cars were most of the major financial backers and boosters of the

The vacant lot in Hudson, Michigan, across from the old Cincinnati, Jackson and Mackinaw Railroad depot, where the Page Fence Giants played Game 2 of their 1896 championship series with the Cuban X Giants. The depot, which is no longer standing, would have been to the far right of this picture. The raised rail bed is still in existence, entering Hudson from the south, and is shown emerging from the woods on the right side (photograph by author).

Page Fence team. From the fencing company was founder and president J. Wallace Page, his son, Charles Page, cousin and fellow fence inventor Charles Lamb, and Walter Clement, an officer of the firm. Mr. and Mrs. Len Hoch and both Rolla and Howard Taylor and their wives were on the train. Not on the Hudson trip was Gus Parsons, who was waiting for a missing umpire to appear at Lawrence Park for an MSL game between the Demons and Owosso that same afternoon. Parsons was probably hoping to get his wish granted to act as the substitute umpire and pay back the earlier robberies the Owosso Colts had committed against both Adrian clubs.[69]

If there was any doubt as to who the media contact was for the Giants, it was Parsons. Neither the *Daily Times and Expositor* nor the *Evening Telegram* appeared to have sent a reporter to the big Hudson-Giants game. The *Expositor* had only a story a few sentences long, while the *Evening Telegram* printed one with the byline of "Special to the Telegram."[70] Whenever Parsons was back in Adrian, the public flow of information from the Page Fence club would be sparse to non-existent.

A great crowd estimated at between 500 and 700 fans packed Recreation Park just south of Hudson's downtown business district on Monday afternoon, July 15, 1895. The lack of rain all summer was on people's minds as the Page Fence Giants and the Hudson team warmed up. Unfortunately, despite being adjacent to the progressive town of Adrian, both Hudson papers followed the lead of many others and used negative stereotypes to describe the game action and made sure everyone knew the Giants were a black team. It appeared that the *Hudson Post* and the *Hudson Gazette* were in a competition to see who could use the most racially tainted and flowery language to detail the day's events. The *Post* referred to the black gentlemen as "the dusky cannibals" and "nine shadows."[71] The *Gazette* called them "base ball brunettes" and said the Hudson club had ordered "dark meat with dressing" for the game.[72]

These comments aside, the two Hudson weekly rags were quite complimentary of the style of play the Giants brought to town. Page Fence won, 13–2, as Hudson scored two runs in the first inning on a walk, single, a double and some throwing errors. The Giants' Billy Holland then settled down and struck out the final two Hudson batters in the opening frame on curve balls, and the "curtain dropped on Act 1 Scene 1 of the tragedy—The Death of base ball!" Now it was time for the Giants to answer, and they did so with four runs in their half of the first inning. Hudson pitching phenom Corwin "C. J." Brunskill was said to be very fast, "but like the California girl at a water resort, a trifle wild." In the third inning, he drilled fellow pitcher Holland in the back. Holland dropped to the ground and lay there for several minutes before he gathered his senses and finished the game.[73]

After having the "audacity" to score in their first time at bat, the Hudson club "repented and went to pieces (and those pieces have not been found yet)," and the visitors controlled the rest of the game. Hudson did not score again. The papers agreed that the Giants were simply too much for the overmatched Hudson nine. The home club was intimidated by the size, grace and beauty of the Page Fence fellows, said they now knew "how Stanley had felt in the African wilds."[74] Holland's pitching was fast, his "coaching" antics superb, the Giants base running was a wonder and their fielding was slick. The only highlight of the game, other than the first inning for Hudson, was that the long-standing drought ended when the heavens opened and washed out play after seven innings. A terrific wind and rain storm came roaring through the county and after a half-hour wait, umpire Richards declared the game concluded.[75]

The *Post* couldn't let the rain go without one last jab at humor about the color of the

Giants' skin. The *Post* claimed that Richards had to call the game "not knowing whether they were fast colors and warranted to wash, or weather [*sic*] Hudson people would be held responsible if the goods were returned in a faded condition."[76]

Hudson manager Pease was delighted at the attendance and wanted to plan more games with the Giants. They claimed general admission gate receipts of $112, plus another $15 from patrons who paid to sit in the new grandstand.[77] Like Adrian's Lawrence Park, whose outfield was set beneath some bluffs and had allowed freeloaders to watch games from the higher ground, Hudson had the same dilemma. Not only was Hudson's new Recreation Park set beneath a large hill to its west, but a raised dirt embankment for the C, J and M Railroad tracks to the southwest allowed freeloaders to stand and watch the game without having to take out their wallets and purses. At least 700 fans had paid the general admission fee, "while the balance of the population contented itself by viewing the sport from hilltops, housetops, freight cars and side tracks," and were "dead beats."[78]

Back in Adrian, the league-assigned umpire never appeared for the series opener with Owosso. Local teenager and league substitute umpire Pearl Southland worked behind the plate and "did very badly" in his first MSL game.[79] The *Evening Telegram* noted, "Southland umpired the game with the assistance of the grand stand." The paper said he had faulty decisions, the crowd was on him all day, and they "roasted" him even worse when the Demons finally dropped the game to the Colts.[80] Parsons' dream of revenge against Owosso never materialized with Southland present. However, Parsons was still irate at Owosso and was earlier quoted as saying "it would have been dark before the first inning was over, if he had umpired the game."[81]

The game in Hudson that brought with it the much-needed rain was a watershed moment for the Page Fence Giants, too. It was Bud Fowler's last game as a member of the club. He had played left field and batted fifth, behind the recently inserted starting second baseman, Sol White. The *Adrian Evening Telegram* announced in its July 16 edition that "Bud Fowler has severed his connection with the Page Fence Giants." The paper said it was "a mutual understanding between himself and the managers," and now Rolla Taylor, Len Hoch and Gus Parsons "have full charge." Grant Johnson remained as shortstop and captain of the Giants and would be on a salary. This move almost mirrored what was revealed on May 1 from Wisconsin, when Fowler and Johnson were put on salary and were no longer members of the management team. Whether the May decision was rescinded until now was unclear, as was what had transpired in the meantime among these five men. However, those reading Willard Stearns' gossipy *The* (Adrian) *Weekly Press* were more up to date on the Giants' internal management conflicts. In his June 7 paper, Stearns questioned how much longer Fowler would remain connected to the Page Fence Giants. Stearns claimed that the old tumbleweed had "not won much good will from the management by his adhesion to the truth." He continued to zing Fowler by noting, "in many respects, he has not been on speaking terms with veracity." The gossip proved to be true, and about a month later Fowler no longer played for his Page Fence Giants.

One newspaper story said Fowler might relocate and play for the Monroe team. However, in a move which showed there were no hard feelings between management and Fowler, he started at second base for the Adrian Demons that Tuesday and replaced Honus Wagner, who was back home in Pennsylvania. Fowler batted cleanup behind Vasco Graham and right fielder George Wilson. Fowler was flawless in the field, went one-for-four at the plate and scored two runs in a loss to Owosso.[82]

So baseball's tumbleweed was on the move again. His stay with the Adrian Demons would last a single game before he made another move. How long Fowler had been contemplating leaving the Giants has been lost to the ages. However, the same day he played his final game in Hudson with the Giants, Lansing Senators owner and manager Ransom N. Parshall sent out a press release announcing his new business partner and plans for a travelling black ball club. The team would begin their games near the end of this summer and would not only challenge the famed Cuban Giants to a world championship series, but also play throughout Europe. The name of Parshall's new business partner was Bud Fowler.[83]

◆ 11 ◆

The Tumbleweed

The last half of July was not a particularly good time for the Giants' and Demons' baseball management. Everything from the smallest issue—Lawrence Park scorecards would now cost five cents—to Bud Fowler leaving the Giants seemed to rear its head.[1]

In the Michigan State League, Parsons saw his competitive squad, once only vying with the Lansing Senators for top honors, now with Owosso thrown into the pennant race. Soon, someone accused the Colts of cheating by exceeding the $500 league salary cap.[2] League finances overall were also becoming an issue, as the gate receipts were low in Battle Creek and Port Huron. The *Evening Telegram* blasted the Battle Creek papers for withholding public support of their MSL club. The *Telegram* bragged that while it "doesn't feel like boasting, but its early start of a reliable ball column stirred up enthusiasm and created an interest" in Adrian, but Battle Creek's club was missing that assistance.[3] Port Huron had never drawn very well and was the last franchise awarded, and it appeared now for good reason.

Publicly, nothing leaked out about any financial problems with the Adrian Demons until late July. On July 24, the management announced that as of July 30, a ten-cent charge would be added for grandstand patrons. MSL teams divided general admission gate receipts but allowed the home club to retain all grandstand fees. However, Adrian was the only MSL town that didn't charge extra for the special grandstand seating. In explaining this charge, team owners said the dime increase was a "necessity." The club claimed it would allow the town to retain its first-class team, put them on the same footing as the other MSL clubs, and keep the league afloat. Several other minor baseball leagues around the country had folded since the Fourth of July, and they didn't want the MSL to join that group.[4]

To help the Demons' gate receipts, another round of games with the Giants was scheduled. Originally, plans called for the single June game and then nothing between the two teams until the MSL schedule was completed the third week of September. Those plans changed due to the Demons' shaky financial standing. A three-game series was announced for July 29, 30 and 31, just in time to reap the benefits of the new, ten-cent grandstand surcharge. Banking on larger than normal crowds, a new section of 150 grandstand seats would be erected in time for the battle of Adrian.[5] The updated schedule quickly changed when two men from Montpelier, Ohio, approached Adrian management and requested one of those three games between the Giants and Demons. Montpelier's Charles Hall and Charles Perry lobbied for the Monday, July 29, contest to be moved to their town, where they would host a "baseball carnival and a general holiday." The pair's efforts were successful, and the newly minted flyers publicizing the three ball games in Adrian were quickly outdated.[6]

There was also a problem with the Demons' roster. First, Honus Wagner returned home, allegedly due to his father's ill health. Then pitcher Jess Derrick requested his release, and the team cheerfully granted it, as he was apparently a troublemaker. Speedy outfielder Billy Smith also asked to be released and mentioned some unrest amongst the players. To be exact, roommates Smith and Maurice Justice had gotten into an argument the morning before a game, which led to a scrap in a back alley. Justice allegedly kicked Smith in the melee, so Smith asked to be released. However, local management refused to cut Smith and successfully convinced him to stay with the Demons.[7] As a result, some new players would be needed to fill the Demons' squad.

The biggest hurdle for Parsons, Hoch and Taylor was Bud Fowler's move. One can only imagine Parsons' reaction when he heard about Fowler's latest scheme, which included stealing some of the current Page Fence Giants! Manager Parshall's press notice in *Sporting Life* was headlined "Fowler Admits It; His Colored Team Going to England with Barnes' White Team."[8] His team? Parshall claimed he and Fowler came to an agreement on July 13, and the squad would be called "The Lansing Colored Capital All-American team." The new club would join with manager John Barnes of the Western League's Minneapolis Millers and play against each other for two months in England. While that grandiose plan was beyond what the Page Fence Giants were going to do in 1895, it was the first half of the press release that must have peeved Parsons, Hoch and Taylor the most.

That opening statement said the new Colored All-American team would be based in Lansing, Michigan, and would travel to New York, playing games along the way. This new team would be in direct competition with the Page Fence Giants. Before embarking for England, the Colored All-Americans had five games on tap with the Cuban Giants, three in Michigan and two in New York, and said they would be playing for the 1895 black baseball championship. The Page Fence club had been challenging the Cuban Giants for the past month, and nothing had come of it. Now Fowler, without any players or without his new club even having ever played a single game, supposedly had a championship series arranged. Or maybe Fowler did have players, as Parshall said this new team would include "several of the Page Fence Giants and two of the Cubans." People were asked to contact Fowler in Adrian for more details.[9] Who was jumping ship now? First, manager Parsons was faced with rounding up two men to replace Derrick and Wagner on the Demons. Would he have to scour the country for more black baseball talent to replace the rumored vacancies on the Giants?

A second national publication, *The Sporting News*, printed a similar story about Barnes' and Fowler's scheme. This one was even more damaging to the reputation of the Page Fence club. *The Sporting News*, August 3 edition, led off with, "The Capital Colored All-Americans, formerly "The Page Fence Giants,' have been reorganized…" and it asked teams to contact Bud Fowler, the manager, who had recently relocated to Monroe, Michigan. Fowler announced that the tour would begin September 15, which was before the conclusion of either the Demons' or Giants' seasons.[10]

Parsons had to do something to combat this attack and, more importantly, his business venture. He fired off a response to the Parshall and Fowler scheme, which appeared in the next edition of *The Sporting News*. The letter was titled in big block letters, "The Page Fence Giants," with a sub-title, "Bud Fowler in No Way Connected with the Management of That Club." Parsons' letter was filled with sarcasm and challenged the very idea of the Capital Colored All-American team. He claimed that as of July 15, Fowler was "in no way connected" with the Page Fence Giants. Fowler, to add to the ill feelings between the two, was now playing second base for the MSL's Lansing Senators. Parsons alleged that Fowler was managing a "myth," as the Capital Colored All-Americans didn't exist. As far as using members of the current Page Fence Giants, Parsons was quite clear about their contract status and the players' feelings about their current arrangement. Parsons said the Giants were booked with games until early October, "are travelling in style, receiving good treatment and have regular paydays," and "will not let go of a sure thing for the sake of chasing rainbows." Parsons said Bud Fowler could tour around the world, but if he planned on beginning in September, he would do it without any Giants players.[11]

One loss Parsons was probably not expecting was that of the cook on the Page Fence train, William Wendell Gaskin, who took a vacation in mid–July. A resident of Jackson, Michigan, Gaskin was not only a very good cook, as none of the Giants' stories complained about the food or the players' diet, but he was also very smart. Gaskin was an active member and office holder of the Michigan Equal Rights Association. During his three-week hiatus from the club, he worked on developing a brochure to solicit funds for the association. About 5,000 copies of the four-page handout were published and distributed around the state, and Gaskin oversaw the project.[12]

In additional good news, J. Wallace Page gained control of the company through a massive stock purchase. In late July, he bought out the 25 percent of the firm's stock from Charles F. Clement, secretary and treasurer of the Page Fence Woven Wire Company. Page was now in charge of the firm again as the majority stockholder. The Adrian plant employed about 150 men, and business was strong.[13]

Adding to the good news, the Owosso club had been drubbed three times by the Adrian Demons, and it was cause for a celebration. A burning red light, apparently a sign of success in the 1890s, greeted the Demons one night as they arrived at Adrian's Wabash Railroad train depot. The players disembarked and were greeted by the city band, and the team's management chartered carriages to take the men to a local restaurant. Local baseball cranks followed along and cheered the victors. At Schwartz and Emmer's diner, someone thought it would be funny to present a watermelon and place one-half of it in front of George Wilson and the other half on a plate in front of Vasco Graham, apparently honoring the famous "watermelon battery." The *Evening Telegram* said the pair "joined the joke as heartily as anyone."[14]

Meanwhile, while Parsons was battling the Bud Fowler plot to disrupt the Page Fence nine, the Giants were playing games in Indiana and Ohio. One contest saw them destroy Bryan, Ohio, 22–0.[15] They split games with Fowler's old team, the Findlay, Ohio, squad. Joe Miller was very good, and the Sluggers couldn't string together enough hits and dropped a 6–5 game.[16]

The next day, Findlay trailed, 4–2, until the eighth inning, when they exploded for ten runs against Billy Holland. Everyone on the Page Fence club committed errors, except for Holland and a new man in left field named Lyons. The infield either booted or threw away seven chances in helping Findlay win, 12–6. The game got off to a bizarre start, as Findlay's starting pitcher, Bill Reidy, who would make his major league debut next year with the New York Giants, was injured by the first batter. George Taylor hit a rocket and Reidy tried to catch it, injured his finger, and had to leave the game. The second baseman, Howard Brandenburg, replaced Reidy in the box, and George Derby, who had been umpiring behind the plate, went in to play second base. Another player, Charley Jewell, took over as an ump, but was so bad and "couldn't see straight" he was replaced after the second inning by another Findlay man named F. Schwartz.[17]

The special train car traveled out of Findlay, went through Toledo, Ohio, and arrived in Adrian on Thursday, July 25. Team management would take the day to discuss September travel plans to the east and review the Bud Fowler scheme, no doubt.[18]

The ticket sales for the Giants-Demons rematch at the end of the month were expected to be hot. Two local establishments, the cigar shop of Charles Robinson and baseball crank and jeweler George Tripp, were spots where you could purchase tickets in advance.[19] It was never revealed how much money the Montpelier boosters had promised to pay Adrian management for the rights to a game, but it must have been enough to make it worthwhile.

After a day or two of rest, the Giants travelled southwest to Bryan, Ohio, and promptly lost a 9–5 game to the farm boys on Friday.[20] They then zipped east, up along the rail line, challenged the Deltas of Delta, Ohio, and won a 5–2 contest on a Sunday afternoon.[21] The short-term substitute Giant, Lyons, played catcher and in the field for a few games, but became sick in Delta and left for home after the game. The team would be down one man heading into the crucial games with the Demons, but had managed to secure the services of William Binga, a player known throughout Michigan for his hitting skills. However, Binga would not be able to leave his team in Pontiac in time for the three-game set with Adrian.[22]

For the first game either 984 or 1,200 people attended the showdown in Montpelier, Ohio, which quickly turned into a route for the Giants.[23] Before anyone was retired in the opening frame, the black gentlemen had scored six runs off Tim Nevins (who was said to have had a massive toothache) and never looked back. Two of the newer Giants started off the big inning. James Patterson drove a Nevins pitch over the right field fence into a cornfield for a two-run homer, and Sol White soon followed with a grand slam. To his credit, Herbert Lentz relieved Nevins after the first inning and gave the Giants only four more runs. Despite the field not being in the greatest condition, the Giants were flawless and committed no errors to back Joe Miller's pitching. The highlight fielding play, though, was turned in by Adrian's speedy outfielder, Billy Smith, who ran between horse carriages that had bordered the diamond to haul in a long fly ball.[24]

While residents reading the game's outcome in the two daily Adrian papers were thinking about which team they had wanted to win, the Bud Fowler scheme was now front and center in town gossip. When Fowler left the Giants, he returned to Adrian for about ten days before moving to Monroe. He was writing letters about his new proposed team, including those in the national sports publications. It's likely his old stomping grounds of the Craig and Reid Barbershop in town was the stage for some lively discussions on the matter. While Adrian's black community most assuredly knew of Fowler's latest scheme almost immediately when it was hatched in mid–July, it took about two weeks for the plan to get coverage in the local newspapers. The tiny staffs of the Adrian papers were likely not scouring *The Sporting News* and *Sporting Life* for any possible little blurbs from Fowler, Parshall and Barnes. It may have taken two weeks for the word to leak out of the Adrian black community, or maybe Parsons, Hoch and Taylor finally wanted to address the plan which threatened their pocketbooks.

Both dailies detailed the Fowler plan but threw cold water on the idea. The *Times and Expositor* said, "the fact is, the Adrian management intends to play the Giants until snow flies, and if they go to Europe it will be without the knowledge or consent of either players or managers."[25] In addition to the ballplaying excursion to Europe in September, a more immediate threat was unveiled by The *Evening Telegram* in an excerpt printed from the *Lansing Republican*. The Lansing rag claimed that members of the Page Fence Giants and the Cuban Giants would replace the Lansing Senators in the MSL. The *Republican*'s source claimed this roster change would take place "at once," but the *Evening Telegram* dismissed the rumor as "very shaky."[26]

Manager Ransom Parshall was so convinced about the success of Fowler's idea that printed material began to circulate for the "Capital Colored All-American Base Ball Club." Allegedly, Fowler was going to invoke some old contracts he had with the current Page Fence Giants and lure them into the fold. Local baseball management claimed these contracts were "valueless," the Giants were being paid on time, and "everything is harmonious." The *Evening Telegram* used an anonymous source, described only as "one of the leading members of the Giants," to answer the MSL and Fowler rumors. This player said, "there is nothing in the Lansing story as to their being substituted for the Lansing team." He added that the Giants would stay with the present management until the close of this baseball season. As for after the season, this unnamed star Giant said a trip to Europe would be nice, if the proper management could be assured. "We shall know that there is enough money back of the enterprise to bring us safe home when the trip is over. We are not going to England to be stranded.... You can rest assured of that."[27]

As to the other half of the ballplaying equation, John Barnes was working his end of the deal. He had already sold his interest in the Minneapolis Millers and was making his way to Michigan. Barnes attended a game in Milwaukee on July 29, between the Brewers and Detroit Tigers of the Western Association. Sitting on the Tigers' bench, Barnes told the reporter he was going to Lansing to interview the manager of the Page Fence Giants about leading the other team on the European trip. Barnes said he would try to arrange ball games, as his club would play the All-American Colored nine in England. This story was published in the St. Paul *Minnesota Daily Globe* newspaper, so the word was out in the city where the Giants had played in April that something was amiss with the Page Fence club.[28]

Something was definitely amiss with the Giants in game two with the Demons. Back home in the friendly confines of Lawrence Park, about half of the 800 people had paid the extra ten-cent charge to secure seats in the grandstand. The other 400 either sat in the general admission section or gathered around the edge of the field by their horses and carriages. Some people had said that having the Giants win the first game would temper the interest in the second one and hurt the gate. There was some talk that game number two was arranged for the Demons to win, but the headline in the *Evening Telegram* of "The Giants Crippled" probably dispelled that rumor.[29]

The Giants began the game with only nine men, and two of them were hurt. The newest Giant, Lyons, remained at home ill, and Jim Chavous had been released or had left the team on his own. Adrian teenager Frank Waters, whom the Giants had recently signed as an emergency fill-in and who had played games in Allegan, was no longer with the club, and Bill Binga had yet to arrive from Pontiac. The nine were juggled around the field, and their fourth-best pitcher, William Malone, started in the box. Billy Holland, coach extraordinaire and one of the best players on the team, had badly sprained his ankle in yesterday's game at Montpelier and was forced to play gingerly in right field. Fred Van Dyke, who had worked his way back on the team since the second Kalamazoo trip and had been taking a turn in the pitching rotation, had a lame arm. As the Giants only had nine men, Van Dyke couldn't rest that day and was forced to play center field. His arm was so bad he could throw the ball only a few yards overhand and was eventually forced to toss it underhand during one play.

Malone was not particularly effective as he walked eight men, hit two and was throwing a "straight ball" with very little speed.[30] He was also mouthy before the game, and the talk was that the Giants would win once again. He walked the first batter, slick-fielding shortstop Maurice Justice, and then Ed Mulhearn was retired on the bases. Batting third that day was Vasco Graham, and as he strolled to the plate, the game was stopped. D. W. Grandon, editor and publisher of the *Evening Telegram*, presented the black catcher with a "base ball stick pin" on behalf of local jeweler J. Will Kirk. Grandon apparently gave a somewhat lengthy and praiseworthy speech aimed at Graham's playing skills and wonderful personality. The young man was being honored for being the only player to catch all his team's MSL games that season. Graham silently accepted the token of gratitude, and the game resumed. The *Evening Telegram* stated that the "presentations speech … was enough to rattle" even a level-headed kid such as Graham. After the presentation, he managed to lift a high fly ball to left field, where Joe Miller cradled it in for the second out of the inning. Paul Craft grounded out to Grant Johnson at shortstop, and Adrian failed to score to open the game.[31]

The Giants did manage to score in the bottom of the first. Lefty George Wilson struck out George Taylor, but then an error, hit and walk filled the bases. Wilson wild-pitched James Patterson home for a run. The next two batters popped out, and the Giants led, 1–0.[32] However, the Giants' injured players began to impact the game negatively, as outfielder Van Dyke allowed Mike Lynch to take an extra base due to his lame throwing arm. In the fifth inning, with Lynch batting again, he drove a ball which eluded the hobbling right fielder, Holland, and rolled into a nearby ditch before the Giant could catch up with it. Holland was so slow on his gimpy right ankle that Lynch circled the bases and touched home, but he had missed third base and was able to run back, touch it and scamper home before being tagged out. That play was the last straw for the Giants, as Holland was summoned to play first base and George Taylor relocated to right field. However, the run after Lynch's fly ball further injured Holland's leg. He was removed after a few batters, and Taylor returned to first. For possibly the first time in their short history, the Page Fence Giants did not field an all-black squad. Herbert Lentz, a white player who had pitched so effectively in a relief role yesterday for the Demons, took right field for the Giants in the sixth inning and finished the game there.[33]

The Giants managed to cut into the Demons' lead when Johnson slammed a ball into the shrubbery in center field and "ran the bases like a greyhound," making the score 7–4 after five innings. The Palmyra Wonder was just too good that day as he struck out ten Giants in posting the 14–5 victory. The Giants were a beat-up and unhappy bunch as they spent their time complaining about the umpire, Christie Reynolds, and kicking about a couple of his calls.[34]

While jeweler Kirk was advertising his wares during the first-inning presentation to Graham, the Page Fence Company also capitalized on the crowd that Tuesday afternoon. Their product design team had constructed a large wire cage and placed it at Lawrence Park, with a sign reading "This is not the house that Jack built, but the fence that Page built." Inside the cage was a young boy, presumably named Jack, who spent the game walking around inside the cage and drawing attention to himself and the wire company's display. Two other little guys also drew attention at Lawrence Park. Len Hoch's son, eight-year-old Willie, and Rolla Taylor's seven-year-old, also named Willie, paraded around in their new blue and white Adrian Demons kid-sized uniforms.[35]

The third game in the series was much like the first. The blue-clad Demons defeated the Giants, 9–3. The rumor swirled that the outcome of the first two games had been arranged to create a buzz for the rubber game of the series. The idea, if true, didn't work as 700 people, or 100 less than the day before, attended the final contest. The Giants' Billy Holland was in the box, but his badly sprained right ankle was still bothering him and his pitches were lacking control and speed. He hobbled fielding ground balls, and whenever a wild pitch or passed ball occurred, Patterson rushed in from third base to cover home plate, instead of the injured hurler. As they did in game two, the Giants tallied a run in the first inning to take a brief lead. Adrian came back with four runs in the second inning and eventually led, 8–2, before grabbing the victory. The two Adrian daily newspapers spent most of their coverage focusing on the play of the Demons and nowhere near as much about the Page Fence Giants. Redeeming himself from Monday's first inning debacle at Montpelier, Tim Nevins earned the victory for the Demons. In the fourth inning, Nevins quickly struck out Van Dyke, Miller and Holland. In the next inning, Holland "turned the tables and struck Nevins out, playing all the time like a clown," and later took care of Paul Kraft, all the while "joshing" with the batter, umpire Jim Mullally, and the fans.[36]

The Giants were playing with a limited roster of nine men and the obviously hobbled Holland and were still able to compete with the Michigan State League-leading Demons, who currently posted a 34–14 record. Even knowing those facts, the *Times and Expositor* was not too kind to the Page Fence-sponsored club. "The Giants are good bicyclists, but they might apparently take some rudimentary lessons in the national game at the hands of the Adrian blue garbed players."[37]

The Adrian baseball management was pleased with the three games, as the gate receipts and whatever Montpelier boosters had paid them were enough to stave off a money crisis. Both the Demons and Giants were now on solid financial ground.[38]

On August 1, the Fowler story overshadowed the third game's news coverage. The tumbleweed, who was still playing second base for the Lansing Senators, announced a major change in plans. No longer would the Colored All-American squad travel from Lansing to the East, battling clubs along the way. Instead, they would travel from Minneapolis on September 1 and head west to play a month of games in California, based in San Francisco. Then the black stars would journey to Honolulu, Hawaii, Australia and New Zealand. The team would return to the States and travel to New York, sail for England, and play their first game in Europe under the watchful gaze of the Prince of Wales. There was no mention of any games with the Cuban Giants or vying for any championship, and nothing about making the current Page Fence Giants the new Lansing Senators. As a matter of fact, to concentrate on this business venture, Parshall announced that his Senators, currently in second place behind Adrian, were up for sale. John Barnes used his connection and said he could lure two of his former Minneapolis players to play for the Lansing squad, to induce a future owner to purchase an improved club. Barnes would also be assembling the white ball club's roster that would challenge the black team over in England. The former Minneapolis manager said his brother's worldwide publishing business connections would also help the team become known far and wide. Bud Fowler's role was to manage and sign the black players. However, the plan to absorb all of the Page Fence Giants was adjusted, and it appeared that maybe only three or four would join the new squad, now renamed the Michigan Capital Colored Champion Base Ball team.[39]

About a week later, old Bud Fowler announced the signing of seven players for this new club, including George Wilson and Vasco Graham of the Giants, who would join the team in late September, following the conclusion of the MSL season. Fowler claimed that five Cuban Giants, pitchers William Seldon and James "Black Rusie" Robinson, center fielder Andy Jackson, shortstop Frank Grant and catcher Clarence Williams, had already agreed to contract terms.[40]

Meanwhile, the Adrian baseball management countered and announced that both Wilson and Graham would return to the Page Fence Giants next year. The *Telegram* proclaimed, "The Giants are winners now, but under the plans proposed will be the greatest colored team in the world." As far as Fowler's Michigan Capital, or the Colored All-American squad was concerned, no records were ever found that it played a single inning anywhere on Earth.[41]

◆ 12 ◆

And Then There Was One

The Page Fence Giants pulled out of Adrian and headed west into Branch County for a tilt against the Quincy club. Pitcher Joe Miller was left behind, as he made his minor league debut with the Demons. It didn't seem to matter who the Giants had in the box, as regular third baseman James Patterson pitched and did just fine in crushing Quincy, 21–7. A large crowd estimated around 1,100 saw the Giants have little trouble with the home team. However, Quincy used a pretty good pitcher named Hilderbrand, who whiffed nine Giants batters.[1]

Meanwhile, Cyclone Miller was locked up in a duel with Lansing's Charlie Ferguson on his way to claim a 7–3 Demons win over the Senators. Making up the Demons' second black battery, Miller and Vasco Graham limited the Senators to just three hits, including holding down Fowler, now with the Senators, who was 0-for-4 at the plate. Miller struck out three, walked five and hit one batter. The other highlight was a home run by the Demons' James Robinson to help clinch the Thursday afternoon win.[2]

Miller then hopped a train to meet the Giants in Three Rivers, Michigan, while Bill Binga finally connected with the team in Allegan for their Saturday game there. The next two and a half weeks would take the Giants through a northern Lower Michigan swing where game specifics and scores became very sparse. They played in cities along the Lake Michigan coastline and north to Traverse City, before jutting across the state's midsection to end August in Detroit. Maybe the scores were sent to the Craig and Reid Barbershop, as had been the plan from early in the season, but they didn't make their way to the two daily newspapers. To be fair, the *Evening Telegram* did a much better job than the *Daily Times and Expositor*. The latter went three weeks in this span and, despite the Giants playing nearly every day, the *Times* reported had only three game scores. Gus Parsons, Rolla Taylor and Len Hoch were most likely not on this lengthy trip, which would partially explain the lack of press coverage. It appeared that Len Hoch rarely, if ever, traveled on the Giants' palatial train car, and Parsons and Taylor were currently focused on keeping the Michigan State League afloat.

Unless the Giants were playing the Demons, most local newspaper stories were one sentence in length, usually giving the score and the battery, and that was it. Occasionally, the teams' hits and errors were mentioned. Line and box scores were nearly non-existent in Adrian newspapers for the Giants' games. In the many towns where the Giants played, it was clear, both before and after the game, when the newspaper editor was a baseball fanatic. Some communities barely mentioned the upcoming game and simply reported the outcome as a win, or usually a loss, for the local boys without even posting the score. In other towns, several preview stories and other game notes, strategically positioned throughout the paper, would include game times, location and ticket prices. Some news stories would remind people about the fancy pregame bicycle parade, while in rare cases a Giants player's name would be used to drum up interest.

Typical was the case of baseball lovers writing for the *Allegan Journal* on August 2, 1895. The *Journal* publicized the contest, telling of a hand-picked Allegan County nine that would play the Giants at 2 o'clock on August 3 at Willow Park. The game time was deliberately set to be early enough "to enable those from the country to get home before dark." The paper previewed the contest with a quite lengthy paragraph. "This famous colored nine—the Page Fence Giants—need no introduction to the public. They are, without a doubt, one of the strongest teams playing ball this year, and have won nearly every game they have played this season. They travel in their own private palace car and each one rides a bicycle, and the parade they give on their wheels will be worth coming miles to see."

The next day, over 1,000 people saw the Giants narrowly defeat the Allegan All-Stars, 12–10. On Sunday, August 4, twice that many people made their way into nearby Muskegon to see either a 12–10 or 19–10 Giants victory (published scores conflict). The *Muskegon News*, which sponsored the team which played the Giants, used the slang language of the day to describe the black players. They headlined with "Cooned Both of Them," as their Tuesday edition included stories on a pair of Page Fence victories. "The darkies put in Miller, their whirlwind but the News boys saw him for 13 hits while Kitson kept the darkies to 10 hits."[3] Kitson was most likely Frank Kitson, who in four years would be a 22-game winner for Baltimore in the National League, en route to 129 major league victories. The 25-year-old right-hander was born in a rural area just outside of Allegan.[4] Unfortunately for Muskegon, "the visitors bunched their hits and the locals their errors," as despite outhitting the Giants, they lost. The Giants made an odd switch in their lineup, possibly due to another injury, as George Taylor, who began the game at first base, ended it behind the plate. Regular backstop Pete Burns made a rare appearance in the outfield.[5]

A much smaller crowd of between 300 and 500 people attended Monday's game. The threat of precipitation probably was the reason, as the game was called after five innings due to rain with the Giants leading, 5–1. Muskegon had imported a "kid pitcher" named Luther from the tiny town of Hart to face the traveling squad. He did a nice job, and the game was close until Muskegon booted the ball around, which led to four Giants runs in the fourth inning. There was no mention of Binga at Allegan or Muskegon, and he was not listed in a published projected starting lineup for the first game with Muskegon.[6]

"The management is reaping a rich harvest just at present," said the *Daily Times and Expositor* about the Page Fence Giants during the first week of August 1895.[7] The Giants were drawing well on the road, where sometimes 2,500 people crowded farm fields and jammed city parks to see the wizards play ball. The management trio was enjoying the Giants' play and the money. Entering their fifth month with the barnstorming gentlemen, problems had been virtually non-existent, except for the Fowler defection and decisions by local umpires. None of the press accounts mentioned troublesome players or reported violent outbursts from any Page Fence Giant. The papers mentioned that the Giants liked to "kick" at the umpire's decisions, but it was obvious by now that many calls were unfairly going against them. The Page Fence ball club had to be exceeding management's and the fence company's wildest dreams.

The Adrian Demons were another story. Over three decades later, Howard Taylor would say that Honus Wagner left the team not due to having an ill father back home, but rather having to play with George Wilson and Vasco Graham—the black players.[8] That same week of Wagner's exit, pitcher Jess Derrick had been granted his release and was branded a troublemaker by the team. Kalamazoo had unsuccessfully protested Adrian's black players, and Lansing was supposedly going to follow suit, but did not. Attendance was not strong across the MSL. One game in mid–September in Adrian, the bellwether franchise of the MSL, drew only 150 paying customers.[9] The Lansing team was for sale, and Battle Creek had just announced it had disbanded its club. During the first week of August, an emergency meeting was held in Jackson to discuss the league's future. Len Hoch was a key player at the gathering, which decided to retain the three strongest franchises, Adrian, Lansing and Kalamazoo, and allow Battle Creek, Port Huron and Owosso to reorganize. Jackson had a team interested in joining the MSL, and the mighty Findlay Sluggers were without an affiliation, as the Ohio State League had folded earlier that summer. The thought was that those two teams or some of their players might fill some of the roster slots on the three struggling MSL franchises.[10] It would take another week of meetings and "good natured discussion" before the MSL felt they were again operating on solid ground. The reorganization had the Jackson club, reinforced with some Findlay players, replace Battle Creek. The new MSL operating by-laws cost Adrian severely. They had been in first place since June 29, but all teams' win-loss records were reset.[11]

Outwardly, things were going fine in Adrian, until another week passed. On August 21, the *Evening Telegram* blared, "Adrian Club Disbands; A Self Sustaining Team Is Impossible," while the *Daily Times and Expositor* had "Leave the League; The Enterprise Does Not Pay."[12] Businessmen Hoch and Taylor decided to foot the Demons' cost overruns no longer and announced that the game that afternoon would be their last. The Adrian community was shocked as nothing had been heard about financial problems, other than the recently imposed ten-cent grandstand surcharge. Hoch and Taylor regretted the decision, but the nation's still sagging economy (in the second year of an economic depression) and lagging attendance played a major part in shutting down the team's operations. Adrian baseball fever had apparently run its course. However, the Page Fence Giants continued, and current Demons George Wilson and Vasco Graham would now be transferred back to that club. To add to the local sting, the baseball management said they had no plans to return any of the season ticket money, even though the schedule was supposed to run for nearly another month. The Demons' management rationale was that the season ticket passes allowed one to see all of the year's games played at Lawrence Park, and they had.[13]

The next day, the Adrian baseball cranks came to the rescue. The *Daily Times and Expositor* had a story entitled "Must Not Disband," while the *Evening Telegram* was led by "Not to Disband." A hurriedly arranged agreement allowed the Demons to travel to Owosso to play three MSL games. The players agreed to forfeit their salary and asked just that their expenses be paid. Hoch accompanied the team to Owosso that Thursday and said that the Adrian community had three days to raise additional financial support, or the Demons would quit the MSL. Both Hoch and Rolla Taylor dumped another $25 into the team's coffers as a show of good faith, even though they claimed to have lost $150 apiece so far.[14]

Having a first-place team cease operations did not sit well with the local baseball cranks. In a matter of two hours that Thursday morning, as the Demons were on their way to Owosso, 18 local men pledged five dollars each to the club in the form of a second season ticket. Among those joining the cause was Seymour Howell, apparently back active in the baseball booster world, local physician F. E. Andrews, and *Evening Telegram* owner D. W. Grandon. The whole idea was hatched by Alanson Bennett, who somehow raised $90 in a short time. A plea was put into the *Evening Telegram* that other ball cranks could drop off their team ticket or donation dollars at the newspaper office.[15]

Meanwhile, along Michigan's west coast, the Page Fence Giants continued playing on the diamond and shut out Hart, defeated Manistee in two close contests, and split two games with the Traverse City Hustlers and the Charlevoix squad. The Giants then swept a pair of games from Petoskey and just nipped a Midland team with two runs in the bottom of the ninth inning, as George Taylor pitched and Sol White caught, as a way to make the game more interesting.[16]

One of the region's major newspapers, the *Detroit Free Press*, often offered more game summaries than either of the Adrian daily papers, and proved the Giants' popularity across the state. For a game with Kalkaska, the *Free Press* provided its baseball fans with a line score, the batteries and a two-sentence summary. The Giants won, 10–6, with the battery of Grant Johnson (pitcher) and William Malone (catcher), which indicated a possible injury or illness to regular catcher Pete Burns.[17]

The following day, the *Free Press* headlined "A Dull Game at Reed City" and added that it was a "stupid game." Burns was back behind the plate for the Giants, and Malone earned the victory in a 12–6, seven-inning contest.[18] The *Reed City Weekly Clarion* previewed the contest by saying, "Those who have seen them play, say that in addition to being first-class ball players, they make a great deal of sport and to see them play is the next thing to going to a circus."[19] The next week's *Weekly Clarion* praised the Giants, who "toyed with our local nine" and "are a great nine" themselves.[20]

In "baseball mad" Flint, the Giants ran into some problems and lost, 8–5, on August 26 and then 11–8 the next day. In the first game, the Giants' fielding was of "high order," with Grant Johnson and Joe Miller earning rave reviews. However, the Giants failed to score after the third inning in their loss. In game two, Billy Holland got knocked out of the box after allowing five runs in the fourth inning and another four in the fifth inning, as the Giants dropped two in a row. One thousand people attended the second game as Flint outplayed the Giants all over the field.[21]

The powerful Page Fence crew then dropped another game, their third in a row. Were the wheels coming off the cart, so to speak? The lucky team was the Holly Cyclone Midgets, sponsored by a local fence company. Holly won this abbreviated, seven-inning game, 6–3, after rain showers that wiped out the last two frames.[22] The mighty Giants had not lost three games in a row for over two months and apparently decided to take their frustration out on their next team. In what the *Daily Times and Expositor* called a "splendid game," they shut out Pontiac, 11–0, behind the pitching of the great coacher, Billy Holland. Apparently, Pontiac's pitcher, Henley, was quite impressive as he would strike out two and three Giants an inning. However, it obviously wasn't enough, as the Giants logged the lopsided victory and regained some of their pride from the previous three losses.[23]

The Page Fence train car headed north to the farming community of St. Louis, nestled along the banks of the winding Pine River in Central Michigan. On August 30, the *Alma Record*, published just a few miles away and served their neighboring town with news, noted, "It isn't generally known that Alma has a band of white caps. For further information consult George Sharrar."[24] Whether Sharrar was the leader of the Ku Klux Klan or possibly a target of the vigilante group is unknown. However, when the word "white caps" and a person's name was associated with them in a sentence, printed on the front page of the local paper, the secret was out that the Klan was alive and active in the area.

The Giants coming to St. Louis was a big event for this mid–Michigan community.

The Detroit, Lansing and Northern Railway offered reduced fares from nearby Ithaca for a trip north about eight miles to St. Louis. The D, L & N cut their regular fare in half and offered two morning rail trips to the farming community.[25] Was the game simply a big sporting event to watch two good ball teams, or would Klan members show up and make their presence known? It's likely that the word got back to the Giants and their management. Adding to the drama, the game would be a close contest between St. Louis and the Page Fence Giants.

The railroad's bargain ticket plan was successful as "a great many people" boarded in Ithaca for the game in St. Louis.[26] A very large crowd, estimated at 1,500 to 2,000, witnessed the Giants pull out a 7–6 victory over St. Louis. The *Alma Record* called it a "pretty game," and the *Gratiot County Herald* said it was "hotly contested."[27] William Malone started for the Giants, lasted five innings, and was lifted while trailing, 4–3. Home Run Johnson entered the game and earned the pitching victory, as the Giants scored in the sixth inning to take the lead and then held on for the narrow one-run win.[28]

The Giants left St. Louis and headed south to Detroit for weekend games with the always tough city Athletic Club. The *Evening Telegram* used the *Detroit Free Press* story, which recorded a Giants 18–7 victory. Home Run Johnson lived up to his moniker as he slammed one in the sixth inning to the Cass Avenue fence that was said to be the longest ever hit on the DAC grounds. The two DAC pitchers were both battered, their team fielded poorly, and the Giants "laid against the ball like fiends."[29]

The two Adrian teams then took their show on the road to the northern Ohio town of Toledo. This baseball-loving community sent 700 people to the game who saw the Giants wallop the Demons, 15–5. Star lefty George Wilson, still with the Demons, was defeated by the loud coacher, Billy Holland, in a game where few details made their way back to Adrian. Apparently, whatever contract stipulation Wilson had used in June to avoid pitching against the Giants was no longer followed in this game.[30] The Demons returned home for MSL games with Port Huron, while the Giants remained to play the Toledo Unions on Labor Day, Monday. The fancy train car would then head west along the Air Line rail route, for games in Swanton and Wauseon, Ohio, before crossing over into Indiana and contests in Kendallville, Butler and Elkhart.[31]

When the Demons arrived home from Toledo, they were greeted with more rumors swirling about the financial straits of their blue-clad club. One story had them folding altogether sometime early next week, while the second had them quitting the MSL and playing as the permanent opponent for the traveling Giants. Monday's game with the Port Huron Marines drew only 250 people to Adrian's Lawrence Park, below the goal of 400 Hoch and Taylor had projected to ensure financial success. The Demons' 7–8 record had them in fourth place in the newly constituted MSL standings. Newcomer Jackson was on top with a 12–6 record, but Adrian was only a game or two behind both Lansing and Kalamazoo. Rolla Taylor strenuously denounced the rumor of the Adrian Demons' imminent demise and said the plan was to play out the 1895 season.[32]

The Demons also underwent a roster shuffle that impacted the Page Fence club. It was announced that Billy Holland would be transferred from the Giants to the Demons to play third base and occasionally pitch. Holland would replace the feisty Mike Lynch, whose last game with the Demons was in Toledo. To fill Holland's spot on the Page Fence Giants, George Wilson would be sent to the all-star club. The *Daily Times and Expositor* said the switch would likely disappoint Wilson's local fan base, but assured Demons boosters that Holland was "a better ball player and funnier than a minstrel show."[33]

The Demons also tried their best to match the influx of talent that Jackson had inked. The Demons signed Frank Belt, who hailed from shortstop Maurice Justice's hometown of Jacksonville, Illinois, Ben Ireland, an infielder from the Findlay club, 17-year-old second baseman Ervin Beck from Toledo, and pitcher William Martin "Bill" Carrick of the Warren, Pennsylvania, team. Carrick came recommended by former second baseman Honus Wagner. The former Demons infielder wanted to return to the still integrated Adrian MSL club (which would dispel Wagner's anti-black player allegation). Demons management had sent Wagner a train ticket, but he was unable to get out of his contract with his current Warren team.[34] Before the end of the decade, two of the new Adrian signees would make it to the major leagues. Beck played for four teams, including a year with the Detroit Tigers, and Carrick pitched for both the New York Giants and the Washington Senators. Despite being in Adrian for only a few weeks at the end of the season, Carrick fell in love with a local girl, Minnie Carpenter, and they eventually married.[35] The influx of these new players was a delight to Gus Parsons, who had made it publicly known that he was against losing the popular and boisterous Holland to the Demons. It appears that Belt never made it to Michigan, and Beck departed after playing just one game for the Demons. However, Ireland and Carrick stuck with the club, which allowed Billy Holland to remain with the Giants, much to the delight of Parsons.[36]

The *Daily Times and Expositor* dedicated seven paragraphs, a line score and game notes to the Demons' 13–4, Tuesday afternoon victory over the Port Huron Marines. Game attendance was even worse than the day before, totaling only 150 customers at Lawrence Park. Beck, in his only appearance for Adrian, helped start two double plays and mashed a home run over the head of the center fielder, after the ball became lost in the weeds along the creek bank. Wilson picked up the win, while catcher Graham injured his hand in the fourth inning, when he split a finger, but remained in the game. The Marines complained long and loud about the umpire, who one paper said "was erroneous on both sides." The same newspaper allocated five paragraphs to the Demons' new arrivals, though one never made it to town. As comparison, on the same day, for the Page Fence men all the *Expositor* printed was "The Giants defeated Swanton, O. team by a score of 6–5 yesterday."[37]

To boost home attendance, Demons management declared this Saturday's game with Jackson as "Ladies Day" and would admit the "fair sex" to the grandstand without the standard charge.[38] While the Demons' business ledger was weak and management hoped this new female bargain day would help the box office, the Page Fence Woven Wire Company had its own struggles. For about seven weeks that summer, the company experience a work slowdown when unable to secure enough wire to weave its unique fence. Even with sales ahead of last year, production was lagging, costing the firm profits.[39]

On the diamond, the Demons and the MSL had another batch of problems. When James Stevens traveled to Lansing at the end of August to watch the Demons play the Senators, he was forced to be the umpire. He spent much of the game dodging rocks that were thrown by unhappy Lansing fans, even though the Senators won the tilt.[40] In another game with the Senators, Lansing pitcher Charlie Ferguson hit Wilson in the back of the head while the Demon was running between first and second. Wilson fell over second base "like a dead man," and the crowd went silent. Doctor F. E. Andrews was called and revived the Palmyra Wonder. Some feared that Wilson was going to die, as when he came to, he "writhed and struggled." He recovered sufficiently to be led from the field, but Tim Nevins took his place in the lineup.[41] About a week later against Jackson, stellar catcher Vasco Graham split his right throwing hand between his fourth and pinkie fingers. Doc Andrews was in the stands for this game and worked to repair Graham's hand. Andrews apparently stopped the bleeding, but he declared that Graham would likely miss the rest of the season. The *Evening Telegram* said the fans were distraught that their pennant hopes were hurt with Graham's loss, but added that he was a crowd favorite due to his "quiet and gentlemanly deportment."[42]

As far as the league went, another team was now out—this time the Owosso Colts threw in the towel. Owosso officials said they had managed to make enough money over the Labor Day weekend to make their players' pay current and meet the club's outstanding bills. The Colts' ownership claimed they had lost money all season, as had the "majority of cities in the league." They thanked all the Owosso boosters for their support and said they were able to make it this far into the season with their fans' help. The ball diamond, owned by the Owosso Athletic Association, would be turned into a skating rink.[43] Owosso wasn't the only troubled MSL town in early September. Lansing, whose team was up for sale by manager Ransom N. Parshall, couldn't bring a full squad of players to Adrian for one game. Bud Fowler, Charlie Ferguson and catcher Bert Elton didn't board the train in downtown Lansing. When the Senators arrived in Adrian, they grabbed two local men named Miller and Carleton and played the league game, but lost, 23–12. Afterward, Ferguson and Elton went on strike for back wages and, when it wasn't paid, they remained in Lansing. The club claimed that Fowler's absence was due to the fact that they had just released him after he didn't board a train bound for Owosso for an earlier game. One wonders what Fowler felt about his new business partner, Parshall, being unable to pay his bills and cutting him from the Senators roster.[44] A few days after Owosso called it a season, Port Huron, the final club to be admitted that spring, defeating the Hudson bid, quit the league. The MSL was now a four-team race between Adrian, Kalamazoo, Lansing and Jackson.[45]

The Page Fence club rolled through their schedule with only a few scores making it back to Adrian. Victories against Butler and Fremont, Indiana, and Defiance, Lima, and Wauseon, Ohio, were published in at least one of the daily papers. By this time, the baseball coverage was centered on the Demons and their 1895 pennant chase, while the Giants were rarely mentioned. The accuracy of game reports was still an issue, as the *Evening Telegram* printed the Lima-Giants game as played in Hinkelville, Ohio, which didn't exist. The *Daily Times and Expositor* reported the same game as a 12–8 Giants win played at the Hicksville Fair, a small town near the Indiana-Ohio border.[46]

Most of the time, by this point, specific Giants players were only mentioned in terms of how they impacted the Demons. Bill Binga had evidently arrived and was playing for the Giants, but his presence in Adrian baseball was first verified only when he was transferred to the Demons to catch. Vasco Graham's recent hand injury was too severe, as Doc Andrews had predicted, and the minor league club needed a backstop. Adrian management tried to sign a catcher from the Iron and Oil League out east, but was unsuccessful, so a Giants player was summoned. Binga caught only a few games with the Demons before both he and the injured Graham were sent back to the Giants. The word was that the Giants' Pete Burns was a better hitter, so he joined the Demons for their late-season pennant run. Whether this statement about Binga was true or not, there is some doubt. In one game, Binga went 2-for-5, scored two runs, made no errors, and "caught a faultless game." He was announced as the Demons' catcher for the rest of the year after that contest, only to be substituted for by Burns a day or so later.[47] However, Binga managed to stay with the Demons long enough to participate in a wild scrum of a game at Jackson.

Jackson, made up largely of Findlay, Ohio, players, was battling Adrian for the league title. To begin the final week of MSL action, Adrian had defeated the Jackson Jaxons in a quite convincing fashion, 16–8, on Sunday.[48] That result didn't go over well in Jackson, which resulted in a mini-riot during Monday's game. Square in the middle of it was George Wilson, who had not been sent to the Giants, as predicted. The young lefty was in the pitcher's box when the home plate umpire began to call some clear strikes as balls, while Jackson was trailing late in the game, creating the uproar.[49]

Billy Madden was a local substitute umpire, replacing regular MSL official James Grogan, who could not make the game. After rejecting an offer by Adrian to have one man from each team ump, Madden went to work. The *Daily Times and Expositor* said that the ball game being played just west of the state prison in Jackson was a nice metaphor for "the rankest steals on record." In the opening inning, and during the leadoff batter's appearance, Wilson had walked off the diamond in protest of Madden's work. After stewing for five minutes and hearing Madden promise to do his best umpire imitation, Wilson returned to pitch. Adrian was already playing the game under protest, claiming that Jackson's new pitcher, Ike Butler, was still under contract with the now-defunct Port Huron squad. Butler would later reach the majors for a single season in 1902 as a pitcher and outfielder for the last-place Baltimore Orioles.[50]

It was obvious to the partisan Demons fans that the fix was in that afternoon. Even though umpire Madden promised a "square deal" for Adrian as part of luring Wilson out of his first-inning funk, it wasn't the case. Wild pitches were called strikes on the Adrian club, but Wilson's missiles cutting the middle of the plate were called balls. Several plays along the bases eliminated members of the Adrian nine when they were clearly safe. The final straw came with Adrian trailing, 6–3, in the ninth inning. The first two Jaxons were awarded bases on balls when Adrian fans thought they should have struck out, including Ike Butler, who one paper claimed "couldn't hit a balloon." Wilson had nearly reached his boiling point again, and he lobbed the next pitch, which was roped for an RBI hit. Wilson bore down and fired one across the heart of the plate to the next batter. Umpire Madden called it a ball, and Wilson walked off the field in disgust and headed toward his bench. Captain Ed Mulhearn, along with Howard Taylor and James Stevens, met Wilson near the bench area and tried to convince the young hurler to go back out and pitch. During this discussion, a crowd of diehard Jackson fans stormed the field, jostled and jeered Wilson, and prevented him for making a timely return to the pitcher's box. In some archaic 1890s rule book section, there was a time limit in effect, which was not lost on Jackson's manager, Todd. He dashed onto the field and shoved a pocket watch in umpire Madden's face. By this time, police officers had taken the field and tried to separate Wilson from the unruly mob. Apparently convinced that Todd's timepiece was correct, Madden declared a forfeit win for Jackson due to Wilson's failure to return to play within the prescribed time limit. Todd threw his hat into the air and yelled joyfully about the victory. To exit the field, the Demons passed two groups, amongst the 1,300 ball fans, who pelted them with rocks, hitting Mulhearn above the eye and Maurice Justice in the chin. Several players demanded a train home to Adrian that evening and vowed they would not return for the series' final two games.[51]

The *Daily Times and Expositor* was upset with the game's outcome. The paper noted that Wilson outpitched Jackson and recorded 11 strikeouts and five "so called" bases on balls. His counterpart, "Butler 4, so called" strikeouts and "according to decisions" walked only one batter.[52] This was the paper's not so subtle way of highlighting the umpire's poor work.

Word of the debacle made its way back to Adrian, and Len Hoch immediately hopped on the train and headed to Jackson. He convinced the Demons to remain and play the final two crucial, pennant-drive games. Pitcher Joe Miller must have been on the same train as Hoch, as one paper late Tuesday reported that the Giants' hurler might make his second appearance of the year for the Demons.[53]

Luckily, the third game was a much calmer affair. Hoch had secured police officers to protect his team, which likely helped persuade the Demons to stay and play in Jackson. Adrian management demanded a new umpire and got to choose between a man named King or long-time, Jackson-area baseball star and brief major leaguer, Jim Tray. King was selected and complaints were few, even though Jackson won, 12–6.[54]

The fourth and final game, on Wednesday, September 18 was an ugly, vile game with the target being the young Palmyra Wonder. Early in the game, the foul-mouthed baseball cranks were on Wilson, screamed "watermelon" and called him a "n----r." Some of the Jackson players joined in jeering Wilson and violating other 1890s baseball rules regarding the official "coacher," designated to razz the opponents. Umpire King did very little to calm down the obscene Jackson rooters and the extra "coachers." One newspaper account declared that characterizing umpire King as incompetent was way too charitable.[55] Wilson's control was off and he was wild, walking three batters in the opening inning. Catcher Pete Burns allowed a passed ball, and the Jaxons scored twice without a hit. The second inning was more of the same, as Wilson walked a man and then one of his deliveries was so wild, it shot past Burns and rolled near the fans who had lined the field. "The ball went into the crowd and one of the hoodlums held it until the runner had scored" amid a loud applause.[56] Wilson managed to settle down and fanned the next three batters, but the damage was done. The youngster was soon lifted for newly arrived righty Bill Carrick, but it didn't help, and the Demons dropped a 13–4 game, to split the four-game series (Sunday's game and a forfeit victory on Monday for Jackson using the ineligible Ike Butler), in their eyes at least. A police patrol escorted the Demons off the diamond and to the Jackson train depot.[57]

The Demons had two more games remaining on the inaugural MSL schedule, both at home with the Kalamazoo nine. Adrian dropped the first, 12–5, but won the Saturday finale, 19–1, on a Wilson four-hitter. Burns went five-for-five at the plate, and the Demons declared they had won the MSL championship.[58] But so did Jackson claim the pennant. To his credit, league president Walter Mumby upheld the Adrian protest over Ike Butler's illegal contract and tossed out that loss. Then Adrian argued that they had won both halves of the split season, even though it was agreed during the recent league reorganization not to count the first-half standings. Adrian management said their aggregate record was 59–29 for a .670 winning percentage, good enough for the Michigan State League championship. Adrian and Detroit papers calculated the winning percentages differently, and it took several days before Mumby, safely tucked away in his Corunna home, announced Adrian as the pennant winners.[59]

Now those loaned Page Fence Giants such as Wilson, Miller, Binga, and Burns could return and strengthen the already powerful travelling team. The Giants, even without those men, kept winning, defeating Wauseon, Ohio, Hudson, Michigan, and an always tough Homer, Michigan, team, 9–7. Homer led, 5–3, after two innings, and the game was tied 7–7 in the seventh inning before the Giants secured the win. Grant Johnson pitched for the victors in a rare appearance in the box.[60] The Giants then destroyed a hand-picked nine from the Mason area, 16–1. There was much fanfare surrounding the game, as Detroit Mayor Hazen Pingree threw out the ceremonial first pitch to Mason Mayor Harper Reed at Webb Park. About 600 people attended, which was declared the city's largest attendance ever. The *Ingham County News* was quite complimentary of the visiting Giants, predicting the score could have been "100 to one," and even so, the locals were still happy with the game.[61]

The next day, in Fowlerville, organizers had vowed to bring in a professional battery to help their cause, even though "the home club contains some of the best fielders and baseman of any team in this vicinity." It didn't work, as Fowlerville lost, 18–4.[62] The next day, the Page Fence men traveled north and defeated a team at Ovid, 19–8.[63]

With the Demons' season over, Hoch and Parsons could focus their efforts on having the Giants finish strong, when they weren't writing letters to the paper or giving their opinions about the disputed MSL title. The day the Demons clinched their pennant, Giants management announced the Page Fence team was booked with additional games through October 7. Their opponent for at least two of those contests would be the Adrian Demons, with match-ups tentatively set for Montpelier, Ohio, and Hillsdale, Michigan. The extended season benefited both management and the players. The Giants could continue generating profit, and the Demons players could pad their ballplaying salary from the recently completed season.[64]

A few days after announcing the two road games, three home dates were added. Len Hoch and Rolla Taylor needed the additional cash, as on September 23, two days off their pennant win, it was publicized that the championship Demons had actually lost money! The management group said they were down $300, even with the late-season influx of $150 from rabid boosters. In an odd twist, the *Daily Times and Expositor* said the Demons' prospects for the 1896 season looked good, largely due in part to the Lawrence Park improvements. However, it quickly noted, "the same management, however, will not undertake the administration of a second season."[65]

On the other side of the ledger, Hoch told the paper that the Page Fence Giants were a profitable endeavor and would be on the road again in 1896. However, the profit margin was thin, and he claimed that if the weather turned for the worse next week, the Giants would financially close the season about even. To add to the stakes in the Demons-Giants series, the winning team would share a special bonus pot of $25. In addition, category bonuses were dangled before the players. A single dollar would be split among those turning a double play; two dollars for a "clean home run hit"; five dollars for the most base hits over the course of the series; and five dollars to the pitcher who gave up the fewest hits per game.[66]

As the Giants wound down their season, they continued posting a string of wins, sprinkled among a rare loss. A Sunday game in Defiance, Ohio, was one of those rare losses, 6–2 to the Greys. On Monday, the Giants showed up in Romeo, Michigan, a small village outside of Detroit. Apparently, after they quickly sized up the opponents, the Giants premiered a new pitcher in the box, William Wendell Gaskin. The wonderfully talented team cook tossed a five-hitter as the Giants rolled, 18–3. This was not the first time the train staff was thrown into a game. Recently, "the porter [Albert C. Carter] … went into the box the other day," which most likely would have been in one of the blowout wins against Mason, Fowlerville or Ovid.[67]

On Tuesday, September 24, the Giants rolled over Pontiac for the second time in a month. This match-up featured the same fire-balling Henley who had battled them in late August, even though the Giants won that contest, 11–0. This time around, the Giants battered Henley and two other pitchers to post another lopsided win. No one was really sure of the final score, though one Adrian paper said it was 25–8. The confusion was due to the scoreboard operator stopping after the fifth inning, when the Giants scored 15 runs. The *Pontiac Daily Gazette* claimed the final score was 24–8 with the game called after seven innings. There was no special Giants pitching experiment that day, as Miller started and was relieved by Malone. The *Gazette* properly summed up the afternoon affair: "Yes, it was quite a circus, but it would have been more interesting if there had been two teams playing, instead of one."[68]

The Giants' victory was a warm-up for the first game in the year-end series with the Demons. There had been a rumor that George Wilson would not be available for the Demons, as he was going to play in an exhibition game in Kalamazoo. This would not be just any game, but for the Kalamazoo Celery Eaters against the major league Cleveland Spiders, led by star pitcher Cy Young. Of course, Kalamazoo was the same town that protested Wilson and Graham's presence on the Demons' roster, but apparently the color line was forgotten when you needed an ace pitcher. One paper called Wilson's planned appearance "a momentous occasion for the young man," but it never happened. The one-day-long rumor was quashed, and Wilson was not summoned to Kalamazoo for some unexplained reason.[69] Instead, the Demons' Jess Derrick, along with youngster Colbert Van Giesen, faced the Spiders and won. When Kalamazoo rallied in the seventh inning to take the lead, the Cleveland major leaguers asked for their pay, took the cash and promptly left the field.[70]

The Demons warmed up for the opening game with Adrian by crushing the Jackson team 12–4 on the same day the Giants were bashing Romeo. The game was played in Findlay, Ohio, where the bulk of the Jackson team hailed from, as a sort of home game away from home. The victory proved to some that Adrian would and could beat the Jaxons anywhere but in Jackson.[71]

The Demons-Giants opening game on Wednesday, September 25, in Montpelier, Ohio, was a stroke of good luck for the Adrian management's bottom line, and they scheduled a second one there that week. The first game featured the Demons' battery of William Carrick and Bill Binga, with Billy Holland and George Taylor for the Giants. The teams played a close game, as each club recorded six hits and two errors, in a 6–4 Page Fence victory.[72]

The competitive nature of the first game drew 4,000 spectators to the following Thursday morning contest in Montpelier. Tim Nevins battled Joe Miller in a high-scoring affair, and the Giants won again, 11–10. Two Demons errors allowed key runs to score at a crucial moment in the game. The Demons did have the best batter on the day as Billy Smith, normally known for his swift legs, slugged a pair of two-run homers off Cyclone Miller. In order to eliminate any potential problems with the umpire, Giants advance agent James Stevens was behind the plate, calling the balls and strikes.[73]

The popularity of the two teams allowed Hoch, Parsons and Taylor to schedule additional contests above what was supposed to be a five-game series. On Friday, the two squads were in the regularly scheduled stop in Hillsdale, and the Page Fence Giants were again victorious. They won, 11–3, as Malone outdueled Wilson. That evening, the Page Fence train car left Hillsdale and chugged 15 miles west to Quincy, Michigan, where the clubs would play on Saturday. While the players' car was being switched in the Quincy train yard, it was bumped by a train pulling a load of coal and was "badly damaged." The Page Fence home on wheels was immediately shipped to the Lake Shore and Michigan Southern train yard in Adrian, where it was repaired on Sunday. However, speculation was that the custom car would not be needed for the rest of the season, as the remaining games were in Adrian plus three the following week in Detroit against the Western League's Tigers.[74]

Adrian brought in a new pitcher for the Saturday game in Quincy named Van Giesen (either Colbert, who had just faced the Cleveland Spiders in Kalamazoo, or Fred, whom the Demons released during the pre-season). Aiding the new hurler was Vasco Graham, whose hand had finally healed, behind the plate for the Demons. The new pitcher was enough to defeat Billy Holland and the Giants, 8–3. Adrian's team was especially sparkling in the field and committed no errors, as was the Giants' Holland, who made three "one-handed stops" on shots back through the box and converted them to outs.[75]

More games meant more money, and after a Sunday off-day the two Adrian clubs began another week of games. On Monday, the location is unclear, as one Adrian paper said it was to be in Fremont, Ohio, and another said Fremont, Indiana. One score later noted the game as a 12–10 Demons victory, but played in Angola, Indiana. The next day in Hudson, Indiana, the Demons won their second game in a row, 15–13.[76]

Between the first and second series with the Giants, the Demons arranged for a single game with the Lansing Senators. To help aid the Demons, Billy Holland, James Patterson and Grant Johnson were added to their roster. Johnson replaced the Demons' regular short-stop, Maurice Justice, who had been injured the day before while attempting to field a ball off the bat of Fred Van Dyke.[77] The substitution worked as Nevins pitched the Demons to a 12–8 victory and newcomer Patterson drilled a home run.[78] The Lansing team then was paid, in full, for their season and disbanded that Wednesday evening. Senators manager Parshall was unable to sell the team and complained that this baseball venture had cost him $1,000. No word on what business partner Bud Fowler felt about his future partner's financial straits.[79]

On Thursday, the final game between the Demons and Giants was witnessed by a relatively small crowd. About 300 souls showed up at Lawrence Park for the game, which began at 2:30 under bright Lenawee County skies. The Giants won a 13–4 "sloppy game," but the real focus was on the special prize pool of money which had been set aside. The Page Fence Giants had won the series, four games to three, which meant a $25 bonus for the men. Apparently, the bonus money for the fewest hits allowed by a pitcher wouldn't be awarded to the young lefty, Wilson. One newspaper stated that this pitching statistic seemed to be the focus of the final game, when the outcome was all but settled. Wilson gave up 11 safeties in the contest and lost, while Miller let only six hits come off the Demons' bats and apparently snagged the bonus for fewest hits allowed in the series. The cash for turning double plays had the Giants' Grant Johnson, Sol White and George Taylor turn two for two dollars each, while Adrian's Ed Mulhearn and Paul Kraft turned one and earned a buck. No one received the home run bonus money, but Johnson and Mulhearn each legged out a triple in the series. The Giants' Billy Holland's work on the field and as a coacher was also singled out for good work, but no bonus cash accompanied that role.[80]

With the series outcome settled, the game became a bit loose. Local resident Al Miller took the field for the Demons, as did regular Giants catcher Pete Burns, who played right field. The substitute Adrian shortstop was outfielder Billy Smith, who did his best, they said, as Maurice Justice was still too hurt to play but did hobble around as the umpire. When James Patterson was knocked out of the game due to being hit in the shoulder by Wilson's pitch, the Giants' mascot was inserted into the lineup. In a rare mention of the Giants' mascot, "Whang" Green was the "colored urchin who travels with the club," and he had himself a day. Green played an inning or two in right field and then got to bat against the Palmyra Wonder. Wilson played the part of a good sport, even in the losing cause, and "lobbed" his pitches to Green. The youngster managed to get a base hit off Wilson, advanced to second on a passed ball and eventually advanced to third base, somehow, complete with a fancy slide. To top off Green's day, when Wilson threw wildly to first on a ball hit back to the mound, the youngster crossed home plate for a run and amused the audience with his trip around the diamond.[81]

Someone had the idea to schedule another game between the two Adrian clubs. The final game of the year for the Adrian Demons was an exhibition against the Giants as part of Ladies Day at Lawrence Park. The discounted female grandstand seats did not exactly entice fans to the contest, as only a small crowd gathered. The *Daily Times and Expositor* drolly announced that the game "was about as enlivening as a funeral," as the Giants won, 18–12. The Demons were greatly shorthanded due to injuries which had moved players out of their regular positions. Mulhearn just missed a grand slam when he hit a bases-clearing triple to center field off Malone, and two more runs scored when Holland dropped the Demons' first sacker's fly ball in left field later in the game. However, those were about all the Demons' highlights, and the game was called after seven innings. Miller was the Giants' winning pitcher, and Wilson, who was in the box on Thursday, also lost this Saturday contest.[82]

However, Wilson's Saturday game highlight was not his pitching for the much-ailing Demons. During the game, a group of Adrian businessmen, headed by L. A. Browne, his manager on last years' Light Guard team, presented the young man with a gold watch. Browne was credited with finding "the Palmyra Wonder" and had contacted baseball cranks for donations. Over 20 individuals and businesses responded to the plea to thank the young pitcher for being the best pitcher in the MSL and possibly in the state. Browne gave money to the fund, as did the team management of Len Hoch and Rolla and Howard Taylor, along with loyal fans such as Seymour Howell, William Sheldon, John E. Bird, James Gough and the firm of Shepherd and McCracken. The gold piece was so popular that Wilson loaned it out for a few days to be displayed in the window of Sheldon's jewelry store in downtown Adrian.[83]

The Giants also spent some time Saturday evening at Barnum's photography studio in Adrian. The photographers took both team and individual player shots. The pictures would be used in next year's promotional flyers around the country.[84] The brothers' picture business must have been the unofficial Adrian baseball photographers, as they had snapped the previous year's Light Guard squad, too.[85]

A few days later, league president Mumby released the Adrian Demons' official statistics for all players who appeared in at least ten games. Unfortunately, that requirement left the Page Fence Giants who subbed throughout the year—Fowler, Burns, Binga and Miller—unrecorded, at least in the printed records in the *Adrian Evening Telegram*. However, the famed black battery easily exceeded the minimum game limit and posted very strong totals. Graham's batting average in 71 games was .309 (94-for-304), with two homers, two triples, 16 doubles and 70 runs scored. His fielding percentage as the team's regular catcher was .951, third on the team. Wilson hit .333 (67-for-201) in 50 appearances, with one home run, two triples and 11 doubles. His .960 fielding percentage was second on the team. By comparison, 12 of the 16 men hit above .300, with Robinson's .451 in 24 games leading the way. Future great Honus Wagner, in his short stint of 16 games, batted .385 for the Demons, second-best on the team.[86]

While bonus money, a gold watch and photos are nice, another reward was on the

The Burnham Brothers Photography Studio, which became the company of choice for the official Page Fence Giants team and individual player photographs. It is pictured on the upper right of this postcard from 1907, along Adrian's West Maumee Street (author's collection).

horizon. Thanks to their outstanding winning record, Adrian's baseball management thought it would be a good idea to end the season by challenging the Detroit Tigers of the Class A Western League. Not only that, but with the major league season about over, some of the top players would be added to the Tigers' regular roster. The Detroit league team was probably concerned as they had finished the season in fifth place and failed to reach the .500 mark. Earlier in the year, the Giants had struggled with their new lineup against some of the Western League teams, but they had improved over the course of the 1895 season. Three of the game's biggest stars were among those slated to appear against the Page Fence Giants. Two future Hall of Famers—Kid Nichols of Boston, who racked up 26 wins in 1895, and Sam Thompson of the Philadelphia Phillies, who had led the majors in home runs and RBI—along with Albion, Michigan, resident and Washington Senators catcher Jim "Deacon" McGuire, were to be in the Tigers' line-up. McGuire's teammate and infielder, Detroit-born Frank Scheibeck, was to join fellow natives Ed Stein, a pitcher for the Brooklyn Grooms, and minor league infielder Ed Egan, on the Tigers' roster. The plan was for the Giants to go to Detroit for three straight day games, beginning on Tuesday, October 8, and then the Tigers, with their added stars, would play a pair of contests at Lawrence Park.[87]

To tune up for these high-stakes game, the Giants hit the road. The black gentlemen thumped Defiance, Ohio, 24–7, on Sunday and then swept a Monday doubleheader against the highly regarded Chicago Unions in Albion, Indiana. The doubleheader was publicized for many miles, and schools and businesses closed for the event. The Unions, who apparently claimed to be the Western black ball champions, were no match for the Giants, as the

Adrian club rolled to 26–7 and 24–6 victories, according to the *Evening Telegram*.[88] The *Daily Times and Expositor* printed the final scores as 20–11 and 21–6 and placed the games in La Porte, Indiana. In the second game, the Giants slugged five home runs, all of which cleared far-away outfield fences. The popularity of the two teams was evident, as over 4,000 people watched the twin bill, a figure about which both Adrian papers agreed. Following the two-game sweep, the Albion ball cranks wanted to bring in a National League squad to town to face the Giants next year.[89]

Excitement for the Detroit contests was high, and the Lake Shore and Michigan Southern railroad cut its fare in half to one dollar for a round trip, providing they could convince at least 50 Adrian people to purchase tickets. The well-respected James Grogan would work the games, a rare umpire who never was embroiled in any controversy with the Giants. The opening game would feature Kid Nichols versus George Wilson, who had just posted a 29–4 record with the Demons.[90]

While the Giants were playing on the road earlier in the week, the three Detroit games became shrouded in doubt. The Detroiters tried to cancel the series, which was also a benefit game for their players. There seemed to be difficulty in securing a city ball diamond this late in the year. Adrian native and now Detroit businessman John F. Navin stepped in and solved the issue. He notified Len Hoch in a Monday telegram: "Just completed arrangements. Everything is O.K. Nichols of Boston will pitch one game. Come on boys."[91]

The Lake Shore and Michigan Southern Railroad was also scurrying around to clarify their special Adrian to Detroit fee structure. They increased their required passenger count from the original 50 customers to 100, before they would implement their half-off charge. Otherwise, a more expensive ticket would take you to Detroit Tuesday morning, and you could return home on the first Wednesday morning train.[92] The target number was achieved and then some, as 153 people boarded the Lake Shore in Adrian Tuesday morning and chugged east to Detroit.[93]

Detroit and Adrian papers published the lineups in their Tuesday editions. The Giants' battery of Wilson and Vasco Graham would face major league stars Nichols and McGuire. The other previously named major league stars would start, and a few highly skilled amateurs would be sprinkled among the Tigers' professionals. The *Detroit Free Press* informed their readers that the Page Fence Giants were "better known throughout the state and western country" than they were locally. They paper added the team played "fast, daring" ball and were the best black team since the old Cuban Giants.[94]

The anticipated Tuesday match-up would have to wait. The weather was too cold for the players and only a few people, by Detroit standards, made it to the diamond. The *Free Press* declared, "it would have been uncomfortable for spectators and unsafe for players," and the game was postponed. It was cold, as snowflakes were seen in nearby Pontiac and at the horse track in Ypsilanti, west of Detroit. The daytime high reached only 43 degrees and was buffeted with a light, wintery breeze out of the northwest. The Adrian fans were given rain checks for one of the later games in the series. Promoting the series, the *Free Press* again printed the projected lineups and said the game would begin at 3 o'clock Wednesday afternoon on the Western League grounds.[95]

The game began the next day as scheduled, but not with the all-star lineup. None of the professional major league players appeared, blaming the cold weather that afternoon. The conditions were almost a repeat from the day before, as temperatures hovered around 40 degrees. The wind had shifted to the west and died down a bit, but it was still not a good day for baseball. The Detroiters were left scrambling for players and had to grab some from the amateur ranks to fill their squad. It did not matter. Joe Miller retired the first three batters, and then the Giants batted. Leadoff hitter and first baseman George Taylor smashed a line shot over the left field fence off Barrett, and the rout was on. According to the *Free Press*, the Giants tallied 16 runs to just two for the team dubbed the "Picked Nine." The *Daily Times and Expositor* and the *Evening Telegram* printed the score as 18–3. All three papers agreed that the game lasted just seven innings. Joe Miller scattered six hits, walked three and struck out seven. However, the *Times and Expositor* stated that George Taylor pitched the game. Every Giant apart from Grant Johnson had base hits, with Holland also slugging a home run. The small crowd, estimated to be only about 150 fans, was said to have a good time, aided by the Giants' "chipper" mood. Additional pre-game entertainment came in the form of Len Hoch pitching batting practice, until he tried to catch a hot one back through the box, badly bruising his hand and ending that experiment. Detroit's old catching star, who had made his major league debut in 1878, Charlie Bennett, sat through the cold weather to view the game. Adrian baseball cranks who made the trip included furniture magnate A. E. Palmer, local *Evening Telegram* reporter B. J. Kingston, Father Ternes of the Roman Catholic Church, John Navin and Demons pitcher Tim Nevins.[96]

The Thursday game was even worse for the Detroiters. The Giants threw their ace, George Wilson, who tossed a three-hit shutout and won, 15–0. The Giants slugged out 16 hits and were nearly flawless in the field. Another small crowd showed up at Detroit's league park to witness what was supposed to be an all-star contest. Reportedly, five major leaguers took the field for Detroit, but the *Free Press* never printed any game account. The stories in Adrian's daily newspapers were devoid of most game details.[97]

A steady rain and cold weather on Friday morning in Adrian caused local management to telegram Detroit and inform them that the two games there could or would not be played.[98] "The season of the colored club is therefore ended. The management has not yet decided whether it will continue the enterprise next season." The second sentence was an odd thing to print, since it had been announced earlier that both Wilson and Graham were to be assigned to the Giants for the entire 1896 season. The Adrian management group had also said that the Page Fence club had made money, and it was printed, more than once, that the Giants would be back on the field next season.[99]

With the weekend cancellation of the two games with Detroit, the Giants disbanded, and the players could head home for the winter months. However, four of the players—Miller, Holland, Burns and

Dewise (Deweeze) Barrett Wilson was apparently a close friend of Gus Brooks, as he served as one of the pallbearers at the graveside service at Oakwood Cemetery. Wilson later, with William Wendall Gaskin, published the *Adrian African American Journal* (courtesy Lenawee County Historical Museum).

Van Dyke—hopped a train to Chicago, where they planned to join the Unions for a game on Saturday.[100] Following the Unions game, Miller would travel west to Denver, Colorado, Holland to Aurora, Illinois, Burns south to his home in New Orleans, and Van Dyke to western Michigan and the tiny hamlet of Vandalia. Malone left Adrian and went directly to Detroit, while Johnson went to Fremont, Ohio, Sol White to Bellaire, Ohio, James Patterson (wrongly named as George in the *Evening Telegram*) to Starkville, Mississippi, and George Taylor to join Miller in Denver. Bill Binga, who had bounced around between Pontiac and Lansing during the 1895 season, before playing with both the Giants and Demons, remained in Adrian for the time being, as did Vasco Graham. The Palmyra Wonder, George Wilson, went a short distance down the road to his Lenawee County village for the winter.[101] The *Evening Telegram* was giddy over the ball team and their players. "They constitute a gentlemanly club of colored men, who have conducted themselves in order in their tour over the country, and have given Adrian a good advertisement wherever they have gone. They will be heartily welcomed next year when the season opens again."[102]

The Giants' record printed in the October 18 *Evening Telegram* has often been massaged over the years. The monthly win and loss breakdown was April 5–13, May 16–5, June 18–5, July 22–4, August 23–5, September 26–3, October 8–1, with two ties for a record of 118–36–2 in 156 games. However, a few years later James Stevens reported the 1895 record as 152 games played and a record of 121–31, which was four fewer games, but three additional wins from what was originally reported. Where did the four games and two ties go?[103]

The Giants played games in Illinois, Indiana, Iowa, Michigan, Minnesota, Ohio and Wisconsin, and in 112 cities, towns, villages and hamlets. Gus Parsons' year-end report noted that the bulk of their losses came in April, when the original roster was not strong enough to challenge the higher level professional clubs. Parsons wondered how the Giants would have fared with a stronger early lineup and pointed to their success at the end of the season with Detroit's club.[104]

All of the Giants' success motivated the team cook and one-day substitute hurler, William Wendell Gaskin. Within a week after the players had scattered, Gaskin tackled a new and quite lofty project. He was going to create an "Afro-American journal, directory and biographical sketch book."

Gaskin's goal was to capitalize on the Page Fence Giants' spirit and highlight Adrian's black residents in the same manner. His focus was on local black people who were known for their "character and integrity," and who held "responsible and honorable positions." The idea was to print between 3,500 and 5,000 copies and distribute them throughout the area. Early feedback was that Adrian's business community

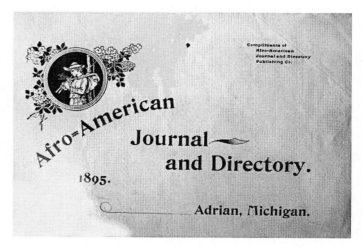

The cover of Gaskin's and Wilson's *African-American Journal*, distributed, free of charge, to the black residents of Adrian in 1895 (courtesy Lenawee County Historical Museum).

was receptive to his idea, and the directory was meeting "with very good success." However, later Gaskin was quoted as saying the project was completed "under discouraging conditions."[105]

Gaskin shouldn't have been so discouraged. The *Daily Times and Expositor* called it "a very creditable production" when they received their copy in mid–November.[106] The paper noted the fine work of Gaskin and D. Barrett Wilson in creating such a work. In 1895, Adrian's total black population was 500 people, and they paid property taxes on $84,000 worth of land.[107]

Both the Page Fence Giants and the Afro-American Directory had been unique projects for this southern Michigan community. Whether the two enterprising men would produce another booklet was unknown at the time. What was known was that baseball fever would return in 1896, and Adrian had to decide how it would treat its sports affliction.

◆ 13 ◆

The Second Season

When the 1895 season ended, Len Hoch and Rolla Taylor were not going to reconstitute the Adrian Demons, and the Page Fence Giants' status was a somewhere between a yes and a maybe. However, as the calendar turned to 1896, the city again looked to possibly field two baseball teams for the upcoming season.

By mid–January, plans were afoot to join a new minor league configuration. Adrian's baseball men—Hoch, Taylor and James Stevens—were right in the middle of the mix again this year. Plans were in the works for a much larger minor league that might include travel outside of Michigan. Kalamazoo, Port Huron, Jackson and Adrian would be the potential Michigan entries, while cities in Ohio and Indiana might support teams. Discussion also centered on what to do about the baseball sin of playing on the Sabbath, which was banned in some places, and how that would impact the league's finances.[1]

At a contentious meeting in late January, held in Detroit, Jackson's Leigh Lynch, still miffed at the Demons' 1895 MSL title, ignored the Adrian contingent. Lynch attempted to steer the meeting away from locating teams in smaller communities such as Owosso and Adrian. He also supported more expensive salary caps which would play into his idea to secure much larger towns out of state for this new league. Lynch also threw out the race card and proposed that "no coons" be allowed in this new league, an obvious dig at Adrian and their famed battery of Wilson and Graham, among others. Hoch, Rolla Taylor and Stevens were bothered by the entire Lynch affair. Taylor announced that Adrian would not join this proposed league.[2]

When a subsequent meeting in Detroit was held in early February, the Adrian men were noticeably absent. Word leaked back to Lenawee County that Lynch had taken Jackson's entry and left for greener and much larger pastures. President Mumby contacted Rolla Taylor and begged Adrian to send someone to discuss the 1896 MSL proposal. Both Taylor and Hoch jumped on an afternoon, eastbound train and headed to a subsequent meeting in Detroit. When they arrived, they discovered the Jackson rumor to be wrong, and they were still in the league mix. The trio left the meeting without submitting an entry for Adrian. They also figured the yearly expenses to be $3,228, and they would need sponsorship of between $800 and $1,000 just to begin the season.[3]

Jackson and Lynch pushed for an increase in the monthly salary limit to $600, a league forfeiture penalty of $300 (an increase from $100), and a guaranteed visiting gate boost from $25 to $35 per game. These were steep increases and much too rich for Adrian. Hoch said as much but also left the door open when he addressed the league owners prior to Lynch making his appearance. The Adrian postmaster believed "Jackson holds the key to the league" and felt that without that town, the league would fail. He also described the ill will between Adrian and Jackson over baseball, but still knew Lynch's entry was vital to the league making money. Jackson representatives got wind of Hoch's statement and were very happy. A Jackson paper noted that the Jackson delegation felt "doubly pleased" by Hoch's statements.[4]

Even though Adrian had not submitted an entry and had earlier said no officially, the baseball fever was still gripping Adrian. At the Hotel Emery, local banker W. H. Waldby and the usual cranks, Len Hoch and Seymour Howell, were named to the proposed team's board of directors. Everyone seemed to agree that the Demons were a great boon for the town last season, attracted visitors and gave people something to do in the "dull season." They decided to raise money to support a team in 1896.[5]

About a month after the latest baseball fever hit, the Adrian boosters claimed to have raised $765 of the needed $1,000 for the upcoming season.[6] The team's entry fee, which was $250 for what would be a Class C minor league in 1895, would jump to $300 for a Class B designation in 1896.[7] Developing rosters was still well over a month down the road. Local boosters thought that only two players from last year's Demons roster—Herbert Lentz and Elmer Smith—could be resigned. Honus Wagner, Maurice Justice, Ben Ireland and Billy Smith had already signed contracts elsewhere for the new season.[8] There was no discussion, at least in public that was recorded, as to using black players on this new team.

Hoch traveled to Muskegon for a baseball league meeting in mid–March.[9] It seemed the Adrian prospects weren't so bleak, and he believed an eight-team Interstate League, with the much larger Toledo and Fort Wayne communities battling Adrian, Jackson, Kalamazoo, Lansing, Muskegon and Saginaw, would be adopted.[10] That plan initially seemed promising until Gus Parsons traveled to Lansing to discuss the Fort Wayne and Toledo entries.[11] Within a day, Jackson's Lynch seized control and negotiated the formation of a new league, of which he was to be the President. The salary level was dramatically increased to $1,000 a month, which forced Lansing and Kalamazoo to leave the league. Lynch had replacement entries from Terre Haute and Port Huron, which would significantly boost travel costs. Adrian wanted to remain in the league, but the travel expenditure gave them cause for concern. Former league president Walter L. Mumby summoned Len Hoch, and the pair met in Detroit to discuss Lynch's latest actions.[12]

While all this Michigan State League negotiating was easy for the public to follow in the paper, the financially successful Page Fence Giants were basically ignored. The good news was that the team, without much about it in the local papers, was also approved for a second season. In late February, the new Page Fence Giants' uniforms were proudly displayed in the Taylor Brothers Hardware store. They were different outfits from the previous year, which had been black jerseys with maroon lettering and tan socks and caps. The prestigious Albert G. Spalding Company in Chicago had made the 1896 version of black and maroon-striped uniforms emblazoned with gold letters that read "Page Fence Giants" across the chest. The Giants' heads would be adorned with black caps, with their legs covered with maroon stockings. Club management declared the design to be the "best make" and of the "finest quality," which "make a neat and striking appearance."[13] Their fancy Monarch train car was being refurbished at the Lake Shore rail yard in town and would leave for the start of the exhibition season on March 30, bound for Peoria, Illinois.[14]

The Monarch Cycle Company was again the manufacturer for the bikes the Giants would ride in the pregame parade. Local merchant William Sheldon would furnish 11 shiny new bikes for the 1896 season.[15] The Monarch firm had cross-promoted with baseball in the major leagues in 1895 and awarded their best-selling bike model to Bill Lange, star outfielder for the Chicago Colts. Ballots were attached to Chicago baseball scorecards, and Lange garnered over 26,000 fan votes as the team's most popular player. The dashing Lange easily beat teammates Walt Wilmot, George Decker and even old Cap Anson.[16] Much like the Page Fence Woven Wire Company, the cycle company enjoyed creative advertisement. *The Sporting News* featured a wood cut of bike champion Tom Cooper wearing a fancy Monarch Bicycles shirt, complete with its lion's-head logo. The company's slogan was simple: Cooper "Rides a Monarch and Keeps in Front."[17]

The Giants' 1896 roster was much the same as the team that ended 1895. Grant "Home Run" Johnson was back as the star shortstop and team captain. Vasco Graham was the starting catcher, with Bill Binga and Pete Burns described as change catchers. The infield was nearly the same as last season, with George Taylor at first base, Johnson at short and James Patterson at third base. Charles Grant, the "new man from Cincinnati," would play second base. The pitching staff consisted of right-handed Joe Miller and lefties Billy Holland and George Wilson. This lineup would put the roster at 11 men to start the season. The mysterious George Patterson, listed in one news account in late 1895, does indeed appear to be James W. Patterson. The *Daily Times and Expositor* and the *Evening Telegram* both mentioned Charles Grant as the only new man on the team. That means Patterson played last year for the team. If James Patterson were new, that would make two new players, and if he had indeed replaced a George Patterson, the papers would have brought that name coincidence to their reader's attention. They didn't. James Patterson also indicated in later years that he had joined the Giants in 1895 and played with them in 1896. So George Patterson's tenure as a member of the Page Fence Giants is incorrect. Some of the

A promotional calendar for the Page Fence Woven Wire Company which featured the Giants. This photograph was probably snapped during the 1896 season at Burnham Brothers studio on West Maumee Street in downtown Adrian. The inclusion of Charlie Grant (1896–1898) and the appearance of Fred Van Dyke (1895–1896) place this portrait as from the 1896 season (author's collection).

familiar names from 1895, such as Bud Fowler, Jim Chavous, Fred Van Dyke and William Malone, were not listed in the opening season previews.[18]

Two people who spent a lot of time together on the train car would be returning. Gus Parsons was back as the Giants' business manager and busy booking games across the country. The first six weeks of the season, to mid–May, were already scheduled before the train car even pulled out of Adrian.[19] The other important cog was William Wendell Gaskin. Fresh off writing, editing, printing and distributing the "Afro American" directory in Adrian, he would again be the team cook. Gaskin was a busy man who had split his time over the past few years between living in Adrian and Jackson. He had also used his legendary fine handwriting skills to secure a job, which already awaited him at the close of this season. Gaskin entered a national penmanship contest sponsored by Payne's Industrial College in Lebanon, Missouri. He defeated 11 other contestants, and his entry was described as "a rare specimen of penmanship." As the winner, Gaskin secured a position as a teacher at Payne's, which would begin in November.[20] Albert C. Carter, the second Giants personal staff member from 1895, did not rejoin for year two. He was replaced by an Adrian native, Robert Henry, whose step-sister, Lida Pate, was an award-winning English student and recent graduate of the high school.[21]

As had been the case in the inaugural season, the palatial train car was previewed with more detail in the papers than any of the Page Fence players. The car was the same one as last year but with added improvements, all completed at the Lake Shore Railway Company.[22]

> It has been entirely refurbished, the color being a rich dark brown. On the upper crown board are painted in gilt letters, the words, "Page Fence Giants Base Ball Club, Adrian, Mich." A new Brussels carpet now covers the floor, while new Monarch car curtains adorn the windows. It is also fitted up with richly upholstered revolving chairs, and all in all, it is one of the most convenient and roomy cars on the road.[23]

If fans wanted to see the latest version of the Giants, they needed to get to the Lake Shore depot on the east side of town in late March. With the establishment of a minor league team in town still up in the air, the Page Fence Giants' schedule still consisted of mostly away games. They would be hard-pressed to return to town, especially if a minor league team did not materialize and the Lawrence Park field sat unused and untended. Team management was pretty sure they could get the Giants back in time for a game in late May as part of Adrian's Decoration Day festivities. They just had to find an opponent. As they had done in 1895, the bulk of the Giants' first month would be games against Western League and Western Association minor league clubs, with the opener set for Saturday, April 4, in Peoria, Illinois.[24]

On Monday, March 30, the newly gussied-up, dark brown Page Fence Giants train car hooked itself to the Lake Shore and Michigan Southern run out of Adrian and headed toward Chicago. Once arriving in the Windy City, they would be hooked to a Chicago and Rock Island train and pulled south to the middle of the state. After a few days of practice, they would play two games with Peoria and then head to Indianapolis and Terre Haute, Indiana, Grand Rapids, Michigan, Milwaukee, Wisconsin, and then St. Paul and Minneapolis, Minnesota.[25] The first season only Gus Parsons, W. W. Gaskin, Albert Carter and William Malone were on the initial ride out of Adrian. News reports did not indicate who made the trek out of Adrian this time, as some players were again going to meet the team at the spring training location. One to travel on his own was captain Grant Johnson, as he left

Findlay, Ohio, and stopped off in Lima on his way to Illinois to be the "guest" of Miss Capitola Gant. His very presence in Lima was reprinted in one Ohio newspaper, the *Daily Herald* of Delphos, which like Adrian was baseball crazy.[26]

On the day the Giants opened their 1896 season in Illinois, advance man James Stevens, back for a second year, hopped on a train. Stevens headed to Minneapolis with "a trunk full of printed matter" (presumably with some of the Page Fence Giant calendars) as he looked for potential cities and dates for the Giants. The *Evening Telegram* bragged about the team and the entire organization in its April 4, 1896, edition. "The Giants are gradually getting in line with the best teams of the country, and are developing step by step to be a first-class business institution."[27]

The Giants were slated to open their 1896 season, after a few days of practice, against the Peoria Distillers. This version of the Page Fence Giants was much more prepared for the minor leaguers the second time around. They had learned that weak links on the diamond or at the plate would be costlier against the professionals than against some group of highly skilled amateurs.

The Distillers were managed by 31-year-old Peoria native Dan Dugdale, a ballplayer with ten years of experience that included two seasons in the majors, most recently with the Washington Senators.[28] The Giants dropped an 8–6 decision with lefty Billy Holland, the excellent coacher, taking the loss, when he blew the lead by issuing eight walks in the eighth inning. A large Saturday crowd witnessed the game, which was the season opener for both squads. Adrian papers offered few details, but George Wilson started the game and was followed by Joe Miller and then Holland. Grant Johnson was the hitting star and lived up to his nickname, as he slugged a home run to go with a triple and a single.[29]

The second game, a Sunday affair against Peoria, went much better as the Giants rolled to either an 11–4 or 13–4 victory. The Western Association Distillers, a Class B minor league team, was held to just six hits through a combined pitching performance by Miller and Wilson. Peoria's Jimmy Burke, who reached the majors in 1898 for his first season of a seven-year career, played shortstop for the Distillers and was held hitless. *The Sporting News* simply noted in its box score, "The Page Fence Giants gave Peoria a bad beating."[30]

The Giants left central Illinois and headed east to step up in play against the Indianapolis club of the Class A Western League. The *Indianapolis News* touted the contest, and an advertisement noted that general admission tickets were 25 cents, with grandstand seating 50 cents. The game would begin at 3 o'clock that Monday afternoon, April 6.[31]

The exhibition tilt saw the Hoosiers throw two pitchers early in the game, neither of whom would make the club that season. A man named Weimer (possibly lefty Jack Weimer, a three-time 20-game winner in the major leagues with the Reds and the Cubs) and Kid Monroe, a minor league veteran of nearly a decade, held the Giants scoreless during their pitching stints. It wasn't until midway in the contest, when manager Bill Watkins inserted Bill Dammann, that the Giants tallied their only three runs of the game in a lopsided 16–3 blowout loss. After 1896, Dammann would play the next three years for the Cincinnati Reds and post winning records in each season.[32] The *Indianapolis News* of April 7 was not kind to the Giants' ballplaying skill, declaring "the colored lads gave an exhibition of how base-ball should not be played." That same paper did single out Johnson at shortstop and Vasco Graham behind the plate as demonstrating "good ball."[33] George Wilson was not effective against George Hogriever, last year's nemesis while coaching third base in the Cincinnati Reds exhibition, who drilled two round-trippers. "John "Jack" McCarthy, already a two-year major league veteran with the Reds, was also strong at the plate for the Hoosiers.

Manager Watkins called the game after eight innings, much to the relief of the 200 spectators who witnessed the "farce."[34]

The Giants boarded the Monarch train car and zipped to southwestern Indiana for a three-game series against the Terre Haute nine. The first game went to the visitors on a close 4–3 score. The Wednesday and Thursday games were scheduled, but scores were not sent back to Adrian.[35]

The information blackout came from the fact that both Hoch and Taylor were busy trying to salvage the Interstate League. Even though in October of 1895 the former Adrian mayor declared that he and Taylor were not interested in running year two of a minor league club, they spent four months in trying to create one. Hoch was so focused on making this work that he temporarily held the franchises for both the proposed Adrian and Saginaw clubs. His plan was to visit Saginaw and find someone there who could run the team. The latest Interstate League proposal included Saginaw, Jackson, Fort Wayne, Toledo, Adrian and maybe a Lansing entry, with a hefty $800 salary limit.[36] All this wheeling and dealing took place during April when the Giants were playing their early-season schedule. As a result, game details were not sent back to Adrian for printing in either of the daily newspapers.

By the fourth week of April, the *Daily Times and Expositor* screamed "Final Failure" and declared the 1896 Interstate League dead.[37] The constant threat of low gate receipts was always the top concern. Toledo, with a history of playing much larger cities, was worried about drawing fans in places such as Adrian and Lansing. Michigan's capital city's bid was stymied when city leaders would not rent out last year's park for a ball diamond.[38] Hoch, along with President Mumby, eventually pulled the plug on the Interstate League, and the towns were left scrambling for summer baseball plans. The *Daily Times and Expositor* said that while Mumby worked hard, no one worked harder to get the Interstate League off the ground than Len Hoch and Rolla Taylor, as one or both had attended every organizational meeting over the past few months.[39]

In an interesting plug for baseball in Adrian in 1896, the *Daily Times and Expositor* offered this bit of advice: "after the delightful experience of last year, if you want baseball, go support the Adrian College team." There was no mention of the Page Fence stars in that bit of advice, and the paper reported only a few of the Giants' scores in the entire month of April.[40]

Hoch and Taylor were not the only Adrian baseball men to struggle to field a team in 1896. Bud Fowler, whose long-publicized but never materialized, Lansing-based Capital Colored All-Americans never left port for Australia, New Zealand or Europe, said he was looking for a team, too. Fowler was living in Muncie, Indiana, and managing the Colored Creole Giants, previously known as the Rock City club from Nashville, Tennessee. A Muncie business magnate decided to go into the baseball business, hired Fowler, and wanted both to emulate the Adrian club and to play the Page Fence Giants sometime in 1896.[41] Fowler's team included Harry Hyde, Bill Stewart, W. Marshall Coffee, Jaspar Dunstan, Billy Daily, Harry Saitbaw, Moses Cain, Will Jackson, Kid Ware, and two men named Hucknow and Demoss. Coffee would play second base and act as captain, while Fowler would play right field and manage the team. One interesting fact is that each of Fowler's new players was an accomplished musician. Word was that they had games already booked throughout the East and West and in parts of Canada. If there was any doubt about who was the best black ball club, *The Sporting News* headline said it all: "Colored Championship; Fowler's Team Will Strive to Wrest It from the Page Fence Giants."[42]

The Giants played at least one of their three games in Terre Haute and then headed several hours north and across the Michigan border to play Grand Rapids. The Giants had an off-day to travel on April 10, before the Gold Bugs would host the Adrian team on April 11, 12 and 13. The Grand Rapids club had handled the Giants in 1895 with the assistance of the infamously rank umpiring of the now-departed Bobby Caruthers.

In 1896, Caruthers was long gone from Grand Rapids, and the Gold Bugs, under Jack Carney, would again battle for a top spot in the Class A Western League. Carney felt the Gold Bugs could win the league title in 1896, and their opener was a crushing 10–2 win over the Giants. The *Detroit Free Press* printed a line score, a story about the game, and two paragraphs that previewed the Gold Bugs' season. One of the Adrian dailies simply printed the final score. The *Free Press* said the Grand Rapids team won "with remarkable ease," and "at no stage of the game were the Giants in it at all." Lefty Jack Hewitt, who had pitched in four games in the majors last year for the Pittsburgh Pirates, held the Giants in check. The highlight of the game was when the Page Fence men loaded the bases and the next batter had a 3–0 count, but Hewitt responded by striking him out to end the threat.[43]

The Gold Bugs and Giants squared off on a rare Sunday game in Grand Rapids, as management kept an eye out for the local police, challenging the local ordinance banning baseball on the Sabbath. Last year, the Gold Bugs and Giants were forced outside of the city limits in Reeds Lake to play a Sunday game. This year, Recreation Park was the setting for game two of the series, and 2,700 people jammed in to see Sunday afternoon baseball and to commit a sin. George Wilson was the Page Fence starter and allowed six runs. An article out of Grand Rapids and printed in *The Sporting News* on April 18 exclaimed, "Wilson … without a doubt [is] one of the best pitchers in the business." Unfortunately for Adrian's men, Leon Wolters, who had pitched for Manistee, Michigan, last year, was a bit better. After the Giants jumped on Wolters for five runs in the first two innings, he settled down and the held them scoreless the rest of the way for the 6–5 victory. The Gold Bugs management expected the successful Sunday event would allow them to go to court and get the city law abolished.[44]

The teams played two more times, and the minor leaguers won both games. Why did the Giants get swept in Grand Rapids? Well, just like last year in Grand Rapids and many other locales, the umpire was not fair. The *Evening Telegram* ran a headline after the four-game set: "Umpiring Said to Be Like a Jug Handle—All on One Side." The Adrian paper wished the Grand Rapids club good luck on their season, but hoped they didn't fall into any umpires like the ones the Giants saw there. Sunday's game was "pretty bad," but Monday's loss was just a "little short of villainous." The *Evening Telegram* said that when a local umpire is paid by the home team, the calls will not go toward the Giants. Giving credit to the Grand Rapids club, the *Evening Telegram* said they were a good team, but after the series of games, could also give the Giants "pointers in dainty bits of robbery." The paper warned that if the atmosphere continued, the Giants would be lucky to escape town with "their bicycles and palace car."[45]

To add fuel to its argument, the *Evening Telegram* printed an excerpt from the *Grand Rapids Evening Press*, which echoed Adrian's view of the situation. The west Michigan newspaper praised the Giants' high quality of play, especially in the field, and said they had even outplayed the Gold Bugs. "Grand Rapids has a good team, but they cannot expect to defeat the Giants in every game, unless it is by rank umpiring."[46]

The Page Fence gentlemen probably couldn't get out of Grand Rapids quick enough and headed around Lake Michigan and into Wisconsin. One Giant who apparently didn't agree with that sentiment was Grant Johnson, who managed to miss the train out of Grand Rapids and thus the next two games in Milwaukee.[47] The Milwaukee Brewers, also a member of the strong Western League, opened their exhibition season before a large crowd with a 10–3 loss to the Giants. Wilson was the winner as the Giants stayed busy slugging 15 hits against Fred Barnes and Kirtley Baker. The latter had already logged three years in the majors, albeit with a dismal 6–28 record, for Pittsburgh and Baltimore. A humorous story which later came out of this game was Wilson's match-up with Fred Hartman, who had hit .319 for the Pittsburgh Pirates in 1894. As Wilson was preparing to deliver a pitch to Hartman, the slugger began to taunt the Palmyra Wonder. "Hurry up, Lefty, put her through and I'll put you out of the business." Wilson continued his pitching gyrations, and Hartman continued. "Put her through, Lefty, and I'll send you home to your mother." Wilson dropped his left arm to his side and told the former major leaguer, "Oh, sugar, you don't look like a hitter." Wilson went through some more pre-pitch antics, and Hartman yelled, "Come, hurry up, Lefty, and I'll smash your legs off." The Palmyra Wonder let go a beautiful curveball which arched over the plate, and Hartman flailed at it. Two more times, Wilson delivered his curve, and two more times Hartman swung and missed. The hometown Milwaukee crowd appreciated Wilson's wizardry and gave him a hearty cheer for his pitching talent.[48]

The travelling stars were to play another game with Milwaukee and then go to St. Paul and Minneapolis, Minnesota. However, no scores got wired to Adrian, so local baseball cranks were left out in the cold. Not coincidentally, it was during this time that Len Hoch and Rolla Taylor were both back in Adrian.

The Page Fence men showed up in Rockford, Illinois, in mid–April and were drilled, 14–4. They faced Elmer Horton, who later that year would pitch in the majors for the Pittsburgh Pirates, and Carlton Molesworth, a 19-year-old lefty phenom, who had pitched in four games for the 1895 Pirates. Molesworth was the more effective of the two, as his "shoots kept the colored nine breaking their necks in the effort to stack up hits." He managed to change speeds, and his curveball kept the Adrian men off-balance.[49]

The Giants eventually ended up back in central Illinois for another game with the Western Association Peoria Distillers. In one of their worst losses since their formation, the Adrian contingent lost, 18–1. Uncharacteristically, Miller and Wilson combined to give up 21 hits, and the Giants committed six errors in the bad loss. Holly Souders gave up an opening inning run and that was it for the rest of the way, as the Giants were dismal at the plate, knocking out only five hits. The Distillers had been a bit short-handed in the first two games the Giants won earlier in April and would have been motivated, to say the least, for this rematch.[50]

For nearly two weeks, there is no information on the whereabouts of the Giants back in Adrian. Earlier stories indicated the club was booked up into May. It is possible the games were rained out. However, it is more likely without the "white club," baseball fever was now limited to Adrian's black community and the town's diehard baseball cranks. The town suffered another baseball blow when the Interstate League did indeed form, just without an Adrian entry. Jackson managed to scrape up enough money to join Saginaw and Toledo as part of an eight-team league. Those cities which originally worked with Mumby, Hoch and Taylor, were joined by clubs in Wheeling, West Virginia, Youngstown, Ohio, New Castle, Pennsylvania, Washington, D.C., and Fort Wayne, Indiana. They formed as a Class C minor league team and bypassed last year's MSL power brokers.[51]

The Mankato, Minnesota, club faced the Giants in late April. The Maroons lost, 5–0, on April 27. The Page Fence train car had been in the town for at least two days before the contest. A second game was slated between the two clubs for Tuesday. No scores were reported to Adrian for the second contest.[52]

To begin the month of May 1896, the Giants won a five-inning game against Winona, Minnesota.[53] A few days later, the Giants squared off against some college boys at the University of Wisconsin. The Giants shut out the Madison club, 9–0. The Giants' phenom, George Wilson, won the game and was said to be "doing some magnificent pitching this season."[54]

During May, as had been the case for much of April, the Page Fence Giants did not get the news coverage back home that they had in 1895. Possibly to combat that fact, team management arranged for two games on July 1 and 2, in Adrian against the Grand Rapids Gold Bugs. To drum up support and to keep the rivalry alive, the *Evening Telegram* reminded readers that the Gold Bugs had two months ago "robbed" the Giants of four games, and the Giants planned to get even.[55] Grand Rapids had apparently replaced Jackson and Monroe as Adrian's mortal baseball enemy.

In mid–May, the *Evening Telegram* gave a brief summary of the 1896 Giants' success. Their article supported the fact that the team's press coverage was nowhere near the level afforded the Adrian Demons last year, and not even close to what the Giants had experienced in their inaugural season. "So far, the Giants have played, as near as can be estimated, about 26 games and out of these they have won 18 and lost 8."[56] The *Evening* Telegram couldn't even provide their readers ("estimated") with an exact game total or record. Their competitor, the *Daily Times and Expositor*, gave the team even less ink, about a dozen total mentions of the team in May and June.

While the papers were ignoring the team's exploits, what little did find space in the paper was almost always positive. The community was proud of these gentlemen and wanted to let the world know that fact. James Stevens, home from his advance work, told one paper in May of the high esteem he had for the players and complimented their work ethic. He singled out Wilson for both his pitching and fielding and Grant Johnson for his overall play. The paper added, "no doubt" a large crowd would welcome the team home in early July.[57]

The Page Fence Company was also doing good work during this time. They always seemed to struggle in keeping up with demand, which was good for them, but not so much for the waiting customer. On Monday, May 18, the company accepted its "largest one-day order ever," for a total of 89 miles and 77 rods (1 rod= 5½ yards) of fencing.[58] Things were not so bright for their former business partner, Bud Fowler. He was in the process of disbanding his Muncie, Indiana–based black team, as "many of the southern teams would not play them, drawing the color line." In an odd move, Fowler's club had played a team in a town called Alexandria, and then he split for parts unknown with the $25 gate receipts.[59]

While it was believed the Giants' record was 18–8 by mid–May, their overall skills added to their allure when they arrived in a town. Despite some losses, newspapers printed stories about the Giants being nearly invincible. One Indiana paper told its readers the team had won 27 games in a row, as the Logansport club was awaiting their arrival.[60] In Michigan's Upper Peninsula, a Calumet paper tried to lure the Giants there and told its readers, even though they played nearly every day, the club had lost only one game in 1896! While no date had been set, Calumet was aiming for the Giants to play on Decoration Day, which, unbeknownst to them, had already been booked with some other town.[61]

Where would these papers receive this information about all the lengthy winning streaks and overall record? Well, it was easy to blame the personable Fowler during his stint with the club, as he had been puffing his age for many years. Now that task was left to Gus Parsons. The team's business manager had already on at least one occasion the previous season claimed a ten-game winning streak, when that was not the case. In an interview with the *Logansport Reporter*, Parsons was "the genial manager of the Giants." Parsons told them of the 27-game winning streak over such clubs as Dubuque, Iowa, Rock Island, Illinois, Terre Haute, Indiana, the University of Wisconsin, Peoria and Bloomington, Illinois, along with some lesser teams.[62] As part of this streak, a swing through Wisconsin saw the Giants whip teams at Stevens Point, Chippewa Falls, Dodgeville, Jefferson and Madison.[63] When the team arrived in Logansport, Indiana, they had just finished blasting Bloomington, 27–2 and 15–0, with Miller winning game one and Wilson game two. Bloomington was said to be one of the strongest, if not the strongest team in Illinois.[64]

While this impressive winning streak was inaccurate, the Logansport paper quoted Parsons as saying they had lost close games to the Cincinnati Reds last year and defeated the college boys in Madison this season, 9–0. Those two points were accurate. However, the same article noted that Parsons told them the Giants had split two games with Grand Rapids, when in fact they had been swept in four. This supports the contention that Parsons would only credit losses in games umpired fairly, as he had revealed in a story last year. With scores rarely printed back home, it was hard to challenge Parsons' account. As a double bonus, the mighty winning streaks were great for intimidating a waiting foe and boosting those local ticket sales.[65]

The Giants arrived at the Wabash train depot in Logansport on the morning of May 26 and headed for the driving park in town.[66] The opening game with manager Kelly and the Logansport Ottos was a one-sided affair, even though some had speculated it might be a close contest. The winning streak continued as the Giants roughed up the Indiana club, 15–2. Billy Holland earned the victory for the Giants, who jumped out to an 8–0 lead and never looked back. Following the game, Fred Van Dyke returned home to Vandalia, Michigan, due to the death of his mother. Team officials noted that this was a "serious loss," but thought they had located a replacement pitcher, Ed Wilson, and a catcher, Herman Sanders, to fill roster spots.[67] Game two was like the first, as the Page Fence men jumped out to a six-run, first-inning lead and were ahead by double digits before the Ottos managed their only run. Wilson and Burns were the battery for the Giants as they cruised to a 12–1 win.[68]

The baseball-crazed town of Montpelier, Ohio, again entered the picture as they planned another day of sporting activities, which featured Adrian's black ball club. On June 4, they would host a game between the Giants and the always tough Defiance Greys. To end the festive day, a 15-mile bike race, with $500 in prizes, would conclude the gala.[69] It was reported that many Adrian people would travel down and take their first look at the 1896 Giants.

Before all that fun, the Page Fence club was poised to tackle their rival, the Chicago Unions. South Bend, Indiana, had booked Decoration weekend games and decided to bring the Unions to town. To build the excitement and to get Adrian people on the train, the *Evening Telegram* billed the match-up as "the colored baseball championship of the west."[70]

◆ 14 ◆

The First Championship Series

The simple headline in the *Evening Telegram* on June 1 told the entire story: "Champions No More."[1] The Chicago Unions had claimed to be the black champions of the West entering the two-day series in South Bend. That claim ended quickly.

The opener was looking good for the Chicago men. The Unions' Harry Moore, a Detroit native, was facing Joe Miller, and a couple of hits and a sacrifice put the Unions out in front early in the game.[2] The Giants tied it 1–1 when Grant Johnson sent Moore's pitch as far as anyone could recollect at Studebaker Park for a solo home run. The score remained tied until the eighth inning, when the Giants tallied four runs, thanks to hits by Charles Grant, George Taylor and Johnson. The score bulged to 5–1, and the *Evening Telegram* dubbed Miller the "Neligh wonder." He closed out the Unions' half of the ninth, and the Giants claimed the opener.[3]

The word on the street must have been quite positive, as the largest crowd to ever fill Studebaker Park showed up for the rematch. Holland "pitched the game of his life," allowed a first inning single, and that was it as the Giants destroyed the Unions, 19–1. The Page Fence gentlemen battered three Unions pitchers, starting with Harry Hyde. Leading 4–0 in the fourth inning, a man named Jones took the mound in relief of Hyde. That proved to be a poor move as Jones promptly allowed eight runs on four singles, a double and two homers. By the game's halfway mark, the crowd became more concerned as to whether the contest would be a shutout. One spectacular play by Johnson kept the whitewash intact for the time being. The slugging shortstop ran after a Texas Leaguer, dove, and caught the ball among the massive crowd of people, horses and buggies which ringed the playing field. The story goes that people could not believe Johnson had made the catch, without flying. Johnson explained that it was only a long jump and no flying was involved. Eleven of the Giants' 15 hits were for extra bases, including Johnson with four doubles and a home run. Holland, Taylor and Van Dyke all had round-trippers, and catcher Pete Burns slugged a pair of doubles.[4]

The outcome left no doubt as to who was the best Western black team. The two victories were also without the benefit of using their ace pitcher, George Wilson. A report in a St. Paul, Minnesota, paper carried an update on the Page Fence club during their series with the Unions. The *Globe* noted that the Giants had not lost in six weeks and said that "Young Wilson … has won all his games of late, scoring six shutouts within a month."[5]

As appears to be the regular schedule pattern, Monday was an off-day and probably a travel day for the Page Fence club. To warm up for their battle with Defiance, the Giants clubbed the Milford, Indiana, team, 10–2, on Tuesday.[6]

When the Page Fence club and the Defiance Greys squared off, they played in Montpelier,

Ohio. The town had successfully arranged a baseball festival last fall for the Giants-Demons appearance, so they planned another one this June and "devised plans to make the day a gala one."[7] And a gala one it was, except for Greys fans. The Giants shut them out, 4–0, shocking the Defiance boosters, as their team came into the game with a 19-game winning streak, including several victories over Interstate League clubs. Holland won the game from the pitcher's box, while Johnson was stellar at shortstop and drilled a first-inning, two-run homer. The shutout marked the Giants' 32nd consecutive victory, and the 1,200 people at the baseball gala went home after watching "the best contest they had ever witnessed."[8]

The outcome didn't sit well with Defiance, and a doubleheader rematch was scheduled for a few days later. The Greys got the best of the Giants, 5–3, on Sunday, but dropped the Monday contest, 3–2, behind the visitors' battery of Miller and Burns.[9] However, the Monday loss may be in error, as one local paper mentioned that the Giants' winning streak was still intact, which simply added to the confusion surrounding the club's lore.[10]

When the Giants' train car pulled into Adrian's Lake Shore and Michigan Southern Depot on Wednesday, June 10, a large crowd welcomed the team. The car was attached to the 12:17 p.m. Lake Shore, as local baseball cranks and members of the Page Fence Company cheered the arrival. There was also a buzz in the air as people spoke of the Giants' return in July to play the Grand Rapids Gold Bugs.[11]

The team's stop in Adrian was a short one, as they had to head west about 35 miles to play the Hillsdale College nine later that afternoon. The game in Hillsdale was the first of a long swing of 40 dates around the state of Michigan during the next six weeks.[12] Wilson and Graham combined to hold down the Hillsdale College club, 14–5.[13] The Giants rapped out 18 hits and were up, 12–0, after five innings.[14] The *Evening Telegram* claimed it was the team's 35th victory in a row.[15]

The following day, Miller and the Giants shut out Homer, 6–0, in what was called a "good game."[16] However, details of the Giants' games were still hard to locate in both daily Adrian papers. The *Evening Telegram* managed at least to record a score for many of the games held in Michigan, Ohio and, to a lesser extent, Indiana. However, the *Daily Times and Expositor*'s coverage of the black gentlemen was much less frequent. The sport of baseball was still being reported in the *Expositor*. In the same *Expositor* edition which noted only the score of the Giants/Homer games, they printed an Adrian College box score. The paper's front page, almost daily, printed the line scores for all the games in the 12-team National League, whose closest clubs were in based Chicago and Cleveland. Adrian's baseball fever was still being promoted, just not so much involving the Giants.[17]

The excitement of the alleged long winning streak was high going into the second weekend of June. The Factory Notes section of Saturday's *Evening Telegram* crowed, "Page Fence, like the Page Fence Giants, is pushing Adrian."[18] A stop in Manistee, along the coast of Lake Michigan, was very competitive for the Giants. Manistee was so good they halted the vaunted Giants' winning streak with a 10–9 victory on Saturday afternoon. The Giants managed to load the bases in the ninth inning before Manistee turned a double play and sealed their upset victory. Manistee was led by a man named Gleason in the box, while Grant Johnson pitched for the Page Fence men.[19] The Giants got back on the winning track on Monday with a 12–8 victory.[20]

The Giants next traveled to St. Louis, Michigan, in the middle of the state. The town was full of baseball fanatics and had even secured a coveted July 4 game with the Page Fence club. They were excited to host the mighty Giants twice within a month. A damper on that enthusiasm came on Wednesday afternoon, June 17, when the Giants drubbed the

St. Louis Brown Stockings, 11–0. It was a battle of a pair of young Palmyra left-handed pitching phenoms, as 19-year-old Harvey Bailey was imported to face 20-year-old George Wilson. Bailey, who had also recently played on the Adrian College team, was making his first appearance for St. Louis. The *Evening Telegram* noted that the hired arm, Bailey, held the Giants to 12 hits, but offered no details about the Page Fence shutout victory that afternoon, except that Wilson and Burns were the Giants' battery.[21]

The Giants now had to face a setback when Billy Holland's playing and coaching duties took a break. Following a Thursday, June 18, game at Ionia, an 8–7 win for the Giants, Holland headed back to Adrian. One account described Holland's ailment as "ill health, the result of an injury." Speculation was that Holland just needed some rest, but should be ready for the games against the Grand Rapids Gold Bugs in Adrian in about two weeks. He was to remain in Adrian and reside with Will Henson. The Giants won the second game with Ionia the next day, 8–5, without Holland.[22]

The team then narrowly defeated Kalamazoo with Home Run Johnson pitching. However, the loss of Holland meant one less arm, so cook Wendell Gaskin made another rare appearance in the box for the Page Fence Giants. The team rolled him out against the Nashville nine, only to see him knocked out of the box after one inning, replaced by Wilson. The Giants managed to rally for a 10–9 win.[23]

With their coacher's injury, the Giants were now short a man, and it was obvious that playing the team cook was not a long-term answer either. James Patterson's name also had not been mentioned for some time, and he was likely absent during this portion of the season. The comings and goings of Giants players were rarely covered in the papers, unless it was the pre-season preview or the year-end summary. Holland's loss placed them in a bind, and someone reached out again to Adrian teenager Frank Waters, who was signed and sent to meet the Giants in Grand Haven. Waters had been a member of the fledgling all-black 1895 Powers Clothing Company team, had previously pitched for Adrian College, and was an emergency Giants fill-in briefly in 1895. Waters was the son of Frank and Jeannette Hairston Waters, was born and raised in Adrian, and had just turned 17 years of age.[24]

The Adrian native got his chance to play for the mighty Giants in a game with Flint, but Waters lost a 9–6 decision, throwing to catcher Vasco Graham. The Flint squad featured slugging Ed Mulhearn from last year's Demons team, along with University of Michigan and Owosso Colts ringer John Bloomington. Even though Waters was born and raised in Adrian, and this was his second, albeit brief, go-around with the mighty Giants, oddly neither daily paper focused on a story of the "local boy makes good" angle either this year or last year.[25]

The hot summer ticket in Adrian was for the upcoming Grand Rapids-Giants matchup in about a week. The rush caused backers to arrange advanced ticket sales at Robinson's Cigar Store and Tripp's Jewelry until noon of game day. Organizers issued a warning to patrons that the grandstand would not be oversold, so that all who purchased those special tickets would have enough room to sit. Tickets were priced at ten and 25 cents. To add interest and to get patrons out to Lawrence Park, framed photographs of the Giants were tacked up around town.[26] Well-respected umpire Jimmie Grogan of Detroit was assigned to call the games.[27]

While Adrian ball cranks were focused on packing the stands for the Gold Bugs battle, the Giants still had to go out and win ballgames. In Flint on Saturday, the Giants won an exciting 6–5 game in the bottom of the tenth inning when Johnson drove in Bill Binga, who had doubled. About 1,500 people attended the game, and it was dubbed by the *Detroit*

Free Press "by far the most exciting game ever witnessed" in Flint. The home team tied the game with two runs in the seventh and loaded the bases in the eighth and tenth innings, only to have double plays end the threats. Wilson and Flint pitcher Robb were very effective, while Johnson and Charlie Grant were singled out for their stellar infield work. The *Free Press* gave a jab at the Page Fence team and said there should have been no issue with umpire Miller, but the Giants didn't agree. "Although the game was umpired in a fair and impartial manner, the Giants were continually kicking and acted more like a lot of savages than a team of ball players."[28]

The Giants finally left the state to play a pair of games in Defiance, Ohio, against the Greys. The Ohio town was very motivated to win one against the Giants, and there were rumors that the Greys might even skip a scheduled Saturday game to rest up for Sunday's tilt with the Michigan men. The Defiance *Daily Republican* remarked that the rest was a good idea, but wasn't sure it would have much of an impact on the outcome. "The home team will be in good shape by Sunday and are going to defeat the Page Fence Giants, if such a thing is possible."[29]

Joe Miller, whose name had not appeared lately as pitching for the Giants, won a close, 3–1 affair with Defiance. The Greys clubbed out eight hits and led 1–0 until the fourth inning, so maybe their planned days of rest were paying off. However, the batting of Page Fence stars Johnson, Van Dyke and Wilson, who each had two hits, with George Taylor adding a triple, was too much for the home club. Shoddy fielding was also blamed for the Greys' Sunday afternoon loss.[30]

The Monday afternoon rematch was set to begin at 3:30 in Defiance. Jerry McCarty was the umpire today, as he had been in yesterday's close affair. He called the balls and strikes in a tilt the *Daily Republican* titled "Rocky Game; Greys skunked in the Contest at Ball Park Monday." Oh, but the headline missed the very important fact that George Wilson had thrown a no-hitter! Wilson out-dueled a man named Wagner as the Giants won, 6–0. The Defiance paper used only two sentences to describe Wilson's heroic feat, and the *Adrian Times and Expositor* devoted about the same length. The *Expositor* did add that Wilson had struck out nine Greys and that only one ball had been hit to the outfield. The *Evening Telegram* was a bit better and longer in detailing Wilson's no-hitter, saying "the outcome added new laurels to Wilson's fame," and probably to Vasco Graham too, the Giants' catcher. "The whole team put up gilt-edged ball, but Wilson's work in the box was the feature."[31]

The Gold Bugs were to arrive from Columbus, Ohio, by train Tuesday afternoon and make their way for an evening stay at the Hotel Emery. They surely had learned of Wilson's no-hitter in Defiance, and that would have added more excitement to the games in Adrian. The 14 Gold Bugs were ready to exert their Class A minor league ball skills over the professional black gentlemen. "The Giants will meet a team of mettle, as well as one with plenty of substitute players eager for the fray."[32]

Adrian baseball cranks eagerly anticipated the two games with Grand Rapids, as there was still bad blood emanating from the April four-game sweep. It was a hot day when the first of the two games began at Lawrence Park. The thermometer had already hit 90 degrees by 12 noon, and the July sun would bake the field for another three hours before the first pitch.[33] Jack Carney's squad, lagged near the tail end of the Western League standings, wanted to show the Giants they were again literally and figuratively not in their league.

The *Daily Times and Expositor* called it "a game with few redeeming characteristics," and the *Evening Telegram*'s four-layered headline included the phrase that the Giants "Had lost their ginger jar."[34] Eleven hundred people jammed Lawrence Park and witnessed a

12–5 loss at the hands of the Gold Bugs. Righty Joshua "Jot" Goar kept the Giants in check, as the Grand Rapids team jumped out to an 8–0 lead after just three innings. Joe Miller pitched for the home team, and the loss was due to poor fielding and his "wretched work in the box."[35] The Giants were out of sorts as the normally slick-fielding team committed an unusually high six errors. There were some positives for the Page Fence men. Billy Holland marked his return to the team after his layoff with two fine catches in left field. Charles Grant recorded "clever work" at second base, while Grant Johnson slugged a home run. However, Binga struggled at third base and Miller was also weak in the field "and could neither pitch nor throw."[36] Detroit umpire Johnny Grogan earned his money's worth, as it was said all his rulings were "fair and just."[37]

The locals were not happy with the one-sided affair. For the first time, the town's two dailies were no longer stridently supporting their Giants. They began to fall into the same writing style as some other papers had, by denigrating the black men and their character. The Gold Bugs also played a part, as they decided to bring a new mascot to the game. Their mascot of choice was a small baby raccoon, which was said to be as "playful as a kitten." The *Evening Telegram* claimed that the tiny animal "struck terror to the hearts of the Giants." That statement was wholly unlikely and was demeaning to the Page Fence team. Grand Rapids third baseman Robert Plantagenant Llewellan "Lew" Camp had picked up the stray raccoon at a game earlier in the season in Indianapolis. Whether Camp innocently corralled the raccoon as a team mascot or thought the furry animal would come in handy to mock the Giants later in the year, is long lost to history. The visual message of the "coon" with the Giants on the ball diamond would have been lost to absolutely no one in 1896.[38]

The mascot's appearance was just the start of a "poky game" that afternoon for the Page Fence Giants. The second inning was particularly bad, as Miller issued two walks, two singles, a double, and a triple, and the fielders behind him were not much better. That concoction contributed to six runs and took the air out of the Giants and the local baseball cranks. The *Daily Times and Expositor* combined the national bimetallism issue, the use of copper and gold to back the country's paper money supply, and the Giants' skin tone, to illustrate the feelings after the second-inning meltdown. The visitors' scoring burst gave the locals "little confidence in the free and unlimited courage of copper." When Leon Walters relieved Goar in the fifth inning and allowed all the Giants' runs, one paper noted, "the Giants found the latter easier, but hardly a watermelon." The "courage," "copper" and "watermelon" words were additional examples of the change in the newspaper tone by the Adrian papers in their coverage of the locally sponsored team.[39]

Behind the scenes, there was also trouble brewing with one of its star players. Pitching wizard Joe Miller wanted off the Page Fence travelling bicycle show and ball team. The rumor was serious enough to make it into one of the Adrian papers following this first-game loss to Grand Rapids. The rumor was that Miller had thrown the first game, figuratively and literally, in order the get out of his contract. Manager Gus Parsons was not happy about Miller's alleged activity. The word was that Miller wanted to join the Bryan, Ohio, team, where he would receive a pay boost to $125 a month.[40]

Day two of the Grand Rapids series was played under another hot sun, as the temperature was a bit warmer at noon, 92 degrees, than the day before. The Giants would have their ace, Wilson, facing Monte McFarland, a right-handed pitcher who, like Goar the day before, had already spent a brief time in the majors. The Palmyra Wonder was described as "an immovable object" for the first four innings, as both teams were scoreless. Rain then doused Lawrence Park, flowed into the creek surrounding the outfield, and caused a half-hour delay. When play resumed, Leon Wolters replaced McFarland, but the Giants decided to keep Wilson in the box, and he was drilled for five runs on five hits in the fifth inning. When Johnson bobbled a ball at short in the sixth inning, the Gold Bugs added a run and now held a 6–0 lead. Johnson redeemed himself, blasted a two-run shot and "buried the ball over the lowlands" and into the wet grass, where it was lost. When another run came across, cutting the deficit to three runs, the Adrian boosters became "jubilant." The Giants continued their comeback and scored two more runs in the eighth inning to whittle the Grand Rapids lead to 6–5. In their last turn at bat, Wilson led off with a fly out to center field, and Grant bounced out to Camp at third. With two outs, Holland singled and so did George Taylor. The tying and winning runs were now on base, and fine-hitting third sacker Bill Binga came to the plate. Binga swung and Camp, ignored the "distracting din" of the crowd, cradled the ball into his glove, making 900 people sadly depart Lawrence Park.[41]

However, baseball fever was back in full swing in Adrian. The newspaper accounts of this second game offered none of the derogatory comments seen following game one. Grand Rapids club officials were happy with the crowds, and the word was that they wanted to return. The excitement around the Page Fence club fueled rumors that plans were in the works for Flint and Defiance to make appearances in Adrian that summer.[42]

Both teams remained in Adrian the evening of July 2 and left the following morning for games. The Gold Bugs went to Detroit to play a Western League game with the Tigers that afternoon. The Giants had two games set in St Louis, Michigan—one this afternoon and then the big July 4 celebration with the Brown Stockings on Independence Day.[43]

While a big crowd in Adrian was anticipated for the July 4 celebration, the Giants had earlier been booked in Gratiot County. Len Hoch scurried to find a game for his town on Independence Day and booked the Flint and Pere Marquette Railroad-sponsored club to play the Kalamazoo nine. One game would be played in the morning, with the second in the afternoon. The ball grounds would also feature a free concert by the Adrian City band.[44] Why the Giants were not scheduled for this festive holiday occasion is a mystery. However, St. Louis was a hot ball town, and maybe their guaranteed money was too good to pass up in 1896.

◆ 15 ◆

Sinister Legislation

Why the sudden turn in the Adrian newspaper coverage surrounding the Giants? The 1895 Adrian daily newspapers, other than the occasional use of the "watermelon battery" in describing Wilson and Graham, were mostly supporters of the team. The newspapers probably believed the food stereotype was simply a descriptive term as opposed to a negative portrayal of the gentlemen. Even when the Adrian Demons, the mostly white minor league team, lost to the Giants in June of 1895, the two papers were complimentary toward the Giants. They both also blasted Wilson's lackadaisical efforts but didn't resort to the racially charged name-calling often common at the time. So what had changed? A little-known 1892 arrest could have contributed to this shift.[1]

Down in Louisiana, Homer Adolph Plessy boarded a train on June 7, 1892, and when the conductor summoned the local police, Plessy was promptly arrested.[2] Plessy's crime had been that he was born ⅛ black but sat in a train car on the East Louisiana Railroad designated for white people. New Orleans Judge John H. Ferguson ruled that the law was just, and the court battle began. Unlike the 1955 Rosa Parks arrest on a Montgomery, Alabama, city bus, the rail company wanted this legal challenge. Due to an 1890 Louisiana state law mandating separate or partitioned cars for blacks and whites, the rail line had to pay for the added cars and altered compartments. This discriminating legislation hit the pocket book of Louisiana railroads, which had no interest in increasing their business costs. As a result, a local citizens' committee and the train company decided to fight the law. So Plessy jumped on the wrong car, which began the long, four-year legal tussle.[3]

The attack on civil rights, and specifically those of black people, began with the collapse of Reconstruction. Congress passed The Civil Rights Act of 1875 to make it a crime to deny people their constitutional rights. However, with the infamous 1876 Presidential election deal ending the Northern presence in the former slave states, civil rights laws were now routinely attacked. In 1883, the Supreme Court struck down the 1875 Civil Rights, Act and the word was out that targeting the rights of black citizens was fair game. When Florida in 1887 passed a segregated rail car law, Louisiana followed suit in 1890, which led to the Plessy and East Louisiana Railroad incident.[4]

By the time the Plessy case wound its way and was ruled upon by the United States Supreme Court, it was May of 1896. In a 7–1 decision, Justice Henry Brown, hailing from the state of Michigan and writing the majority opinion, ruled that the rail car segregation law was legal. Brown was a Massachusetts native but had moved to Detroit before the Civil War, which helped to launch his thriving law career. While large swaths of Michigan could be deemed progressive during the war, Detroit was not one of those. The city's leading newspaper, the *Detroit Free Press*, was an anti-war, Copperhead publication, and the city was the scene of one of the country's biggest anti-draft riots. This setting is where Brown began his legal career, which likely influenced his interpretation of black people's civil rights. He was apparently no abolitionist either, and despite his Northern upbringing, he didn't join the Union Army in the Civil War.[5]

His majority opinion ruled that separate facilities were not illegal, and if the "colored race" believed so, "it is not by reason of anything found in the act, but solely because the colored race chooses to put that construction on it." He added that it was folly that "social prejudice" could be solved through legislation and disagreed that the "commingling of the two races" was the only way to secure equal rights. Justice Brown danced around the 14th Amendment, passed to ensure that all Americans held civil rights, and which he agreed was legally accurate. However, Brown's logic followed that "if one race be inferior to the other socially, the Constitution of the United States cannot put them upon the same plane."[6] He felt that the 14th Amendment was a nice law in theory, but impossible to legislate in practice.

In a somewhat bizarre twist, the only Justice to rule against the Court's decision was Judge John Marshall Harlan, a former slave owner from Kentucky. In a blistering dissent, Harlan stated that the Louisiana law was "inconsistent" with and "hostile" to the United States Constitution. He added that while slavery was illegal, states could now pass "sinister legislation" which would "interfere with the blessings of freedom." The result, Harlan feared, would be "to place in a condition of legal inferiority a large body of American citizens … called the people of the United States."[7]

The decision unleashed a torrent of "separate but equal" possibilities across the country, as Justice Harlan had correctly predicted. Some states had already written laws that schools should be segregated, with whites in one school and the "coloreds" in another. The Plessy ruling gave creative segregationists, in both the North and South, federally supported legal justification to follow the separate but equal philosophical doctrine.

Depending on where you lived, the ruling was a major event or just another Supreme Court ruling. At least, that is the way it was reported. The *Detroit Free Press* noted the Plessy case within a short article about four Supreme Court rulings and referred to it as the "Jim Crow car case." The Detroit paper listed the Plessy ruling after a patent infringement complaint concerning the Singer Sewing Machine company and a Kansas mortgage penalty case.[8] The *Chicago Tribune* devoted only 47 words to the entire case and tucked it safely away on page 10.[9] The *Inter Ocean* of Chicago announced that the ruling "legalizes the line" but only covered the topic in one paragraph.[10] The *Wall Street Journal* was similarly scant with its coverage.[11] The *Boston Post* headlined "Supreme Court for Discrimination— Harlan Dissents" and claimed that there would be no impact on interstate commerce as the ruling concerned only intrastate passenger travel.[12] The *New York Times* did publish a much longer version than many other Northern papers. A large section of its story focused on Judge Harlan's "very vigorous dissent." It quoted the Judge who "saw nothing but mischief in all such laws." The *Times* offered a new scenario where the rail companies provided passenger cars to separate Catholics and Protestants and those of the Teutonic and Latin races, too.

However, as you moved South, the papers provided a chronological history of the Plessy case in the entire four-year legal battle. While the Northern papers either didn't understand the repercussions of the Plessy ruling or felt their readers were not impacted by the court's decision, that feeling was not shared in the South.

A Kentucky paper reported on the "Jim Crow" ruling and said a Federal Circuit Court from the Kentucky district had ruled a similar law as unconstitutional, and the case was now before a Court of Appeals.[13] The *Roanoke* (Virginia) *Times* noted that Brown's majority opinion was short and added a brief case history. It also printed Harlan's view that the decision was "repugnant to the 13th Amendment," which outlawed slavery in the United States following the Civil War.[14]

The newspaper stories in the state of Louisiana did not bury the ruling within other Supreme Court decisions. The *Times-Picayune of New Orleans* even briefly previewed the case in its Sunday, April 12, edition, the day before arguments were to be heard before the Supreme Court.[15]

When the ruling was announced a little more than a month later, the *Louisiana Democrat* in Alexandria was quite blunt, stating, "the Senegambian must now relinquish his ambition to ride in railroad coaches with white people."[16] The *Times-Picayune* said the ruling clarified the state law and claimed it did not create a situation of inequality between United States citizens or any races but actually provided "equal privilege" for interstate rail passengers. The article's final sentence also portrayed dissenting Justice Harlan as "following his course in the civil rights cases," which was either an insult or compliment and depended upon your feeling about the Plessy ruling.[17]

The former slave owner and only dissenting Justice sounded very much upset with the verdict, as was the *Richmond Planet*. The Virginia-based paper was founded 14 years earlier by 13 former slaves and had a circulation of a few thousand people. The *Planet* deemed the Plessy loss one which showed that the country's law was influenced by public sentiment. "We can be discriminated against, we can be robbed of our political rights, we can be persecuted and murdered and yet we cannot secure a legal redress in the courts of the United States." The paper announced that "evil days" had arrived, and the power of the federal government was being limited by state laws. It predicted that at this rate, one day it would be better to be a Governor than the President.[18]

In the Page Fence Giants' hometown, the Adrian papers reported nothing. As a matter of fact, from the day of the ruling for the next week, neither the *Adrian Evening Telegram* nor the *Daily Times and Expositor* printed anything at all about the Plessy case. The two dailies would have certainly been aware of the ruling through other papers and from their subscriptions to the national news services. For whatever reason, they ignored the Plessy outcome. Or did they? Was this a contributing factor to the change in tone when writing about the exploits of the Page Fence Giants? The federal government now sanctioned the separate but equal philosophy among the races. Maybe the two dailies were beginning to embrace this ruling as an acceptable way to treat their black Adrian neighbors.[19]

With the Supreme Court ruling fresh in the minds of those paying attention to such things in the summer of 1896, the Giants rolled out of Adrian and into St. Louis, Michigan, on Friday, July 3. The same town where just one year ago the "white caps" were mentioned on the front page of the local paper was again hosting the black all-star team. Their Independence Day celebration would feature the Giants.[20]

A crowd of over 1,000 saw the Giants nip the St. Louis club, 8–7. To help battle the professionals, the hired gun, Harvey Bailey, Wilson's fellow left-handed Palmyra neighbor, was again signed to pitch for the Brown Stockings. Last month he had lost, 11–0, but apparently showed enough then for a return engagement. Everything went well for the local boys until shoddy fielding in the sixth inning put the Giants ahead. The poor fielding was a constant theme for the day, as St. Louis fumbled their way to nine errors. The fine coacher, Billy Holland, earned the victory for the Giants. Bailey gave up nine hits, all singles, while

Holland was bashed for 12 knocks, four of which were for extra bases.[21] Two years later, Bailey posted a winning record with the major league Boston Beaneaters as he shared a spot in their rotation with future Hall of Famers Kid Nichols and Vic Willis.[22] Despite recording two losses that summer against the Giants, Bailey made it to the majors, and his victorious mound opponents, George Wilson and Billy Holland, did not.

"The greatest crowd in the history of baseball in St. Louis," the *Detroit Free Press* led off its July 4 game story. The *Free Press* said the crowd was more than double than the previous day at 2,250, which was cooled off thanks to a 45-minute, fourth-inning rain delay. The visitors won, 11–7, and both the *Free Press* and the *Evening Telegram* noted that the star of the game was the Giants' Holland, for his wizardry in catching fly balls in left field. The Detroit paper called his work "sensational," while the Adrian paper labeled it "brilliant." Both teams scored multiple runs in the opening inning as neither Pangborn for St. Louis nor Miller for Page Fence was terribly effective. The Brown Stockings scored six of their seven runs in the opening inning, but the Giants countered with seven in their next two stanzas and held on to win.[23]

Back in Adrian, why the Page Fence Giants management didn't reserve July 4 for a home contest is a question left to history. Only one game of the scheduled doubleheader between the Kalamazoo and Flint and Pere Marquette Railroad teams was played, possibly due to the same rainstorm which interrupted the Giants' contest in St. Louis. The railroad club won the game, 6–3, in front of a small crowd and a far cry from the thousands who showed up in St. Louis for the two games with the Giants. To make matters worse, the *Daily Times and Expositor* characterized the local game as "poor" and "uninteresting." Even the baseball challenge match that evening between the Adrian Fats and the Adrian Leans sounded like a dull affair, as the hefty boys won, 18–6.[24]

For the next week, details of the Giants games against the F & PM, Marine City and Milford nines and any other teams were minuscule. A motivated Giants fan, even by reading

A postcard of the sprawling Page Fence factory grounds on the east end of Adrian (courtesy Lenawee County Historical Museum).

both Adrian dailies, would have a hard time finding more than a score at this point in the vseason. One game highlight, if one could call it that, was when George Wilson drilled Milford's pitcher, Yerkes, in the head with a pitch, knocking him out and fracturing his skull. Yerkes was still suffering the effects of the beaning near his ear the next day. To add insult to injury, the Milfordites dropped a 9–5 decision in a game witnessed by about 800 people at the local fairgrounds.[25]

The *Daily Times and Expositor* continued its trend of covering less and less of the Giants in year two of the team's existence. Very little news concerning the 500 black Adrian residents made its way into the newspaper in 1896. In mid–July, the paper omitted scores of several Giants games but managed to report that a fund was being established to bury General Lee. He was described as "the old colored shoemaker" who had died recently, and his body would be buried in Ann Arbor, for some reason, which was unacceptable to some people in Adrian. Lee's funeral was held at the Second Methodist Episcopal Church on Friday, July 11. However, no word was ever given as to whether the fund-raising goal was successful or not.[26]

Following a Giants win at Milan, the team returned to Adrian on July 11 and stayed overnight, before leaving the following morning for a game in South Bend, Indiana. The Giants squared off against a team from Bryan, Ohio, where a couple of familiar names dotted the Ohioans' roster. Maurice Justice, the speedy shortstop from the Adrian Demons, and William Malone, an 1895 Page Fence Giant, donned the Bryan uniform. The Giants won, 6–5. One Adrian paper claimed that all the South Bend papers were raving that it was the best game of ball they had seen in their town in 20 years.[27]

As the Giants were reeling off wins, their sponsor was enjoying its own success and was undergoing a building boom during July of 1896. Local contractor H. N. King had been hired to erect another storehouse on the Page Fence factory site. The building's location was between their manufacturing plant and the warehouse on the east end of Adrian and would be 30 feet high and well over 100 feet in length. The estimate was that this new structure could hold over 600 miles of finished woven fence.[28]

The company was also excited that the Giants would return to town to play another game. The Flint Champions, led by the former Demon and well-traveled Eddie Mulhearn, would face the Giants at Lawrence Park. The *Evening Telegram* claimed that the town wanted to see "the Giants, [who] are favorites here, and as baseball has been scarce," believed this game would draw well.[29] The Champions were no ordinary club but rather an all-star team from the previous season's Michigan State League. In addition to Mulhearn, infielder Ben Ireland and pitcher O. Hicks from last year's Demons squad were on the Champions, along with Kalamazoo's slugging and boisterous Shadrack McHoverter, Albert Fisher from the 1895 Owosso Colts, and professional ringer and University of Michigan athlete John Bloomington.[30]

"A fair sized crowd" showed up at Lawrence Park to see the Giants edge the Flint Champions, 5–4, in mid–July. The Adrian crowd was happy to have high-quality baseball back at Lawrence Park and gave hearty applause to the familiar Giants faces and to former Demons Mulhearn and Ireland. As he had been the case over the two seasons, Billy Holland stole the show with his fielding, base running and coacher antics. The comedian delighted the crowd on several occasions. Once, while Holland was on second base, Grant Johnson hit a low liner, and as the coacher broke for third, he had to hurdle the shortstop and made it safely to third. Later, while Holland was pitching, a Flint player hit a ball back to him. He took his sweet time and "looked the ball carefully over to see the stitches were all perfect" before he lobbed it over to first base to retire the batter. In keeping with the fine tradition from 1895, a nice group of freeloading patrons, perched on the bluffs overlooking the diamond, contributed to the festive occasion by letting their cheers reign down on the field below.[31]

"The Giants infield was like a stone wall," said the *Evening Telegram*, as the Giants posted a second victory over Flint, 6–2. Third sacker Bill Binga, who had struggled in the field in yesterday's contest, "put up the cleanest and snappiest third ever seen on the diamond." As a matter of fact, one report had the Giants' victory as one of the better games ever played in Adrian—"simply ablaze with brilliancy." A total of 525 fans paid to watch the event (there was no mention of an attendance figure for the freeloaders on the bluffs) in a game played in one hour and 40 minutes, which was quite lengthy for its era.[32]

Wilson pitched for the Giants, but the cool weather that day was cited as a contributing factor in a rocky outing. However, the standards were very high for the local fans as Wilson set down Flint in order in the first and allowed only single base runners in the next three innings. Wilson allowed two runs in the fifth inning, thanks to a Johnson error and a Wilson mistake in the field. The Palmyra lefty finished the game, allowed only one more hit and struck out eight. The fielding wizardry of Burns' strong arm behind the plate and Fred Van Dyke, robbing McHoverter of a home run, were two examples of the Giants' "brilliancy." Adding to the highlights was the sparkling fielding of the Champions' Dennis Lowney. One account said that if Lowney could improve his hitting, he "would shine in the National League."[33]

Both teams spent the evening in Adrian and left the following morning to play a third straight game, this one in Genesee County. Their goal would be to bring the previous two baseball games' excitement to Flint.

The Page Fence Giants management was always looking to create an event which would attract large crowds. At the end of July, a game was scheduled against the always competitive Homer, Michigan, team as part of a celebration at Devil's Lake, a resort only a few miles north of Adrian. The game would be in affiliation with the Maccabees, a fraternal life insurance organization, holding a family camping retreat at the lake and ensuring a large crowd.

There was also excitement surrounding an official, national black baseball championship series. The first word of the event began to leak out in mid–July, and plans were in the works for three games to be held in mid–September, in Adrian. The *Daily Times and Expositor* called it "the amateur baseball championship of the world," and it would be against "that other colored congregation the Cuban Giants."[34]

The other type of excitement was one the club did not want to deal with during their season. Stellar pitcher Joe Miller was no longer on the Giants. The rumor of Miller not doing his best or even "throwing" the game had persisted since his efforts against Grand Rapids earlier in the month. He did not pitch in the first game against Flint and was released that evening. Gus Parsons was still not pleased with Miller's performance against the minor league Gold Bugs, and "facts came out" which led management to believe he had to go. Miller promptly boarded a train out of Adrian and headed southwest to Bryan, Ohio, to sign a new and improved $125 monthly contract. Miller would not find things any calmer in Bryan, as the Ohio club had stormed off the field Thursday in an eighth-inning dispute, while tied 1–1 in Defiance against the Greys. Unlike earlier in the year, when the Giants scrambled to find a replacement pitcher and snagged Adrian teenager Frank Waters, they were better prepared this time around. They simply summoned James H. Chavous again from Marysville, Ohio, to fill Miller's roster spot. Chavous had pitched and played in a few games last year, "but was unable to get in prime condition" and was not retained for the beginning of the 1896 season. The plan was for Chavous to pitch the club's game in Flint.[35]

Chavous' hometown paper, the *Marysville Journal-Tribune*, was very proud to see their hometown lad make a return to the mighty Page Fence club. "Our crack ball pitcher … was so satisfactory … they felt they must have him again this year." The newspaper told its readers to expect good things from Chavous and the Giants. The article concluded with the opinion that few could beat Chavous, who he "has lots of speed and can pitch a veritable serpentine ball."[36]

While one newspaper account alluded to money as the main dispute between Miller and the Giants, the *Evening Telegram* said it was ego. "The real trouble with Cyclone Joe was that he could not endure the supremacy of Wilson as a pitcher. His jealousy of the Palmyra Wonder made him lose his head. He was a star last season but has done very indifferent work this season."[37]

"Chavous is O.K.; Manager Parsons New Pitcher Seems to Be of the Right Sort," rang the headline in the Saturday, July 18, *Adrian Evening Telegram*. The new addition helped to complete the three-game sweep of the Champions, in a 6–4 victory on Friday. While the Ohio pitcher was hit hard, his teammates supported him with fine glove work and bailed him out in his first appearance for the Giants in 1896. Both teams' scintillating fielding work was on display, with second baseman Charles Grant and shortstop Grant Johnson combining for seven putouts, eight assists and no errors. The Flint nine had former Adrian Demon Ben Ireland rob Johnson of a base hit with a wonderful catch, and Shadrack McHoverter stole a home run from Binga by diving into a ditch to catch a long fly ball.[38]

The Giants scored all their runs early off a pitcher named Walsh, who was ill and was relieved by a familiar face. Pitcher Hicks from the old Demons went to the box and held the Giants scoreless the rest of the way. Page Fence players Johnson, Van Dyke and George Taylor slugged doubles, while Flint's Bloomington and Ireland notched triples. Over 1,000 people "yelled themselves hoarse" in Flint and cheered every wonderful pitch, hit, and catch.[39]

While the game went well and Miller's mound replacement recorded a victory, the Giants' visit to Flint was not a smooth one. The ugly racial prejudice against black ballplayers was evident and reported in both Flint and Adrian newspapers. The bad calls by racist umps and racially tainted jeers were noted in newspaper reports of the time. However, almost nothing was written about segregated conditions in some of the towns where the Giants played. There were no accounts of how often the team was forced to eat and sleep on their train car, as opposed to how often they could venture into town and be treated civilly by hotel keepers and restaurant operators. In Adrian, the *Evening Telegram* reprinted a shameful report of how the Champions and Giants were treated when they arrived in Flint. Both clubs pulled in on the Flint and Pere Marquette 10:44 morning train, with the Champions most likely in regular passenger seats and the Giants riding along in their palatial Monarch car. The two teams exited the train and headed into Flint for lunch. The Champions went to their regular spots, but the Giants ran into a "snag," as it was characterized. The black gentlemen were refused admission to not one, but two Flint hotels, who would not serve them food because of their skin color. The talented and accomplished American men had to trudge through Flint and look for a lunch stop. A combination of anger, shame and humiliation no doubt enveloped them, before they entered Walter's Restaurant, which had no issues with the black men. "They found the latch string out and a welcome that wasn't any less cordial on account of their color." The Adrian paper called it what is was, the "color line," but added that the Giants had been in many Michigan towns and had "been accorded the best of treatment by hotel keepers." The Adrian view was that Michigan was a progressive state, but there were still places where civil rights were a "dead letter." Flint, Michigan, proved to be one of those places in 1896.[40]

In the late 1890s, Michigan was still largely inhabited by white farmers and businessmen. The automobile industry was still about a decade away from blooming. The large influx of firms recruiting Southern blacks to fill jobs in the Michigan factories was still about 20 years away. Contact with black people, in many communities, would have been a rare occurrence. Racial problems were likely not going to be discussed, unless thrust upon the national stage, as they were not seen as an issue to a largely white state of Michigan. A combination of I don't know and I don't care led to the racial and civil rights questions being easily ignored by those choosing to do so. The fact that the 1893 Depression was still hurting the country in 1896 allowed people the excuse to focus on their economic straights and not the lives of a handful of citizens who just happened to be black.

While it was noteworthy that the Flint racist event made it into the newspaper, the *Evening Telegram* did not follow up with an indictment of the Giants' treatment. There were no calls for boycotting Flint merchants or cancelling future games in that town. There were no calls for a public rally of Adrian citizens to support the civil rights of the Giants. There were no editorials demanding equal rights for their town's black all-star team. Maybe, coming off the *Plessy v. Ferguson* case, this was the new and legally acceptable way to treat your fellow countrymen, who just also happened to have black skin.

Hey, Don't Drink the Lemonade

The Giants' next local appearance was in northern Lenawee County at Devil's Lake. Forsaking a horse and buggy, one could take the train west out of Adrian on the Lake Shore to Hudson, hop aboard the northbound Cincinnati, Jackson and Mackinac, and arrive at Manitou Beach. A short jaunt around the southwest side of Devil's Lake would place you at Oak Grove Park. The popular resort community would be overrun with members of the Maccabees, whose families were there to swim and play for a few days in late July. The lake earned its name when Pottawatomi Chief Meteau's daughter, who was said to be a fine swimmer, drowned. Her body was never recovered, and the Chief declared that the devil must have snatched her, and thus the lake's name.[1]

Farther away, the Giants continued to play ball after their mistreatment by the businesses in Flint. They lost in Saginaw to the Flint and Pere Marquette Railroad-sponsored team on Saturday, but won the rematch the following day.[2] The Giants headed out of Saginaw toward the northwest part of the lower peninsula. One of their next stops was picturesque Traverse City, a community which sat in a bay off Lake Michigan, to play the hometown Hustlers. The locals had always prided themselves on their good ball teams and supportive fan base. The Giants won the games, and a reprint of the *Traverse Bay Eagle* newspaper said the locals had no reason to complain about the outcomes. The Hustlers were skilled, but the Giants were "brilliant players."[3]

The Giants' management was attempting to schedule additional dates against competitive teams in Adrian, as the Defiance Grays would later visit Lawrence Park and the Grand Rapids Gold Bugs were still in discussions. Along that same competitive realm, over a week after plans had been leaked to the press for a black baseball world championship series, there were no additional details circulating.[4]

The Giants at this point of 1896, had to reassert its claim as the state's top independent team. The Flint Champions declared that they were Michigan's best, but they had just recently been swept by the Giants, while the Flint and Pere Marquette Railroad team had taken two out of three from the Champions. By some odd reasoning, the railroad company club now claimed to be the state's best, even though the Page Fence nine had won three of four games against them this season. "The independent championship of Michigan must belong to Adrian," declared the *Evening Telegram*. "It is well enough for Adrian to step in and say, 'hands off.'" The paper added that the city could also rightly claim to be the independent champions of the world, for their success in 1894 too! Doing so, they claimed, apparently with a straight face, would not be an "over reach" either.[5]

As a warm-up to the big contest at Devil's Lake, the Giants rolled into Homer, just south of Albion in Calhoun County, and lost a 5–4 decision. The Homer club had managed to secure the services of a pitcher named Ferguson, who was most likely Charlie Ferguson, from the 1895 Lansing Senators. Ferguson, a big, blonde right-hander, had found himself without a team when the Tacoma, Washington, Rabbits had disbanded in June. He returned to Michigan and was on his way to follow his Tacoma manager to Toledo, but that wouldn't be until mid–August.[6] Ferguson and a man named Robinson, who started the game, managed to hold the Giants to four runs and grabbed the victory. Returning Giants hurler James Chavous could not secure the win, and Pete Burns was again behind the plate, as Vasco Graham had been battling a hand injury for a few weeks and had difficulty playing that position.[7]

The next day, the two teams squared off at the tourist resort at Devil's Lake. Homer wanted a sweep of their two-game series, and the Page Fence Giants wanted revenge. Even though this rematch was played not too far from Adrian, very few game details exist. The Giants won either 10–4 or 9–4, as the two Adrian dailies conflict. The game was played at Oak Grove Park, a diamond carved out of what was called Green's Landing, on a large swath of land owned by Orson Green on the southern shoreline of Devil's Lake. Green's acreage was just east of Beardsell's property, which also sat along the lake's edge, adjacent to the Manitou Beach tourist development.[8] Several thousand people, probably mostly Maccabees, attended this hotly contested ball game. In a rather odd twist, two umpires were used, as Homer provided a man behind the plate and the familiar Jim Mullahy surveyed the bases.[9]

To be accurate, the actual odd twist came out of the concessionaire at the third annual Southern Michigan Maccabee Association at Devil's Lake. Will Parsons (no relation to Gus of the Giants) had won the bid to be the summer retreat's sole soft drink provider. He mixed ten gallons of water with over a dozen freshly squeezed lemons, along with some other concoctions, and sold drinks to spectators and other Maccabees. The *Evening Telegram* was quite reserved in its headline, calling Parsons' drink "Hot Stuff."[10] However, the *Daily Times and Expositor* was quite a bit more honest with its coverage and called Parsons' mixture one that "Poisoned Picnickers."[11]

Neither Adrian daily newspaper had much to say about the ball game, as they spent their print space writing about the lemonade fiasco, throwing up, or both. It was a very warm day, and over 100 people quickly purchased a glass of lemonade, drank the liquid, and 30 minutes later found themselves sprawled around Green's Landing, too sick to move. Three physicians happened to be attending the ball game and treated the ill. One observer said the place looked like an outdoor hospital, and many people thought they were going to die. The effect was so strong that a bicyclist became so ill, he fell off his ride.[12]

One of the people who ingested the lemonade was the Giants' Gus Parsons. He couldn't send his usual game report back to the newspapers, as he spent two hours rolling around the ground in agony. That fact is probably another reason neither Adrian paper had much to say about the game between Homer and the Page Fence men. Parsons must have walked into the *Daily Times and Expositor* office the following day, as that paper had a detailed account of his suffering. Parsons drank half a glass of lemonade before an unknown man leaned over to him and said, "That'll make you sick." Parsons, upset at the late notice, retorted, "Well, why the deuce didn't you tell me that before I drank any of the stuff?" The mystery man replied, "Oh, I didn't want you to waste your money." Parsons claimed he thanked the man, whom he sarcastically dubbed "the kind economist," and promptly lay down under a tree and prepared to die.[13] Needless to say, Parsons did not die, and neither did anyone else from drinking the lemonade. People began to feel better once they experienced "extreme retching," but Parsons was not alone in a belief they were all going to heaven that afternoon.[14]

Almost immediately, an investigation took place to see what was wrong with Will Parsons' fresh lemonade. Someone in the medical community figured that when Parsons asked at a drug store in nearby Hudson to purchase tartaric acid, to add a bit of a kick to his lemonade, tartar emetic, a poisonous, crystal-like powder, was wrongly substituted. The poison was used as an expectorant for parasites, and it effectively did its job that afternoon at Devil's Lake.[15]

While the Giants were at Homer and Devil's Lake, the Defiance Grays spent the better part of the past week slugging it out in a series of games with rival Bryan. The Greys and Bryan were literally fighting it out on the diamonds of northern Ohio. An ugly brawl occurred in the Thursday contest at Delta, Ohio. Defiance led by three runs in the ninth inning when their catcher, Greenwald, was tripped by a Bryan player named Holmes, which allowed two runs to score. When Greenwald grabbed Holmes to repay him for his "villainy," the benches emptied onto the diamond. Greenwald took on the first seven or eight Bryan players who ran up to him and more than held his own. Outside the main Greenwald scrum, former Giant and current Bryan player William Malone was tussling with a member of the Greys. The Defiance *Daily Republican* said, "During the melee Julius Castle distinguished himself by kicking Malone, the n-----, who plays 1st base for Bryan." It took 12 minutes to restore order. When calmer heads prevailed, Defiance retired the last batter and took their winnings home. Heavy betting to the tune of several hundred dollars added to the game-day tension. Bryan's boosters were hopeful that three last-minute ringers would bring a victory, and they wagered large sums to win both the game and the betting pot. There was no mention of the recently released Joe Miller playing for the Bryan team.[16]

The after-effects of the brawl with Bryan apparently carried over the next day for the Defiance nine. The self-proclaimed Ohio champions had a hard ride to Adrian, covering 46 miles on rickety 1890s railroad tracks. They were tired when they arrived and didn't put up much of a fight. The Giants absolutely drilled the Greys, 13–1. By one story, Defiance committed nine errors, while another said there were a whopping 12 fielding miscues. The Greys' infield was a virtual sieve, committing seven errors and basically eliminating any chance of beating George Wilson and the powerful Page Fence crew. As a matter of fact, the Greys' single run came on a Bill Binga throwing error. The *Evening Telegram* again singled out Billy Holland, who "was funny, as usual, and incidentally played star ball." Other highlights included the fielding work of "Cinci," Charles Grant, "the modest second baseman of the Giants, [who] covers all the territory, and allows nothing to break through," and the all-around play and daring base running of George Taylor.[17]

The *Daily Times and Expositor* used many food-related adjectives to describe the thrashing the Giants administered that day. Defiance was "nearly starved" and "they kept trying to climb into the pantry window until it was slammed down and bolted on the inside." The Giants were "voracious club-swingers [who] made a hearty meal of the Defiance visitors."[18]

The second game between the clubs had the *Evening Telegram* call it "another easy one." The Defiance boys did a bit better than the day before, only losing by a count of 6–2. The victory placed the Giants' season record at 80 wins and 19 losses. Billy Holland's coacher antics kept the Greys off-balance at the plate and everyone else in stitches. His pitching was superb and his "monkey-shines, as usual … kept everybody in good humor—even the fellows who couldn't locate his curves." The paper claimed there wasn't much difference between Holland and star hurler George Wilson. "He is hardly less a wonder than Wilson, though his pitching is so much covered up by his antics that it is almost lost sight of in the games." It took 90 minutes for the Giants to chalk up another victory. However, both dailies noted that the Lawrence Park crowd was smaller than expected. The *Evening Telegram* was especially disgusted with the lack of support shown for both teams. It complained that Adrian would have a hard time claiming to be a great baseball town with small crowds and that what was being played at Lawrence Park was "far superior to anything that can be seen outside the Western League."[19]

The Giants left for a 15-day trip across Ohio. On the schedule were stops in Defiance, Tiffin, Norwalk, Galion, Gibsonburg, St. Mary's, Wapakoneta and Bucyrus.[20] How many of these games were played is up to debate. Over the next two weeks, only a couple of the game scores made it back to either the *Evening Telegram* or the *Daily Times and Expositor*.

The Giants' roster included only ten men at this point of the season. The infield was manned by first baseman and usual leadoff hitter George Taylor, with Charles Grant at second, Bill Binga at third and Grant "Home Run" Johnson at shortstop. The outfield was Billy Holland in left field, Fred Van Dyke in center, and Pete Burns in right. When they were not pitching, George Wilson and Jim Chavous would also roam the outfield. Vasco Graham was the main catcher, with Burns acting as his substitute.

Over the next two weeks, Giants baseball coverage was at a two-year low. The team defeated the Greys again on Sunday, August 2, in a game in Defiance, 13–8, behind the pitching of Chavous. The next day, in Tiffin, Ohio, the Giants narrowly nipped the Gibsonberg team, 2–1.[21] The results of other games played during this Ohio swing were not reported back to Adrian.

However, the big news now was that the Buffalo Bill Wild West Show was coming to town. Performing two shows on Tuesday, August 4, the troupe, featuring Buffalo Bill Cody, trick shooter extraordinaire Annie Oakley, the usual appearances of "Cowboys and Indians" and assorted "foreigners," attracted 15,500 paying customers to Lawrence Park. The Buffalo Bill Show was so popular that when it was next performed in Jackson, at least 400 people boarded the train in Adrian and went to see it again.[22]

Whatever excitement surrounded the town with the traveling Western show, it would be dampened later that month. In 1895, tragedy had struck the ball club when Gus Brooks died in Hastings, Michigan. This time, the team's management suffered the blow when Rolla Taylor's wife, Maude, unexpectedly died on August 17. Her death certificate said she died due to complications from childbirth.[23] However, the couple's youngest child, Adelaide, was born four years earlier, and their grave site at Oakwood Cemetery does not include any infants. So it is possible that Mrs. Taylor suffered for several years of poor health before she died at the young age of 34. A large crowd gathered at the couple's home at 52 Broad Street to honor Maude (Ayers) Taylor, who "was of a sprightly, vivacious disposition," was very kind and considered a pillar in the Adrian community. Her home at the corner of Broad and Butler Streets was filled with many floral arrangements sent by grieving friends. In the 1890s, a lengthy newspaper article about a deceased woman was rare, and Taylor's death and those who subsequently attended her funeral were carefully noted in both the Adrian dailies. Len Hoch served as one of her pallbearers. Taylor and Hoch attending to funeral duties certainly contributed to the lack of press for the ball club back in Adrian in August.[24]

The day following Mrs. Taylor's death, the Giants posted a 6–2 victory in Dundee, Michigan, over the Flint Champions. The contest featured a woefully out-of-touch umpire,

Frank Treadwell, who followed the old baseball rules of 1886, which created "some laughable breaks," according to Gus Parsons. The game was an eight-inning affair as lefty Wilson was particularly effective, striking out about one Flint man per inning.[25] Wilson was apparently cruising toward a shutout when the "generous coiled spring hustlers" gave away two runs in a put-up job," as they "couldn't bear to shut them out." The Giants must have entertained the Dundee crowd with their best performances, as Parsons claimed, "everybody enjoyed the game immensely." One paper reported, "The inimitable Page Fence Giants, half-minstrel, half-boyish aggregation of athlete stars," demonstrated a "happy-go-luck style, making witty sallies at their luckless opponents and consummating the slaughter with professional sang froid."[26]

As great and entertaining as the team was on Tuesday, the Giants were the opposite for a Wednesday game in Tecumseh against Flint. Baseball management remained in Adrian for Maude Taylor's funeral, while the Giants demonstrated a lack of focus as they lost to Flint, 12–10. Billy Holland was hit hard, and Vasco Graham, in a rare relief appearance, tried his hand in the box. Ed Mulhearn was Flint's hitting star, and shortstop Dennis Lowney was again a slick fielding wizard for the Champions. Grant Johnson slugged a round-tripper for the Giants, but it wasn't enough to offset his team's shoddy fielding.[27] The Giants didn't like to lose but had defeated Flint several times this summer and were probably more concerned with their rematch the next day with Grand Rapids.

Coming off his Tuesday victory against Flint at Dundee, Wilson was the choice to face Deacon Ellis' Gold Bugs at Lawrence Park on Thursday, August 20. The game was highly publicized to push people to attend the game. The Giants' lineup was printed in one paper a day early to motivate the locals to dig into their pockets and pay to see these two outstanding teams. For the Page Fence stars, Taylor (1b) would do his customary leading off, followed by Binga (3b), Johnson (SS), Burns (C), Holland (LF), Wilson (P), Chavous (RF), Grant (2b) and Van Dyke (CF).[28]

Only 300 people paid their way into Lawrence Park to see Wilson and the Giants defeat the mighty Western Leaguers, 6–4. The visitors put a strong team on the field, as eight of their nine starters had either played in the majors or would in the future. Righty pitcher John Slagle started for the Gold Bugs and whose major league claim to fame was one appearance to earn what would now be called a "save" for Cincinnati's Kelly's Killers in 1891. Slagle allowed 11 hits, while he struck out one and walked two. Wilson allowed ten Gold Bugs hits, walked three and struck out four batters in winning the contest.[29]

However, there was an undercurrent to this game, even with the Giants' victory, which was not prevalent in Adrian last season. The ill feelings overshadowed a wonderful game by Fred Van Dyke, who had three hits, knocked in the winning run and saved at least two others when he "scooped up" a fly ball just before it hit the ground. The Giants believed that umpire Jim Mullahy was not giving them fair calls, again. In the second inning, Grant Johnson was caught in a rundown between first and second. The Giants alleged—led by Charles Grant—that one of the Gold Bugs had held Johnson so the star shortstop could be tagged out. The exchange between Grant and umpire Mullahy became so heated, it was believed a fight would break out. The *Adrian Daily Times and Expositor*, apparently after speaking with Gus Parsons, offered more details. The business manager claimed that Mullaly told Grant, "Oh, go on, play ball, you can't win out anyway." Grant threatened to strike the umpire and had to be forcibly restrained. However, before being grabbed, Grant bumped into Mullaly. The umpire, who was standing with his feet crossed, lost his balance and fell.[30]

The rival *Evening Telegram* covered the incident briefly the following day. The Johnson tag out play involved no fight, and "the matter was amicably settled." There was no mention of the bump or of Mullaly falling, and there was no accusatory quote from Parsons either. Their paper never mentioned Charles Grant being involved in the incident. The *Telegram*'s next two days of coverage of the Giants' win was filled with comments from all over the board. They derided Gold Bugs manager Deacon Ellis, who said that Lawrence Park needed to be groomed better, since it still showed the wear and tear of the Buffalo Bill extravaganza. The paper also wanted to know what was wrong with the Palmyra Wonder. It said, "Binga's efforts to win deserve recognition. He is in the game to win," and predicted the Page Fence team "would make many of the National League take water."[31] The *Evening Telegram* also acknowledged the black gentlemen's attitude toward umpiring. "The Giants seemed to feel that they always get the worst of the umpiring on the home grounds. It is a mistaken idea, however, that Adrian people are not in sympathy with the Giants."[32]

However, the following day, a very troubling racial comment appeared in the *Evening Telegram*. "Our Giants, are as quite [*sic*] and gentlemanly a set of boys as can be found anywhere, but they won't stand it to be called n-----s and we don't blame them. But, they can play ball can't they."[33] Well, who was calling them that foul name? Was it umpire Mullaly who touched a raw nerve in the normally laid-back Charles Grant? Were players from the Grand Rapids club causing problems and adding a racial epithet? Was the name-calling coming from the paltry crowd that showed up at Adrian's Lawrence Park? If the use of the word was so troubling, why didn't the *Evening Telegram* identify the culprits using this foul language? The *Daily Times and Expositor*, while originally printing a more detailed account of the Grant and Mullaly confrontation, was silent on any the use of the "n" word.

Whatever negative feeling emanated from the stands or from the Gold Bugs about the Giants, it was not the case across the entire country. A few days after their win over Grand Rapids, an unnamed manufacturer presented the Giants a dozen new wooden bats. A note accompanying the package said there was no charge for the 12 gifts.[34] A Paw Paw, Michigan, newspaper, publicizing a future appearance of the Giants in their town, was highly complimentary. "The colored gentlemen composing the team are not only ball players of high class, but they are merry makers as well and their good natured raillery and unique coaching keep the spectators in a roar of laughter."[35] Another Michigan town, which had unsuccessfully tried to lure the Giants for an 1895 appearance, advertised that "Binga will be here Tuesday, September 1, with the Page Fence Giants (All colored)."[36] As would be the case for the Giants' entire existence, the treatment of them as ballplayers and as men varied from town to town and was mostly out of their control.

A few days after broaching the racial discord, the *Evening Telegram*, in maybe a slight aimed at the Adrian baseball cranks who were less than supportive of the town's black ball players, printed this nugget: "No city in Michigan has shown more courtesies to Adrian's famous ball team than Saginaw. They are always received there with a royal welcome." The Saginaw-based Flint and Pere Marquette Railroad team would soon play the Giants in Adrian. Giants management was even adding a balloon ascension to increase the number of fans at Lawrence Park. It was just one year ago that Adrian had claimed to be the baseball capital of the Michigan, and now it was forced to add a side show to boost attendance. The baseball management let the Saginaw people know they appreciated the way their town had always treated the Page Fence nine and urged Adrian residents to come out and show positive support. The balloon display, featuring black Professor Osseo Phillips from Manitou

Beach, went off without a hitch. Unfortunately, the ball crowd was the opposite of positive and turned unruly and violent.[37]

The throng of freeloading patrons hoping to witness a game at Lawrence Park again appeared in full force. Five hundred people paid to see the game and the balloon launch, while another 500 took it in for free and stood along the bluffs adjacent to the ball field. Even though last season's canvas wall reappeared on the north side of the field, it did not dissuade the freeloaders. A second group of people, mostly young boys and men, crowded around to the right of the grandstand and tried to gather a free peek at the festivities. They attacked a special one-man security force, hired just for this occasion, pushed and pummeled him and ripped his vest. When Adrian town marshal Henig, along with a few city policemen, arrived, the unruly mob calmed down. The fans resumed to watching the balloonist and the baseball game.[38]

The game wasn't much to watch for those rooting for the Page Fence men. They saw Palmyra's Harvey Bailey defeat Billy Holland, 9–2, thanks to four F & PM runs in the opening inning. The Giants responded with one run of their own in the first, but Bailey held them to just six hits, all singles, and easily won the game. The Giants' highlight was nearly turning a triple play on an infield grounder in the eighth inning, but Graham dropped the ball (probably at home) to nullify the attempt.[39]

The balloon ascension began in the ninth inning, but Phillips needed some help, and a group of neighborhood boys came forth to help on the inflation. Once airborne, Phillips tossed out advertising cards on the way up, and when he rose to an estimated 800 feet, he parachuted out of the balloon. On his way down, Phillips "performed on the bar" and finally landed near the flag pole in left field, about 150 yards from where he took off. Without the parachuting Phillips' weight in tow, the balloon rose to about 2,000 feet and drifted west of the park, before dropping to a rest on Greely Street. The combination ball game and balloonist was a profit maker for the local organizers.[40]

The two teams were to play again Saturday and Sunday, but in Saginaw, the home base for the railroad's Flint and Pere Marquette nine. The Giants were probably looking forward to visiting the area in Michigan's thumb region, whose citizens had been very hospitable toward them over the past two years. However, neither Adrian daily paper provided details of the games, though they still printed, nearly every day on the front page, the National and Western League scores and standings.

Saginaw baseball cranks were excited to have the Giants in town. There was no mention of the bike parade before the game, but the promoters did say the "Giant quartette of Chicago" would sing during the game.[41] For the second time in as many days, the F & PM squad defeated the Giants. This contest was much closer than the day before in Adrian. The Saginaw squad's Toby Ferry allowed five runs in the first inning, due to some timely hitting and daring Giants base running. However, Jim Chavous was not able to keep the Saginaw men in check. One tough-luck play came in the second inning, when Eddie Cull's fly ball hit Fred Van Dyke in the hand. Instead of catching it, Van Dyke deflected the ball into the stands for a home run.[42]

In the ninth inning, with the local men trailing, Cull's dramatic, two-strike, two-out home run over the right field fence tied the game. His blast was so unexpected that the crowd sat in hushed amazement. When former Adrian Demon Ben Ireland singled up the middle, the Saginaw men had a shot at winning. John Bloomington then drilled "the longest hit of the year, way out among the geese that pasture on the common." The hit drove in Ireland and put the Saginaw squad in the lead, 12–11. The Giants went quietly in the bottom of the ninth and dropped the game. However, Billy Holland did not go quietly after the team's loss. He announced for the entire world to hear that the Giants would win tomorrow's game.[43]

Around 750 people had attended the Saturday affair, which was satisfactorily umped by a man named Howe. Both teams approved of his calls, and it was hoped he would also work the Sunday game in Saginaw. Instead, for some reason Frank Callahan, a former Saginaw minor leaguer and a Detroit native, worked behind the plate. The *Saginaw Courier Herald* said Callahan was better as a player than an ump. George Black, a local player, an acquaintance of Len Hoch and a local baseball crank, was also available to ump, but somehow Callahan got the job.[44]

The Giants made good on Holland's promise from the day before and beat the F & PM club, 13–10. Nearly twice as many people attended Sunday's game, which featured the Palmyra boys, Wilson and Bailey, squaring off in the pitcher's box. Wilson got little fielding help from his fellow Giants as they booted the ball in the fifth inning, which led to seven unearned runs. Wilson became quite upset at his team's poor play and catcher Burns' inability to "hold his speedy curves." "Wilson was up in the air in this inning, but it was enough to send any pitcher skyward," was the view of the *Saginaw Courier Herald*. On the other side, Bailey's defense was little better, as infield bobbles and hits barely eluding players led to his demise.[45]

The town of Saginaw continued its fine treatment and acceptance of the Page Fence club. They were especially glowing in praise of George Wilson, who they felt should be in the major leagues. "With a good catcher and proper support in the field, Wilson would make it interesting for any team in the country in or out of the National League. His underhand raise ball is simply unhittable. The batter usually reacts about three feet under the ball, which usually skims along about knee high until the batsman gets ready to swing at it, when it shoots upward almost to his shoulder."[46]

While the win against Grand Rapids was nice and the finale against the F & PM club was satisfactory, the Giants were aiming their sights at the upcoming contests with the Cuban Giants. The management of these two fine professional baseball teams had decided that a lengthy series, much longer than the three games originally announced, would be played, starting in mid–September. The games, 15 in all, would be contested in Michigan, Indiana and Ohio, and would decide, once and for all, the black baseball championship of the world.

◆ 17 ◆

Here Come the Giants

To bide their time before the big world championship, the Giants continued to play games with local clubs and against professional players. The Giants probably hoped to have easy games between now and the championship series and likely prayed that no one on the ten-member team got hurt.

They ended August in the southwestern Michigan community of Paw Paw, where a large crowd saw them rip the locals, 22–1.[1] The community decided that day to hand out awards to fine plays in the field. When imported ringer Susby Lawton crossed the plate for a Paw Paw run, one of the town's fair maidens presented him with a basket of fresh flowers. That gift would be the extent of the day's giving to the home club. The Giants responded with 22 runs, and one paper said they could have scored another 22 if they had "tried hard." When one of the Giants slugged a home run, a Paw Paw resident "promptly and appropriately presented him a mammoth watermelon" that was said to better than a bunch of flowers anyway. "A lively scramble" ensued as the black players devoured the award and showed the audience "that the darkeys can play ball." The Paw Paw paper complimented the Page Fence club, saying they were a "merry, jolly, gentlemanly lot of fellows, who keep the spectators hugely amused and good natured," all while slaughtering the home team.[2]

The Giants began September as they had ended August, with a big win. The Flint and Pere Marquette team of Saginaw was again their opponent as they appeared in Williamston, Michigan, about 20 miles east of the state capital. The *Williamston Enterprise* claimed the clubs were "two of the best teams in the state, outside of the Western League" and urged people to attend the game at Riverside Park.[3] This was the community which had featured Bill Binga in its preview story for the game. Before he joined the Giants late in 1895, Binga had played games at Riverside Park, both as a hired ringer and as a member of his short-lived, all-star, all-black team. The Giants won in Williamston, 20–5, over the Saginaw men in front of a very large audience who braved high winds to view the contest.[4] The next day, the Giants made their way to Laingsburg, about ten miles to the north, and beat the locals, 17–1, again in front of a large crowd of fans.[5]

The Giants then played Flint in Flint and lost, 12–9, as Holland was hit hard. The only Giants highlight was a Grant Johnson round-tripper described as "a corking line hit over the race track," during a ninth-inning rally which fell short.[6] The Giants then appeared again in hospitable Saginaw for a Sunday afternoon tilt with the F & PM team. A special excursion train from Yale to Saginaw was added to the regular passenger schedule, and a 90-cent ticket would get you to the game and back. A Yale newspaper said the contest would feature "a scientific game of base ball played by the most amusing club in the country."[7] Grant Johnson out-dueled Harvey Bailey, 1–0, to secure the win. Both pitchers were effective as they surrendered only nine hits. About 500 people attended the game, with no word on how many took the special train out of Yale.[8]

The Giants had plans to play a game on Labor Day against a semiprofessional squad in Detroit's new Bennett Park. Instead, they played two games against a team called the Athletics. The Giants won, 12–3, in the morning game and came back and took the afternoon contest, 11–2. The *Detroit Free Press* said the Giants outplayed the Athletics in every phase of the game, and their wins both came easily.[9] Bennett Park was at the corner of Michigan and Trumbull and featured a 5,000-seat, large wooden grandstand behind home plate. It stood until 1911, when it was torn down by the new owners of the Detroit Tigers, who incidentally had family ties in Adrian, and replaced with Navin Field. The site was the same corner as the later Tiger Stadium.[10]

A day later, September 8, the Giants were to play the Jackson Wolverines of the Interstate League at Adrian's Lawrence Park. Considering all the ill-will between Adrian and Jackson and the near-riot last year in Jackson, it was amazing that the game was scheduled in one of the communities. However, the game was soon moved to the more neutral Dundee, Michigan. To add to the spectacle, the victorious club would keep the gate receipts along with a nice $250 bonus prize.[11] A supportive crowd from Adrian made the trek to the tiny southeastern Michigan community to see Wilson and the Giants whip the Interstate League entry, 7–0.[12] The Palmyra Wonder, who had been both verbally and physically accosted in one of last year's games in Jackson, undoubtedly enjoyed the moment and the cash that was about to be split among the victorious Giants. The winning nine returned home for a night in Adrian, before they left the following morning on the Wabash Railroad for a game in Bryan, Ohio.[13]

The actual game in the northern Ohio community was uneventful, as Jim Chavous mowed down the Bryan boys, 12–1. The visit to Bryan was anything but uneventful as ex-Giant Joe Miller appeared at the diamond and caused a ruckus. It was unclear whether Miller was now on the Bryan team, after the $125 contract had been dangled in front of him to leave the Giants. Cyclone Joe was upset with the Giants' management and claimed they had refused to pay him $24 in back salary. Miller decided that if he wasn't going to get paid, he would grab $24 of Page Fence Giants' property. He managed to snag "two uniforms and a worthless chest protector," but was unsuccessful in attempts to grab more Giants property. He did demand additional PFG uniforms, but "most of the men refused to comply" and stated that they were personal items. Team management's view was that when Miller left the Giants, he failed to give the required two-week notice. His action cost the team money for a replacement player. Gus Parsons was not pleased with Miller's stunt, and the rumor was that if the former Giants pitcher showed up in the state of Michigan, he would be arrested for larceny.[14]

Len Hoch, when not carrying out his postmaster's duties in town, took pen to paper and sent *The Sporting News* a note about the upcoming black baseball championship battle. He praised the Giants for their wins against Grand Rapids, Milwaukee and Jackson, Michigan. He also singled out George Wilson for pitching in 32 games and winning 27, including nine shutouts. Hoch claimed that going into the championship tilt, the Page Fence men had recorded a record of 130 wins and 20 losses. The scheduled games against the Cuban Giants would begin on September 13 in Lima, Ohio, followed by contests in Montpelier, Ohio, Adrian, Hudson, Lansing and Allegan, Michigan, South Bend, Indiana, and finally to Hastings, Grand Rapids, Quincy and Detroit, Michigan.[15]

The Page Fence men had been able to rest a couple of days, while the East Coast–

based Cuban Giants defeated a team in Titusville, Pennsylvania, 12–4, on Friday.[16] Both teams had to make their way to Lima, Ohio, for their Sunday, September 13 contest, the first of 12 games to settle the championship baseball debate. The games garnered national attention. Len Hoch sent stories to *The Sporting News*, and later *Sporting Life* printed game-by-game scores. The *New York Sun* reported the first game score and even correctly printed the contest as the Page Fence Giants versus the Cuban X Giants.[17] There were actually two Cuban Giants teams playing that year. However, no one in Adrian managed to realize it until after the series was completed. The Page Fence Giants were competing against the Cuban X Giants, an off-shoot of the original Cuban Giants.[18] Their opponent was always referred to as the Cuban Giants, and it wasn't until the series was well over that the local management included their foe's "X" designation.

The Page Fence roster remained at ten, as it had since the departure of Joe Miller in mid–July. The infield was George Taylor, Charles Grant, Grant Johnson and Bill Binga. The outfield was Vasco Graham, Fred Van Dyke, and Billy Holland, when he wasn't pitching. Pete Burns was behind the plate, and Jim Chavous and George Wilson were pitchers and change fielders.[19] The Cuban X Giants had three former Page Fence Giants on their 12-man roster. James W. Patterson finished the 1895 season with the Giants and was supposed to have begun 1896 with the Page Fence men, except that no game results mentioned him with the Adrian club this season; he was at second base for the Cuban Giants. Sol White, Bud Fowler's 1895 Page Fence Giants replacement, was now manning shortstop for the Cuban Giants. A man named Miller was also on the Cubans' roster. Over the years, there has been a dispute as to who it was, with Frank Miller usually referred to as this man.[20] However, in a story after the season, Len Hoch said the Cubans pitcher was Joe Miller. If Hoch was correct, and there was no reason to believe he would lie about this person, the former Page Fence hurler would be facing his old team for the championship. The two remaining infielders were Ed Wilson (who had been rumored as an emergency candidate in May for the Page Fence Giants) at first base and William Jackson at third base, with Andy Jackson behind the plate. In the outfield were Bob Jackson in left, Oscar Jackson in center and George Terrill in right. The pitching staff, in addition to Miller, consisted of William Selden, veteran left-handed star George Stovey, and a man named Banks.[21]

In the opening championship game in Lima, Ohio, the Cuban X Giants came from behind to grab an 8–6 victory over the Page Fence men. A crucial outfield error opened the door for a five-run seventh inning which helped sink the Adrian men. The error was blamed on a rough field, which indicated that the ball must have eluded a Page Fence Giants outfielder, or he fell in pursuit. The Palmyra Wonder started the series and held the Cubans to six hits. William Selden, a veteran of nearly ten years of professional ball, earned the victory, even though the Page Fence crew hammered out ten hits.[22]

Hoch's report in *The Sporting News* claimed that baseball fever was so high that nine train carloads of fans made the trip from Adrian to Lima for the series opener.[23] The Lima Northern Railroad offered low rates from Adrian and at all stops along the way, so "that every one [*sic*] can afford to go and see the great game."[24] Hoch called the opener, despite the losing score, "an immense success," and claimed it was the largest crowd in Lima baseball history.[25] Both Giants clubs jumped on the rails and headed back to Adrian to spend the evening.[26]

The teams left Adrian Monday morning for Montpelier, Ohio. It rained, so the Monday afternoon game was postponed and the teams rode the rails back to Adrian. Games two and three would now be played in Hudson, Michigan, as part of four days of Free Street

Fair festivities, which ran along Main to Market Streets.[27] The morning tilt was postponed due to wet grounds, but either Mother Nature dried the field or workers expended yeomen's efforts to prepare the grounds, as the afternoon game was contested.[28]

The diamond was in a field east and across from the Cincinnati, Jackson and Mackinaw Depot, on the south side of Hudson. Detroit mayor Hazen Pingree, running for Governor of Michigan, made a speaking appearance at the depot to a crowd of about 500 people.[29] Those same 500 people, plus 500 more, hung around to watch lefty coacher Billy Holland try to even the championship series.[30] It worked for a time, as the Page Fence nine jumped out to a 7–0 lead. Something happened to Holland at the midway point of the game, and he gave up runs in bunches. In the sixth inning, Holland was pummeled for 13 runs as the Cuban X Giants took control of the game and won, 20–14. Holland took the loss and despite the slaughter pitched a complete game, while Banks earned the victory for the Cubans.[31]

The town of Hudson had at least three newspapers at this time, and each reported the game details in its unique style. The weekly *Hudson Post* exclaimed that the Cubans won, 22–12, the game was well attended, and "the Adrian club was being beautifully whipped."[32] The weekly *Hudson Republican* referred to the championship contest as from "darkest Africa" and characterized it as a "battle royal of giants." They said the final score was 20–12.[33] The daily *Hudson Gazette* was more cordial toward the black players, calling them "experts." The field conditions were still poor due to the earlier rain, and it was hard to find a dry spot on the soaked grounds. The *Gazette* also said that Holland was victimized by many fielding errors which contributed to his poor overall pitching effort. The *Gazette* praised umpire Gil Seewald, noting "although, as a usual thing, the gents of color are hard to please, not a kick was heard on the young man's decisions." The daily paper also correctly reported the final score as 20–14, unlike the two weekly rags.[34]

The Page Fence Giants managed to record their first series win in game three, with a crushing 26–6 victory, Wednesday at Quincy. Jim Chavous and Vasco Graham were the successful battery in securing the initial Page Fence victory. Former Page Fencers Joe Miller and James Patterson both pitched for the Cuban X Giants.[35] The winning Giants scored all their needed runs in a seven-run fourth inning and slammed out 22 hits. In the field, they were just as dominant, committing just a single error. The Cubans club posted a sloppy six errors in the field, which had been their team's total in their first two wins.[36]

The series became even at two wins apiece on Thursday, September 17, in Lansing. In a battle of lefty hurlers, George Wilson bested Cuban X Giants ace George Stovey, 5–2. One Adrian paper recorded the score as a 4–2 win for the Page Fence Giants.[37] The young Wilson tossed a seven-hitter as his team led from start to finish. The next game, scheduled on Friday, had been originally been set for South Bend, Indiana, but had been relocated to Lansing. It ended up being rained out.[38]

The two clubs traveled for a Saturday game to the western Michigan community of Allegan, located between Kalamazoo and Grand Rapids. The Adrian men chalked up their third win in a row and doubled up the Cuban Giants, 14–7.[39] Almost no game details made their way back to Adrian, and one paper reported the score at 15–7.[40]

Even though this series was touted as the championship of black baseball, the often bragged about baseball fever was waning in Adrian. It was obvious that the Adrian daily papers didn't send reporters to any of the early games, and whatever details Gus Parsons telegraphed back to town were not enough for even a paragraph-sized story. The two Adrian dailies rarely printed Giants box scores, unless they were playing the Adrian Demons, and that obviously lasted for just one year. The *Daily Times and Expositor* failed to print even the less detailed line scores. However, to its credit, the *Evening Telegram* did print line scores every so often, but it wasn't with any regularity. So the 1896 championship series was no different from the policy the papers had followed since the club's inception.

The Lansing rainout, which was originally slated for South Bend, was returned to the Indiana community, and the series' sixth game was played on Sunday, September 20. The Adrian club extended their winning streak to four with a 10–7 victory. The win placed the series at four games to two in favor of the Page Fence crew. Chavous was the winning pitcher with Graham behind the plate. It was reported that game six was "one of the prettiest games ever played in that city."[41] Fatigue was apparently becoming a factor in this playoff series, with fresh legs and arms becoming keys to victories. With the teams playing nearly every day, one printed blurb explained the Page Fence success as "the younger team is winning by superior fielding."[42]

Game seven was at a town that had not been listed on either of the two preliminary schedules. Hartford, Michigan, a tiny hamlet of about 1,000 people in far western Van Buren County, about 12 miles from the Lake Michigan coastline, lured one of the black championship series games to its community. Michigan Senator Julius S. Burrows' speech preceded the afternoon affair and added to the large crowd at the ball game. A narrow-gauge railroad, to drum up more spectators, offered reduced fares for a 16-mile trip from nearby Paw Paw to Hartford.[43] Residents jumped at the offer as "quite a number of people" rode the railroad to see Senator Burrows' speech and the ball game.[44] The Page Fence winning streak ended in a "hotly contested game," a 3–2 victory for the Cuban X Giants.[45]

The next day, Tuesday, September 22, the two teams squared off in another small Michigan community. Buchanan, just a few miles from the Indiana border near South Bend, was also not on either original schedule. The Adrian gentlemen won a close contest, 4–3, and held a five-to-three advantage in the 12-game series. The Page Fence Giants were just two victories from the title.[46] As usual, no other game details made their way back to Adrian, so residents had to rely on word of mouth for anything other than the final score. The next three contests would be played in Adrian, and that promised better news coverage.

However, it appears by this eighth contest in Buchanan that additional games were being added and the best of 12 format was no longer being followed. Additional games raised the number of contests one of the clubs had to win to clinch the coveted black baseball crown. Later published reports claimed that the updated series would consist of 15, 16 or 19 total games![47]

For some reason lost to history, Adrian's Lawrence Park was not the site for games between the Page Fence Giants and the Cuban X Giants. Whether the Buffalo Bill Wild West Show's damage was too difficult to repair, the Adrian fairgrounds, on the city's east end and a few blocks from the massive Page Fence company complex, would be the location for the championship battles. About one week before the teams' appearance in Adrian, grounds crews were trying to enhance the ball diamond. "The fair management is making several improvements on their ball grounds…. The sod is being removed from the diamond and bleachers will be erected with seating for a capacity of 1,000." The additional grandstand seating would add 15 cents to whatever was charged for general admission to the game.[48]

Residents of Adrian awoke on September 23 to a heavy frost covering the Lenawee County lawns and farm fields. "Much damage" was done to area crops, with grapes, tomatoes and melons especially hard hit.[49] If it warmed enough for the frost to melt, the teams were to play one game that Wednesday afternoon and then a morning and afternoon double-header on Thursday, September 24.

The Cubans nine, despite being atrocious in the field, bungling their way to eight errors, defeated the hometown club, 8–5, on Wednesday. The Page Fence team got off to a solid start, tallying three runs in the first inning and another one in the second, to lead 4–0, But the local Giants could not hold on and dropped the contest. The game was rather loosely played until the score became tied in the fifth inning, and then the intensity increased. Joe Miller defeated Page Fence Giant James Chavous over the nine innings. The Page Fence hurler was ineffective, allowing 11 hits and walking another seven Cuban X Giants. Billy Holland's outstanding play in the outfield saved the Giants on several occasions and kept the score close. One story said that if not for Holland's work, a "stampede" of X Giants would have crossed the plate. Costly errors by the Page Fence first and third baseman (likely Taylor and Binga) sealed their fate and handed the game over to the out-of-towners.[50] Former Adrian Demons second baseman and now local saloon owner Paul Kraft was behind the plate as umpire. About 800 people paid to attend the Wednesday game at the newly revamped fairgrounds diamond.[51]

At 10 o'clock the following morning, more fans showed up at the fairgrounds to see the first of two games that day. The *Evening Telegram* called the morning affair "the best game ever played in this city," and it was in front of a large crowd, too.[52] To add to the excitement, the teams needed 11 innings to settle the matter, before the local men earned an 8–5 win. The Palmyra Wonder pitched the whole way, as did his left-handed counterpart, George Stovey. The Page Fence men had to rally from a one-run deficit to tie it up in the ninth inning. "The all-around playing of Wilson and Holland were the features. Wilson's work in the box was particularly fine." Whatever crowd control was put in place was not effective as one of the Cuban X Giants named Jackson, while running for a catch in left field, managed to run over and cut the face of young boy named King.[53] Even though this was the best game ever played in Adrian, one paper had no line or box score, while the other had a simple line score and the batteries. For a world championship game and series, the Adrian daily newspapers were not pulling out all the stops by any stretch of the imagination to cover the event. While battling for the prize as Michigan's baseball capital in the summer of 1894 was important to the town, the loss of the mostly white Adrian Demons had tamped down the game's fever by 1896.

The largest crowd of the three Adrian games came out to the fairgrounds in the afternoon and witnessed what the *Evening Telegram* called a "pounding match from start to finish." The pounding was mostly done by the Page Fence gentlemen to a tune of 17–8 over the visiting Giants. The same paper also characterized the game as a "farce" when compared to the morning contest. Poor fielding doomed the Cuban X Giants, and the blowout win was also only a seven-inning affair for a reason that was never revealed. In the pitcher's box, Billy Holland beat William Selden, as the latter was touched for 18 hits and blew a 3–1, first-inning lead. Another former Adrian Demon and member of the 1896 Flint Champions, Ed Mulhearn, was originally assigned to umpire the last of the three-game series. However, someone protested (the story wasn't clear as to which team), and Page Fence Giants pitcher Jim Chavous was selected to call the championship game instead. That odd selection was a clear indication that a black player was a preferred umpire over the well-known professional white player.[54]

The most notable event of the big win was an injury to Charlie Grant. While, fielding a ball at second base, he was hit "in the stomach by a hot ball," promptly threw the batter out at first, and then "went into a slow faint, lasting some five or ten minutes." Probably flashing back to the Gus Brooks tragedy the previous season in Hastings, the Page Fence men rushed to Grant's aid. Soon a large crowd gathered around his prone body. Some vigorous massaging brought him out of his comatose state, and he recovered and managed to finish the game.[55]

Adrian's hosting the championship series brought back some of the luster to the town. The fairgrounds' grandstand was jammed full of people for both the morning and afternoon games, and the ball park vendors did good business. A teenager from Quincy was also busy that day, picking pockets, and was locked up in the local jail.[56]

With their doubleheader sweep in front of their fans, the Page Fence Giants needed just one more win to secure what was now scheduled as a 15-game championship event. The series stood at seven victories for the Adrian club and four wins for the Eastern-based Giants. If the Page Fence Giants could win just one more game, they would have the bragging rights of black baseball all to their own. The potential pennant clinching game would come in a town not on the original schedule, which had been added in a revised edition— Caro, Michigan.

The Tuscola County community is in the thumb region of Michigan's Lower Peninsula, along the Cass River. How a town with a population of less than 2,000 managed to secure a potential world championship title-clinching game has long been lost to history. The Cuban X Giants left Thursday evening for Caro following their doubleheader loss on the Wabash Railroad. The Adrian men stayed in town and on Friday morning, the Page Fence crew hitched their Monarch train car to the Wabash and headed north to Tuscola County.[57]

The pride of Adrian was now at stake in what could be the deciding game of the world championship tussle. Meanwhile, the black community was using the Giants' success to further their positive impact on Adrian. Following the 1895 season, team cook Wendell Gaskin, along with friend Duweize Barrett Wilson, created the Afro American Directory and distributed it throughout the town. Their entrepreneurial spirit was again in full gear during September of 1896. The day the Page Fence Giants swept the doubleheader from the Cuban X Giants, the *Michigan Representative* appeared around town. The *Adrian Evening Telegram* proudly boasted itself as the print shop for the *Michigan Representative* and published not one, but two glowing stories about the new black newspaper. Gaskin, with all his connections from traveling with the Giants, was the paper's business manager. He journeyed throughout Michigan, Ohio and Indiana to drum up support and secure advertisers for his latest business venture. Duweize Wilson was named the president of the paper, with Henry Harris as vice-president, Walter Burton as secretary and Horace Craig, popular local barber and Bud Fowler confidant, as the treasurer.[58]

The *Michigan Representative*'s first issue was a four-page, seven-column newspaper printed on Thursday, September 24, 1896. The *Evening Telegram* described the paper's goal as "dedicated to the best interests and highest elevation of the colored people."[59] Gaskin's three-state trip provided the paper's boosters with optimism, as he told one reporter the idea received support from both blacks and whites. Reportedly, 28 cities would send in news that impacted their black community. In addition, 25 special writers had been contacted to contribute to the new enterprise. The *Evening Telegram* noted that those 25 "are among the foremost writers" within the black community.[60] In Michigan, the paper's first edition had news and information "interesting to the colored people" from Detroit to Ann Arbor to Grand Rapids and across other parts of the state.[61]

Locally, three members of the business team would also be involved in the writing. Burton would act as the editor, with Craig and Harris as associate editors. Adrian High School grad and public speaking wiz, Miss Lida Pate, who was the step-sister of the Page

Fence Giants' traveling porter and barber, Robert Henry, would be the paper's city editor. The *Michigan Representative* would be a political supporter of the Republican Party and endorsed the fall Presidential ticket of William McKinley and Gus Hobart. The *Evening Telegram* wished all the best to the paper's organizers and wanted it to have a "long life and a fat pocket book."[62]

With his latest business venture just evolving, whether Gaskin was on the Page Fence Giants train car or not, you can bet the Adrian newspaper was being read by the team on its way to Caro. A Friday afternoon victory would allow the Page Fence team to put to rest the claims by the Chicago Unions, the Cuban X Giants, the regular Cuban Giants, or any other black team as to who were the world champions. For some reason, maybe the several-games cushion, the Adrian club started Grant Johnson in the clinching game. Maybe it was an honor, due to his and Bud Fowler's work last year in first organizing the club. Of course, Wilson and Holland had both pitched in the doubleheader the day before, and Chavous, who usually needed more rest than the two staff aces, had been in the box on Wednesday. Maybe Johnson was just doing his part to win the championship. Whatever the reason, Home Run, more known for his bat, now had a chance to secure the title with his arm.

The Friday affair was much like the Thursday afternoon game, as the Page Fence Giants bashed the Cuban X Giants and won by a large margin, 16–8. Johnson's victory clinched the world black baseball championship for the Page Fence gentlemen! The Adrian club had won eight of the first 12 games of the 15 scheduled contests. Both Adrian papers gave glowing accounts of what the victory meant to the town and the team, but printed very few game details. The *Daily Times and Expositor* gushed that the Cuban X Giants had always claimed to be the world champions, and that was no longer the case. The paper believed that with the series victory, the Giants should also add the amateur championship of the United States and of the entire world to its crown. The championship would also improve the business fortunes of the Page Fence Giants, as plans were to play "a great part of the time next season" out East in territory once controlled by the two Cuban Giants squads.[63] The *Evening Telegram* said, "The western youngsters have proven themselves too fast for the eastern Giants, not only in the field, but also at the bat, where it was feared they would prove weak against the famous sluggers of the east."[64] For years the East Coast club was known for its success at the plate, but Wilson, Holland, Chavous and Johnson, with a few exceptions, shut them down. The *Telegram* agreed with the *Times'* assessment that the title would help the club's business outlook, as their name recognition was now blared across the entire country. The *Telegram* concluded their tribute with "hearty congratulations" and anticipated the team's return to Adrian to be "their triumphant homecoming."[65]

However, the Giants winning the series eight games to four did not end the series. There were still stops in Hastings, Grand Rapids, and two at Detroit's fancy new Bennett Park. How much enthusiasm would there be at these Michigan towns? The championship series had mathematically been concluded, and a winner had been declared and crowned.

Hastings saw the largest crowd of any of the series games. Estimates were that over 2,000 people paid to witness the Saturday contest, which saw the Cuban X Giants record an 11–6 victory in game 13.[66] The following day, September 27, the Page Fence crew won, 10–2, in game 14, played in Grand Rapids.[67]

The final two games of the series were to be in Detroit on September 29 and 30, which would make the final championship series 16 games. With the win in Grand Rapids, the Page Fence Giants had now secured nine victories, so they had also won the championship in a best of 15, 16 or 17-game series, too. There was a rumor of a hastily added game Monday in Adrian, before the final two contests in Detroit. That rumor was quashed almost as soon as it was leaked. Monday's game was scheduled for Laingsburg, and the Page Fence men won that contest, 6–2, to raise their record to ten wins against five losses. Writing about the series over a decade later, Sol White of the Cuban Giants and the 1895 Page Fence second baseman, agreed with the 15-game series schedule. He agreed that after the second game the Page Fence club "won as they pleased." He added that his former club was physically "in the pink of condition and played great ball." On the other hand, White claimed his Cuban X Giants were "bad, physically, as a team in spring practice."[68]

While the two clubs were busy traveling and playing, Len Hoch was in Detroit, planning for the final two games at Bennett Park. However, the threat of rain caused the cancellation of both contests before either team apparently even made the trip to Detroit. If either of the two original schedules had been followed, it would have ended the series at 15 games. However, capitalizing on their championship, the Page Fence Giants wanted to keep playing. The Cuban X Giants, having made the trek into the Adrian club's backyard, just kept raking in the money, too, and had an opportunity to save some face with the additional games. Another game for Thursday, October 1, in baseball-crazed Montpelier, Ohio, was quickly added to the schedule. James Chavous pitched and won, 8–6, for the Page Fence club. It was finally announced that the last game of the series would be at Lawrence Park on Friday, October 2.[69]

The Adrian game on Friday lasted only five or six innings (game accounts differ), as the Cuban X Giants had to catch the train for games with the Chicago Unions that weekend. The Cuban X Giants' William Selden defeated George Wilson, limiting the Adrian club to just five hits. The final score was 5–3 in front of only about 200 people, who braved the October Michigan weather to watch the game. To keep active and warm, both teams engaged in much banter in what was described as a "talky game."[70] The series ended at 11 wins for the Page Fence Giants and six for the Cuban X Giants.

Each of the players on the championship Adrian team was awarded a fine sterling silver medal of a bar and a pendant. The design featured the work of local jeweler and baseball crank J. Will Kirk, who had awarded similar prizes to Lawrence Park ballplayers over the past two seasons. The silver bar was engraved with the player's name and the pendant with "1896. Page Fence Giants. Champions." The *Evening Telegram* called the medals "handsome pieces of work" and declared the gentlemen should be proud of all their hard work to earn the jewelry.[71]

Gus Parsons apparently gave another interview to the *Adrian Daily Times and Expositor* about the team's finances for the 1896 season. "Professionally it has been a triumphant one, but from a financial point of view so much cannot be said. The wet weather which marked earlier and later portions of the season exercised disastrous effect." There was some hesitancy to exclaim publicly that the Page Fence Giants would return in 1897, even though that had been advertised as the plan for much of the summer. Parsons wanted to wait on plans for the Western League before committing to fielding the team for a third season. He also claimed that several of the Cuban X Giants, "all of whom would like to travel under him," might be added to the 1897 Page Fence roster.[72]

Apparently whatever hard feelings existed between the two clubs, at least in one case, weren't too harsh. Pete Burns jumped ship and would play in the weekend games in Chicago for the Cuban X Giants. The remaining members of the newly crowned championship squad remained in Adrian. They toured the Page Fence Woven Wire Fence Company plant on Saturday morning. The players showed off their new championship medals to the factory

This picture from 1909 shows J. Will Kirk (#15), an Adrian jeweler who designed gifts for the Page Fence Giants and Adrian Demons. James Stevens (#26), a local tobacco merchant, was the Adrian Demons' official scorer in 1895 and later was hired as the advance agent for the Giants from 1896 to 1898 (courtesy Lenawee County Historical Museum).

workers and to Gus Parsons, Rolla Taylor, Len Hoch and advance man James W. Stevens, who accompanied the team on the plant tour.[73]

Even though the Page Fence club was officially disbanded for the season, the two championship series clubs were not done trying to earn additional money. It was revealed that the two teams would play a few games in Ohio "on the cooperative plan." The Cuban X Giants went to Chicago to play the Unions over the weekend and then made their way back east to Ohio.[74]

The details surrounding the status of these games now become murky. The Cuban X Giants went to Lima, Ohio, on Monday, October 5, to play the Page Fence club. A second game was also set for later in the week on Thursday afternoon in Delphos, Ohio, at the Fifth Street Grounds.[75] The Adrian dailies had put the team to bed for the season, and their game coverage ended for 1896. However, scores later sent to *Sporting Life* noted that the Lima game was apparently actually played in Findlay, Ohio, with the Cubans winning, 7–4. On Wednesday, October 7, the two clubs faced each other in Paulding, Ohio, where the Cubans won again, this time 8–4.[76] The Thursday afternoon game in Delphos was never played. According to the *Daily Herald* newspaper based in Delphos, someone called their town Wednesday evening and said that both teams had disbanded following the game in Paulding and would not play the scheduled Thursday game.[77] So finally, the battle for the championship between the two outstanding black baseball clubs had concluded, at least on the field.

An end of the year wrap-up story appeared in the *Evening Telegram* on Saturday, October 10. The curious lead sentence said that "the Page Fence Giants practically ended their season at their game at Lawrence Park, but since have been filling a few dates on their own account." The story noted that the team made money "and shows three figures on the right side of the ledger." The paper noted that Gus Parsons had not yet found any full-time work for the winter months and informed readers where each of the Giants would head in the off-season. The *Evening Telegram* said that none of the Giants remained in Adrian. George Taylor had already left for Denver, Colorado, and Vasco Graham to Omaha, Nebraska. Pete Burns and Billy Holland returned to their homes in Chicago, Charlie Grant to Cincinnati, Grant Johnson to Findlay, and James Chavous to Marysville, Ohio. Of the three Michigan men, Fred Van Dyke went to his home in Vandalia, Michigan, while Bill Binga moved back to Lansing and George Wilson moved in with his parents, down the road a few miles to Palmyra.[78]

The gentlemen were proud of their championship and shiny medals. Chavous was seen walking around his Marysville town sporting the "handsome silver medal."[79] Unfortunately, no image of the medal exists today, and the Adrian papers didn't print a picture of the award.

While the tussle for the baseball crown finished in early October, the follow-up battle, a war of words, continued for well over another month. The Page Fence Giants' advance agent, James Stevens, sent a summary of the championship series to *Sporting Life* in late October. In it, he listed 16 games and ended the championship series with the October 1 game in Montpelier, Ohio. Stevens' report listed the roster of both teams, including the three former Page Fence Giants, "Sol White, … Patterson … [and] Miller" with the Cuban X club. He noted the dates and locations of each contest and the final scores. He added a closing opinion that the Cuban X Giants "are all large men and hard hitters, while the Page Fence Giants are small, but they showed their Eastern rivals that they also knew how to hit, as they out-hit as well as out-fielded them." Stevens predicted a major swing through the East in 1897 for the Page Fence Giants in the backyard of the New York–based Cuban X Giants.[80]

Without a doubt, E. B. Lamar, Junior, manager of the Cuban X Giants, read Stevens' article. He responded with his own series summary, which was printed two weeks later, November 14, in the national sporting magazine. Referring to his team as the Cuban X Giants, he publicly took issue with Stevens' contention that the Adrian nine outslugged the Cuban gents. Lamar was upset that Stevens mentioned that fact and claimed "he [Stevens] failed to state how his team won the series of games. While we acknowledge they are champions for this year, we deny that they out hit us." The earlier murkiness entered at this point in Lamar's story. He included the three late Cuban X Giants wins, following the end of the official championship series in Laingsburg. His series record was 11 to 8 for the Adrian men, but had his team out-hitting Page Fence, 187–173. It is not even clear whether Lamar accompanied the team following the game in Hastings. His game accounts in Grand Rapids, Laingsburg, Montpelier, Adrian, Findlay and Paulding had scores which did not match the Adrian papers. Lamar had his Laingsburg loss as only 10–6, while the Adrian club said that it was 10–2. Lamar also had incorrect dates for several of the contests, so his information contained flaws.[81]

Lamar also claimed that the Cuban X Giants were badly injured, the Page Fence Giants quit the series early, and his team would win in a rematch. "We were at a disadvantage in playing the majority of these games, owing to the fact that for nearly two weeks six of our players had to be in the game, while disabled from charley horse and sprained ankle." Despite adding games to the original 12-game series, Lamar claimed that the Page Fence team didn't finish the schedule, which may have changed the outcome. "The only reason they gave for not playing the balance of the games was that we might beat them out for the championship and would take no chances." After his excuses, Lamar tried to convince the readers, "we don't feel sore over our defeat" and said they wanted the "pleasure of meeting them next season" and would probably beat them, too. To add to his team's resume, Lamar added into his logic the three wins in Chicago (reportedly with Page Fence Giant Pete Burns on his club) over the Chicago Unions and the Chicago Eelyaro club.[82]

In Adrian, the Page Fence men had their fancy medals and likely ignored the revisionist history from the greatly biased Lamar. The status of Adrian's baseball fever took a mighty hit late in the year. Len Hoch and one of the Taylor brothers made their way to Detroit and surmised that the old Michigan State League from 1895 would not be reprised in 1897. Taylor said the Interstate League was covering too much ground and was too expensive for a town of Adrian's size to attempt to field a competitive entry. Taylor bragged on the Giants, though, and declared it was now the town's "crack professional team." The attendance in 1896 was not as strong as it had been in the inaugural year, and Taylor claimed the Giants lost 35 games to bad weather which negatively impacted their earnings. So Adrian, in 1897, would be a one-team town again.[83]

◆ 18 ◆

Lima Northern

A story in the *Evening Telegram* in late 1895, though unrelated to baseball, would cast an ominous shadow over the Giants ball club for the 1897 season.[1] Probably no one expected the arrival of Adrian's new rail line literally to derail the Page Fence Giants in their third year of operation. If anyone had the inclination that the Lima Northern would basically end baseball in Adrian, it may have been Willis T. Lawrence.

The Lawrence family for decades had owned the spread of land on the west edge of town, nestled under the Greely and River Street bluffs. The South Branch of the River Raisin ran near the east edge of the property. On the southwest end of the site was the "old mill track" near Race Street, a little nub of a road off West Maumee. A small creek called the "old channel drain" ringed the park's north and west sides. The creek, only a few feet wide and not very deep, funneled the rain run-off from the bluffs above and drained it into the River Raisin. When the first white settlers arrived in the 1820s, Lawrence Park was a Pottawattamie campground, and the "old channel drain" was the River Raisin, before its course changed, probably with the building of the mill.[2]

Not content with having park land in his family's holding, in late 1894, Lawrence announced plans to erect between 25 and 50 cottages on the property. He planned to tear down the site's wooden floral and mechanic halls and use the lumber for the new homes. Lawrence's development would sit on the western edge of the park, and he claimed that the baseball diamond would not be negatively impacted. He proposed improving the diamond by leveling and rolling the field. His ambitious plans also called for Race Street to connect with Springbrook Avenue and for a new street to be constructed to intersect with Greely "in front of E. C. Sword's residence." In the same edition of the *Adrian Daily Times and Expositor* paper, local ice dealer Henry C. Bowen touted his plan to rent a section of Lawrence Park for horse racing in 1895.[3] Neither Lawrence's housing development nor Bowen's business plans were ever adopted.

A year later, Adrian Alderman Allen quoted Lawrence about his dislike of Sunday baseball games on the land he had rented out to the local ball cranks. However, the park was rented out for the popular Demons and Giants in 1895, and Lawrence collected his money and remained silent. Little did anyone know that the new railroad would solve Willis T. Lawrence's moral dilemma of playing on the Sabbath. The glory days at Lawrence Park were about to end.

After the 1895 baseball season concluded, there were rumors of the Lima Northern Railroad coming to Adrian. In November, the Ohio railroad claimed to be arriving in the "near future." As a show of their business strength, the firm had authorized an increase in their capital stock offering from $300,000 to $2.4 million.[4] A month later, it was predicted that the Lima Northern would have track to Adrian by April of 1896.[5] If true, the Lawrence Park ball diamond and its grandstand would be impacted, as revealed in negotiations which were not made public until a few months later.

In early 1896, local bigwigs, including J. Wallace Page, were lobbying the railroad to come to Adrian. A February 1896 meeting unveiled the tentative track design with a switch yard near the water works plant on West Maumee Street. A new depot would be erected "on the river flats," which was near the Lawrence Park ball field.[6] A few days later, one newspaper announced that there were plans for Lawrence Park to be "converted into a thriving industrial district."[7] With that excitement in the news, the Lima Northern began to play two towns against each other. Railroad officials leaked a proposal which had their tracks leaving Wauseon, Ohio, and heading north over the state line to Morenci, Michigan. The railroad's two proposed plans were to leave Morenci and lay the track to either Adrian or Hudson.[8] The town which pledged to purchase the most Lima Northern stock would obtain the rail line.

The railroad battle captivated Adrian, and the town quickly assembled a team of high-powered lobbyists. The Page Fence Giants' Rolla Taylor and Len Hoch, along with Seymour Howell, Willis T. Lawrence and J. Wallace Page, were committee members. Page went so far as to say that his company would be "liberal" in subscribing to the Lima Northern and even gave a great speech to area residents, backing the line.[9]

With Adrian all in a twitter about the Lima Northern, another unexpected new rail proposal was floated. At a meeting in late February in Defiance, Ohio, it was announced that plans were in the works to use the old rail bed of the planned, but never built, Columbus, Lima and Milwaukee line. Their route would impact the proposed Lima Northern line. To add to the rail fever, a few days later another investment group mentioned their plans to finally develop the Columbus, Lima and Milwaukee line. Both of the C, L and M groups claimed to have secured the right to use the road bed. One of the groups even claimed to know nothing of the second C, L and M proposal![10]

The Adrian papers throughout 1896 reported each and every move of the local railroad lobbyists plus news from the Lima Northern and the proposed C, L and M idea. Taylor and Hoch spent much of their early months of 1896 working on the rail plan, along with unsuccessfully organizing another minor league team and operating the Page Fence Giants. They should have stuck to the latter. The Giants began and ended their 1896 championship season, and the Lima Northern was still just a rumor in Adrian.

Adrian already had a pair of railroads in town: the more established Wabash and the Lake Shore and Michigan Southern. The LS & MS had numerous workers in their Adrian car yards and was for many years the town's largest employer. Their long-alleged competitor, the Lima Northern, by October 1896 had bridged the Maumee River in Napoleon, Ohio, but were nowhere near laying tracks into Adrian. Land acquisition negotiations had bogged down, and financial issues had delayed their entry into town. As late as November 1896, there was still a strong rumor that the line would entirely bypass Adrian and instead travel into Hudson.[11] The *Evening Telegram* declared that those local pessimists who believed the new rail line was doomed for failure "are not up to date."[12] The paper was correct.

The Lima Northern had made their way into Adrian in October 1896, but not on their own line, but rather renting pre-existing rails owned by the Wabash Railroad and Lake Shore and Michigan Southern Railroad. A new Lima Northern "Hogg" brand locomotive had recently delivered 52 train car loads of precious Ohio coal. That figure was coupled with 235 other car loads over the past few weeks into Adrian. The coal was sold to towns in southern Michigan, including Detroit and rival Hudson. Within the next month, via the Lima Northern, nearly twice as many car loads of coal would be brought to town. A company official stated that the road was "doing a good business and will prove of advantage to Adrian in many ways."[13] Still, by the opening of 1897, there was no Lima Northern track in Adrian.

While Adrian's papers usually waited until closer to spring to report on the Page Fence Giants, that was not the case for the national sporting publications, *The Sporting News* and *Sporting Life*. These two magazines printed stories in January and February 1897 about the Page Fence club and their rival, the Cuban X Giants. As one might expect, despite what Ed B. Lamar claimed last year about no hard feelings existing between the two clubs, that was simply not the case. For proof, Lamar and Gus Parsons spent the winter months trying to steal players from each other's roster.

During the 1896 championship series, the Cuban club had been called simply the Giants by members of the Adrian contingent. As later press accounts circulated, an X was added to the name Cuban Giants and used as the war of words began between those Giants and the Page Fence crew. The reason for the confusion was due to a split at the beginning of the 1896 season between the two East Coast organizers of black baseball. One team, led by J. M. Bright, remained the Cuban Giants, while the Cuban X Giants were led by Lamar.[14] No one in Adrian apparently picked up on this difference, and they didn't begin using the "X" until well after the end of the championship series. The Page Fence Giants were more accurately playing the "X" Giants for the title. Bright and Lamar battled over the next few years over the use of the name Cuban Giants, causing much confusion at the time and in subsequent years.

An early January story submitted by James Stevens to *Sporting Life* noted that the Page Fence 1897 goal was to field the strongest black team possible. Stevens claimed that their 1896 record featured 165 games with only 21 losses. The data would support a record of 144–21, but as Gus Parsons had been known to refigure games they were cheated out of as wins, or at least not losses, this record may be questioned. Stevens also said they had won a 17-game playoff against the Cuban X Giants, which added to the uncertainty of the actual length of the championship series. Stevens mentioned that the champion Giants would also look to play games in the East to "compete with the famous Cuban X Giants for supremacy." He also felt as if the game receipts would be a bit healthier out East. He announced the 1897 roster as "Bill Holland, the king of all coachers; George Taylor, who has few equals at first base and no superiors; George Wilson, the boy wonder, Patterson, Grant, Burns, Binga, Johnson, Shaw and Van Dyke." Stevens closed by saying they were still looking "for several more men equally as famous" to join those he had already named.[15]

As expected, Stevens' Page Fence Giants report was carefully scanned by the Cuban X Giants and E. B. Lamar. Two weeks later, the same national sporting publication offered a rebuttal to some of Stevens' writings. A reporter covering New York baseball said Lamar was "surprised" at Stevens' letter and claimed the Cuban X Giants would have the strongest black team this year. To add to the argument, the proposed X Giants roster included some of the same names that had supposedly already agreed to contract terms with the Adrian club; specifically, Billy Holland, George Taylor and J. W. Patterson. The story glowed at the acquisition of Taylor, considered the Page Fence Giants' best player last season. They also announced that a contract had been sent to shortstop Grant "Home Run" Johnson in hopes that he would join his three buddies on the Cuban X club. In addition, John Nelson, who had played a handful of early games for the 1895 Page Fence club before being released, also joined the New York–based team.[16]

Not to be outdone, Len Hoch used his writing skills and fired off a response to Lamar. A week after the *Sporting Life* story was scanned by readers across the country, Hoch sent a lengthy article to *The Sporting News*. Hoch said that 9,000 souvenir calendars, featuring the Page Fence Giants team, had been sent out as a promotional gift to publicize the club and the company. Hoch said Gus Parsons was back for his third year as business manager and would be fresh for the task, having just returned from a two-month vacation with his wife in Kansas City, Missouri. Named on the Page Fence Giants roster were J. W. Patterson, Grant Johnson, George Taylor, George Wilson, Pete Burns, Billy Holland, Charles Grant, William "Bill" Binga, Fred Van Dyke and Robert Shaw. Hoch said the bulk of the season would be played in the East, where the champions could perform in front of a new audience. Holland, Taylor and Patterson, claimed just two weeks earlier to be playing for the X Giants, were on Hoch's 1897 Page Fence roster.[17]

Local newspaper coverage about the Giants began to trickle out to Adrian residents in early March. One erroneous report was that Len Hoch was no longer associated with the Giants and that Parsons and Rolla Taylor, with assistance from James Stevens, would be the team's management group. Two days later, Hoch got word to the paper that he would take a backseat from daily club operations, but still was "financially interested."[18]

At this same time, in a visit to the *Adrian Telegram* office, Gus Parsons and James Stevens informed the newspaper that the Page Fence Giants, shockingly, would not play any games in Adrian in 1897. No reason was given for this decision either. The same interview revealed the club's early season schedule, which would start with the Class A Indianapolis Indians of the Western League on April 2. A series against fellow Western Leaguers, the Columbus Senators, would follow, as the Giants began with four games against teams in the highest level of the minors. Class B Interstate League foes Dayton and Springfield, Ohio, would occupy the schedule, and then back to the Western League to play three games against their fierce rival, Grand Rapids. The Giants would then travel to Fort Wayne, Indiana, and south with two games in Terre Haute, Indiana. They would take on their first college team of the year with the boys at Wabash in Crawfordville, Indiana. The remaining April games would be against a smattering of teams from the Western League, Western Association and college clubs.[19]

The 1897 Page Fence Giants roster was also now locally announced, as part of the Parsons and Stevens interview. There were new names joining the old regulars. The pitching staff would again be led by the "Palmyra Wonder," George Wilson, along with the great coacher, Billy Holland. A pair of new faces, Robert "Bob" Shaw from Los Angeles and another hurler named Jones, were on the roster. The infield would be nearly the same as last season, with George Taylor at first, Charlie Grant at second, and Grant Johnson at shortstop, but Bill Binga, who had played third base, was moved to left field. James W. Patterson was to play third base, even though he ended the year with the X Giants. A story placed in *The Sporting News* by the Cuban X Giants' E. B. Lamar seemed to confirm that Patterson would appear for the Adrian club. Lamar's roster was released a few days before the Page Fence's, and had no mention of Patterson with his club.[20] Pete Burns would be back as the main Page Fence catcher, and there was no mention of the return of Vasço Graham. A man named (Bert?) Wakefield was also signed as a substitute player.[21] An earlier roster had indicated that Fred Van Dyke would again be on the Giants team, but this latest preview omitted his name.[22]

The battle for the star black ballplayers continued as the Chicago Unions publicized their roster of men around this time. Their plan was to invite 16 players to early practice and cut down to 12 for the upcoming season. Detroit native Harry Moore and Ed Woods, from Mason City, Iowa, would be two of the featured pitchers, while an 1896 Bud Fowler find, Harry Hyde, would be the Unions' third baseman. In 1896 the Unions claimed to have been dubbed the "Black Wonders" due to their skillful ball playing at their home diamond at Butler and Thirty-Seventh Streets in Chicago. Frank Leland, the team secretary, said that the Unions were to play the Cuban Giants in June "for the colored championship" and wanted to arrange games with the Page Fence Giants, too. Leland added that all through the winter months, two members of the champion Giants, Billy Holland and Pete Burns, had played indoor baseball with the Unions. The Page Fence Giants would probably be happy to return to Chicago to play before large crowds in a major American city and chalk up some easy wins, too.[23]

When the Unions told the world they were the black baseball champions of the West, Hoch didn't take long to jump back into the fray. In a letter to *The Sporting News* in mid–March, Hoch claimed the Giants won ten of the 15-game series against the Cuban X club and rightfully earned the championship title. He added that the Giants and the Unions had played five games in 1896, all won by the Adrian men, and included the game scores, four of which weren't even remotely close. "It takes a pretty vigorous claim agent to keep in the game after such a series of drubbings, but the secretary of the Unions is equal to the occasion," Hoch sarcastically quipped. He continued by saying the Unions were "not in the same class with the Giants," and this season they would give the Chicago team a five- to ten-run handicap, wager the entire gate money, and the Adrian men would still win the game and the cash.[24]

While Leland's Chicago Unions wanted to stage a black baseball championship that summer, so did Bright of the genuine Cuban Giants. Bright listed the "crack colored clubs" he hoped would attend, with the rival Cuban X Giants not mentioned. Bright did list the Page Fence Giants as the first team invited to his version of the world championship. Bright added Leland's Chicago Unions, followed by the Pittsburgh Keystones, Norfolk Red Sox, New York Gorhams, the Pinchbacks of New Orleans and his own Cuban Giants.[25]

East Coast fans of black baseball now had to contend with a second confusing season following the Cuban Giants and the Cuban X Giants. In early April, Paterson, New Jersey, defeated the Cuban X Giants, 20–9. A few days later in Lancaster, Pennsylvania, the Cuban Giants lost, 13–4. The next day, the Cuban X Giants came to town and lost to Lancaster, but in a closer 17–6 outcome. Reading, Pennsylvania, then hosted two games with the Cuban Giants and beat them twice, which probably confused many Pennsylvania residents as to what team was playing whom, and where, and when.[26]

While all this arguing, scheduling, and roster wheeling and dealing was taking place, the Page Fence Giants still faced a major issue—there would be no home games in 1897. The situation became even clearer in March. The March 16 *Evening Telegram* screamed the multi-lined headline: "Lima Northern Depot Will be placed at the Entrance to Lawrence Park; Deal has all been settled; The Park Buildings all have to be moved." The business deal was struck between the railroad company and Willis T. Lawrence. The Lima Northern officials claimed to have plans ready to construct a massive and expensive $5,000 stone depot "just west and south of the entrance to Lawrence Park." As a result, two quaint homes, an old mill, a red barn, park fencing, and some other buildings, "including the grand stand on the park," would be moved. The grandstand would be relocated "about 600 feet west of where it now stands and the ball grounds will be located near floral hall."[27] While the relocation might save the large wooden seating structure, it was doubtful that baseball could be played at the park, as a new ball ground would have to be created while working around the construction of a depot and the laying of railroad tracks.[28] Plans called for the Lima Northern track to run through the park entrance, near where two little houses stood, and the new depot would be built on the east side of the tracks. Lawrence also included a plan to connect the short park entrance road, dubbed Race Street, north and through to Springbrook Avenue. A railroad official claimed to have given Lawrence $2,500 for the property, while another said it was only $1,000. The two daily papers also reported that Lawrence would be able to operate a coal yard out of the old floral hall.[29] As far as losing the baseball site, Lawrence was later quoted as saying that he had envisioned over 25 years ago that a railroad would eventually come through his park property, and now it was coming true.[30]

By the end of March, several of the Page Fence Giants players had arrived in town for their trip to Ohio. The original opening game of the 1897 season was no longer in Indianapolis, Indiana, but in Columbus, Ohio. Some of the Giants would go directly to Columbus, including new Los Angeles–based pitcher Bob Shaw. He had previously pitched for a California team called the Trilbys, but had now signed with the famous Page Fence championship club. A report out of his hometown noted that Shaw was "not only a great pitcher, but a wonderful batter."[31] However, he was also taking with him an injured throwing arm, which had "little speed," though he had earned a victory in a recent game out west.[32] The players leaving Adrian would be Bill Binga, arriving from Lansing, along with James Patterson, George Wilson, Peter Burns and Billy Holland. The five would climb aboard their train car on Thursday, April 1, and head a few hours south to central Ohio.

When the players left Adrian, they were greeted by a chilly Lenawee County morning. The thermometer was below freezing as the sun was rising in the east on the April morning.[33] The team management—Gus Parsons and Jim Stevens—had left the previous day and were making plans for the club's arrival in Columbus.[34] Rolla Taylor would not make the sojourn to Columbus until Friday and would stay to watch the opening game of the season, which had already been pushed back a day to April 3.[35]

Excitement in Adrian also surrounded the new railroad. Clark Decker had been awarded the bid to construct a freight storage building at Lawrence Park for the Lima Northern.[36] Charles Havens, who had been laying the tracks into town, arrived early in the week with 59 horses and mules and a crew of workmen. He was to extend the Lima Northern line five miles out of Adrian and north toward Tecumseh.[37] The rail cranks were probably just as happy for this work, as the ball cranks had been just as sad to see the end of Lawrence Park.

The opening game on Saturday with the Columbus Senators, who were led by former major league player and manager, Tom Loftus, was a loss. The Giants dropped a 7–3 decision to the Western Leaguers, and the lefty Wilson took the defeat in the pitcher's box. Few details made it back to Adrian, even with it being the season opener, except to say the Giants "played a stiff game."[38] However, the *Adrian Daily Times and Expositor*'s final score disagreed with the *Telegram*'s. The *Times* said the actual score was 10–7, with both Wilson and Shaw pitching in the Giants' loss. The paper blamed the defeat to James Patterson's throwing error from third base in the opening inning, allowing three men to score. The Adrian paper added that even with the loss, the *Columbus Journal* had praised the efforts of the Michigan club.[39]

Both clubs had Sunday off as it rained. The second game in the series on Monday resulted in another Giants loss, 13–8, this time in ten innings.[40] The Giants managed to notch ten hits, but could not overcome 35-year-old and six-year major league veteran George Tebeau's two home runs. Columbus managed 16 hits off the Giants' pitchers in the victory. Again, few details made it back to Adrian, but one story noted that the Page Fence gentlemen were "fearfully robbed" in the final inning. That phrase again likely related to an umpiring controversy and either his lack of game-calling skills, his lack of honesty, or both.[41] The third game between the clubs, scheduled for Tuesday, was rained out, according to the *Evening Telegram*.[42] However, the *Chicago Daily Tribune* printed a game story, as the contest was evidently not postponed. The Giants dropped their third straight game to Columbus, this time 11–6.[43] The Senators threw three pitchers at the Giants, all lefties, to earn the win. Oscar Streit, a 6'5", 23-year-old southpaw who later briefly made it to the majors, began the game. He was followed by Peter Daniels, who posted a 12–3 record for the Class A Senators, played in the majors back in 1890, and would do so again in 1898. Daniels came into this game 30 to 40 pounds lighter than last year and was the most effective Senators pitcher that day.[44] The third player was William Dinsmore, whose stint with Columbus would last only a few games this season. The trio threw to Ike Fisher, who the following year would play nine games, mostly at catcher, for the Philadelphia Phillies. The Page Fence Giants battery in the loss was Joe Miller and Pete Burns.[45] Whatever bad blood there had been between Parsons and Miller was gone, as Cyclone Joe was back in the fold for the Page Fence men in 1897.

The Columbus correspondent to *The Sporting News* heaped praised on the Page Fence club. He stated that the Adrian men were a bunch of "lively players" who "will make many a club bite the dust before the season is over." The Giants' left fielder did "sensational work," and the lefty Wilson "is plenty fast enough for the Western League." For some reason, while heaping his praise, the writer felt it necessary to describe the various players' skin tones. "They range in color all the way from Shaw, the California pitcher, who is a very light fellow with rosy cheeks to 'Mr. Johnsing' [sic] the shortstop, upon whom charcoal would make a white mark." This type of description would not occur when discussing any of the white players.[46]

The Giants had more success on Wednesday against the lower-level, Class B Interstate League Dayton Old Soldiers. The conditions were less than ideal for the season's first win, as game reports said it was cold and windy, which caused a sparse crowd. Bob Shaw and George Wilson combined to win the game, while Bill Binga was the catcher in the 18–11 Giants victory.[47]

News about the Page Fence Giants remained sparse in Adrian. Railroad fever had definitely replaced baseball fever in town, as the day-by-day excitement about the Lima Northern supplanted the Giants' game scores and stories. Now, sometimes a week or more would pass before either the *Adrian Daily Times and Expositor* or the *Adrian Evening Telegram* would even mention the club. Without the mostly white Adrian Demons involved in baseball and no longer having an adequate diamond for local games, the Page Fence Giants legacy was now being recorded by the many towns and villages they would visit over the next two years.

◆ 19 ◆

The Homeless Season

If you wanted to find out that the Adrian public school eighth graders surprisingly defeated the town's older ninth graders, 11–3, in baseball, that would be in the local dailies. Rumors about another attempt at establishing a Michigan State League could also be found in the local papers. Of course, the nearly daily updates featuring the Lima Northern in town were easily found, too. Just don't try to locate anything about the world champion ball team sponsored by one of Adrian's largest employers.

Once the regular season was underway, *The Sporting News* and *Sporting Life* turned their focus of publicizing baseball news and box scores of the professional, white-men-only leagues. Occasionally, a report from one of their many stringers would include a paragraph about the Page Fence Giants, when they were in town and playing the local professional white clubs. A year after *Plessy v. Ferguson*, the equal but separate American philosophy was in full force. Unfortunately, there was no media police, so separate became very clear, and equal morphed into non-existent coverage.

One such exception was an early April report in *The Sporting News* of a new black baseball league, based in all the major cities along the East Coast. A man named A. J. Carter of Washington, D.C., had the idea. Two black players in Boston were said to be early supporters of Carter's plan. Details were still sketchy, but Carter had financial backers who would pay the travel expenses of representatives from the Eastern league cities to the nation's capital to discuss the matter. The plan was to get teams based in the nation's capital, along with Boston, to join with Baltimore, Brooklyn, New York and Philadelphia. Carter wanted to work and possibly use the major league stadiums for his baseball league, so that any games would not conflict with the white clubs. The league would be owned and operated by black businessman who knew about baseball and would work hard at the endeavor. The story also praised the marketability of black teams, proclaiming "their playing is more picturesque to look at than the pale-faced brothers. They put more ginger into the sport."[1] Needless to say, Carter's league never got off the ground.

The Page Woven Wire Fence Company was doing a "booming" business in the spring of 1897.[2] Seymour Howell, who spent 1894 and 1895 as an influential baseball crank, now spent his time riding his bike on long trips and vacationing around the country. The ousted Adrian Light Guard manager, L. A. Browne, was busy with his law practice in town, but was scouting around for better job prospects. Howard Taylor apparently let his brother handle the family business with the Giants, as his name was no longer mentioned as a member of the club's management. Len Hoch and Rolla Taylor were the only original Adrian baseball moneymen still spending their cash on the club. Bud Fowler was long gone, and Grant Johnson was still on the Giants' roster, but no longer as part of management.

As the Page Fence gentlemen made their ballplaying treks through Michigan, Indiana, Wisconsin, Ohio, Iowa and Illinois, unless the factory or one of the black barbershops posted scores, the Giants were out of the spotlight. The *Chicago Daily Tribune*, a few hundred miles west of Adrian, surprisingly was a source of box and line scores and sometimes a game story. The much closer *Detroit Free Press* rarely covered the Giants unless they were playing a local team.

The Giants, though, were still popular on the road. One game in mid–April reportedly attracted over 2,000 people to pack Peoria, Illinois', new grandstands. The weather was poor for the game and the "dust was so thick that a thrown ball could hardly be seen from the grandstand," and still they crammed fans into the ball field.[3]

When the Giants rolled into Madison, Wisconsin, in late April, and blasted the college boys, 15–1, the *Chicago Daily Tribune* had a nice write-up, along with a box score. The Giants tallied the bulk of their runs in the first half of the game and were never threatened. The Chicago paper reported that Giants pitcher Bob Shaw's speed was slow, but he was hard to hit. When one of the cardinal-wearing Wisconsin boys managed to put the bat on the ball, it was quickly scooped up or hauled in, and the batter was retired. In a rare 1897 printed box score, the Giants lineup led off with Holland in left field, followed by Patterson at third, Johnson at shortstop, Taylor batting cleanup and playing his usual first base, Burns at catcher, Binga in center, Grant at second, Shaw the pitcher, and batting ninth and last was Miller in right field. Every Giant scored at least one run and all recorded a hit, except for the usually dependable Taylor.[4]

The Giants boarded the specially outfitted Monarch train car and headed west for about a week of games in Iowa. Bob Shaw defeated the Cedar Rapids Rabbits of the Western Association in one contest, as the Giants "struck the town like a cyclone and imagined everything would go their way." However, the Adrian men dropped the follow-up game to the Rabbits. The Page Fence men were well received in Cedar Rapids, and hopes were high that they would make another appearance later in the season. The Iowans embraced the visitors' playing skills and their antics. "The Giants fully kept up the reputation for rollicksome humor [and] there was never a situation too complicated to debut some ludicrous remark or grotesque caper."[5]

The Giants continued their Iowa slate and headed into Des Moines for a pair of weekend games. The Iowa town was excited about the visitors' arrival as the Giants departed their special car and checked themselves into the Aborn Hotel. The team watched the rain drop out of the skies from their hotel room, which simply added to the area's flooding problems.[6] Lost games meant lost revenue, and no one had to remind the Giants' management of the 35 lost games during the 1896 season, due to wet weather.

Des Moines bragged about the Giants' world championship and of the talent of the Palmyra Wonder in order to drum up fans for the weekend series. "They have with them Pitcher Wilson, who it is said would be a $5,000-year man if his color could be bleached out a few points."[7] The *Iowa State Bystander*, the "official paper of the Afro-American Protective Association of Iowa," reminded its readers that while Saturday's game was in Des Moines, the Sunday contest was at Walnut Creek Park. The *Bystander* urged residents to hop on either of the special Sunday afternoon train cars leaving the Union Depot at 2:15 and 3:00, headed for Walnut Creek Park.[8] Unfortunately, the heavy rain of Friday continued Saturday, and when it finally stopped, the field was so full of mud that both weekend games were cancelled.[9]

One interesting development was that a new player had joined the Giants. A Des

Moines newspaper printed the two teams' rosters, and the Giants now had 11 players on their squad. The infield was the usual Taylor, Grant, Johnson and Patterson, with Burns behind the plate. The outfield was Binga, Miller and Holland. The pitching staff was Wilson, Shaw and a new man named Broadest.[10] With the Adrian papers not as excited as they had been in 1895 and 1896 about their black ball team, Broadest's background and how he signed with the Page Fence Giants was a mystery. The original one- or two-sentence long backgrounds of any new Giants were now a thing of the past.

How long the Giants waited out the rain on Sunday is unknown. However, by Monday they had made their way to the Mississippi River community of Burlington, Iowa. The Colts, also members of the Western Association, were the Giants' next victims. Wilson, called by one Des Moines newspaper "the crack colored pitcher of the world," struck out 12 men in a narrow, 3–2 Giants' win.[11] However, in keeping with the unreliable reporting, the *Evening Telegram* claimed the winning margin was 5–3 and said Wilson had struck out 13 men. The Page Fence club came back and defeated the Colts the next day by a more convincing margin of 13–8.[12]

Railroad fever was in full swing by this point in Adrian. A pair of Lima Northern Railroad officials arrived in town in late April and told the public that passenger service would begin in a matter of days. A temporary depot had been built at the entrance of what had formally been Lawrence Park. The railroad was eager to begin collecting money from Adrian residents to help pay for the construction of the LN's proposed elaborate and expensive stone depot. However, company officials publicly complained about their efforts to bring a third rail line to Adrian. A company spokesman decried the efforts by some residents along the track route, who held up the line by asking for right of way fees three and four times higher than the Lima Northern believed they were worth.[13]

After leaving Burlington, Iowa, the Giants crossed the Mississippi River to play in Beardstown, Illinois. The black gentlemen eked out a slim, 2–1 victory.[14] Back in Adrian, wet weather had slowed the railroad's track-laying progress. However, that didn't stop the planned celebration of the Lima Northern. As April came to an end, Willis T. Lawrence took a sledge hammer and drove a special train spike into a metal rail at the entrance of Lawrence Park. It was part of a special ceremony to welcome the new rail company to town. Lawrence commented that he was quite pleased with the ceremony and giddy about the train crossing his property.[15]

During this same week, baseball fever was also evading Adrian once again. Yet another attempt to create a Michigan State League was underway, and these prospects appeared promising. The 1895 MSL commissioner, W. H. Mumby, was back in the fold and leading this latest round of negotiations. Unlike 1895, when the Adrian Demons claimed the disputed league crown, the Lenawee County community would sit out this version of the MSL. The 1897 lineup looked very similar to what had been created just two years earlier. Lansing, Kalamazoo, Port Huron, Saginaw, Jackson and Bay City would all start the 1897 season with a low, Class D minor league classification. Mumby was his typical upbeat self in making the announcement. The league would "commence under the most auspicious circumstances ever known to a Michigan State League." Mumby added that the problem with some of the previous leagues was the failure of owners to follow the constitution, including the agreed-upon salary limit. The 1897 version would have a $600 salary cap, and Mumby said that if the owners could adhere to the agreement, the league would last for a long time.[16]

While not joining this latest reincarnation of the Michigan State League, some of the familiar faces from 1895 would be involved. Umpires James Grogan, an Adrian and Page

Fence Giants favorite, along with W. A. Doyle and O. G. Hungerford from Kalamazoo, would work the MSL games. The Demons' slugging first baseman, Ed Mulhearn, who led the 1896 Flint squad, was on the Kalamazoo roster, Bay City signed slick glove man D. J. Lowney, and catcher Bert Eltom was back with the Lansing Senators. Unlike 1895, there would be no George Wilson or Vasco Graham, or substitutes such as Bill Binga, Bud Fowler, Pete Burns, or Cyclone Joe Miller on the original rosters. While nothing was mentioned in Mumby's announcement, this latest league would be for whites and not for black professional ball players. There would be no star-studded "watermelon batteries" this time around.[17]

Baseball was still growing its fan base across the country in 1897. The *Evening Telegram*, nearly every day, printed the line scores of the country's highest and only major league organization—the National League. They also printed scores for the eight-team Western League, which included the Detroit and Grand Rapids clubs in the Class A minors. One level lower, the eight-team Class B Western Association, whose clubs were in Illinois, Iowa and Missouri, also had their scores in the Adrian papers. In some cases in 1897, Adrian readers would go a week or two before coming across a single sentence about the reigning black baseball champions, their Page Fence Giants.

Unbeknownst to Adrian residents, the Chicago Unions wanted another crack at trying to defeat the Page Fence club. The Unions claimed that a game at their home grounds at 37th and Butler Streets in Chicago would be for the world black baseball title. Originally the Page Fence Giants were to play three games with the powerful and all-white Chicago Dalys during the second weekend in May.[18] Somewhere along the way, the third game with the Dalys was replaced by one against the Unions.

The Dalys played their season opener against the Giants on May 8 on their home grounds at 39th Street and Wentworth Avenue. The Giants won easily, 14–6, with a new pitcher named Ed Woods hurling for the Page Fence crew. The Giants slammed four home runs, coming off the bats of Holland, Johnson, Burns and Wilson. The Dalys were a popular team in the Windy City, so the *Tribune* printed a box score. Taylor at first base led off as usual, followed by Patterson at third, Johnson at short, Holland at cleanup and in left field, Burns catching, and then Wilson, Grant at second, Binga in center and Woods ninth. The new pitcher gave up eight hits, walked five and struck out five.[19]

The next morning, the two clubs squared off again. The 10:30 start didn't change the outcome as the Page Fence Giants won in convincing fashion, 10–0, behind the battery of Miller and Binga.[20] The Dalys remained behind at their ball field and awaited the Whiting Greys for an afternoon contest. Meanwhile, the Giants ventured onto the Chicago Unions' home grounds, a few blocks away at 37th and Butler Streets, for a 3:30 game.[21]

Union Park was the site of this championship battle, at least in the eyes of the hosts. The Page Fence Giants had clubbed the Unions all five times in 1896 and were probably not too worried about this contest. If so, that was a mistake. The Unions held on to a 7–6 win and bested the Palmyra Wonder.[22] The Adrian men once led, 4–1, as they faced the Unions battery of Harry Buckner and Robert Footes, who were effective both in the field and at the plate. Buckner helped himself and slugged a homer off Wilson, while Footes notched a double. According to the line score printed in the *Chicago Daily Tribune* the next day, none of the Page Fence men recorded an extra-base hit. It is possible, though, that the Chicago paper just focused on the batting exploits of the home team that day, as it is hard to imagine scoring six runs without the benefit of an extra-base hit.[23] How much the Giants were aware of the game build-up by the Unions is anyone's guess. A few days later, a northern

Indiana newspaper reported that the Sunday afternoon affair had been "for the championship of America."[24]

The Giants left Chicago and headed into Michigan, where at least some of the teams would not be as difficult to play as the professional Chicago Unions club. After having their usual Monday off, they ventured to Ionia. The Barry County community was excited for the match-up with the powerful Giants. They had done their best to import some better players for their squad and had just lost a 12-inning affair to the always tough Muskegon club. The *Ionia Daily Standard* claimed their town's 8–6 loss on Sunday to Muskegon was "one of the finest games of ball ever played in amateur ranks in the state," and Ionia lost "due to bad luck."[25]

The *Daily Standard* touted the upcoming contest with the Page Fence club as something for all to see. In a rare occurrence, the paper used Giants players' names to promote the tilt. "Come and see the best game of ball ever seen in Ionia…. Pangborn and Poff will be the battery for Ionia, and Wilson, the great south paw and Burns for the Giants." Pangborn was coming off a 12-strikeout performance in their Sunday loss to Muskegon, adding to the town's excitement. The paper also mentioned the pre-game parade, which was rarely publicized any more. Maybe the Giants' fine ballplaying no longer required the drumming up of curious fans with a fancy parade. Or maybe the parade was just the normal operating procedure for the past two and a half years and was simply no longer mentioned. Whatever the case, the street parade, featuring the nattily clad, bike-riding Page Fence men, would begin at 2 o'clock and would be led by the Ionia city band.[26]

When the parade kicked off on May 11, it was a gala event. In addition to the Giants on their bikes and the city band, several horse and buggies carted the mayor and other local dignitaries to the ball diamond. The Ionia mayor, a man named Ellis, was there for the event and not for the baseball game. Reportedly, he had no idea where to go to toss out the ceremonial first pitch and had "to be led to the pitcher's mound." The Mayor's aim was so wild that the honorary opening pitch zoomed past catcher E. R. Bailey. Mayor Ellis was given at least one opportunity and possibly more to deliver the ball successfully in the direction of home plate.[27]

Mayor Ellis' feeble ball-tossing was just a precursor to what occurred on the field shortly thereafter. The Giants drilled Ionia, 10–0, in front of 400 people. The diamond was in terrible condition for any type of ball game, not to mention one hosting the black champions of baseball. "The grounds were simply terrible—a mess of mud glazed over the top with a thin crust of dry earth. A ball struck the ground with a dull punk, either making a hold for a final resting place, or rolling feebly to one side." The players spent most of the afternoon slipping and sliding around the yard while either running the bases or fielding the ball. The shutout was not the least bit troubling to the Ionia ball cranks, who believed with more practice they would have a strong team that summer. The Giants' elegance on the ball field was evident, and there was no debate as to their skills or ability to humor the audience. "The gay nonchalance and easy indifference of the darkey boys was exasperating, although they are a whole show in themselves, and kept the boys and girls tittering with their monkey-shines and droll remarks."[28] As far as specific game details in the local paper, there were none.

The next day, the two teams squared off again and the results were nearly the same, as the Giants won, 11–1. Ace pitcher Pangborn, who was supposed to face Wilson in game one, was held out until game two. The Giants apparently pushed Wilson back to this game, too, as Miller was the winning pitcher in the first game.[29] The home team turned three double plays, managed only four hits, two of which were doubles, but that was about it. The field was again a sea of muck, and for the second day in a row the Giants were the more skillful players. A reporter claimed the Giants were used "to all sorts and conditions of grounds, and they just slid around in the mire, and got there in the nick of time, and smiled."[30]

Some baseball and much railroad fever were still going strong in Adrian in the spring of 1897. Excitement grew as Adrian High School decided to join a statewide athletic league, with a two-day championship competition scheduled in early June. The Lenawee County community would join Detroit, Ann Arbor, Lansing, Jackson and Grand Rapids in sending teams to the state tournament. The local baseball excitement was quickly tamped down when Ann Arbor drubbed the local high school boys, 23–4, just a few days after the statewide competition was announced to the public.[31]

The finishing touches on the Lima Northern railroad were also taking place. First, as either an ominous sign of shaky financial issues or a glimpse at future riches, there was a new name for the railroad in town. The company was now known as the Detroit and Lima Northern Railroad, as investors bought into the existing firm.[32] Track crews had crossed Lawrence Park and were headed north out of town, already about three miles from Tecumseh.[33] The temporary passenger depot opened on Monday, May 17, and a week later two dozen Adrian residents plunked down a dollar each, hopped aboard from there, and traveled to Detroit. Capitalizing on the town's baseball cranks, a special Adrian to Defiance excursion was advertised for later in the month, when the Giants would be there to play the Greys.[34]

In the meantime, the Page Fence men were busy clubbing some of the better teams from around the state. A mid–May weekend showdown in Saginaw saw the Giants post two shutout wins against the always competitive Flint and Pere Marquette Railroad-sponsored team.[35] The Giants came back on Monday and Wilson defeated Bay City, 9–4.[36] The Adrian men then chugged south into Mt. Clemens, a town north of Detroit. The Giants played the Detroit Athletic Club there and won a narrow 4–3 victory. Former Brooklyn Bridegroom and Detroit native Ed Stein was a ringer for the Athletics. While he had pitched in the previous seven seasons for the major league club, he was placed at first base for Mt. Clemens.[37] Wilson gave up three first-inning runs and then held the Athletics to four hits, before the Giants won it on Patterson's 12th-inning home run. The *Detroit Free Press* singled out the good play of four Athletics and the pitching of Wilson as bordering on "phenomenal" and claimed, "the style of ball put up would do credit to many professional league teams."[38]

A few days later, the *Free Press* was less than gracious in covering a rematch, which saw the Giants blast the Athletics, 11–4. The paper's headline was "Giants Walloped the 'White Trash,'" and the game account was biting this time around. The *Free Press* claimed the Athletics were a bit short-handed, though they still put up a good game, and the defeat was "like eating a watermelon for the Page Fence Giants." A crowd of about 500 attended this game, held in Detroit and featuring the usual Giants superior play and clowning antics. "The Giants are a gingery lot of players with not a dinky arm in the outfit and it is as good as a circus to watch their antics on the field." The Athletics jumped to an early leady off Ed Wood(s), who went eight innings, only to be relieved by Holland, who also gave up a run. Both Wood and Bill Binga, as the Giants' battery, were singled out for their fine performances, as was Patterson's three-run homer to right field. The margin of victory could have been larger, but when Wilson was caught in a rundown off third base, Charlie Grant thought it would be a good idea to race past his teammate. Both were declared out and were considered part of the "clowning antics" of the day.[39] The *Daily Telegram* reprinted the entire

Free Press story and allowed Adrian residents their first in-depth glimpse of the Giants in about a week.[40]

Following their success in Detroit, the Giants crossed the border and headed into Canada. The black gentlemen were scheduled to be a part of the Queen's Birthday celebration in Guelph, Ontario. The Guelph Maple Leafs, reportedly one of Canada's strongest baseball teams, were the Giants' opponent. The American men managed to beat Guelph, 3–1 and then 8–0, as over 5,000 people attended the two games. The Giants headed back to Adrian and dropped off Billy Holland. The star pitcher, outfielder and noted coacher was said to need some rest and would remain in Adrian for a "spell."[41] A few days later, the same paper noted that joining Holland for some rest were George Wilson and Charlie Grant.[42]

The latest excitement for the Adrian baseball cranks was that locals would be able to travel south to Defiance, Ohio, to witness their team in action. Games on Sunday, May 30, and Monday, May 31, would hopefully attract fans from far around to Defiance. The newly unveiled Detroit and Lima Northern was offering a special set of passenger cars from Adrian to Defiance to provide the Giants with some support.[43] The *Defiance Democrat* was even more specific on the train route, saying it would leave from Tecumseh, stop in Adrian, travel to Napoleon, Ohio, and use the Wabash Railroad's tracks to chug through Okolona and Jewell before arriving in Defiance. The paper urged fans to attend the games, as they would be the last chance to see the Giants before they embarked on a tour through the Eastern part of the United States.[44] The Napoleon, Ohio, paper echoed that sentiment and told people to be ready for a pair of great contests at the Defiance ball park aimed at "lovers of a good exhibition of the National game."[45]

The three resting players returned to the team, and the Giants were coming off a convincing 25–4 victory on Saturday against the Ann Arbor Browns at the town's fairgrounds.[46] It was believed that the Defiance Greys would offer a much tougher nine.

Many people followed the newspapers' advice as a total of 175 people rode the special excursion into Defiance and swelled the game attendance to about 1,000.[47] The train left Lawrence Park at 8:30 in the morning, with a one-dollar fee for the round-trip excursion. Expectations at the fence company were high as the Factory News column in the *Evening Telegram* bragged, "The Page Fence Giants continue to make it smoking hot for every team they meet."[48]

At first, the Ohioans were very pleased with the game, as after six innings their pitcher, Herbrand, managed to keep the mighty Page Fence Giants off the board. Wilson was equally sparking, limiting the Defiance club to a single run. However, the Giants exploded for 12 runs in their half of the seventh inning, as the Greys succumbed to a case of "razzle dazzle." An error opened the door for the Giants, causing Herbrand to lose his composure. Runs came so quickly that the *Daily Crescent* reporter "thought it would be necessary to get the Central fire department to put the Giants out." Wilson continued his fine work on the mound and struck out 11 Greys, while Johnson was the Giants' star at the plate, drilling a home run, a double and two singles.[49] Following in the spirit of news reporting from the era, three different final scores were published. The *Daily Crescent* and *Defiance Daily Republican* printed a 13–1 outcome, while the *Adrian Evening Telegram* had it 14–1 and the *Adrian Daily Times and Expositor* had it 14–0.[50] The Detroit and Lima Northern special excursion then left Defiance at seven that evening and arrived back in Adrian by 10. A story proudly noted that the new line was on time at each stop along the way.[51]

The following day, the Defiance Greys were much better and gave a strong performance, as the game was tied 6–6 going into the ninth inning. However, the Giants scored the winning run on a daring base running maneuver by Johnson. The Giants' Woods had pitched a good game, but star lefty Wilson relieved him in the final stanza and earned yet another victory. The Greys out-hit the Giants and had fewer errors, but still lost, 7–6.[52]

Monday's Defiance crowd was just as large as the Sunday gathering. However, it was observed that Sunday's crowd was mostly men, while the rematch was much more balanced between males and females. This even mix led to a livelier audience, as "men threw their hats in the air, women waved their parasols, children yelled and the whole crowd shouted themselves hoarse."[53] While Defiance loved their baseball, their news stories, after the Giants had come to town, referred to the team as "dusky boys," "darkeys," or worse yet, "coons." The town was no stranger to black people, either, as one of the Cuban Giants teams was scheduled to appear later that month to play the Greys.[54]

The Page Fence men headed out of Defiance and east to Wadsworth, Ohio.[55] The game in eastern Ohio featured a pair of National League ringers for the battery. Someone in the town of Wadsworth wanted badly to defeat the 1896 champions of the world and contacted the major league Cleveland Spiders. The club was not likely to offer staff ace Cy Young to the Ohio town, or any of their other more experienced hurlers. The Spiders did decide that right-handed pitcher John Pappalau, who was on the roster but had yet to make an appearance in the majors, along with catcher, Lou Criger, would travel south and face the Giants. The 22-year-old rookie was nervous at the start, and the Giants jumped on him for four runs in the opening inning. The Palmyra Wonder was fine the first time through the order, until the Ohio team tallied three runs in the fourth inning. Fortunately, the Page Fence nine tacked on additional runs and earned a 7–5 victory in front of 700 hopeful fans. Six days later, Pappalau would make his major league debut for the Cleveland squad.[56]

The long-term plan had been to travel east and capitalize on their championship over the Cuban X Giants to make more profits for the Adrian investors. However, for some reason, that Eastern travel plan came to an abrupt halt. Len Hoch told the *Evening Telegram* that the Page Fence Giants were not going to play out east. Hoch claimed that the club's advance agent, James Stevens, had tried to book ball games for the champions and had come up empty. Hoch claimed that Eastern baseball prospects were very poor. Stevens' claim was much bleaker and described it as "simply dead."[57] It's possible the Eastern towns were boycotting the newly crowned Page Fence champions out of loyalty to either of their Cuban Giants clubs. The original Cuban Giants and their owner, John Bright, were apparently suffering financially now, too. The Cuban Giants, of the genuine variety, were sitting idle in New York and trying to schedule games somewhere out west.[58] Meanwhile, the other East Coast black baseball powerhouse, Ed B. Lamar's Cuban X Giants, did manage around this time to make it to Defiance, where they lost to the Greys, 6–0.[59] Hoch's early-June interview also seemed to indicate that the next Giants game was on June 27 in Grand Rapids.[60] If correct, that would mean a two-week layoff for the Page Fence club. The future was not looking too bright for the black baseball champions of the world.

◆ 20 ◆

Losing Things

The Page Fence Giants may have been taking a hit at the box office without their anticipated Eastern tour. However, that wasn't their major concern as they entered the summer months. One of their original and best players was released.

Billy Holland, the crafty left-handed pitcher, excellent coacher, and slick outfielder, was no longer a Page Fence Giant. Whether his rest spell following the club's Canadian trip was a tip-off that something more serious was wrong is unknown. Maybe there was a larger problem behind the scenes, as both Wilson and Grant had been rested along with Holland. The *Evening Telegram* posted a two-sentence story that Holland had been released, with a general explanation that "Billy became too numerous for the management." To add to the drama, Holland had decided to join the rival Chicago Unions, who still claimed that due to their one-run victory over the Page Fence Giants in May, they were the new black baseball champions.[1] The Unions and Chicago would be a familiar spot for Holland. He had come to the Giants in 1895 from the Unions, where he had played alongside the late Gus Brooks and catcher Pete Burns.

Another familiar baseball face in Adrian was also lost. Adrian Light Guard manager L. A. Browne announced that he was moving out of town. Browne had recently passed the bar exam and would join the law firm headed by H. C. Dodge, in Elkhart, Indiana. Dodge's firm was rapidly growing, and he needed help in handling cases. The *Evening Telegram* praised Browne as a smart law student who had a "brilliant future before him." The former Adrian baseball crank planned to establish his law career in Elkhart and later send for his family.[2] In 1894, Browne was credited with signing the teenaged George Wilson from nearby Palmyra and placing him in the pitcher's box for the 1894 Light Guard team.

With the Giants in eastern Ohio, they completed a three-game sweep of the Taylor Grays. Two of the victories were played in Clyde, Ohio. The final contest was played before a large crowd, numbering around 2,000 spectators, in Lima, Ohio.[3] When the Giants' James Stevens returned from his failed Eastern booking tour, the team focused on adding more games in Michigan. Club management's concern over a two-week idle stretch in June was negated when Michigan was more receptive than the East Coast, and games were quickly added to the Giants' schedule.

The Giants and the Detroit Athletic Club held a rematch in Mt. Clemens, and the Page Fence men won, 22–2.[4] The Giants then made their first-ever appearance in the tiny town of Perry, in Shiawassee County, halfway between Lansing and Flint, on June 16. The Giants recorded a 10–0 victory. More importantly, a replacement for the popular Billy Holland had been secured. The Giants' battery in the Perry game was Johnson and Johnson.[5] Grant Johnson was most likely the pitcher, as he had tossed a few games in his previous years with the Giants. The new Johnson was George Johnson, a young catcher who would go on to have a long career in black baseball, also known as "Rat" and "Chappie." A few days later in a game in St. Louis, Michigan, in front of 1,100 fans, the new Johnson hit a triple, to support "Home Run" Johnson on the mound in a narrow 12–11 win.[6]

A week later, the Giants would lose another man, but not by choice. Playing the Lansing minor league team in the tiny southwestern Eaton County hamlet of Bellevue, James Patterson was badly injured while trying to field a ball. Senators catcher Bert Eltom hit a hot shot to Patterson in the fourth inning. Patterson, probably manning his regular third base position, saw the ball take a funny bounce, striking him in the left shoulder and promptly breaking his collarbone. The good news was that the Giants managed to win the game, 18–5, behind the battery of Miller and Binga.[7] Now, Gus Parsons would have to locate another man for the Giants or play with a reduced roster.

The next day in Hartford, the Giants' lineup moved Binga from behind the plate to third base to replace the injured Patterson. Pete Burns was moved from the outfield to catcher. Newly signed George Johnson was put in left field and batted in the cleanup position. In one of the tightest contests of the season, the Giants won, 3–0, as Wilson tossed a one-hitter and struck out 13 opponents. The Hartford pitcher, Summers, held the Giants to just four hits, with the new Johnson's double the only extra-base knock. Fifteen hundred people paid to attend the game, as the Page Fence club remained a great draw.[8]

The reportedly tough Muskegon Reds were no match for the Giants, as Miller again pitched a victory and defeating the home club, 20–6. About 1,000 spectators witnessed the Sunday afternoon affair, which was closely played until the Giants tallied 11 runs in the fourth inning.[9] On Monday, a day the Giants usually had off, they visited another small Michigan town, Sparta, and posted a 10–0 whitewashing of the local gents.[10]

The next contest, on June 29, was one where the awful details have been lost to the ages. Whatever happened that day was not good, as the Giants stormed off the field in Saranac, Michigan and refused to finish the game.[11] There were few words in the local or the state's major newspapers about the incident. The Giants had played over the years in nearby Ionia, a few miles east of Saranac. The team had also made game stops in Lowell, just over the Kent County line. So the Giants would have been aware of the area's racial climate, if that was the case. If the cause of the problem was a financial one, you would think that would have been easily stated. The fact that no reason was ever publicly stated leads one to expect the worst, rightly or wrongly.

The Saranac Advertisers baseball club was chomping at the bit to play the famous champions. The *Ionia Daily Standard* wrote a few days before the game that "the Advertisers are said to be strong enough to make an interesting game, and a big crowd is expected."[12] The combination of playing the previous day on a usually idle Monday, and now facing a large and excited crowd, and a highly motivated Saranac club, ended up hurting the Giants. The *Detroit Free Press* said the Giants forfeited the game to the Saranac Advertisers and added, "it was a hot game up to the fifth, when the Giants left the grounds."[13] The *Adrian Daily Times and Expositor* printed a mysterious two-sentence story, with its information apparently gleaned from a Gus Parsons telegram. "The Page Fence Giants, for the first time since the organization of the team, left the grounds at Saranac after the fourth inning. The dispatch does not state the nature of the trouble."[14] The following week, the *Ionia Daily Standard*'s Saranac correspondent submitted a two-sentence story. "The Page Fence Giants vs. the Advertisers were the attraction here Tuesday afternoon. The Advertisers didn't win."

Their report contradicted the *Detroit Free Press* story that the Giants had lost the contest with Saranac due to a forfeit.[15]

What exactly was said or done to make the Giants so upset that after two and a half years of being the target of verbal assaults and crooked umpiring, they had reached the point of walking off the ball diamond? George Wilson had vacated a diamond during a wild game in Jackson, but he was with the Adrian Demons at the time. Giants second baseman Charlie Grant had once bumped an umpire, who then awkwardly fell during a heated dispute, but the game continued when cooler heads prevailed. At Grand Rapids, Bobby Caruthers' umpiring debacle and another similar fiasco in Fort Wayne did not cause the Giants to march angrily off the diamond. In those stolen games and in countless others, both documented and undocumented, the Giants endured abuse and finished the game. This was not the case in Saranac, Michigan, on June 29, 1897, and the reason has been lost to history.

To add to the strange events of the day in Saranac, the Billy Holland-led Chicago Unions were playing about 20 miles to the south in Hastings. The Unions defeated the Hastings team, 15–12, two weeks and two years from the day Gus Brooks died.[16] Whether the proximity of the Unions, Holland, and their continued claims of being the black champions played any part in the Saranac incident is left to conjecture.

The details surrounding the Saranac incident were never investigated by the Adrian newspapers. Fortunately, the Giants left the state of Michigan for games in Wisconsin and Illinois. Their train car made its next stop in Sheboygan, Wisconsin, and this train trip appeared to be one of their longer ones between one game and another. The East Coast swing was no longer in the plans, so the Giants would be visiting some friendly stops during the summer heat.

The scheduling of games was still an issue for this traveling Page Fence team. In mid–June, around the time James Stevens informed the Giants' management that baseball out east was "simply dead," a Philadelphia paper advertised a local appearance. The paper, obviously somewhat confused, said the Page Fence Giants, from Chicago, would play three games in the first week of July in their town.[17] However, the East Coast swing had been long abandoned by Page Fence backers. Green Bay, Wisconsin, was the city where the men played over the Independence Day holiday and not Philadelphia.[18]

For the first half of July, almost no information about the club made its way back to the Adrian dailies. Parsons must have been home for the July 4 holiday with his wife, or he had just decided that the local news appetite was pretty light now when it came to the Giants. When mid–July arrived, a few scores made their way back to Adrian, as "our Palmyra Wonder," George Wilson, the *Evening Telegram* noted, tossed a one-hitter in beating La Crosse, Wisconsin, 9–0. The game was actually played on Saturday, July 10, but the result wasn't printed until July 14.[19] Wilson pitched a few days later and won in a "great game" played in Beardstown, a river city in west central Illinois.[20]

The Giants had not lost a game in many weeks, if you disregard the Saranac forfeit, which Gus Parsons would undoubtedly do. The Giants won by large margins over town clubs in Clinton and Mason City, Illinois, and the Page Fence men were "winning everything and playing to good crowds."[21]

The baseball fever in Adrian was probably relieved a bit, when the 1897 edition of the Michigan State League began to fall apart. By the end of July, the six-team league was down to four cities, after both Lansing and Jackson dropped out. This latest configuration of the MSL consisted of Bay City, Flint, Saginaw and Port Huron. Even with these four remaining clubs in operation, one news story said the league was basically "about done."[22] The decision by Hoch, Taylor and other Adrian baseball cranks to skip joining the reorganized league now appeared to be the correct one.

The *Evening Telegram* periodically kept everyone in town apprised of one of their former Demons, albeit for less than a month. Honus Wagner, who the *Telegram* said was known as "Johannes" during his short Adrian stay in 1895, had just been signed by the National League's Louisville Colonels. The story claimed that he had earlier been paid a nice sum of $4,000 by the Paterson, New Jersey, Silk Weavers minor league club. The Adrian paper believed Wagner was now ready for the majors and characterized him as "a phenom."[23]

As for the Page Fence team, the local baseball fever for them was ramped up a bit, when the club challenged the Chicago Unions to another game. The Adrian nine was perturbed that the Chicago team continued claiming to be the best black ball club in the West, off their one-run victory in May. The Page Fence management wanted a rematch to "play a game of ball for the colored championship."[24] Likely miffed at the Unions' bragging ways and the fact that the Giants had defeated the Chicago club in five of six contests over the past two years, the gauntlet was thrown down in the final week of July. Plans developed that the winning team would net a $100 bonus, in addition to the gate receipts, and the game was tentatively scheduled on September 28 in Hart, Michigan. To add some excitement, the local story about the proposed match noted that Billy Holland was now on the Unions, but had been replaced "by George Johnson, of Bellaire, Ohio, who is said to be a very fast player."[25] The same championship challenge was reported in a Chicago paper about two weeks later. The *Chicago Times-Herald* version noted that the rematch had grown from a single contest to either a three- or five-game series. The Illinois story verified the earlier monetary arrangement and added that the games could be played anywhere, except in Chicago or Adrian.[26]

How did this Page Fence Giants challenge of the Unions develop? A few days before the idea was leaked in an Adrian paper, the *Dixon* (Illinois) *Evening Telegraph* unveiled a similar plan. In its July 23 edition, it claimed that some of their Dixon baseball cranks had contacted both the Giants and the Unions and offered a $100 bonus to play in their town. The idea was for "the winner to take the money."[27] Dixon residents predicted that a large crowd would witness the battle, as "all would want to see them play."[28] The offer came after the north central Illinois town, nestled along the Rock River, was drilled, 21–3, by the Giants the day before. The locals were said to be grateful they managed to score the three runs they did off George Wilson.[29] It's possible that the Dixon cranks put the rematch idea in the mind of Parsons.

The Giants continued to beat up on small-town ballclubs in Illinois as July ended. The team and their Monarch train car eventually made their way north along the railroad tracks into Wisconsin. The final day of July saw the Giants lose for the first time since June, 3–2. "In one of the finest games ever seen" in Green Bay, a bobbled ball by the Giants' center fielder in the ninth inning allowed the winning run to score, as the runner barely beat the throw to home plate.[30] Grant Johnson pitched for the Giants, and the game featured "pranks characteristic to the colored race," said the *Oshkosh Daily Northwestern* on August 3, 1897.

The next day, the Giants' ace twirler, Wilson, was on the mound. The euphoria surrounding the Green Bay win led to four times as many people attending the Sunday afternoon rematch as had paid on Saturday, as crowd estimates was near 2,000 spectators.[31] The Giants jumped out to an early lead and recorded a 7–2 victory. A Green Bay paper described

Wilson as "a lightening south paw" who allowed runners on base, but few to cross the plate.[32] Another Green Bay paper, whose story was reprinted a few days later in Adrian, heaped praise on the Giants' ballplaying and comedy skills. "Their coaching was full of slang phrases that were fresh to the ears of almost all that were present and their good-natured thrusts at the home boys kept the spectators laughing all through the game." The Green Bay paper also noted their local connection with one of the Giants. The Page Fence center fielder, Wood, who had also pitched for the Adrian club, was born in Green Bay 24 years earlier. The paper added that his mother was Lizzie Wood from Natchez, Mississippi, who moved to Green Bay and married a man with the same last name of Wood.[33] Subsequent articles said the player's name was Ed Wood.[34]

Around this time, the Giants may have begun a stretch of being short-handed. Maybe homesickness hit Wood, as it was reported that he had left the team and now pitched for a Wisconsin city club. A team from Waupun, all salaried professional players, inked Wood for a game against the Oshkosh Colts. Wood was being touted in the Oshkosh paper as possibly the best pitcher in the country.[35] One wonders if this was a mistake and George Wilson had been signed instead, or simply a ready-made excuse, when the all-amateur Oshkosh club lost to the professionals. In an August 3 game, Wood came in from right field and pitched two innings in Waupun's shocking 10–7 loss to the amateurs. About a week later, Wood pitched his Waupun team to a 10–2 victory over Green Bay. The *Green Bay Press-Gazette* said Wood "formerly of the Page Fence Giants … was jolly and kept the crowd laughing but he pitched ball all the time." A sign of the times, the same paper headlined Wood's victory with "An ex Page Fence Giant Coon Twirled for Them."[36]

By this time the Giants had spent the week following their Green Bay stop crushing a team in the booming lumber town of Menominee, Michigan, 11–0, 14–4 and 11–4.[37] The state's Upper Peninsula would continue to be the locale for the next set of games, as they drilled a team from Escanaba, 17–0, then "badly outclassed" Marquette, 11–0.[38] The next day, a very large crowd watched a considerably closer rematch, which the Giants won, 6–4.[39]

The *Adrian Evening Telegram* printed a glowing report of the Page Fence club after their pair of victories in Marquette. The *Telegram* claimed that the team had won "70 straight games, and have had 21 shut outs to their credit this season."[40] Apparently, the disputed forfeit loss to the Saranac Advertisers in late June and the 3–2 defeat at the hands of Green Bay were all but forgotten for this story. The Adrian local then reprinted a *Marquette Mining Journal* story which offered a glowing account of the Giants' talents. The Upper Peninsula paper claimed that the Page Fence men were a "little if any short of national league speed and the only thing that keeps half its members from playing the big fellows is an accident of birth which gave them black skins." It told about one baseball "magnate" who hoped "Home Run" Johnson was light-skinned enough to pass as white, but found him "several shades darker than the ace of spades" and had to end the major league dream. The Marquette paper described Wilson as the "swiftest ever seen" in town and said he had top control and "the ball comes from his delivery as if shot out from a cannon." With that, the Giants headed south and back into Wisconsin for more games.[41]

A mid-week series with Oshkosh, Berlin and Omro, Wisconsin, saw a new name appear on the Giants' roster. Sherman Barton was signed to replace Wood. A pre-game lineup for the game against Oshkosh listed either Barton or Wilson as possible center fielders, with Burns in right and Patterson, with his injured shoulder and far away from the infield in left. The infield was Taylor, Grant, "Home Run" Johnson and Binga, with George

Johnson behind the plate and Joe Miller on the mound.[42] Barton was a 22-year-old native of Normal, Illinois, and had played at least one year of organized ball. He was also a former Chicago Union, and his signing probably allowed Gus Parsons to gloat a bit and helped to heal the wound of losing Billy Holland to the Illinois club.

Barton was the leading batter against Oshkosh, even while in the ninth spot, by getting three hits and scoring two runs. In the field, he caught a fly ball as the starting center fielder and was flanked by right fielder Burns and Wilson, who subbed for the injured Patterson, in left field. The Giants won the game, 8–4, as Miller defeated the Colts at Athletic Park. Miller's pitches were impressive and his "speed was marvelous." The Giants' infield was also praised as several balls that would have been hits against other teams were turned into outs. The Page Fence ball skills and general demeanor impressed the 1,800 fans who packed the main grandstand and adjacent bleachers. "They were an orderly, gentlemanly lot of fellows, who know how to coach without being offensive."[43] The Giants rolled to victories over Berlin and Omro, Wisconsin. They then chugged their way on their Monarch coach to the Michigan coastal city of Manistee for weekend games with another team named the Colts.

Manistee had prided itself on the strength of its ball clubs over the years and were ready for the black gentlemen to invade the town. The *Manistee Daily News* said, "the Colts will give them a hard hustle this time" and dubbed them the "colored whirlwinds."[44] The paper also promoted the Giants' star hurler, Wilson, as "the phenomenal pitcher ... and two great games are anticipated."[45]

The locals were a bit concerned that heavy rain from the previous weekend was still leaving its imprint. The Recreation Park infield clay was now floating, and the grounds crew was rolling the infield and hoping it would be satisfactory for the games against the Giants.[46] The crew's efforts worked, and the Giants and Colts managed to play that weekend.

Joe Miller was ineffective as the Colts tagged him for several runs in the opening inning. The highlight was an Amos Haynes grand slam over the left field fence, leaving the Giants looking at a quick early deficit. Haynes was paid a $1 bonus for his homer, which undoubtedly added to his joy. Miller temporarily settled down and fanned the next batter for the first out of the inning. However, Miller's recovery was only temporary, as the next batter singled to right. When Fox hit a comebacker to the mound, Miller used his mighty arm to peg a throw so wild to first base that it didn't come to a halt until it rolled to a stop against the outfield fence. Before anyone was settled in their seats, the Giants were staring at a 5–0 deficit.[47]

Miller made it through the second inning unscathed, but gave up two more runs in the third, and the Giants were now facing their biggest deficit in months. The Giants eventually responded with three runs in the third and fifth innings to cut the Colts' lead to 8–6. "Then in the seventh the balloon went up for the Colts." The Giants managed to lift a pair of fly balls off pitcher Quinn to center fielder Gleason, who promptly dropped both. Buoyed by the miscues, the Page Fence men tallied six runs, finally grabbed the lead, and secured a 12–8 win. The Giants' infielders also recorded two double plays, which offset their unusually high eight errors, and the winning streak continued.[48]

"Twas Manistee's Day!" screamed the *Daily Advocate's* Monday headline. The *Daily News* led with, "They Play Hot Ball, Colts Down the Page Fence Giants, Robb the New Pitcher Shows up Well."[49] The mighty Giants were taken down Sunday afternoon in Manistee by a score of 6–4. Clay Robb had been shipped in from the Flint team of the latest reincarnation of the Michigan State League, which had conveniently folded a few days earlier. Robb was originally announced to play in the Saturday game, but was not in the lineup for the Colts' loss.[50] However, his insertion into the Sunday afternoon lineup immediately impacted the rematch.

Robb's game didn't begin too well, as the Page Fence men scored three runs in the opening inning. That offset a run the Colts had made off Miller, who, for some reason, started in back-to-back games. Manistee's Robb settled down in the box and added some fielding wizardry. The import stopped one batted ball with his foot and turned it into an out, and later nipped a speedy Giants runner at first with a laser throw to the bag. In the fourth inning, after giving up four runs and the lead, Miller was relieved by Wilson. George Taylor slammed a long homer over the center field fence in the fourth inning to cut the deficit to 5–4, but that was all for the Giants. The home club scored a single run off Wilson to boost their led to two. The Page Fence men sensed the urgency and knew their long winning streak was in jeopardy. Risky base running in the eighth inning saw all three Page Fence outs come from being tagged out while aggressively attempting to reach second base on singles. When the Giants were set down in order in the bottom of the ninth inning, the 1896 black baseball champions had lost to Manistee, 6–4.[51]

The *Adrian Daily Times and Expositor* added few details following the rare Giants loss. "After winning eighty-two straight games," the Page Fence men had lost was about the extent of their coverage for this mighty feat.[52] The *Evening Telegram* said the loss was contested "in a square game," so the umpire would not be blamed in this defeat, as many had been over the past three seasons.[53] Parsons was quoted in one Manistee paper that this was the Giants' first fair defeat since early June, which implied that both the Saranac and Green Bay losses were tainted.[54] Interestingly, there was an actual umpire controversy before the Sunday afternoon affair. A man named Alex Lamberg was hired to call the ball and strikes. The *Manistee Daily Advocate* maintained that when Lamberg made his first appearance on the diamond, the crowd's "howl" and "some kicking among the players" caused him to be yanked and substituted for by W. D. Gohn. The same paper characterized Gohn's work as "fair and impartial and gave general satisfaction."[55]

People coming from as far away as Clare and Ludington raised the attendance to nearly 1,000 people at the new Manistee ball park. The large throng of baseball patrons added to the day's excitement. The occasion became even more festive when Gus Parsons and the local baseball folks hatched a new deal. Following the completion of the seventh inning, the Manistee boosters announced to the crowd that the Giants would stay in town for an extra Monday game against the Colts.[56]

The additional game was a joyous occasion for the local ball cranks, but not for everyone in northwestern Michigan. James Kehoe, a Traverse City baseball booster, was "hot" and was expecting the Giants in his town for a Monday game.[57] The Traverse City Hustlers claimed to be a very competitive team and anxiously awaited the contest. The Page Fence Giants had previously played in the Michigan resort town, so the locals knew what to expect from the travelling professionals. Kehoe bragged to one town newspaper that the Giants were just a notch below the major leagues. He claimed that this year's Hustlers squad was better than last year's, and he fired a jab at the Page Fence men. Kehoe said the Giants "scoop every amateur team they play, with the exception of an occasional game with such a team as the Hustlers, when they frequently get let down." He expected a large paying Monday afternoon crowd, including many riding the rails from the surrounding communities.[58]

When word leaked back to Traverse City of the seventh inning announcement, Kehoe and another baseball crank, William D. C. Germaine, hopped on the train. The pair arrived in Manistee Sunday evening with "blood in their eyes." The two accused the Manistee boosters of robbing their northern baseball rivals of a chance to play the Giants and felt the town tried to keep the black ball club all to themselves. This, of course, was true. However, the Manistee men denied the charge, and Gus Parsons supported the locals. No doubt, two strong gate receipts persuaded Parsons to abandon the Traverse City trip, too. In his defense, Parsons claimed the Giants would not be able to travel to Traverse City on Monday and then take the train many miles across the state to play in Corunna on Tuesday.[59] Kehoe's and Germaine's complaints fell on deaf ears, and the Giants remained in town and downed the Manistee Colts, 5–4, on Monday afternoon at Recreation Park. A good-sized crowd saw the lefty, Wilson, toss curve balls to Pete Burns to earn the victory.[60] To support their game-stealing scheme, Manistee backers claimed that Traverse City was a poor ball town, and a recent three-game series there netted the Colts only $10. They added that Traverse City organizers would only pay $25 of the $40-dollar travel expenses, so another game in the better ball town of Manistee made economic sense for the Page Fence club.[61]

Kehoe was the ticket agent and depot manager for the Chicago and West Michigan Railway in Traverse City and could read a train schedule.[62] Kehoe claimed he had found a travel route from Traverse City to Corunna without much difficulty. He also claimed that considerable expense had been incurred in printing the "attractive" game posters now nailed around the Traverse City area. The rumor that a third Manistee game would be more lucrative than a single stop in Traverse City did not sit well with Kehoe. He pointed out that three teams from around the state—St. Louis, Muskegon, and the Grand Rapids Heralds—had each played a series in both towns. In each case, Traverse City netted the clubs more money than they had gained in Manistee. Kehoe added that a July 4, 1896, doubleheader in town between the two cities raised only three fewer dollars at the gate ($255) than had four games during last month's July 4 weeklong celebration in Manistee ($258). Kehoe closed his public airing of grievances by saying that the Hustlers were a better team than the Colts and would have drawn better even on a Monday than Manistee did with its large Sunday afternoon crowd.[63]

Actually, the only hustler here was Gus Parsons. Monday had normally been an off-day used for travel, so the Giants simply remained in Manistee and scheduled an additional game. Even with the added game, Parsons was at least able to rest his players by eliminating 50 additional miles of travel and boost the club's profits.

With the Giants unable to reach Corunna from Manistee due to a wreck along the Flint and Pere Marquette rail line, Tuesday became an off-day.[64] The club eventually made its way out of town and entered St. John's, Michigan, on Wednesday. The contest was against the local nine, who were under-practiced and were "entirely outclassed." The Giants crushed them, 20–5, at Athletic Park in front of 650 paying customers. The *St. John's News* reported, "the antics of the colored boys created much merriment. They compose one of the best teams in existence and have only been beaten one game this season on its merits."[65] The newspaper's win-loss information was undoubtedly coming from Parsons, whose creative statistical analysis of the team's record was becoming quite well-known around baseball circles.

This juggernaut of a team was in its third year of positively promoting the Page Fence Woven Wire Fence Company and the town of Adrian. It also appeared that as the 1897 season was winding down, the Giants would not play a single game in Adrian. One of their closest games would be in Elkhart, Indiana, to face the Whiting Grays in early September. The Adrian ball cranks, anxious to see Wilson, Taylor, Binga and the two Johnsons, would have to jump on the train and travel. They would not be the only Midwestern town excited to see the Giants. It was predicted that Whiting, Indiana, a growing town on the south shore of Lake Michigan about 15 miles from Chicago, would add 15 passenger coaches to shuttle their fans to the game. Meanwhile, South Bend railroad officials would order ten extra passenger cars to transport all their ball cranks wanting to see the Giants in Elkhart.[66]

To prepare for the Grays game, the Giants cruised through towns and chalked up victory after victory. They defeated Battle Creek, 8–4, in front of 1,500 fans. Sherman Barton threw a seven-hitter and Grant Johnson slugged a home run.[67] The Calhoun County town was totally unprepared for the large audience, which included fans on special train cars from Adrian. Battle Creek's Athletic Park's grandstand was jammed full, and the overflow spilled by the hundreds along the edge of the diamond.[68] It was the largest baseball crowd anyone had seen in years, despite the fact there were special admission fees. The town had previously allowed women to attend the ball games for free, but the Page Fence Giants contract did not allow for that arrangement. Battle Creek boosters claimed they were forced to charge women and children 15 cents a ticket and men 25 cents, to meet the Giants' terms.[69] The fans were not dissuaded by the added fees, as the advanced promotion worked to its full effect. One Battle Creek paper claimed that local baseball fans had come to witness a team posting an unheard-of record of 75–1 in 1897![70]

The Giants ripped off wins against Hastings, Corunna, and Angola, Indiana, and tiny Burr Oak in rural, southern Michigan. In the final week of August, the Giants were finally able to make it to Corunna. A large crowd had assembled for their postponed game due to the train wreck, and Corunna cranks now had their chance to witness the visitors' ballplaying exploits.[71] The misnamed Corunna Stars were drubbed by the Giants, 20–1, as the Adrian men scored in all but one inning. Wilson fanned eight men and surprisingly surrendered his only score on a home run. The Giants recorded 19 hits with seven doubles, three by newcomer Barton, along with one triple and two homers. Wilson hit a double, triple and homer to help his own pitching performance. Reportedly, the Stars were a strong team, but not so on this day. Someone surmised that the Giants must have hypnotized the Corunna Stars. In addition to

The cover of the 1897 Hudson, Michigan, Street Fair booklet, which featured games by the Page Fence Giants, the Battle Creek Independents and the South Bend Green Stockings (courtesy Hudson Museum).

Corunna's home run, umpire Bert Amsden's work was singled out as the game's other local highlight.[72]

The Giants were now going to face tougher competition as the month of September arrived and the potential to make lots of money. Baseball management was anticipating a huge crowd in Elkhart. A nice purse was also anticipated for Labor Day in South Bend, and as part of a tournament at the Hudson Street Fair. A return trip to Battle Creek would be good for the bottom line, too. To add to their coffers and to their prestige, there was still that September 28 date in Hart, Michigan, with the Chicago Unions for the black baseball championship. September could be a very profitable month for the Page Fence Giants.

◆ 21 ◆

Large Crowds and
the White Giant

The Thursday game at Burr Oak was the final tune-up before the anticipated match-ups in Elkhart and South Bend, Indiana, and against stiffer competition than the farm town provided.

The Monarch train car rolled into Elkhart with the Page Fence team, ready for a competitive affair against the Whiting Grays. Estimates were that about 5,000 people made their way into the ballpark, many likely coming to town on those special train coaches. However, for some reason almost no one from Adrian boarded the train for the game, as only about "eight or ten people" went to Elkhart.[1] As the train came closer to its destination, the enthusiasm picked up, and so did the numbers on the train. Sturgis, Michigan, only a few miles from the Indiana line, loaded 57 passengers. Another Michigan border town, White Pigeon, collected tickets from over 100 riders. As the train crossed into Indiana, even more people stepped into the cars, as it stopped in Vistula and Bristol before reaching Elkhart. The depot was packed with travelers as "there were excursion trains in there from every direction."[2]

The throng of train passengers made their way to the ball park and soon overflowed the place. The grandstand seated 2,700, and it was completely jammed with baseball fans. However, they now needed spots for another 2,300 people, and that became a problem. The grandstand overflow spilled to the edge of the ball field "so that the men had but a limited space in which to play." Elkhart boosters claimed they collected tickets from over 4,300 people, while at least another 500 freeloaders hopped over a fence and never paid anything to see the game. What a game it was! The Palmyra Wonder led the Giants to a 10–7 victory over the talented Whiting Grays. The boomtown, located near the Illinois border, imported a hired battery from Chicago in a move to defeat the world champions. The *Evening Telegram* said that Wilson "pitched the game of his life" in the Sunday victory. Casting a dark cloud on an otherwise successful day, the Grays' manager fell seriously ill and died during the game. In the common, blunt writing style of the day, the *Evening Telegram* minced few words. "[A] Mr. Clark, town clerk, was taken with heart disease and was taken home a corpse."[3]

A doubleheader was on tap for Monday's Labor Day celebration in South Bend. Another massive crowd greeted the Giants, estimated at 3,500 spectators. The Giants won both games over the South Bend Green Stockings by identical 8–7 scores. Sherman Barton won the morning contest against Litchfield, Michigan, native Colbert Van Giesen, and Cyclone Joe Miller beat 20-year-old Lee Faurot, who had pitched for Jackson to finish out the 1895 MSL season, in the afternoon affair.[4]

The Giants headed back to Wisconsin for a pair of weekend games against the Oshkosh Colts. The Saturday game was close until pitcher Barton helped himself at the plate and slugged a bases-loaded triple in the eighth inning to break the 2–2 tie. He held the Colts to four hits, a double by Nicolai the only extra-base knock. The 5–2 Giants win "was as fine an exhibition of baseball as was ever seen in the city." A relatively small crowd for this time of the season of 300 fans saw the Giants play Oshkosh on Saturday, in a game which took only 78 minutes to play.[5]

However, for some reason the Sunday afternoon game drew five times as many people to the ball field. Maybe it was because the Giants would not field an all-black lineup. They had fielded a cook, their porter and even their little mascot over the previous three seasons. However, this time the black gentleman would play alongside a white man and face one of their own pitchers.[6]

The Colts found themselves without a quality pitcher, as Blakely was spent from the previous game. However, the Giants had no such problem as they temporarily traded Sherman Barton for Colts outfielder Nicolai. He was the same man who had drilled a double off Barton in yesterday's contest. Barton did pitch for the second day in a row, gave up seven hits and five runs to his former teammates, and lost for the Colts, 5–0. Barton managed to strike out two of his Giants buddies and hit Bill Binga with a pitch. The Giants didn't score until the fourth inning and were helped by a sloppy eight errors by the Colts. The Colts had committed only two errors the day before, and the large increase was either due to bad breaks or maybe some players didn't want to help a black pitcher. One game summary hinted that the Giants would not have scored without the aid of all the errors. An Oshkosh paper mentioned that after the temporary player trade, the game became "something of a farce and much of the interest in it was lost." The Page Fence Giants took the game seriously, as Miller held the Colts to three hits in the shutout. Nicolai, the one-day Giant, failed to get a hit, but did lay down a successful sacrifice bunt as the white Giant batted eighth, between pitcher Miller and catcher Burns. Nicolai recorded zero putouts in right field but also had zero errors. This 75-minute baseball game may have been the final time that integrated professional teams faced each other for the next 50 years.[7] The Gentlemen's Agreement and the country's Jim Crow atmosphere, buoyed by the *Plessy v. Ferguson* ruling the year before, contributed to that fact.

On their way back to Michigan, the Giants swapped back Barton for Nicolai and decided to stop off again in Angola, Indiana, to play a single game. They Adrian men had narrowly won a ten-inning affair a little more than a week earlier, and the Indiana town enjoyed the team. "The Page Fence Giants are a well-behaved and comely lot of colored individuals." The rematch was so popular at the local Linder and Ramsay Stave Factory that the owners had to cease production, as so many men went to the Giants game rather than report for work.[8] This latest Angola game was more of a romp as the Giants won, 9–1.[9]

Baseball fever was creeping closer to Adrian, as advance agent James Stevens was working to schedule a game near the home of the Page Fence factory. The closest he could come was Hudson, Michigan, as part of their Street Fair to be held for four days in mid–September. Stevens had left from South Bend the day after the doubleheader and traveled to Hudson. His goal was to negotiate some type of game contract for the Giants.[10]

Around this time, a representative of the Detroit Tigers of the Class A Western League wanted to tap into the Adrian baseball fever. A club official telegraphed Howard Taylor and requested a midweek game in Adrian between the Tigers and a fellow Western League foe, the Grand Rapids Bob-o-Links. However, Taylor quickly replied that there were "no respectable ball grounds" for such a game, which ended that idea.[11]

Meanwhile, Stevens was successful in securing Hudson for the Giants, as they would be a featured attraction of the Street Fair. The Page Fence club would play only a few miles to the west and on the closest diamond they had been to Adrian all year. The Giants would face two competitive teams who would also draw well. As the Giants had played in front of nearly 9,000 people in a series of games during the first week of September in northern Indiana, the thought must have been to see if those numbers could be replicated in Michigan. Originally, it was thought that the Whiting Grays and the South Bend Green Stockings would be the two teams in Hudson to face the Giants.[12] However, the Grays dropped out for some reason, and the Battle Creek Independents took their place.

The Giants left Angola, Indiana, and pulled into Adrian on Monday evening, September 13. They took the train to Hudson the following morning for their first game.[13] Hudson was quite proud of the second year of their Street Fair, as they were credited with being the first town in the state to hold such a gathering. A 50-page booklet, touting local businesses and listing the four days of activities, was readily available.[14] Hudson was again hoping for thousands of people to visit their fair city and leave some money behind, to help the local merchants. The Street Fair organizers planned on a variety of events to draw people into Hudson. In addition to the baseball tournament, bicycle and horse races, a balloon launch, and the Davidson Military Band from West Unity, Ohio, were on the schedule.[15] Without a doubt a major draw would be the black gentlemen from Adrian, as they were scheduled to play on all four days of the fair.[16]

A large, electrically illuminated "Welcome" sign arched over the entrance to the downtown Hudson business district. The Street Fair occupied Main, Church and Market Streets, and an assortment of 12' × 16' tents blocked the thoroughfare and marketed the wares of the downtown businesses. Organizers hoped last year's fantastic turnout would help the locals, as the national economic depression called the Panic of 1893 had now continued into 1897. With "ample capital" and following "strict business principles," the "little white city," as it was known, lured citizens from miles around. Hucksters and fakirs separated people from the money in their wallets and purses, while children's pets, farmers' prized livestock, and horticulture displays dotted the streets.[17]

The first Page Fence game had to be a major disappointment to baseball boosters, as only about 200 people showed up Tuesday morning to see the Giants play the South Bend Green Stockings.[18] The likely main reason for the small crowd at Island Park, across Bean Creek at the end of Church Street, was that both teams arrived significantly late.[19] The scheduled 10 o'clock game started "considerably" after 11 a.m.[20] The weather was also a factor, as one report said it was 92 degrees in the shade by the time the first pitch was delivered.[21] The game was said to be entertaining for the first few innings, and then the Indiana club began kicking the ball around and the Giants won, 16–6. One of the Page Fence Giants' Johnsons slugged two homers, and some "pretty plays" in the field were also featured.[22]

A much larger crowd made it to Island Park for the afternoon game with the Green Stockings. The makeshift park was on a slab of an island created when the local grist mill rerouted a portion of Bean Creek to provide itself with water power. About 800 people saw the Giants shut out the South Bend gents, 5–0, in a game which was close until the seventh inning, when one of the Johnsons hit a bases-clearing triple. The biggest news on day two of the Hudson Street Fair (at least according to the *Evening Telegram*) was that over a dozen people had been victimized by a still yet to be located pickpocket gang.[23]

On Wednesday afternoon, a six-inning affair, shortened to allow the Green Stockings time to board the fast mail train back to South Bend, ended with a 3–2 Page Fence victory. This game was called a "fast and furious one," as it had to be, as the six-inning contest began at 4:30 and ended in time for the South Bend club to board the 5:50 train out of town.[24]

Thursday was the featured and best day of the fair. The morning would feature the always popular horse racing. Hot weather was blamed for keeping down the attendance the first two days, with several Street Fair goers being overcome by the heat.[25]

Luring fairgoers to town on Thursday was over $700 in purses for riders and horses at the new Hudson driving park, on the south end of town. It worked, as about 2,000 people made their way into Hudson, with 375 arriving from Adrian on the westbound Lake Shore train.[26]

That morning the Battle Creek Independents, the replacement team for the Whiting Grays, lost to the Giants, 9–6, in what the *Hudson Gazette* characterized as a "pretty exhibition of scientific base ball."[27] The Battle Creek club had picked up players from Albion, Homer and Jackson to strengthen their squad and may have aided in keeping the game close with the Giants.[28]

It was reported that many of those horse race spectators later made their way a few blocks north and across Bean Creek to the Island Park ball diamond.[29] The Thursday afternoon game was a 5–0 Page Fence victory over Battle Creek. Both teams were slick in the field and turned double plays, and the competitive nature of the teams greatly pleased the crowds.[30]

Friday was another Page Fence Giants doubleheader sweep of the Independents. The morning game was a very close, 4–3 win, while the afternoon affair was an 11–1 blowout victory. The thrashing of the South Bend and Battle Creek teams took on Biblical proportions to a writer at the *Evening Telegram*. The Friday afternoon victory would have been another shutout, if not for a throwing error by the Giants' unidentified third baseman. The Battle Creek squad "bravely fought," but like "the Assyrian(s) of old, the Giants 'swooped down like a lamb on the fold,' and snatched the victory.[31]

While during the week, the hot weather and a dash of rain were blamed for keeping attendance figures lower than the first year, everything changed by Saturday's wrap-up story. Hudson organizers claimed that 25,000 people jammed their hamlet on Thursday. The report said that the Cincinnati Northern Railroad had to drop off passengers in Hudson and then return to depots both north and south of town to pick up patrons who were left behind due to the capacity filled train cars.[32] Even though the farmers brought their wholesome wares to town for the array of exhibits, it was said that the saloons did the best business for the week.[33] One travelling vagabond entertainer, tabbed with the unenviable "fakir" label, had $40 snatched from him, but few in the crowd cared and felt as if he deserved to lose the money. The crowds were so impressive and orderly that representatives of four other towns visited Hudson to see if they could pull off a similar event. Apparently, Kalamazoo officials were so happy with what they had witnessed that they hired one of Hudson's organizers to create a similar street fair for them in October.[34]

The string of victories at the Street Fair apparently ended the Page Fence Giants' 1897 season. A week after their seven straight wins in Hudson, Gus Parsons told both Adrian newspapers that the team had concluded the year with a poor financial record. The *Adrian Daily Times and Expositor* noted that early-season poor weather had cost the Giants 57 games, which had obviously negatively impacted the team's bottom line. The Giants' record was 124–12.[35] Keeping in the spirit of conflicting records, the *Evening Telegram* said the record was 125–11, which they rightly characterized as "phenomenal." The *Telegram* echoed Parsons' report from their rival paper that bad weather had sapped profits from the traveling club.[36] Other papers continued to brag about the Giants' prowess on the diamond, as the *Delphos*, Ohio, *Daily Herald* and the *Steuben* (Indiana) *Republican* both printed a 126–10 record for the Adrian club.[37]

The poor bottom line must have weighed heavily on the Giants' management, as two last-minute games were scheduled after the end of the season. On Saturday, September 25, the Giants took the train to Albion, Michigan, made their way to a baseball field carved out of the horse driving park in town, and defeated a Battle Creek team, 6–3. A small crowd witnessed the game set along the banks of the Kalamazoo River on the city's south end. A few double plays turned by the slick-fielding Giants made it an "interesting" affair, nonetheless.[38]

The following day, on the opposite end of Calhoun County from Albion, the Giants played in Battle Creek. That city was extremely giddy to host the Giants' final game of the year. As a bonus, star hurler George Wilson was to pitch the season-ending contest. The *Battle Creek Daily Journal* dubbed Wilson the "colored wonder" and claimed he was "without a doubt, the greatest colored pitcher in the country." Someone told the paper that when Wilson pitched in 1897, the Giants did not lose a single game. To counter Wilson's immense talent, the Independents attempted, but were unsuccessful, in securing the talented Danny Friend, one of the starting pitchers in the rotation for the National League's Chicago Colts.[39]

About 1,000 people made their way to Athletic Park in Battle Creek Sunday afternoon, September 26, to see the Giants win the season finale, 8–1, over the Independents. A man named Stinson pitched for the Battle Creek team, and shoddy fielding behind him led to six unearned runs. Wilson's curveball made local history when he hit an opponent with the pitch. In the eighth inning, the Palmyra Wonder, tossing one of his "cannon ball in shoots," broke the left arm of John "Silver" Fyanes. Reports were that Fyanes would now be laid up for several weeks.[40] With this latest victory, the second, official season-ending game occurred for the Page Fence Giants. There had been no mention in weeks of the September 28 game in Hart, Michigan, against the Chicago Unions for the black baseball championship. The game just disappeared from the schedule. The two championship-claiming clubs would face each other just once in 1897.

Maybe the rivalry could be rekindled on the diamond next season. Maybe more than one game could be scheduled between the two black Western baseball powerhouses. If both sides wanted to play, it was surely possible. It had already been announced that the Page Fence Giants would be on the road next year and that their 1898 season opener would be on April 4 in Columbus, Ohio. "Manager Parsons will continue to be their guiding star."[41]

While the organized Page Fence Giants team may have now finally reached the end of the 1897 season, the players were not finished playing ball. Battle Creek swooped up Joe Miller, Bill Binga and James Patterson for an upcoming game at the Calhoun County Fair. The small town of Homer had enough money to hire the battery of George Wilson and Pete Burns as their ringers. The two towns would square off for a single game the following week at the fairgrounds.[42] During this lull, at least two of the Giants had plans for something a bit bigger than baseball and would skip the Homer–Battle Creek tilt; first baseman George Taylor was getting married.

One of the original Page Fence Giants was at the St. Joseph County courthouse in Centreville, Michigan, on Tuesday, October 5. With Taylor was his 19-year-old bride-to-be, Edith Weaver, as they filled out their marriage license. Taylor was 30 and considerably older than Weaver. Taylor listed his occupation on the marriage license not as a professional baseball player, but as a tinner. The teenaged bride-to-be noted on the license that she was a housewife. The following day, Wednesday, October 6, the couple was wed in Three Rivers, Michigan, by William A. Frye, a white minister of the gospel. It is unknown how many Giants made the trek to Three Rivers and witnessed the wedding ceremony. Reportedly, George Wilson and Peter Burns left Battle Creek for Homer that day, or maybe it was more accurately for Taylor's wedding.[43] Former Giant Fred Van Dyke lived only a few miles away in Vandalia and may have been in attendance that Wednesday. However, Charles Grant was definitely at the wedding. The starting second baseman and member of the team since 1896 was Taylor's best man.[44] While some records have George Taylor as born in Kansas, an interview noted that his home was in Three Rivers, when he began his professional ballplaying career in 1889 with Aspen of the Colorado State League.[45]

To show off their new-found ringers, the Battle Creek Independents hosted a team from Kalamazoo and won, 13–4. One of the Ganzel brothers on the Western League's Minneapolis Millers smacked two homers off Joe Miller. Cyclone Joe later yelled at Ganzel, "You won't get another," and he didn't. The three hired Giants all played well, and Bill Binga assumed the role of coacher. "Binga displayed a wit at coaching which kept the faces of the large crowd of spectators wreathed in a continuous smile."[46]

Some of the Giants, possibly newlywed Taylor and teammate Grant, scheduled a game in Paw Paw, Michigan, on Thursday, October 7. The game would be a part of a community celebration, which also featured high wire artists, bicycle and running races, acrobats, a balloon launch and a band concert.[47] No results of the game were printed, and one wonders if there were enough available Giants to play the contest.

The build-up to the Homer-Battle Creek battle highlighted the use of the Page Fence ringers. "A great rivalry exists between Wilson and Miler and each will do his utmost to win," one paper publicized the game. Battle Creek's Athletic Park was the scene of the affair, as the site for the epic contest was moved from the county fairgrounds. Tickets would cost 25 cents for men, plus ten cents extra for grandstand seating, but the ladies would be admitted to the grounds for free. On Sunday, October 10, the Homer team upset the Battle Creek Independents, 11–9, even though Joe Miller was said to have outpitched the Palmyra Wonder. The *Battle Creek Daily Journal* claimed that Homer was loaded with ringers from the Page Fence team (Wilson and Burns), along with a Ganzel brother and another man named McKinney. The Independents allowed four unearned runs and lost in a game "they should have won handily." A large crowd witnessed the game, which was "intensely exciting throughout."[48] The week-long hype was accurate, and the players scattered for the winter months.

Some of the Giants returned home, while some apparently still wanted to play ball. James Patterson wrote to the Page Fence Company, where he was going to work in the factory during the winter, that he was busy on the ball diamond until October 21.[49]

At this point in the year, the railroad fever was again high in Adrian. There was the repeated announcement of the beginning stages of the elegant, large stone depot for the now recently renamed Detroit and Lima Northern Railroad. The depot would be modeled after the beautiful Lake Shore and Michigan Southern train station in nearby Hudson, with a "high cupola … [and] a covered driveway" and would sit upon "handsomely" adorned

The elaborate brick and stone Lake Shore and Michigan Southern train station in Hudson, Michigan, which was to be the model for the Lima Northern depot in Adrian. The Adrian version was never built, and the Hudson depot building was torn down over 40 years ago (courtesy Hudson Museum).

grounds.[50] The proposed depot's spring Lawrence Park groundbreaking, whose plans had robbed the Giants of their home ball diamond in 1897, had been delayed for months. It now appeared that the project would commence. The Lima Northern had not experienced a smooth entrance to town, as the rail line had already been purchased, the name changed, and the new elegant depot was slow to develop. These were not good signs for Adrian's third rail company.

For some reason, the *Detroit Free Press*, never particularly supportive of the Giants, printed a lengthy and praise-filled letter, which lauded the skill and character of the Page Fence gentlemen. It was an excerpt printed a few days earlier from Sturgeon Bay, Wisconsin, in *The Sporting News*.[51] The letter appeared in the Detroit paper's November 1, 1897, edition. A Wisconsin man wrote:

> You can't go and see the Giants without having a good laugh and don't think for an instant that laugh producing is the limit of their abilities. Not much, they are ball players—ball players that play the game with a snap and vim that is wonderful. They make double plays that are things to marvel and wonder at in days to come. Wilson is a southpaw that could jump right into the National League

and more than hold his own and he wouldn't have to play with 'der Browns either. Miller has terrific speed and Petie Burns is a backstop "wat is a backstop." The rest of the team play an article of ball that is a thing of beauty. Color or no color they are good fellows and will do the square thing.[52]

After three years of crisscrossing the Midwest and Canada, the Page Fence Giants were a source of pride for Adrian, the fence company, and the black citizens of the country. Probably exactly what Bud Fowler and Grant Johnson had expected when they first approached the Michigan town in the summer of 1894.

◆ 22 ◆

A War of Words

It seems that as soon as the baseball season is over, another annual ritual begins. The scribes take pen in hand and try to improve their team's standing, all without the benefit of a ball and bat.

The Manistee team posted a 30–18 record, and *Sporting Life* magazine headlined "Michigan's Champions" as "Manistee Lays Claim to High Semi Professional Honors." The team split two games with the Cuban Giants and the Grand Rapids minor league club, took one game from the Page Fence Giants, swept Sheboygan, the Wisconsin League champions, and went 12–9 against fierce rival Traverse City.[1] So someone thought they were the champions of the state of Michigan.

The usual Giants antagonist, the Chicago Unions, were also back in the news during the winter months. Frank Leland wrote *The Sporting News* that his Unions were 128–24, and he still considered them the "Black Wonders throughout the Western States." Leland told of his team "defeating every colored club of note" and reminded readers of their single victory over the Page Fence Giants, when the Adrian management boasted they could spot the Chicago club a bushel of runs and still win. Well, the Giants lost, 7–6. That win, coupled with the Unions' split of a four-game series with the Cuban X Giants, a four-game sweep over the Memphis Cliffords, and three victories over the Genuine Cuban Giants, led the Chicago team to claim the black baseball championship for 1897. Leland continued his jab at the Adrian men, saying that other than the battery of Wilson and Burns, they didn't have much. He felt the Eastern-based Cuban X Giants were a better club. Leland said that due to the Unions' superior record and despite the fact "there is no colored league; we claim the right to be styled the colored champions of the world." Two former Giants, George Hopkins, who played in the first month of 1895, and the ever-popular but high-maintenance coacher, Billy Holland, finished the 1897 season with the Chicago Unions.[2]

In the same edition of *The Sporting News* as Leland's letter, Len Hoch called the Page Fence Giants the "celebrated colored champions," but lamented that the team didn't play in Adrian in 1897, as the ball field was "appropriated by the new railroad." Hoch was more optimistic concerning the team's financial future and believed the Giants' outlook for the 1898 season was "brighter." Contradicting himself by ignoring his complaint to the Adrian papers of a financially losing season, Hoch now claimed Gus Parsons had "made the season successful in a financial sense" and never mentioned the 57 rainouts that reduced profits. The Giants' season record had now jumped up to 138–10, as somewhere about a dozen additional games were considered since the season had ended. Hoch noted that Parsons and his wife would be staying in Adrian during the winter (unlike last year), and Parsons was already planning for the next season. Hoch vowed that the upcoming version of the Giants would be better than ever and "easily the fastest colored team in the country."[3]

Hoch did manage to mention the lack of profits when speaking about the other baseball teams in the state. He claimed that Michigan "was not a bonanza," as the Western League's Detroit Tigers failed to meet their monetary goals and Grand Rapids was supposedly teetering on the brink of insolvency. The Michigan State League was a financial disaster, as some teams failed to make it through the 1897 season, while only six independent teams (Battle Creek, Homer, Muskegon, Manistee, Saginaw and Traverse City) made money.[4]

Hoch also did not let the chance go by in his lengthy letter to expound about the superior Page Fence Giants' financial picture as compared to other black teams. He claimed that both the Cuban X and Cuban Genuine Giants ran out of money and were stranded while on Western road trips.[5]

The former mayor and now recently replaced Adrian postmaster (due to the election of the Republican President McKinley) turned his pen to the newly self-proclaimed black champions, the Chicago Unions. He characterized the Unions as "literally demolished" once they left the city of Chicago to play ball. Possibly hinting at shaky umpire work aimed against the visiting teams, Hoch did not accept the Unions' title. He claimed that their championship pronouncement was weakened because they were trounced in visits to Michigan and Wisconsin. Leland responded by noting that the Unions had won every game in Wisconsin and lost only one in the state of Michigan.[6]

Hoch announced the often-repeated vow to play the Unions in a single game, winner-take-all of the gate money challenge. With a dig at the Unions, Hoch claimed that, despite the best of efforts of many baseball cranks, the Chicago club always seemed too busy to play the Page Fence Giants.[7] Neither Hoch nor Leland ever mentioned the September 28 game scheduled in Hart, Michigan. However, Hoch's last dig may have in fact been a veiled reference to the Unions backing away from that game.

The off-season was not just a battle among the black teams, but also a time to reflect on the racial divide foisted on the game. A year after the *Plessy v. Ferguson* Supreme Court ruling, the nation's color line was firmly in place. Noted black baseball columnist Charles C. Stinson put pen in hand and did his best to persuade the baseball powers to open the game to all men. Stinson's impassioned plea for integration made its way into *The Sporting News*. "There is no reason in the world, why a colored man is not as capable of playing baseball in the National League, as white men or even Indians." Stinson asked for black men to be given a chance to play with whites and believed they would prove to be their equal. He mentioned Weldy Walker, who caught for Toledo years earlier, as better than some of the white catchers who currently were considered "hot stuff." He praised Buffalo's second baseman, (Frank) Grant, and pitcher Frank Miller as two others who could make the major leagues. "The fact is, there are plenty of first class colored players and there is no question as to their ability." Stinson claimed that American society was moving forward, and a man just wanted an opportunity to prove his worth on the ball diamond. The baseball scribe noted that there was "nothing in the laws of the league" which dealt with a player's nationality or color. He also contended that baseball fans came to see a good game and not to "look at the color of the players."[8]

Appealing to the pocket book, Stinson said that black players would attract more black fans to the games, improving attendance and gate receipts. If a black man could sit in a seat in Congress, "then surely he is good enough and capable of playing baseball." *The*

Sporting News headlined Stinson's letter with "Good Players," but the article didn't move baseball forward for the next 50 years.[9]

While interesting letters flowed around the country and detailed the exploits of the black teams, the Page Fence club became the center of a short-lived rumor. In mid–February 1898, a story circulated that Elkhart, Indiana, was going to lure the Giants from Adrian. Coincidentally, Elkhart was the same city where L. A. Browne had relocated his family and established his new law practice. The discoverer of ace George Wilson, Browne somehow must have been involved in this story. The rumor detailed how the Indiana town had organized a "substantial" fund raising effort and hoped the Page Fence Giants would serve as their entry in the new Michigan-Indiana League.[10] The rumor soon lost its legs, the Page Fence Giants remained in Adrian, and the new minor league never materialized in 1898.

Newspaper coverage of the Giants' off-season wheeling and dealing in this fourth year was nearly non-existent. The initial baseball excitement had worn off, and now a single sentence about the black team was all one would usually find in the Adrian newspapers. In March, the newspapers noted that James Patterson would be back, as would Joe Miller and William Binga.[11] Patterson had spent the winter residing in Adrian and working at the Page Fence factory. With the start of the ball season, Patterson had made arrangements for the factory to post the Giants' scores again.[12] Patterson was also named the team captain, as Grant Johnson was rumored to be gone. The Chicago Unions announced in early March that Johnson would be their starting shortstop for the 1898 season. Johnson would join former Giants teammates George Hopkins and Billy Holland on the roster.[13] By the end of March, about a week before leaving for spring training in Illinois, Wilson, Miller and Binga joined Patterson in Adrian and were seen around town practicing their craft.[14] And somewhere along the way, Home Run Johnson returned safely to the Page Fence crew.

While the team was readying for another successful season, the Page Fence Company was rebounding from the nation's nearly five-year economic calamity—the Panic of 1893. The busy Page Fence factory night shift was "the best we have ever had," as they manned dozens of the wire looms. Company reports were that an abundant backlog of orders had shipments of the finished fencing "between twenty and thirty carloads behind." The inside of the now-bustling factory was compared to the city of Chicago. If you stopped moving on the factory shop floor, you would be run over![15]

The Detroit and Lima Northern railroad fever had sapped the Giants' newspaper coverage in 1897. This year, a new fever, surrounding the beginning stages of the Spanish-American War, was the key issue. The accidental sinking in mid–February of the USS *Maine*, moored off the coast of Havana, Cuba, sent shock waves throughout the country, increasing the war fever.[16] Although early reports seemed to indicate an internal engine problem as the cause of the massive explosion, which led to the deaths of hundreds of sailors, the steady drumbeat of war ignored that fact. A sunken U.S. Navy ship fueled efforts to rid a European power, the Spanish, from the Western Hemisphere. Their occupation of Cuba was too close for many Americans, and Spain's rumored atrocities against the locals pushed the United States toward a confrontation. In Adrian, the local National Guard regiment, based in the massive armory building, would likely be called into action. Daily reports of where they boys might be traveling across the globe replaced the coverage of where the baseball boys would be traveling around the Midwest.

Former baseball investor Colonel Seymour Howell soon offered his services in the military to reprise his service to his new homeland. Howell, though born in England, came to this country with his parents and later served the Union in the Civil War. He now wanted to become an active duty officer in the U.S. Army in the Spanish-American War. In his late 50s, the former city treasurer and longtime banker saw his daily exploits covered in the Adrian newspapers. Originally called back early from his annual winter vacation in Florida, he was sent to join the 31st Michigan, stationed at Camp Eaton, near Brighton.[17] Howell promptly flunked his physical, which made state-wide news, as the *Detroit Free Press* blared, "Will Not Be Accepted."[18] After some back-door negotiations, the aged Howell was removed as a battalion leader, assigned as a paymaster in the regular Army, given a pay raise, and allowed to serve his adopted country with dignity.[19]

Another of the major financial backers of local baseball and the Giants, Len Hoch, had changed his focus in 1898, too. Hoch was looking at becoming involved in a major business venture far from Adrian. He had his eyes on starting a new cement plant in Coldwater, a Michigan community about 60 miles west of Adrian. The Coldwater Portland Cement Company was led by Hoch and a group of Michigan businessmen, including Adrian's Rolla Taylor and John Navin. The group raised $300,000 in stock purchases to begin the firm.[20] Many stories of Hoch's grandiose business scheme received print in the Adrian papers and took away from any Page Fence Giants baseball fever.

Hoch had also resumed his efforts in trying to overhaul the nation's tax code, something he had spent a considerable amount of time on prior to his Page Fence Giants days. In 1894, his speech before the Farmer's Institute in Morenci had been turned into a pamphlet, exposing the benefits of famed economist Henry George's "Single Tax" proposal. Hoch sent his speech to newspapers and friends and hoped for broad coverage of his idea.[21] The "Single Tax" was a "land value tax" by which municipalities captured rental fees on public land and used the money for the common good. The idea was to increase the efficient use of property, increase community wealth, create jobs, and act as a hedge against inflation, all very important during the five years of the Panic of 1893.[22] After apparently stepping away from the "Single Tax" mantra for a few years, Hoch addressed a group of Detroit citizens in January 1898 and resumed touting the plan.[23]

With Howell, Seymour and Hoch focusing their efforts on other endeavors, Adrian baseball was without two of its early benefactors. The loss of Hoch was a major blow to the baseball organization. Coupled with Bud Fowler's early first-season departure and the rumor about Grant Johnson leaving the team, baseball and the Giants, specifically, were missing key, enthusiastic boosters heading into the 1898 season.

Unlike the first year, when the newly formed Giants practiced only a few days before facing Gas City, Indiana, they planned a one-week pre-season to begin 1898. Team members would eventually gather in Peoria, Illinois, to work out and then to play an opening season game against the locals. Also, unlike the first season, there was no final roster update or much information of any sort on this latest version of the Page Fence Giants in either of Adrian's daily newspapers.

The Giants were scheduled to spend most of the first month of the season playing minor league clubs. The national sporting publications would print stories featuring the white minor league clubs, and within those, a line or two would mention their exhibitions against the Giants. While Peoria opened the Giants' season, other April stops were also announced for Springfield, Illinois, Ottumwa, Iowa, Milwaukee, Wisconsin, Toledo, Ohio, and London, Ontario, Canada. One previously announced game with the major leagues Cincinnati club was ultimately cancelled by Reds official Frank Bancroft for some unknown reason.[24]

The Giants began 1898 with a 10–7 win over the Class B Western Association Peoria

Distillers.[25] The Adrian men came back and won a second game against Peoria.[26] The Page Fence club's third game of the season was against another Western Association team, the Ottumwa Coal Palace Giants. They defeated those white minor leaguers too, and then tied them the next day, 12–12.[27] The Giants won games in Cedar Rapids, Iowa, including one where the black gentlemen defeated the Rabbits, 13–4. In that lopsided affair, Wilson out-dueled two pitchers, including Dewey McDougal, who had spent two years in the majors and was coming off a 20-win season for Cedar Rapids.[28]

While game details were almost a thing of the past in the *Adrian Daily Times and Expositor* and the *Adrian Evening Telegram*, that was not the case at the Page Fence Woven Wire Fence plant. Someone from the team, probably James Patterson, was getting the word back to the plant floor in Adrian. "The report from each game of the Page Fence Giants is an interesting feature at the factory."[29]

The Giants traveled to Grand Rapids for a series of games against Frank Torreyson's Cabinet Makers of the Interstate League. An earlier schedule had the Page Fence men in Milwaukee on several of these dates, but as had been the case in previous seasons, last-minute changes were the standard operating procedure. The Sunday afternoon game at Alger Park was played before either a "small crowd" or 1,200 people, as news accounts conflicted, and they witnessed a slugfest and a 10–8 Giants victory.[30] Joe Miller pitched a shutout over the last five innings, as the Giants faced a future starting major league lefty, Billy Campbell, and a former Louisville Colonel catcher, Henry Cote.[31] Unfortunately, poor weather cancelled the rest of the games with Grand Rapids that week.[32]

The Giants made a relatively close stop to their home base, with an early-season appearance in late April in Toledo. Their opponent was the 1897 Interstate League pennant-winning Toledo Mud Hens, whom they defeated. "Wilson, who has developed into a heavy hitter, knocked out a home run. He also shows improvement as a pitcher," as the Giants won, 4–3.[33] The "pretty game of ball" was played on the Toledo Armory grounds.[34] In a rare feature story, the *Evening Telegram* reprinted the *Toledo Commercial*'s article, which included a complete box score. Leading off in the victory over Toledo and playing second for the Giants was Charles Grant. He was followed by James Patterson in left, Grant Johnson at shortstop, George Taylor hitting cleanup and playing first base, George Wilson as pitcher, Bill Binga at third, George Johnson, Junior in right, Pete Burns behind the plate and Sherman Barton in center field. Burns and Binga accounted for half of the Giants' ten hits. The Toledo paper was effusive in its praise of the black gentlemen, calling the team "mild mannered," and saying they played "a game that is well worth seeing." The Ohio account also had kind words for Wilson, referred to as "Mistah Wilsin," saying he was "one of the best wrong paw pitchers in the business," as he "gracefully" carried out his ball playing duties.[35]

Another Toledo paper praised the Giants, in yet another article reprinted in Adrian. The *Evening Telegram* used the *Toledo East Side Record* to heap accolades on the Page Fence club, when that role was apparently no longer desired by the local scribes. As usual, the top attraction was the Palmyra Wonder. This Toledo paper noted that Wilson had the "ability to send a globe in two or more opposite directions at the same instant," and the result is that "two or three good batters of opposing clubs are now in insane asylums." The other emerging star, at least in the eyes of the *Record*, was versatile Bill Binga. The third baseman and sometimes catcher was described, at first glance, as a slow-moving man. However, once the game began, Binga "unwinds himself, lets out his joints a couple of inches," took a deep breath and became "a composite streak of dust and darkey from base to base." The *Toledo Record* dubbed him "Binga-from-the-Raisin."[36]

The American club traveled into Canada, shut out a team in St. Thomas, and swept a pair of contests from London, Ontario.[37] The Canadian trip became eventful for reasons other than posting a string of victories. Illness and injury sidelined four of the players. Second baseman Charlie Grant had become sick once the train car entered Canada. Around that time, Home Run Johnson became ill and left the team to recuperate at his home in Findlay, Ohio. Following their 9–8 win in London on April 30, the team's two top pitchers, Miller and Wilson, were out walking and taking in the sights that evening. A runaway draft horse emerged from an alleyway, and while Wilson could side-step the animal, Miller was not as lucky or quick. Cyclone Joe was knocked to the pavement, and the frightened horse stepped on his right pitching hand, gashing it in two places. Miller also suffered a bruised left arm, a skinned face and was "very generally used … up."[38] Last year's Canadian trip had also not been kind to the Giants, as this was when Billy Holland complained of illness, remained in Adrian, and was later released from the club.

While these Canadian games were ongoing, the bigger news in Adrian was that the 31st Regiment was pulling out of the Wabash Railroad depot and headed to Camp Eaton near Brighton. The members of the regiment's Company B were excited, and a large crowd assembled to see the men off, as the country was in the beginning month of the Spanish-American War.[39] President William McKinley and Congress had finally declared war on Spain, following months of warmongering by American imperialists. The sinking of the USS *Maine* in February had been the catalyst for going to war, and the expansionists got their wish on April 25.[40] Adrian's news coverage featured the soldiers and the country's possible war strategy, all while the men were being drilled at the camp on Island Lake in Livingston County. These war news articles left little time and space for stories about the star-studded travelling baseball club.

As May greeted the country, the Giants were again not gracious guests. The Giants steamrolled teams in Oil City, Pennsylvania, where Wilson tossed a three-hit shutout, and clubs in Canton, Coshocton, and Massillon, Ohio.[41] "Good Game—Small Crowd," headlined a Massillon paper that was gracious in its praise of the Giants.[42] The Yingling Hill Park crowd was small due to a sky which threatened rain at any minute. At least three ringers from Toledo were imported to strengthen the Massillon club, but they still lost, 5–1. The news account said the Giants were pleased with umpire Robert Featheringham's calls "and not a kick was made," which was apparently a surprise to the locals. The story claimed that the Yingling Park fans had expected the black team to complain and to be "rowdy players," but that was not the case. The *Massillon Item* newspaper explained that the Giants "put up too fine an article of ball to need to resort to such tactics to win." The paper congratulated the visitors on their few fielding errors and noted "their team work was perfect." Even though the Giants' pitching staff allowed only a single run, the story highlighted Massillon's hurler. Snook twice loaded the bases with only one out, and each time held the Giants off the scoreboard. The day's batting highlight came when the Giants' James Patterson drilled a home run.[43]

Back at the Page Fence factory, the plant was about as successful as the ball team. The fence company was so swamped with orders they worked 22 hours a day in order to meet their demand. One report had the company's production schedule behind by some 200 miles of fencing.[44] The company was having some problem securing enough materials to make their patented fencing, causing a major headache in Adrian. How much money was being made and how much was being lost due to the production delays is anyone's guess. However, it was a sign that the Panic of 1893 might finally be coming to an end. While this factory glitch was a major issue for J. Wallace Page, it was probably not the most important thing in his life. The fence magnate was planning the June 1 wedding at his home at 27 College Avenue of his daughter, Bertha Helen Page, to local attorney Leslie B. Robertson.[45]

The ever-active Len Hoch quickly made his way out of town in May of 1898. The former mayor and ousted ex-postmaster had incorporated his cement company and had plans drawn up for building the plant that summer in Coldwater.[46] While Hoch managed to purchase several hundred shares of the $10 stock, his outlay trailed larger investors, Rolla Taylor, John F. Navin and H. F. Cook of Adrian and O. L. Pierce of nearby Hudson.[47] Despite that fact, Hoch was elected Vice-President and Manager of the newly established Coldwater Portland Cement Company.[48] The investors purchased 565 acres of "marl" land, a clay and silt-like substance, in an effort to ensure that the raw materials needed for the cement production were readily available.[49]

For people in Adrian, Hoch's leadership and vibrant personality would be missed by the community. However, for others, word late in the month that the 31st Regiment was heading closer to the war front was in the forefront of many people's minds. The men would be leaving the cozy confines of Camp Eaton near Brighton and riding trains to Camp Thomas near Chattanooga, Tennessee, to await word on their next assignment.[50]

On the baseball diamond, the familiar Detroit Athletic Club team was the Giants' next opponent. Games were set for 4 o'clock Friday, May 13, and Saturday, May 14, and would be held on the ball grounds bordered by Woodward, Cass, Canfield and Forest Streets, about a dozen blocks from the Detroit River and the business district. The *Detroit Free Press* noted that the Giants had a 122–10 record in 1897 and currently were the only travelling ball team using their own train car. The DAC team was "working hard" to "make a good showing" against the Giants.[51]

Two close games were what the Detroiters gave the travelling Adrian men. On Friday, "the Page Fence Giants, who can be both minstrels and ball players on the diamond," won a narrow 9–8 victory by scoring the winning run in the bottom of the eighth inning. The DAC pitched Harwood Bacon, who hurled "a first-class game" and was better than the Giants' Sherman Barton. The "colored joshers" scored single runs in the first four innings, but the Delta men battled back and briefly took the lead. The Detroiters, down by two, appeared on the verge of a rally when the first two men got on base in the ninth inning. But Binga turned a nifty double play by snagging a low foul liner and firing a strike to first, doubling off the base runner. The next man hit a triple, and rather than driving in the tying run, the Detroit club remained a tally short. With the tying run standing on third, the next DAC batter, Guiney, hit a ball to second baseman Charlie Grant, who scooped up the grounder and threw to first to end the threat and secure the Giants' victory. Fine glove work by both teams were highlights of the game, played in front of about 800 people on the DAC grounds.[52]

The closeness of the first contest had the Detroit ball cranks excited for the second game of the series. The Deltas hired a new pitcher, Harris, who was from Tecumseh, Michigan. Harris had some success for Olivet College against the University of Michigan club recently and the previous year against a travelling college all-star team from New York. The Detroit club also made a few changes in their lineup to defeat the Page Fence men. Stoking the day's competitive fires, the *Detroit Free Press* reprinted the Giants' win-loss records over the years. They noted that the club was 121–31 in 1895, 143–26 in 1896 and 128–10 last season, all final records which contradicted anything the Giants had reported back in Adrian.[53]

The Deltas' Saturday afternoon started off badly as for some inexplicable reason Harris failed to show for the game, as did catcher Twomey, who had caught the previous day. George Sheldon, a college boy from Yale known more for his success on the tennis court, replaced Harris. The substitute catcher was a man named Case, who had been on the New York all-star team which Harris had mowed down last year. Sheldon and Case worked together quite well, but were still not strong enough to match the battery of Wilson and Chappie Johnson. The Giants lefty carved through the Deltas and struck out batters in every inning but one, on his way to 12 on the afternoon. However, the Deltas did somehow, momentarily, pull ahead with a wild fourth inning, in which they plated all their day's six runs. Wilson lost his control that inning as he managed to hit three Detroit batters, chucked a wild pitch, and gave up several base knocks, as the Deltas rallied to a 6–3 lead. The Giants pecked away at Sheldon, and a home run by Grant in the seventh inning and a two-run double by George Johnson in the eighth sealed the 7–6 victory. A slightly larger crowd than on Friday, 1,200, attended the contest which was "sharper and cleaner than that of the day before."[54]

The Giants' next game was the season opener for the Flint and Pere Marquette Railroad team from Saginaw and was played at Flint's Dewey Park. The *Adrian Evening Telegram* had the headline as "Giants had fun with F. & P. M." as the 17–5 victory was a blowout from the start. Charlie Grant repeated his slugging from Saturday and drilled another homer, as did Patterson and one of the Johnsons. Miller and Wilson took turns pitching in a game that "was too one-sided to be interesting, but the colored boys kept the crowd in good humor by their clever antics."[55]

In honor of the celebration of Queen Victoria's Birthday on Tuesday, May 24, the Giants were booked for Leamington, Ontario, a city on the banks of Lake Erie and about 30 miles from Detroit. The American club easily defeated the locals, 9–1, before a crowd which consisted of nearly one-half of the city of Leamington.[56]

As the Page Fence men returned to the United States, they stopped in Detroit and were spectators at a Western League game between the hometown Tigers and the St. Paul Saints. The black men's appearance was noted in the *Free Press*, which said the Giants sat in the Bennett Park bleachers, at the corner of Michigan and Trumbull (future site of Tiger Stadium), for the Wednesday afternoon game. The travelling ball stars saw Detroit's Tom Thomas defeat Bill Phyle, 7–6. The first-place Saints lost the game in the final inning to the sixth-place Tigers. Arthur "Old Hoss" Twineham dropped a bunt down the first base line which eluded Phyle and scored the Tigers' Henry "Hunky" Hines from third base with the winning run. Phyle, who later that summer would pitch for the major league Chicago Orphans, slipped and fell while running to field the bunt, which sealed the Tigers' victory. The Page Fence Giants were familiar with Twineham, as he had been on the Grand Rapids roster over the years, after he had served two seasons as a solid-hitting back-up catcher for the major league St. Louis Browns. No doubt the Adrian gentlemen were wondering how many of them would be playing in this game, if not for the color of their skin. Likely in their mind, too, was how many felt they were better than Tom Thomas, Hunky Hines, Arthur Twineham, and Bill Phyle. As a matter of fact, every player in the lineup for both Detroit and St. Paul that day had played, or would play, in the majors. Undoubtedly, some of the best players at the diamond that day were plunked down as paying customers in the Bennett Park bleachers.[57]

◆ 23 ◆

The Last Summer

The day the Giants watched the Tigers-Saints game, President McKinley ordered more fighting troops for the Spanish-American War. The President wanted to add 75,000 enlistees to the already 175,000 in service, bringing the country's men under arms to a quarter of a million soldiers.[1] How many of the Page Fence Giants thought about volunteering for the war is anybody's guess. However, two years following the controversial *Plessy v. Ferguson* court ruling, it's likely not too many wanted to leave the ball fields for the battle ground to fight a European power accused of bullying the Cuban natives. The Page Fence men could look around and see the United States as a racially segregated country. America's limits on their civil rights probably tamped down the spirit to fight the Spanish over the rights of the Cuban natives, while our black citizens had their second-class status reaffirmed by the U.S. Supreme Court. None of the Page Fence men left the team to join the war effort.

The Adrian citizens followed the war in their daily papers. Residents felt that their 31st regiment was going to make the news, as they had been ordered to be the first Michigan unit to head south to the war front. Plans were to travel in 30 train cars to Camp Thomas, near Chattanooga, Tennessee, to the old Civil War battlefield of Chickamauga, just over the border from Georgia.[2] The order in mid–May sent anxious nerves through the town. However, they were quickly soothed when reports from Camp Eaton noted that the regiment remained stuck there. Six weeks later, as June 1898 ended, the 31st was still at Island Lake, along with 36,000 other Michigan soldiers. Without leaving the camp, the 31st suffered its first military casualty, when a young man from Fenton died of pneumonia. Amid great pomp and circumstance, his body was shipped out to family members, and the 31st's initial casualty was not caused by enemy troops.[3]

With war fever running high in Adrian, the Page Fence ballgames basically were dropped from the news cycle. The *Daily Times and Expositor* now only updated the town every two or three weeks in a single sentence about the team's play. From late April to mid–June, Giants results appeared only a couple of times in the paper, even though the standings and box scores were on the front page for the whites-only National League on a nearly daily basis. The *Daily Times and Expositor* also printed the Eastern and Interstate League scores.[4] The *Adrian Evening Telegram* was a bit better with its coverage and was the best paper in town in which to follow the Giants. However, it was also nothing for them to go two weeks without a mention of the Page Fence club. The *Detroit Free* Press, which had ignored the team for its first three years in existence, had changed its stance. The Detroit daily was now easily the best paper to follow the Giants in 1898. The papers in the towns where the Giants made an appearance still appeared excited at the prospects of seeing the ball wizards in action. Their reports were still filled with lively editorial comments and often additional game facts, such as line or box scores. But the time had passed when the Adrian papers would reprint those accounts so the locals, both white and black, could follow their hometown team.

In early June, a game with Chatham, Ontario, would just be another easy win for the Page Fence Giants. The club soundly defeated the minor league Chatham Reds on the Canadians' brand-new Maple City Athletic Association grounds. About 1,000 people saw the Giants' third best pitcher, Sherman Barton, out-duel Rube Waddell in a 9–1 victory. Barton held Chatham to four hits as the Giants scored on a combination of seven hits and seven Reds errors.[5] Waddell was just at the beginning stages of his future Hall of Fame career, and had begun 1898 with the Detroit club in the Western League before bolting to the Canadian club. Waddell eventually ran off a string of 20-win seasons in the majors and was known as one of the true characters of the game. Waddell had made a brief major league appearance in 1897 with Louisville, before they decided he needed more time in the minors.[6] If any scouts had been at this game and seen how the Page Fence Giants treated the prodigy, they would have likely been more impressed with Barton's four-hitter.

The success of the Detroit Athletic Club Deltas both on the field and at the gate pushed them to schedule more games with the Adrian men. Fresh from their shellacking of Waddell's club in Canada, the Giants had two more games on the calendar with the D.A.C. The *Free Press* printed the projected lineups and reminded baseball fans of the fantastic ball skills "and a half-way minstrel show at the same time."[7] The Giants did not let the Deltas gain much confidence in the first game, as they scored 13 runs in the first three innings. Joe Miller gave up seven runs, but it was good enough as the Giants easily won, 21–7. The Giants stole eight bases and hit one double, one triple and four homers. James Patterson slugged a pair of home runs, while Taylor and Grant hit one apiece. The new starter for the D.A.C. was named Barry. He was touched for 17 hits and gave way to one of the Guthard brothers, who weren't terribly effective either. However, all the Giants' fire power at the plate was not the main reason cited for the Deltas' loss. Poor fielding by the left side of the infield was apparently the biggest factor, as Bell was a sieve at shortstop and Miller at third base "did not wake up until the game was hopelessly lost."[8]

"The Page Fence Giants had another batting carnival at the D.A.C. grounds," said the story about the Saturday afternoon rematch. The Giants won, 15–8, but Barton gave up six runs in the first two innings, half of them on a pair of home runs by Henry Dingwell. The D.A.C. substituted Twomey as their catcher, and he shut down the Giants' running game from the day before, limiting the Adrian team to a single stolen base. The *Free Press* said that when the margin stood at 11–8 in favor of the Giants in the sixth inning, "someone whispered that the score was close and with two out, Barton and Johnson, the younger, each cracked out a home run to swell the total." A large crowd of about 1,200 attended the game on the D.A.C. grounds.[9]

In a strange twist, the Giants loaned one of their players to pitch against them in their next game with the Battle Creek club. The Independents, who had hired several of the Giants at the end of last season for their battle with Homer, had George Wilson on the mound. The Palmyra Wonder lost to his Giants, 11–2, due, in part, to Joe Miller having better fielding behind him than Wilson.[10]

The Giants had two games scheduled later in the week in Huntingdon, Indiana. The *Daily News-Democrat* of Huntingdon said the Giants arrived "in a private car, play ball like fury, and advertise the Page Fence." However, Huntingdon baseball organizers eventually pulled the plug due to poor advanced ticket sales. The report was that a projected single-game profit of between $8 and $25 was not enough to cover the Page Fence Giants' appearance fee (between $35 and $50), along with the visitors' expenses.[11]

The Giants swept a pair of games in Logansport, Indiana, and followed with a trip to Danville, Illinois. None of those game scores made their way back to Adrian. The Giants cancelled another game that week scheduled in Mattoon, Illinois.[12] Instead, the Giants pointed their train car toward Clinton, Illinois, for a game that would draw spectators from much larger Decatur and surrounding towns.[13] That game score also did not reach Michigan. Neither paper bothered to call the Page Fence factory for the results, which James Patterson had pledged to send back to his co-workers after each game.

The Giants were practically without Adrian newspaper coverage after the first week of June. Even stories highlighting the upcoming Independence Day celebration no longer pushed an appearance by the celebrity black ball team. In previous years, the Giants did their best to play in front of their hometown. By 1898, war fever combined with few baseball stories placed the team away from the eyes of Adrian's readers. Daily updates of the Spanish-American War were commonplace. But locally, the 31st was still sitting safely out of harm's way at the campground near Chattanooga.

Few mentions of the town's black population were found in either of the daily papers. However, both did mention that the Adrian High School 1898 graduating class did contain one young lady of color. The *Evening Telegram* in mid–June also noted two special prayer services at the black 2nd Baptist Church in town that featured the Rev. S. Henri Browne. However, without the Giants' news updates, it appeared that much less black community news was making its way into print.[14]

Adrian's baseball fever was on its last legs in 1898. Len Hoch was travelling between Coldwater and Adrian and apparently no longer involved with the club. The Giants' advance agent, James Stevens, was retained for the 1898 season, but even his travel itinerary updates were no longer found in the papers. The affable Gus Parsons rarely was quoted anymore about the poor umpiring, the good or bad gate receipts, or praising the Page Fence gentlemen. The Taylor Brothers still owned and operated their successful South Main Street hardware business, but their names were no longer publicly mentioned in connection with the Giants. Quite simply, the initial euphoria of the Page Fence Giants was fading away in the Lenawee County community.

In some of the previous years, in order treat the local cranks' baseball fever, efforts had been made to reserve the Giants or a high-quality minor league team to play on the Fourth of July. In 1898, the town settled for the Adrian-Toledo YMCA single-game challenge. It must have been a low-key affair with very little fanfare. The two main daily newspapers disagreed on the game score and even who had won the contest.[15]

The Page Fence Company kept its name in the news in the summer of 1898, as it capitalized on the current war. In yet another of the company's clever marketing moves, the firm printed maps of Cuba and handed them out around town, with the island being surrounded by, not surprisingly, a Page Woven Wire Fence.[16] The two key founders of the company, J. Wallace Page and Charles Lamb, continued to improve their product and the firm's efficiency. In June, the pair was awarded a patent for a device which controlled the speed of the wire being fed into the fence-weaving machine.[17] The company also decided to create a second "Page Park" in Adrian at a place commonly referred to as the college grove. The park would be stocked with wild and exotic animals (deer, elk, bear, and moose), all protected from the public, or vice versa, by a sturdy, woven wire Page Fence. As a benefit to the locals, admission to the park would be free of charge.[18]

On the baseball end of the company's marketing genius, those hoping for a Page Fence Giants visit in 1898 finally got their wish. The Knights of the Maccabees, a fraternal life, health, and burial insurance society, booked the Giants for a pair of games in mid–August as part of their schedule of family-oriented activities. The fraternal club had recently selected Adrian for their annual summer family encampment.[19] The organization was a "whites only" group, who needed a social safety net during the country's Gilded Age. Families resided in tents during the encampment and while in Adrian would be located at what was left of Lawrence Park.[20] With Lawrence Park's baseball field now being used for the encampment and the Detroit and Lima Northern railroad, a new baseball diamond would be carved out of the county fairgrounds. James K. Wolverton would again use his skills to measure and create an infield at the new location.[21] In addition to the ball games, the Toledo Marine Band was hired to perform a concert in front of Lawrence Park's old baseball grandstands.[22]

The irony of having a black ball team entertaining the fraternal organization's families, a group that the Giants' players and families were ineligible to join, was probably lost on many of the Maccabee encampment attendees. The tentative plan was for the minor Interstate League Toledo Mud Hens to play one game on Wednesday, August 17, and the Giants' rivals, the Chicago Unions, to play the following day.[23] Both teams promised to give the Page Fence club a competitive game. Fueling the excitement was a subsequent rumor that famed coacher Billy Holland would soon rejoin the team.[24] The original two games had now expanded to three contests—a doubleheader against Toledo on Thursday and a Friday morning contest with the Interstate League's New Castle, Pennsylvania, Quakers. The Chicago Unions were no longer mentioned as an opponent.[25]

Work was also done on creating a new ball diamond at the Lenawee County Fairgrounds, on the east end of Adrian, just north of the Page Fence manufacturing plant. In 1895, Wolverton was the same man who was given the chore of upgrading the Lawrence Park diamond for the Giants and the Demons. Over the past few years, he was also hired to groom the Adrian College baseball infield and the YMCA ball grounds. One paper bragged about Wolverton's skill and noted, "it is unnecessary to say that it will be well done."[26]

One would think with the star-studded squad finally making a rare home appearance, newspaper stories would appear in town. That was not the case. Both dailies had ignored the Giants for the entire month of July, other than their mention at the upcoming Maccabees encampment. The famed travelling ball team was quickly becoming a footnote of the town. It wasn't as if the Giants were idle. Following two years of negotiations, they finally made an appearance in Utica, Michigan, in early July and won, 7–2.[27] The following day, July 3, the Giants defeated Bay City's entry in the International League, 11–5. Wilson won for the Giants, even though he gave up 11 hits to the Sugar City club in front of a large Sunday afternoon crowd of 1,200 spectators.[28] There was no word in Adrian as to where, or if, the Giants were to be a featured attraction somewhere for Independence Day.

By the middle of July, the Giants were in Wisconsin. Their games with the Oshkosh Indians were set for the weekend of July 16–17. The Giants would be a part of a string of high-profile and competitive games in this baseball-crazed town. In addition to the Page Fence club, the Chicago Unions and the minor league Detroit Tigers were slated to appear during the latter part of the month. Oshkosh baseball boosters claimed they had "now prepared a menu fit for the most exacting fan and worthy of large attendance."[29]

The Giants rolled into Oshkosh aboard their splendid train car on Thursday evening, July 14, and plans were for some rest and practice on Friday, before the big weekend series.

The rest plan quickly went away as the Indians and Giants sat down and talked baseball that night. Taking center stage for the Giants was slugging infielder James Patterson, while a catcher named Dixon was the Indians' baseball expert. Much of the evening's talk was about the black team, Bud Fowler, and the early originators of baseball. A newspaper reporter present at the gathering wrote of how Fowler organized the Giants in 1895 and "practically the same men" had played all four years, even though Fowler left the team. The Giants' Patterson told of how Fowler "had this team in his noodle for six years before anyone knew it. He is a great schemer ... and if he were here now he would have some scheme for us." Fowler was still playing ball at the age of 55, back in Ohio, and doing some pitching too, even though he had "lost his arm" five different times! Patterson claimed that old Bud Fowler was playing baseball "while Anson was still peeking through the cracks in the fence." Fowler's love of baseball apparently took precedence over making money, as Patterson lamented that the old timer "had all kinds of chance to make money and still he hasn't a cent."[30]

Oshkosh's Dixon claimed that in addition to Fowler, the original baseball men were Anson, Morrissey, Fowler and Harry Wright. Dixon said Wright was dead and Anson was now out of the game, leaving Morrissey and Fowler as active participants.[31]

The Giants enjoyed the stories of old first baseman George Taylor, who seconded the evening's account about Fowler's age. "Can he go back? Well, I guess. He can go back farther than I ever read." The reporter ended his column with the fact that the black ball players adored Fowler. He "is the colored player's champion and they swear by him."[32]

The night's baseball talk wasn't the only excitement of the evening for the visiting Giants. Sometime after the gathering, Gus Parsons released George Taylor from the team. Whether it was for Taylor's public praise of Fowler's Page Fence team idea, or just offering his strong opinion, one of the original Giants was gone. The official word was that Taylor was sent packing for "insubordination." It was announced that the Giants were now looking to add at least two new men to join the star-laden club.[33]

The Taylor release placed backup catcher Pete Burns at first base, with Grant, Johnson and Binga rounding out the infield. Young "Chappie" Johnson was behind the plate. The outfield now had to use two starting pitches for its three spots, Wilson and Miller, while Patterson stayed in left. Sherman Barton was on the mound for game one, and this left the Giants without any extra players.[34]

The sudden jolt of losing Taylor carried over to the ball field, as Barton gave up ten runs to the Indians in the first two innings. The home team's onslaught began "the moment the umpire wigwagged the signal to play ball" and didn't stop until Joe Miller relieved Barton in the third inning. Miller set down the next 12 batters in order, but it was too late and the Giants lost, 10–7. Former Giant Ed Wood, the Wisconsin native, earned the victory for the Indians.[35]

The following day at Combination Park was a completely different story. George Wilson sent a strong message and threw an 18–0 shutout. Even though the Oshkosh paper and community were supportive of the black team, their reporting centered on the hometown Indians. A pitcher named Check started the game and was "hit hard," allowing the longest homer ever at the field. James Patterson hammered the monster shot and was described by the *Daily Northwestern* as the "tall Etheopian." The Giants knocked Check out of the box after five innings, and he was replaced by the tired Woods. The Indians' black player had started the game at third base and after some "lumpy work" there was moved to left field, where he promptly dropped the only ball hit to him. With that as the background, the Indians' management thought it was a good idea to pitch Wood for a second day in a row, but he was ineffective. Wood also struggled at the plate, and looked and played tired. The grandstand apparently ignored his outstanding work and victory the day before and "began to have its suspicions" of Wood being on the take in game two against his former teammates. The Indians' only highlights were when they pulled off both a double play and a triple play which kept the laughable score from becoming even worse.[36]

Wood's effort in the opener should have put to an end any nefarious speculation at Sunday's game. The fact that Sunday's rematch was played in a scorching temperature, estimated between 95 and 110 degrees, obviously had to impact the man who hurled a complete game the day before.[37]

The Giants left Oshkosh and headed north to Green Bay, where they had split a pair of games last summer. The afternoon midweek contests would take place at Washington Park on July 20 and 21. The Page Fence men arrived over the Chicago and Northwestern railroad on Tuesday evening and checked into the Central Hotel for their stay in Green Bay. Prior to the first game, both teams arrived in the morning at Washington Park and held practice sessions. The *Green Bay Press Gazette* heaped praise on the visitors, calling them "almost perfect players and their errors are few." However, the paper wrongly identified the team as hailing from Chicago and not Adrian, Michigan.[38]

The newspaper coverage in the *Press Gazette* was decidedly biased for the home team, which was easily defeated, 9–2. The paper noted that an unidentified Giants pitcher was "hit freely," but Green Bay was "unlucky" due to the placement of the "perfect fielding" visitors. The paper claimed that the locals put up a "strong game" and that the teams were basically about even. The batting highlight came when another unnamed Giant hit an inside-the-park homer when the ball could not be located among the weeds against the outfield fence. The *Press Gazette* stated that the second game of the series would feature a new Giants pitcher, as the roster was down to just nine men and only two pitchers, with the release of Taylor in Oshkosh. However, with Wilson, Miller and Barton, the Page Fence club really had three pitchers, and not two, in their rotation.[39]

The next day, the *Green Bay Press Gazette* claimed that the Giants' new player was named Miller, and he earned a 12–0 victory over the local team. The news story claimed that Green Bay was "mystified by Miller's curves." The game was close until the Wisconsin club's starting pitcher, Schroeder, was knocked out of the box after five innings. Again, few details of the Giants' play were detailed. The paper did inform its readers that the Page Fence crew left Friday morning for a game that afternoon in Marinette and then had a Sunday contest in Sturgeon Bay.[40]

The Oshkosh Indians had just been outscored, 27–2, but they were busy trying to arrange a series of games with the Giants. The idea was for the two teams to stage a week of games from August 8–14 with stops in small cities across Wisconsin. The Oshkosh paper hoped stops could be arranged in Menasha, Waupaca, Omro, Berlin, and Appleton before a big finale back in Oshkosh. Oshkosh dreamed of strong gate receipts. The *Daily Northwestern* believed the games "ought to be a paying venture."[41]

Apparently, the Page Fence Giants' management was not clued in on the Oshkosh plan. Once again, rumors as to games placed the Giants in two places at one. When Oshkosh wanted the Giants in Wisconsin, the club was busy defeating the Chicago Marquettes in Illinois, 3–0. On a day the Oshkosh boosters hoped to face the Page Fence Giants, the Adrian club was actually busy defeating the Niles ballists, 9–1, in front of a large southwestern Michigan crowd.[42] The week-long series with Oshkosh never materialized.

With the hometown Giants about to appear in Adrian, the baseball coverage began to increase in the dailies. The ever-popular Honus Wagner, he of all of three weeks with the 1895 Demons, was now standing 27th in batting with Louisville of the National League as July ended.[43] Another former Demon, Bill Carrick, had made it to the big leagues at the end of July and was pitching for the New York Giants. One Adrian paper reminded its readers that Carrick had married local gal Winnie Carpenter when they had presumably met during his playing stint in town.[44] One paper also noted that Billy Smith, one of the two Smith boys to play for the Demons, was now with the Toledo team and would man center field against the Giants.[45]

Regardless of the amount of newsprint given to the black team, the excitement was growing for their first appearance of 1898. About a week before the games, work was conducted on the fairgrounds to get the athletic park in shape. The Page Fence Factory news column in the *Adrian Daily Telegram* (renamed from the *Evening Telegram* on August 8, 1898) simply stated, "The majority, if not all of our boys will take in the Giants ball game here next week."[46]

When the fancy train car arrived in Adrian from Coldwater at 10:10 p.m. Tuesday, August 16, on the Lake Shore track, the *Daily Telegram* noted that relatively mundane fact.[47] It didn't report the team had just defeated a tough Coldwater squad, 3–1, in front of 1,500 people or that Barton had pitched in "the most interesting game of baseball every played here."[48] However, the *Daily Telegram* followed up its Giants railroad itinerary story and declared "all are well and report a good season."[49] There was no word about the background of the alleged new pitcher by the name of Miller, or the reason for Taylor's release, or what had happened to the lucrative plan to play Oshkosh in a series of games the previous week.

All three Maccabees-sponsored games at the newly created fairgrounds ball diamond would begin at 10 o'clock in the morning. The opening game against Toledo was quite simply dubbed "the finest exhibition of base ball ever seen on Adrian grounds," as the Giants won a close, 2–1 affair. Wilson pitched for the Giants and likely pleased the large Lenawee County crowd. The Palmyra native struck out four Mud Hens and surrendered only a home run to Erve Beck, who would make his major league debut the following season.[50] Beck and Wilson had been teammates on the Demons, as the Toledo native had first began his professional career at the age of 16.[51] Edward Madden, the pitcher for the Mud Hens, was nearly as effective as Wilson, allowing two runs, but one was unearned.[52] The *Daily Telegram* said George Johnson was the "feature of the game" at first base and "made the fans forget there was ever such a man as Taylor."[53] The Giants managed to sign a new player, who was only listed as Smith. He manned center field against Toledo and was said to be a fast base runner and a "cracker jack fielder," too.[54]

While the opening game was exciting, the Maccabees' attendance was not up to what was projected. Michigan Governor Hazen Pingree was a no-show for the parade, which was called a "great event" and witnessed by thousands, even though only about half the participants lined up to march.[55]

Toledo earned its sweet revenge on day two. About 800 paying customers made their way to the new fairgrounds diamond to see the Mud Hens' hitting hero from the day before, Erve Beck, pitch for his club. Beck was normally the starting second baseman, as the Giants didn't face any of the Mud Hens' top three hurlers, including ace Charlie Ferguson, a former Lansing Senator. Beck teamed with the regular starting catcher, Ed Arthur, to down the Giants, 7–6. The Mud Hens defeated the battery of Miller and Burns and led from the start. With the small roster, Wilson was again forced to play the field, made the best of it and slugged a two-run double.[56] Old time ballplayer Christy Reynolds was behind the plate to umpire both games, and no one reported any kicking over his calls.[57] Following the game, the Toledo club hopped on the fast mail train back to Ohio, while the Page Fence men also headed out of town. The third contest against a second Interstate League foe, New Castle, Pennsylvania, which had originally replaced the Chicago Unions, did not take place. The report was that neither the Giants' and Quakers' management could agree on terms of the game.[58]

As the Page Fence Giants left their home base, an odd tidbit appeared in the *Daily Telegram*. Apparently, the lack of local newspaper stories had fueled a rumor that the Giants were not as good as they had been in previous years. With the team not appearing in Adrian until the Maccabees' encampment series, residents were apparently skeptical of the black men's winning record, even though it closely mirrored what had occurred in 1895, 1896 and 1897. However, the *Daily Telegram* responded, following the pair of contests with Toledo, that J. W. Patterson was doing a great job as the team captain and that "the Giants can play good ball is not doubted much as it once was."[59] With that, the Giants pulled out of Adrian, and that was about all that was heard about them for the remainder of the 1898 season.

◆ 24 ◆

Steel Away

The day after the second encampment game, a major economic event was unveiled which greatly impacted the Page Fence Company. At a meeting in New York City, a new, super company was proposed and dubbed the iron and steel trust. Its goal was to acquire as much as possible all the raw materials needed to make iron and steel and to own those foundries and mills throughout the United States. In addition, the trust company would operate many of the rail lines and river barges used to transport both the raw materials and then, later, the finished product. A net worth of around $200,000,000 would make it larger and more powerful than the famed John D. Rockefeller Standard Oil Trust.[1] Rumors circulated as to whether steel magnate Andrew Carnegie and fellow tycoon Rockefeller would be invited to join the trust or be left out of the mega-merger. If approved, this new trust would control much of what was needed to produce iron and steel from Pennsylvania to Minnesota, and included metal fencing in Adrian, Michigan.

What was not known at the time was whether the trust's control would be nearly 100 percent, which it would if they could convince Andrew Carnegie's steel plants to join the business venture. It would place the firms needing iron and steel, such as the Page Woven Wire Fence Company, at the mercy of the trust, at the worst, or choosing between the new group and Carnegie's company, at the best. Costs for raw materials and the shipping of the finished woven wire fence would be largely out of the control of J. Wallace Page.

A few weeks later, in early September, the trust management signed the incorporation papers and officially created this massive business. On paper, the new company was designed to merge Illinois Steel with the Minnesota Iron Company, but that was just a formality.[2] About a month later, at a meeting in Cleveland, frantic railway owners within the Central Traffic Association, who were not swooped up in the iron and steel trust, voiced concerns over the subsequent shipping rate cuts. The new trust was undercutting the Association's rates and offering cheaper freight deals, a tactic called a "weapon in the hands of the trust." Once the new trust ran everyone out of business, they could then boost their freight rates to whatever level they pleased. The Association was so concerned after just six weeks of the iron and steel trust's existence that they even invited western railroad officials, who were not members of their group, to join their secret Cleveland meeting.[3]

Back in Adrian, the Page Fence Company became very concerned over the iron and steel trust and just how it would impact their manufacturing business. How much money could be spent on a travelling all-star baseball team, when the firm's very livelihood was at stake, was a question that needed to be answered. However, things were not all bleak at the Adrian fence company. Their newsletter, the *Coiled Spring Hustler*, which had promoted the Giants back in 1895, underwent a name change. The new title was the *Page Fence Age*, and it would still be sent to their numerous agents around the country to help spread the word about the fine products. There was apparently extra money for the arts, too. Adrian College music professor T. F. Rinehart helped to create the "Page Fence March." The waltz was written by Rinehart, while the words were added by local physician and baseball fan Dr. J. H. Reynolds. The song was printed on a one-page circular and added to the Adrian fence company's unique marketing lore.[4]

The railroad line which had forced the closure of the Lawrence Park ball diamond continued to be a boondoggle. First, the rail line was named the Lima Northern. A few months after arriving in Adrian, it was absorbed and the name was changed to the Detroit and Lima Northern. The elegant $5,000 stone depot, to be modeled after the one in nearby Hudson, was no longer on the drawing board. The adjusted cost for a sparkling new passenger depot was dramatically reduced to $1,800 dollars.[5] With such a massive budget, cut there was no way the building could resemble the elegant Hudson train station.

Even with these revised station plans, the D & LN's only work on the new depot had been to pound down surveyor's stakes.[6] The railroad company had delayed building a permanent depot throughout the summer of 1897. In October, Lawrence filed a lawsuit against the railroad company because they had yet to pay him. "I simply told them that if they didn't pay me for the land I'd commence suit against them. They said they wouldn't pay for it because they understood it was mortgaged. I told them I would give them one hundred dollars for every dollar of mortgage they could find on the property." Instead, they had leased the Merrick Building on the north side of West Maumee Street as a temporary train station and then constructed a wooden passenger's platform for use when boarding the train.[7]

While Willis T. Lawrence may have been ecstatic in 1897 about his dream coming true of a rail line through his property, it put an end to the Giants having a permanent home field. The new rail line spent the early months of 1898 handling legal messes. First, injunctions were requested over their use of rail lines into Detroit, and then the Lake Shore and Michigan Southern filed a complaint over the D & LN's lack of payment for the rental of switching tracks in Adrian.[8] The railroad news continued to get worse. By the first week of September, the Detroit and Lima Northern was placed into receivership.[9]

A few days earlier and before the railroad went belly-up, one of the town's biggest ball cranks moved out of Adrian. Len Hoch had sold his home on the corner of Toledo and Clinton Streets to W. H. Barrett and finally relocated his family to Coldwater.[10] With the sale, Hoch would no longer have to worry about his wife and children back in Adrian and could now focus his full-time efforts on building the Coldwater Portland Cement Company. This move likely ultimately severed whatever, if any, financial ties Hoch had with the Giants.

The 31st Michigan Regiment, which had dominated the newspaper coverage during those crucial early spring months and pushed the Giants aside, failed to earn their war fame. By the end of August, the Spanish-American War was over, and the United States claimed victory, advancing another step toward their expanded imperialist role in world affairs. The 31st remained based in Georgia. They had deridingly dubbed themselves the Chickamauga "Park Police" in honor of their three months' stay at the famed Civil War battlefield.[11]

Another entity robbing the Giants' fame in 1898 was an old nemesis, the Chicago Unions. The club had decided to promote yet another "colored baseball championship" series, but not against the Giants. They could have played the Giants, who were in Chicago the day of their latest stunt. The Chicago Unions invited the Cuban Giants from New York for a Sunday doubleheader in mid–September. The morning game was a 12-inning 3–3 tie, while the Cuban Giants won the nightcap, 6–2. At least three former Page Fence Giants played in the game, Billy Holland and George Hopkins for the Unions and John Nelson for the New York squad. Appearing in the same edition and on the same page of the *Chicago Daily Tribune* as the Unions/Cuban Giants' championship results, was a story about the Page Fence men dropping a contest to a team called the Auburns, 2–1. Wilson was out-dueled by a man named Brown, as both teams combined for just 11 hits. The Giants turned three double plays, but it wasn't enough to seal the victory. The Chicago paper noted that the two teams had played three weeks ago, and this Sunday victory was sweet revenge for the Auburn club.[12]

The whereabouts of the Page Fence Giants over the remaining weeks of the season were hard to follow. In late September, the Giants were in Jackson to play a game "and quite a number went over from here [Adrian]."[13] However, the *Daily Telegram* didn't print a game story the following day. The team went to Marlette, Michigan, for a street fair appearance. The Giants whipped the local boys, 8–3, but the crowd was held down due to a rain shower.[14] A few days later, the Giants defeated the Owosso Masqueraders, 15–3, in Bancroft, as part of the county fair, which also featured running, biking and chariot racing.[15]

The first weekend of October, the black gentlemen were booked for Chicago. However, a game at Daly Park against the Mandel Brothers was postponed when the Giants, for an undisclosed reason, could not make it into town in time.[16]

Neither Adrian daily paper had reported any Giants games scores since they had left the Maccabees' encampment in mid–August. The final 1898 season story about the Giants came in the Saturday, October 22, edition of the *Adrian Daily Telegram*. The blurb wasn't a story, but rather a comment in their special column reserved for factory news. The Page Fence Company noted "Captain J. W. Patterson, of the Giants, is back on the force again, the ball season being closed." The 1898 season would end without the usual financial report from Gus Parsons. No quotes from Parsons about problems with umpires or use of his creatively adjusted win-loss record. No complaints about the weather robbing the Giants of many potentially lucrative dates. There was no wrap-up of where the players were going to live in the off-season. There was nothing about local Palmyra legend, George Wilson, either. The Page Fence Giants articles simply stopped appearing in the papers.

With the baseball season now completed, the off-season maneuvering could begin. Page Fence Giants founder Bud Fowler was back in the news, vowing to return to Findlay, Ohio, to form a professional team in 1899. One man he claimed to have on his roster to play shortstop was his old partner with the Giants, Grant "Home Run" Johnson.[17] However, that Fowler claim was put to rest by the end of 1898 when a man named Myers was signed to play shortstop, and Johnson was no longer associated with stories about the new Findlay club.[18]

Fowler also boasted that he was organizing a second new team, the Black Tourists, who would travel in their own specially fitted train car. The club would take a six-week tour across the country and end up in California in the fall of 1899. Fowler announced, "This great aggregation of colored players will be composed of the best in the country."[19] However, his Black Tourists apparently didn't have any players under contract. Early in 1899, Fowler requested that he would like to hear "at once" from Fred Grant, Bill Seldon, Sol White, Clarence Williams, Robinson and Jackson of the Cuban X Giants, Wilson of the

Page Fence Giants, Billy Holland, Robert Footes and Harry Buckner of the Chicago Unions. His plea also omitted any mention of "Home Run" Johnson.[20]

The Page Fence Giants were also busy in the off-season. They signed John Brown, who had played center field for the 1898 Racine, Wisconsin, team.[21] Game dates in mid–March against Connie Mack's Milwaukee Brewers of the Western League and Cedar Rapids, Iowa, of the Class B Western Association were already being publicized prior to the ball season.[22] However, those games with the Page Fence Giants would never take place.

Behind the scenes, the Giants were undergoing an upheaval. The Page Fence Company was no longer going to have its name associated with the black baseball team. As a result, the future of the Giants was in doubt. Local lore was that the new iron and steel trust was devastating the operations at the Page Woven Wire Fence Company. The word was that the manufacturing company was struggling to obtain the raw materials for making their fences, all courtesy of the new trust. No metal wire meant no fence and no profits. The Page Fence Company was forced to reduce their operation and didn't return to full production until early March of 1899.[23] J. Wallace Page wanted no part of paying the new price scale offered by the trust and devised a plan to beat the monopoly. So with a potential financial crisis looming, operating a travelling all-star black baseball team became a luxury they could no longer afford. Why send a team across the country to advertise their numerous wire fence designs when you might be unable to make the product?

In the fall and winter months, plans were devised to have the Page Fence Company build and operate its own steel plant. The new facility would not be constructed in Adrian, but rather in the heart of steel country—Pennsylvania. The Monessen steel mill was on a fast track for completion, as the plan was for it to be operational by July 1, 1899, in the Monongahela River town about 30 miles south of Pittsburgh.[24] As this business plan was leaked back to Michigan from Pennsylvania newspapers who rejoiced over the building of a new steel mill, panic quickly set in for Adrian residents.

In mid–February, the *Daily Republican* of Monongahela, Pennsylvania, announced in the Monessen News column that the Page Fence Company had already let construction bids and simply awaited warmer weather before beginning its project. The paper gleefully added to its claim that the Adrian fence manufacturer was going to move its entire operation to Monessen.[25] Business expansion was nothing new for J. Wallace Page. The previous February, the firm had purchased the Michigan Wire and Iron Works in Detroit and moved their equipment to Adrian, which added decorative wrought iron fencing to their product line.[26] That move would have been hailed by Adrian, but this latest rumor removed jobs from the town's largest employer.

A few weeks later in early March, a reporter for the *Adrian Daily Telegram* confronted Page about his new business model. Page was unhappy with the news leak and confirmed that "a wire mill is being contemplated" in Pennsylvania.[27] A reprint in the *Daily Telegram* from the *Belle Vernon* (Pennsylvania) *Enterprise* let readers know what was possibly in store for the Lenawee County community. The Pennsylvania paper contended that the Page Fence Company within the next few months would "move bodily" their firm to Monessen. The Adrian firm had already placed a purchase bid on 18 acres of property and buildings at a former industrial plant, and the Pittsburgh & Lake Erie Railroad had laid tracks to the proposed mill. The overall goal was for this new plant to produce the wire, so Page did not have to deal with the iron and steel trust. There were already two existing steel mills in Monessen, employing about 700 men, and Wallace's venture was adding another 600 jobs, including those relocating from Adrian.[28]

Page tried to downplay the impact on Adrian and was visibly upset that his new business venture had leaked back home. Blaming those in the know, Page declared, "they have told far too much." The statement did nothing to reduce Adrian residents' fears of a massive job loss in town. Page repeated his answer that a wire mill was only being "contemplated" for the Pennsylvania site. He added, "the probabilities are that when that is done, we shall do some weaving there," but clarified that the Monessen mill would remain as a branch of the Adrian Page Woven Wire Fence Company.[29]

While this business drama was playing out, the baseball club was no longer part of the marketing plans of the Page Fence Company. In February 1899, *The Sporting News*, in their large miscellaneous baseball column entitled "Caught on the Fly" revealed the move. "The X Page Fence Giants have been organized by Manager J. W. Patterson, 18 Ormsby Street, Adrian, Michigan, who claim that they are the strongest colored team that ever happened. He is booking dates." Adding to the irony, five paragraphs below, was Bud Fowler's scheme for the new Black Tourists baseball team.[30]

The day before Wallace was forced to confront the rumors of the pending move to Pennsylvania, the *Daily Telegram* reprinted an article from the *Toledo Bee* about Gus Parsons. The paper revealed that Parsons would no longer be associated with the Page Fence Giants and that he, along with William "Rasty" Wright and George "Deacon" Ellis, had purchased the Paterson, New Jersey, minor league baseball franchise.[31] Parsons, as he was with the Page Fence Giants, would be in charge of the team's business operation.[32] The Paterson Weavers had been a Class B team in 1898 but would be raised to a Class A classification in 1899 and have their named changed to the Giants.[33] Incidentally, Paterson was not a new stop for Parsons, as it was the same town where he secured the Page Fence Giants Monarch train car in 1895.

Once it was discovered that Parsons was no longer with the club, the team's demise appeared evident. A Green Bay paper in early March 1899 repeated *The Sporting News* note that the club would be called the X Page Fence Giants, but mentioned that a few of the rival Chicago Unions would be added to the roster.[34] When the 1899 season began, the X Page Fence Giants had been dropped and the team was on to its third name in a matter of a few months—the Columbia Giants. However, the team's original name was still often used throughout that season, as the white-owned and operated newspapers were slow to change. Indiana newspapers promoted upcoming springtime games with the Page Fence Giants in mid–March.[35] One *Sporting Life* story from early March featured a request by the Baltimore Giants, the self-proclaimed black baseball champions of the South, who challenged the Page Fence Giants to play them in Chicago.[36]

Unlike the lengthy, multi-paragraph 1894 story which greeted the Bud Fowler creation, and the numerous articles throughout 1895, the end of the Page Fence Giants was covered with much less fanfare. The *Daily Times and Expositor* announced in a brief sentence on March 15 that John Patterson would be the manager of "the Columbia Giants, formerly the Page Fence Giants," and their new headquarters would be in Chicago.[37] A few days later, the *Daily Telegram* repeated Patterson's baseball appointment under its factory news column. The story was quite complimentary of Patterson, who during the winter months had resumed his job at the Page Fence factory. Patterson was referred to as the team captain and had recently been given a leave of absence to train for the upcoming ball season. "J.W. is a first-class man to work, and a fine ballplayer and has a host of friends here who wish him the best of luck in the new venture." The *Daily Telegram* added that "most" of the Page Fence Giants had signed with the Columbia club.[38] Another former Giant, catcher Vasco

Graham, had also spent the winter working at the Page Fence plant. Graham resigned his factory position in early April to play baseball, but apparently not with the Columbia club.[39]

As if the month of March couldn't get worse for Adrian residents, it did. With the potential loss of its largest employer moving to Pennsylvania still vibrating through the town, Adrian's second-largest was now in the rumor mill. The Lake Shore and Michigan Southern Railroad, formerly Adrian's top employer, only to be unseated a few years early by J. Wallace Page's firm, was the target of a massive job transfer. "There has been rumors and rumors for a long time about the Lake Shore railroad shops going out of town," which eventually came true the last weekend of March. The head of Adrian's railroad manufacturing car department was notified to begin plans to move his entire operation to Buffalo, New York. The shop foreman was told it would take place "within a short time," and the Adrian workers, to keep their jobs, were being asked if they wanted to move to Buffalo. The rumor was that with the exception of a single car repair shop, all operations would move to New York. One Adrian paper headlined the bombshell as "The beginning of the end."[40]

To add to the town's misery, the Detroit and Lima Railroad was back in court. A Toledo courtroom saw a $713,000 lawsuit filed by the construction firm which built the railroad, as a way to recoup some cash for unpaid bills.[41]

The former Page Fence Giants were no longer staging operations in Adrian for an upcoming season. Captain James Patterson met his Columbia Giants in Chicago for practice and then scheduled their season opener in Bloomington, Illinois, on Thursday, April 6.[42] But, as was the case with the old Giants, this schedule was changed and the club opened the season in Wisconsin, not in central Illinois. A familiar early stop for the Columbia Giants would be in baseball-crazy Fort Wayne in late April. The northern Indiana town was excited to play this new organization, which they dubbed "the crack colored team."[43]

With the Page Fence Giants no longer having any business connection with Adrian, news coverage of the black gentlemen all but ended. There was no season preview of the new club. *The Sporting News* in mid–April said that the Columbia Giants would train in Chicago for a week, open their season in Milwaukee and play minor league teams from the Western Association, Interstate and Canadian Leagues. The same article listed the Columbia team roster as George Wilson, Grant Johnson, Charles Grant, Joe Miller, William Binga, George Johnson, Pete Burns, J. W. Patterson, Sherman Barton, Harry Buckner, Lewis Reynolds and a man named Jones.[44] A game lineup printed in May by the *Detroit Free Press* was sprinkled with many names familiar to Adrian ball cranks. Burns was behind the plate, George Johnson was slated for first base, with Grant at second, Binga at third and "Home Run" Johnson at shortstop. The outfield was Patterson in left, Reynolds in center and Barton in right. Either Harry Buckner or Jones would start on the mound and face the Detroit Athletic Club team and Harwood Bacon, the "clever southpaw twirler."[45]

The group of young men whose focus had supplanted the Giants in Adrian, the 31st Regiment, was back in the news. While the Spanish-American War ended last August, the 31st Regiment had remained in service. The men finally received their wish when they were shipped out of the states and made two stops, tours of duty in Cuba, but well after the fighting had ceased. Following their soldering duties, they were sent home in mid–April 1899, much to the delight of the state's populace. Ten thousand Adrian residents greeted the boys and lined the streets as the soldiers marched from a train depot to the downtown armory building.[46] When word was received that the boys would be home soon, plans were for made to organize a "good speedy amateur base ball" team. A few of the future key players would be returning with the 31st, fueling the baseball cranks' excitement. James Jay would act as right fielder and manager, and William Groeschow would play shortstop and be the team captain. They would be named the Imperials, and Adrian residents were asked to donate money for uniforms and to buy game tickets.[47]

Lobbying efforts to keep the Lake Shore's enormous presence in Adrian continued in the spring of 1899. A small group of influential Adrian citizens, including J. Wallace Page, managed to secure a 20-minute meeting in Cleveland with the Lake Shore's President, W. H. Newman, and General Supervisor, P. S. Blodgett. The short gathering offered up very little in details, but there was some hope. The railroad revealed that the company was still considering all their options and nothing final had been decided for Adrian. In a public relations move, the lobbyists added that the railroad officials had treated the local contingent "very courteously."[48]

The very day of the Lake Shore meeting, a Pittsburgh paper noted that work was moving forward on the Monessen plant. Additional railroad tracks were being laid, and excavation work for a building foundation was underway. The Pittsburgh reprint in an Adrian daily noted "the way the work is progressing, although it conveys the impression that the whole Page plant is to be moved away." It acknowledged J. Wallace Page's repeated denial of that plan.[49] However, that Pennsylvania optimism did not manifest itself. Soon construction of the steel mill was delayed and would not resume until early September. The steel trust was blamed for not shipping the needed materials to a competitor. The trust also caused a critical work stoppage in Adrian, where ten looms were shuttered "for the want of wire, and it is the direct effect of the trusts."[50] The new Monessen steel mill was eventually completed, and as the company founder had predicted, it served only as a branch of the firm. The Page Woven Wire Fence continued to operate in Adrian for another two decades.

As the baseball season was in full swing on Monday, May 22, player-manager Bud Fowler and his white teammates on the Findlay baseball club hosted the Columbia Giants. The old Page Fence crew was again advertised as "the strongest colored team in the union," with the "great Grant Johnson, George Wilson, the greatest of south paw twirlers, and others equally famous on the diamond."[51] Fowler and the Findlay boys promptly upset the mighty Columbia Giants, 6–5. Joe Miller took the loss. There was no mention of the Black Tourists, either.[52]

What thoughts must have been going through Fowler's mind as his 1894 brainchild played across the ball diamond? Page Fence Giants co-investor Grant "Home Run" Johnson was trying to defeat him, as were former teammates "The Palmyra Wonder," George Wilson, and temperamental pitcher "Cyclone" Joe Miller. The Page Fence holdovers on the newly formed Columbia nine had joined the team after Fowler left the Giants in the first half of the 1895 season. Fowler and Johnson had altered their grandiose business plan in the summer of 1894, after a receptive audience of Michigan baseball cranks cheered on their Findlay Sluggers. When financing was ultimately secured, Adrian, Michigan, and not Findlay, Ohio, was selected as the home for the Page Fence Giants. Now, here was Fowler back in Findlay five years later and managing yet another professional baseball team.

Later that week, the headline in the *Lima* (Ohio) *News* on May 23, 1899, was "Opening, Of the Base Ball Season With Good Attraction, The Page Fence Giants, Will Meet the Findlays at Faurot Park Friday Afternoon." As was often the case this season, the old name was used to describe the new Columbia Giants. Nevertheless, also like the old Giants, the promoted Friday game was cancelled, when Findlay's Fowler declared "circumstances" caused the Lima appearance to be wiped off the schedule.[53]

Fowler continued as one of baseball's tumbleweeds, rolling across the country and playing the game he loved. Whatever he was thinking on those two days in May, one could guess this wily old black gentleman was using "his noodle" for a "scheme," as to how he could create another "crack colored baseball team" as good as Adrian's Page Fence Giants.[54]

Epilogue

The national recognition of the Page Fence Giants name and their outstanding reputation kept Bud Fowler's idea in front of baseball fans for the next 20 years. In several attempts to form other travelling black all-star teams, Fowler used the Page Fence Giants name to boost his credibility. When William Malone was looking for a baseball job in the May 5, 1900, *Sporting Life,* he listed only two of his many previous clubs, and one of them was the Page Fence Giants.

An article in the *Detroit Free Press* on March 17, 1901, erroneously listed the team's winning percentage from 1895 through the 1900 season as all under the name of the Page Fence Giants. At least nine players on this 1901 version ended the 1898 season on the final Giants team, including Wilson, Patterson, Miller and both Johnsons. Even advance business agent J. W. Stevens was still with the team, now based in Detroit. Their new name would be the Royal Tiger Cigar Giants, with another familiar name acting as manager—second baseman Charlie Grant.

The *Detroit Free Press* article noted the team's win-loss totals from 1895, though, still called the team by their old name, the Page Fence Giants of Adrian, and referred to them as the black champions of the world.

The article listed the yearly Win-Loss Records:

1895	Games Played 152	Won 121	Lost 31
1896	Games Played 168	Won 143	Lost 25
1897	Games Played 139	Won 129	Lost 10
1898	Games Played 117	Won 107	Lost 10
1899	Games Played 178	Won 156	Lost 22
1900	Games Played 183	Won 158	Lost 25

A few years later, another Page Fence Giants team, apparently consisting of local factory workers from the Adrian plant, was sponsored and played area teams. However, make no mistake, these gentlemen were not connected with the original Page Fence club.

As far as into the 1920s, a Page Fence Giants team, consisting of all black players, made the rounds in Michigan. News articles promoting them and connecting this latest version were used to drum up support, harking back to the good old days when the team had visited a town. However, this 1920s team was only using the old name, as J. Wallace Page had died in 1916. The company was sold and became the American Chain and Cable Company in the early 1920s. In today's world, this unauthorized use of a company name would result in a lawsuit.

There was only one, true, original and authentic Page Fence Giants. They were the team from 1895 to 1898, based in Adrian, Michigan. They were also the world champions of black baseball in 1896, and all the men had the medallion to prove it.

PFG Master Roster

1895

George Taylor	1B
John W. Jackson/Bud Fowler	2B*
King Soloman "Sol" White	2B
Grant Johnson	SS
James Lincoln	3B
William H. Malone	3B-P
James W. Patterson	3B
George Hopkins	OF
Gus Brooks	CF
? Howard	RF
? Lyons	LF
John Nelson	RF
Pete Burns	C*
Vasco Graham	C*
William Binga	C*
Joe Miller	P-OF*
Fred Van Dyke	P-OF
George Wilson	P-OF*
Billy Holland	P-OF
James Chavous	P
Frank Waters (Substitute and Adrian teenager)	P
Herbert Lentz (Substitute white player from Adrian Demons)	RF
William Wendell Gaskin (Substitute; PFG team cook)	P
Albert C. Carter (Substitute; PFG team porter/barber)	P
"Whang" Green (Substitute; a youngster who was the PFG mascot; exhibition game vs. the Adrian Demons)	—

*Made at least one appearance during the season for the MSL's Adrian Demons minor league team.

1896

George Taylor	1B
Charles Grant	2B
Grant Johnson	SS
James Patterson	3B
Vasco Graham	C-OF
Pete Burns	C
William Binga	3B-C
Joe Miller	P-OF
Billy Holland	P-LF
George Wilson	P
Fred Van Dyke	P-CF
James Chavous	P-RF
Frank Waters (Substitute and Adrian teenager)	P
William Wendell Gaskin (Substitute; PFG team cook)	P

1897

George Taylor	1B
Charles Grant	2B
Grant Johnson	SS
James W. Patterson	3B-LF
Pete Burns	C-RF
William Binga	C-CF-3B
Billy Holland	P-LF
George Wilson	P
Joe Miller	P-RF
Robert Shaw	P
Ed Wood(s)	P
George Johnson	C-LF
Sherman Barton	OF-P
? Broadest	P
? Jones	—
? Nicolai (Substitute white player from Oshkosh Colts)	RF

Fred Van Dyke and a player named (Bert?) Wakefield were said to have been signed to contracts, but I never found them mentioned in any game accounts during 1897.

George Johnson was also referred to as "Johnson, Junior" in box scores. He would later be known with the nicknames of "Rat" and "Chappie."

1898

George Taylor	1B
Charles Grant	2B
Grant Johnson	SS
William Binga	3B
Pete Burns	C-1B
James W. Patterson	LF
George Johnson	RF-C
Sherman Barton	CF-P
Joe Miller	P-OF
George Wilson	P-OF
? Smith	LF

James Patterson later in life was nicknamed "Pat."

Management Group:

Owners: Len W. Hoch, Rolla Taylor, Howard Taylor, J. Wallace Page, Grant Johnson (1895), Bud Fowler (1895)

Team Business Manager: Augustus "Gus" Parsons

Advance Man: James W. Stevens, 1896–1898

Statistics

Adrian Demons—Michigan State League— Official 1895 Season Statistics

Printed in the October 4, 1895, Adrian *Evening Telegram*. Submitted by MSL President Walter H. Mumby.

The Adrian Demon official scorekeeper was James Stevens, later the advance agent for the Page Fence Giants.

The MSL official report combined the statistics of William and Elmer E. Smith into "Smith" for the 1895 season.

Player Hicks was referred in several instances by both O. Hicks and C. or C. E. Hicks.

A paper or league typo has Graham's fielding percentage at .934, but my calculation is .951.

If a man played less than ten games, he was not included in the official MSL report, which eliminates the Page Fence Giants' Bill Binga, Pete Burns, Bud Fowler and Joe Miller, and other Demons such as Erve Beck and William Carrick.

Batting Statistics

	Games	AB	R	H	2b	3b	HR	Avg.	SB
James Robinson	24	104	25	47	9	1	1	.452	2
Honus Wagner	16	70	25	27	4	2	1	.386	16
Tim Nevins	28	108	37	40	10	2	2	.370	10
Ben Ireland	11	54	12	20	5	0	0	.370	5
Maurice Justice	79	375	105	133	14	4	2	.355	65
E. E./Wm Smith	80	380	98	134	28	10	0	.353	31
Paul Craft	70	281	101	97	22	0	1	.345	28
Ed Mulhern	80	360	97	123	18	0	3	.342	37
George Wilson	50	201	49	67	11	2	1	.333	26
Malcolm Whitehall	10	40	9	13	3	0	0	.325	7
Mike Lynch	66	280	75	87	17	4	1	.311	29
Vasco Graham	71	304	70	94	16	2	2	.309	18
Dutch Craft	22	85	17	25	2	4	1	.294	8
Jess Derrick	43	169	32	45	2	0	1	.266	14
Herbert Lentz	36	143	33	34	7	0	0	.238	10
O./C. E. Hicks	12	38	11	9	1	0	0	.237	8

Fielding Statistics

	Games	TC	PO	Assists	Errors	Pct.	Pos
O/C. E. Hicks	12	12	4	8	0	1.000	P-FR
George Wilson	50	304	45	247	12	.960	P-OF
Vasco Graham	71	597	493	75	29	.934/(.951)	C

	Games	TC	PO	Assists	Errors	Pct.	Pos
Ed Mulhern	80	759	691	25	43	.943	1B
Tim Nevins	28	120	19	91	10	.916	P-OF
Herbert Lentz	36	157	44	97	14	.910	OF
E.E./Wm Smith	80	170	130	21	16	.905	LF
Malcolm Whitehall	10	71	30	34	7	.901	2B
James Robinson	24	37	30	3	4	.891	—
Dutch Craft	22	72	46	14	12	.884	2B-RF
Jess Derrick	43	121	35	72	14	.883	P-CF
Paul Craft	70	317	163	114	40	.873	2B-RF
Honus Wagner	16	108	46	48	14	.870	2B
Ben Ireland	11	37	12	19	6	.837	INF
Maurice Justice	79	421	129	216	76	.819	SS
Mike Lynch	66	253	97	101	55	.782	3B

Ray Nemec's Compiled Statistics: Page Fence Giants When Playing with the Adrian Demons During the 1895 MSL Season

Nemec located 13 box scores of games between the Page Fence Giants and teams in the Michigan State League in 1895.

A check will see that Nemec has more "Games Played" for Wilson and Graham than do President Mumby's official MSL statistics.

Ray Nemec's statistical work is from the "Bud Fowler biographical file, National Baseball Hall of Fame Library, Cooperstown, NY" and is reprinted with their permission. Nemec was a founding member of the Society of American Baseball Researchers (SABR) and was the first chairman of the Minor League Research Committee. He won the prestigious Henry Chadwick Award in 2012 for his prodigious research, which he began in the 1940s. Sadly, Ray Nemec passed away in 2015.

Batting Statistics

	Games	AB	R	H	TB	2b	3b	HR	SB	Avg.
Pete Burns	4	18	7	11	15	4	0	0	2	.611
Bud Fowler*	31	139	43	46	59	11	1	0	5	.331
Geo. Wilson	52	208	54	68	86	11	2	1	26	.327
V. Graham	77	324	73	105	134	19	2	2	18	.324
Bill Binga	3	11	2	3	4	1	0	0	1	.273
Joe Miller	1	5	0	1	1	0	0	0	0	.200

*Fowler played 1 game with the Adrian Demons immediately after leaving the Page Fence Giants. The remaining 30 games were with the Lansing Senators.

Pitching Statistics

	Games/GS	GS/CG	IP	Wins	Losses	Pct.	H	BB	SO	R
Geo. Wilson	37	34/30	298	29	4	.879	289	96	280	173
Joe Miller	1	1/1	9	1	0	1.000	3	5	3	3

RAY NEMEC'S COMPILED STATISTICS FOR PAGE FENCE GIANTS VS. MSL TEAMS—1895

Batting Statistics

	Games	AB	R	H	TB	2b	3b	HR	SB	Avg.
Grant Johnson	11	44	17	28	47	5	4	2	1	.636
Patterson*	10	45	20	21	32	3	1	2	2	.467

	Games	AB	R	H	TB	2b	3b	HR	SB	Avg.
Sol White	9	42	12	15	23	3	1	1	2	.357
Bud Fowler	10	45	6	16	21	1	2	0	1	.356
George Taylor	13	56	19	19	23	4	0	0	6	.339
Gus Brooks	4	17	3	5	7	2	0	0	0	.294
Pete Burns	13	56	5	14	15	1	0	0	1	.250
Joe Miller	11	42	7	10	12	2	0	0	0	.238
Billy Holland	12	42	9	8	8	0	0	0	3	.190
Jim Chavous	3	13	2	2	2	0	0	0	0	.154
Fr. Van Dyke	9	35	4	5	7	2	0	0	0	.143
Wm. Malone	12	39	9	5	8	1	1	0	0	.128

*He lists Patterson's first name as George, however, my research leads me to believe it is James W. Patterson.

Pitching Statistics

	Games	GS/CG	IP	Wins	Losses	Pct.	H	BB	SO	R
Joe Miller	7	5/5	52	5	1	.833	52	16	36	33
Wm Malone	3	3/2	21	1	1	.500	22	13	5	19
Billy Holland	4	3/2	24	1	2	.333	28	8	12	25
Fr. Van Dyke	2	2/1	17	0	2	.000	25	6	3	21

Mitch's Lutzke's Page Fence Giants Pitchers' Win/Loss Totals Versus All Teams: Major, Minor, College and Amateur Clubs

Pitching records were compiled using results which were gleaned through the author's research. The chart includes the "Win-Loss" records in games which were not mentioned in the book.

In cases where conflicting names were found in game results, the author used the pitcher named by an Adrian daily newspaper as the pitcher of record.

Albert C. Carter (PFG team porter/barber) was listed as having pitched in a victorious 1895 game, but no other details, as to his total innings, or if he was the pitcher of record, were discovered.

William Wendell Gaskin (PFG cook) was credited with a win as the starter in 1895, but was knocked out of the box early in an 1896 game, in which the Giants rallied to win.

Pitching Records

1895	W-L		1896	W-L
Joe Miller	17–4		Joe Miller	8–2
William Malone	14–2		James Chavous	7–3
Billy Holland	9–8		Grant Johnson	4–1
Grant Johnson	4–0		Fred Van Dyke	1–0
George Wilson	2–5		Frank Waters	0–1
Fred Van Dyke	2–2		W.W. Gaskin	0–0
James Patterson	1–0			
George Taylor	1–0		**1897**	**W-L**
W. W. Gaskin	1–0		George Wilson	15–1
James Chavous	0–1		Joe Miller	9–2
Albert Carter	ND?		Sherman Barton	3–0
			Ed Wood(s)	3–0
1896	**W-L**		Robert Shaw	3–0
George Wilson	19–5		Grant Johnson	2–1
Billy Holland	13–4			

1898	W-L
George Wilson	8–1
Joe Miller	6–1
Sherman Barton	4–1
Grant Johnson	1–0

PFG Career	W-L
George Wilson	44–12
Joe Miller	40–9
Billy Holland	22–12
William Malone	14–2

PFG Career	W-L
Grant Johnson	11–2
Sherman Barton	7–1
James Chavous	7–4
Ed Wood(s)	3–0
Fred Van Dyke	3–2
Robert Shaw	3–0
James Patterson	1–0
George Taylor	1–0
W.W. Gaskin	1–0
Frank Waters	0–1
Albert Carter	ND?

1896 Championship Series Scores

Page Fence Giants vs. Cuban X Giants

Sunday Sept 13	@ Lima, Ohio	Cuban X Giants 8	PFG 6
Tuesday Sept 15	@Hudson, Mich	Cuban X Giants 20	PFG 14
Wednesday Sept 16	@ Quincy, Mich	PFG 26	Cuban X Giants 6
Thursday Sept 17	@Lansing, Mich	PFG 5	Cuban X Giants 2
Saturday Sept 19	@Allegan, Mich	PFG 14	Cuban X Giants 7
Sunday Sept 20	@South Bend, Ind	PFG 10	Cuban X Giants 7
Monday Sept 21	@Hartford, Mich	Cuban X Giants 3	PFG 2
Tuesday Sept 22	@Buchanan, Mich	PFG 4	Cuban X Giants 3
Wednesday Sept 23	@Adrian (CF)	Cuban X Giants 8	PFG 5
Thursday Sept 24	@Adrian (CF)-AM	PFG 8	Cuban X Giants 5
Thursday Sept 24	@Adrian (CF)-PM	PFG 17	Cuban X Giants 8
Friday Sept 25	@Caro, Mich	PFG 16	Cuban X Giants 8
Saturday Sept 26	@Hastings, Mich	Cuban X Giants 11	PFG 6
Sunday Sept 27	@Grand Rapids, Mich	PFG 10	Cuban X Giants 2
Monday Sept 28	@Laingsburg, Mich	PFG 6	Cuban X Giants 2
Thursday Oct 1	@Montpelier, Ohio	PFG 8	Cuban X Giants 6
Friday Oct 2	@Adrian (LP)	Cuban X Giants 5	PFG 3
Monday Oct 5	@Findlay, Ohio	Cuban X Giants 7	PFG 4
Wednesday Oct 7	@Paulding, Ohio	Cuban X Giants 8	PFG 4

Of the four games played in Adrian, three were reportedly at a field at the County Fairgrounds (CF) while the last one was at Lawrence Park (LP).

I listed all the games between these two teams, even the end-of-the-year exhibitions which became part of the debate as to the actual length of the championship series. Following their eighth win, in the game played at Caro, Michigan, the Page Fence Giants considered the series over and declared themselves the black baseball champions of 1896.

Chapter Notes

Chapter 1

1. *Adrian Daily Times and Expositor* (ADTE), Aug. 8, 1894.
2. *Ibid.*
3. *Ibid.*
4. *Ibid.*
5. *ADTE*, Aug. 7, 1894.
6. *Ibid.*
7. *ADTE*, Aug. 3, 1894.
8. *ADTE*, Aug. 8, 1894.
9. *ADTE*, Aug. 15, 1894.
10. *ADTE*, Sept. 25, 1894; June 3, 1895; Aug. 7, 1894.

Chapter 2

1. *ADTE*, Aug. 30, 1894.
2. *ADTE*, April 13, 20, 1894.
3. *ADTE*, Aug. 31, 1894.
4. *ADTE*, June 15, 1894.
5. *ADTE*, June 20, 1894.
6. *ADTE*, July 5, 7, 1894.
7. *ADTE*, June 23, 1894.
8. *Ibid.*
9. *Ibid.*
10. *ADTE*, July 2, 1894.
11. *ADTE*, July 16, 1894.
12. *Ibid.*
13. *ADTE*, July 9, 12, 1894.
14. *ADTE*, July 19, 1894.
15. *ADTE*, July 20, 1894.
16. *Ibid.*
17. *Ibid.*
18. *ADTE*, July 23, 1894.
19. *ADTE*, July 19, 1894.
20. *ADTE*, July 21, 1894.
21. *Ibid.*
22. *ADTE*, July 26, 1894.
23. *Ibid.*
24. *ADTE*, Aug. 18, 1894.
25. *ADTE*, July 26, 28, 1894.
26. *ADTE*, Aug. 2, 1894; and *Adrian Evening Telegram* (AET), Aug. 2, 1894.
27. *AET*, Aug. 2, 1894.
28. *ADTE*, Aug. 3, 1894.
29. *Monroe Democrat*, Aug. 9, 1894.
30. *Ibid.*
31. *Detroit Free Press*, Aug. 7, 1894.
32. *ADTE*, Aug. 6, 1894.
33. *Ibid.*
34. *AET*, Aug. 7, 1894.
35. *Ibid.*
36. *ADTE*, Aug. 7, 1894.
37. *AET*, Aug. 7, 1894 and *ADTE*, Aug. 7, 1894.
38. *AET*, Aug. 7, 1894.
39. *ADTE*, Aug. 7, 1894.
40. *Ibid.*
41. *AET*, Aug. 7, 1894.
42. *Ibid.*
43. *ADTE*, Aug. 8, 1894.
44. *Monroe Democrat*, Aug. 9, 1894.
45. *Monroe Democrat*, Aug. 9, 1894; *AET*, Aug. 9, 1894.
46. *AET*, Aug. 13, 1894.
47. *ADTE*, Aug. 13, 1894.
48. *AET*, Aug. 13, 1894.
49. *ADTE*, Aug. 13, 18, 21, 1894.
50. *ADTE*, Aug. 13, 1894.
51. *ADTE*, Aug. 23, 1894.
52. *AET*, Aug. 23, 1894.
53. *ADTE*, Aug. 3, 1894.
54. *ADTE*, Aug. 23, 1894.
55. *AET*, Aug. 22, 1894.
56. *ADTE*, Aug. 23, 1894.
57. *Ibid.*
58. *Ibid.*
59. *AET*, Aug. 18, 1894.
60. *ADTE*, Aug. 23, 1894.
61. *Ibid.*
62. *Ibid.*
63. *AET*, Aug. 23, 1894.
64. *ADTE*, Aug. 23, 1894.
65. *AET*, Aug. 23, 1894.
66. *AET*, Aug. 24, 1894.
67. *ADTE*, Aug. 23, 1894.
68. *Ibid.*
69. *AET*, Aug. 23, 1894.
70. *ADTE*, Aug. 23, 1894.
71. *AET*, Aug. 23, 1894.
72. *Monroe Democrat*, Aug. 30, 1894.
73. *Ibid.*
74. *Ibid.*
75. *Ibid.*
76. *Ibid.*
77. *ADTE*, Aug. 27, 1894.
78. *Monroe Democrat*, Sept. 6, 13, 1894.
79. *ADTE*, Aug. 27, 1894.
80. *Ibid.*
81. *AET*, Aug. 28, 1894.
82. *AET*, Aug. 29, 1894.
83. *ADTE*, Oct. 2, 1894.
84. *Ibid.*
85. *Monroe Democrat*, Sept. 27, 1894.
86. *Ibid.*

Chapter 3

1. *Cincinnati Enquirer*, Aug. 28, 29; *ADTE*, Aug. 29, 1894.
2. Federal Census, 1860.
3. *Detroit Free Press*, Feb. 15, 1898.
4. Jeffrey Michael Laing and Bud Fowler, *Baseball's First Black Professional* (Jefferson, NC: McFarland, 2013), 65, 133.
5. James A. Riley, *The Biographical Encyclopedia of the Negro Baseball League* (New York: Carroll & Graf, 2002), 294–5.
6. *ADTE*, Aug. 29, 1894.
7. *Ibid.*
8. *The Lima News*, Aug. 27, 1894; *Cincinnati Enquirer*, Aug. 28, 1894.
9. *Findlay Daily Courier*, Aug. 28, 1894.
10. *ADTE*, Aug. 27, 1894.
11. *ADTE*, Aug. 27, 28, 29, 1894.
12. *ADTE*, Aug. 29, 1894, and *Cincinnati Enquirer*, Aug. 29, 1894.
13. *ADTE*, Aug. 29, 1894.
14. *ADTE*, Aug. 28, 1894.
15. *ADTE*, Aug. 27, 1894.
16. *ADTE*, Aug. 29, 1894.
17. *Cincinnati Enquirer*, Nov. 24, 1894.
18. *ADTE*, Aug. 29, 1894.
19. *ADTE*, Aug. 30, 1894.
20. *ADTE*, Aug. 30, 1894.
21. *ADTE*, Aug. 30, 1894; *AET*, Aug. 30, 1894.

22. *ADTE*, Aug. 30, 1894.
23. *AET*, Aug. 30, 1894.
24. *ADTE*, Aug. 30, 1894.
25. *ADTE*, Aug. 31, 1894.
26. *ADTE*, Aug. 30, 1894.
27. *ADTE*, Aug. 31, 1894.
28. *Ibid.*
29. *AET*, Aug. 30, 1894.
30. *AET*, Aug. 31, 1894.
31. *Adrian Daily Telegram*, Sept. 9, 1916.
32. Federal Census 1850, 1860; Find-A-Grave; *DFP*, Dec. 17, 1891; *DFP*, Sept. 29, 1915.
33. *ADT*, Sept. 9, 1916.
34. DAR File J. Charles Morehouse Lamb.
35. *ADT*, Sept. 9, 1916.
36. Federal Census 1870, 1880; *Ancestry.com.*
37. *DFP*, Sept. 29, 1915.
38. *DFP*, Dec. 30, 1896.
39. Jan Richardi, *Fencing the World: Adrian's Page in History* (Adrian, MI: Lenawee County Historical Society, 1999), 1–2.
40. *DFP*, March 27, 1908.
41. *ADTE*, Aug. 29, 1894.
42. *Ibid.*

Chapter 4

1. *ADTE*, Sept. 19, 1894.
2. *AET*, Sept. 20, 1894.
3. *ADTE*, Sept. 19, 1894.
4. *AET*, Sept. 19, 1894.
5. *ADTE*, Sept. 21, 1894; *Adrian Weekly Times and Expositor*, Sept. 28, 1894.
6. *ADTE*, Sept. 21, 1894.
7. *AET*, Sept. 21, 1894.
8. *Ibid.*
9. *ADTE*, Sept. 21, 1894.
10. *Ibid.*
11. *Ibid.*
12. *AET*, Sept. 21, 1894.
13. *ADTE*, Sept. 21, 1894.
14. *Ibid.*
15. *DFP*, Sept. 22, 1894.
16. *Adrian Weekly Times and Expositor*, Oct. 15, 1894.
17. *ADTE*, Nov. 13, 1894.
18. *AWT&E*, Oct. 15, 1894.
19. *Sporting Life*, Dec. 8, 1894.
20. *Ibid.*
21. *The Sporting News*, Dec. 29, 1894.
22. *AET*, Oct. 17, 1894.
23. *TSN*, Dec. 3, 1894.

Chapter 5

1. Hoig L. Gay, *A Capsule History of Adrian, Michigan and the State of Michigan* (Adrian, MI: Adrian Area Chamber of Commerce, Swenk-Tuttle Press, undated c. 1964), 3; W.A. Whitney, *History and Biographical Record of Lenawee County, Michigan* (Adrian, MI: W. Stearns & Co., 1879–80), 11.
2. Whitney, 9–11, 51; Charles Exera Brown, *Brown's City Directory of Adrian* (Adrian, MI: Times & Expositor Printing Office, 1870), 28.
3. Whitney, 13 and 55; Brown, 29.
4. Whitney, 14; Walter Romig, *Michigan Place Names* (Detroit: Wayne State University Press, 1986), 11.
5. Whitney, 14–15.
6. Federal Census 1830, 1840, 1850.
7. Richard Illenden Bonner, *Memoirs of Lenawee County, MI*, Vols. 1 and 2 (Madison, WI: Western Historical Association), 70, 499.
8. Rosalee Corson, editor, *Early Adrian* (Adrian, MI: AAUW, 1965), 81–83.
9. Charles Lindquist, *Adrian: The City That Worked, A History of Adrian, Michigan, 1825–2000*, (Adrian, MI: Lenawee County Historical Society, 2004), 32–33.
10. Lindquist, 24–25.
11. Chapman Brothers, *Portrait and Biographical Record of Lenawee County, Michigan*, (Chicago: Chapman Brothers, 1888), 175.
12. Corson, *AAUW*, 80.
13. Noelle Keller email, Adrian College Librarian, to author, Jan. 4, 2017.
14. Brown, 49.
15. Peter Morris, *Baseball Fever, Early Baseball in Michigan* (Ann Arbor: University of Michigan Press, 2006), 94, 98–100, 108–109.
16. Library of Congress, Map Library.
17. D.W. Wilson, and Wendell Gaskin, "African American Journal of Adrian," *Adrian Daily Times and Expositor Press*, Adrian, MI, 1895 (portions on-line).
18. Brown, 47; Lindquist, 52.
19. Brown, 30–32.
20. Brown, entire directory; Federal Census, 1870.
21. Brown, 19, 151; Federal Census, 1870.
22. Brown; Federal Census, 1870.
23. *Ibid.*
24. Federal Census, 1870.
25. *Ibid.*
26. *Ibid.*
27. AA Journal of Adrian.
28. Lindquist, 106.
29. John I. Knapp, and Richard I. Bonner, *Illustrated History and Biographical Record of Lenawee County, Michigan*, (Adrian, MI: The Times Printing Co., 1903), 328.
30. Lindquist, 106.
31. AA Journal of Adrian.
32. Federal Census, 1870, 1880, 1900.
33. Harry H. Chapin, Adrian City Directory, 1885–86, Harry H. Chapin, Adrian, MI, 1885, 57; Reprint of Mudge Directory of Lansing City, Introduction by David R. Caterino, Historical Society of Lansing, MI, 1991, 35; Federal Census 1900.
34. AA Journal of Adrian.
35. *Ibid.*
36. *Ibid.*
37. *Ibid.*
38. *Ibid.*
39. *Ibid.*
40. *ADTE*, April 1, 1895.

Chapter 6

1. *TSN*, Dec. 29, 1894.
2. *TSN*, Jan. 26, 1895.
3. *SL*, Feb. 23, 1895.
4. *ADTE*, Nov. 17, 24, 28, Dec. 12, 1894.
5. *TSN*, Dec. 29, 1894.
6. Baseball Reference.
7. *TSN*, Feb. 9, 1895; Baseball Reference.
8. *Kalamazoo Daily Telegraph*, May 11, 1895.
9. *TSN*, March 2, 1895.
10. *TSN*, April 20, 1895.
11. *ADTE*, Feb. 2, March 2, 1895.
12. *ADTE*, March 2, 25, 1895.
13. *TSN*, March 23, 1895; *ADTE*, March 25, 1895.
14. *AET*, Oct. 8, 1894.
15. *ADTE*, March 18, 25, 1895.
16. *AET*, April 2, 1895.
17. *ADTE*, March 15, 1895.
18. *ADTE*, Feb. 28, 1895.
19. *AET*, March 20, 1895.
20. *ADTE*, Dec. 15, 1894.
21. *AET*, March 27, April 4, 1895; *ADTE*, April 3, 1895; Federal Census Returns.
22. *TSN*, March 9, 1895.
23. *Chicago Inter Ocean*, Feb. 24, 1895.
24. *ADTE*, April 1, 1895.
25. *ADTE*, April 1, 1895; *AET*, April 3, 1895.
26. *ADTE*, April 1, 1895.
27. *AET*, March 27, 1895; *ADTE*, April 6, 1895.
28. *AET*, April 4, 1895.
29. *AET*, April 4, 1895; *ADTE*, April 6, 1895.
30. *AET*, April 4, 1895.
31. *Ibid.*
32. *AET*, April 6, 1895; *ADTE*, April 6, 1895.

33. *AET*, April 4, 1895; *ADTE*, April 6, 1895.
34. *Marion Chronicle*, April 4, 1895.
35. *AET*, April 9, 1895.
36. *The Indianapolis Journal*, April 9, 1895.
37. *ADTE*, April 9, 1895.
38. *Indianapolis News*, April 8, 1895.
39. *Indianapolis Journal*, April 9, 1895.
40. *Ibid.*
41. *AET*, April 10, 1895.
42. *Indianapolis Journal*, April 11, 1895.
43. *Indianapolis News*, April 11, 1895.
44. *Indianapolis Journal*, April 11, 1895.
45. *Findlay Daily Courier*, April 12, 1895.
46. *ADTE*, April 11, 1895.
47. *Indianapolis Journal*, April 11, 1895.
48. *Findlay Daily Courier*, April 12, 1895.
49. *Indianapolis Journal*, April 11, 1895.
50. *Indianapolis News*, April 11, 1895.
51. *Ibid.*
52. *Ibid.*

Chapter 7

1. *AET*, April 12, 1895.
2. *Ibid.*
3. *Ibid.*
4. *AET*, April 13, 1895.
5. *AET*, April 13, 1895; *TSN*, April 20, 1895.
6. *AET*, April 13, 1895.
7. *Ibid.*
8. *Cincinnati Enquirer*, April 13, 1895.
9. *Ibid.*
10. Baseball Reference.
11. *ADTE*, April 12, 1895.
12. *Grand Rapids Democrat*, April 13, 1895.
13. *Grand Rapids Evening Press*, April 15, 1895.
14. *Grand Rapids Democrat*, April 14, 1895.
15. *Ibid.*
16. *AET*, April 15, 1895.
17. *Grand Rapids Democrat*, April 14, 1895; *AET*, April 15, 1895.
18. *Grand Rapids Democrat*, April 14, 1895.
19. *Grand Rapids Democrat*, April 15, 1895.
20. Baseball Reference.
21. *AET*, April 17, 1895.
22. *AET*, April 15, 1895.

23. *Grand Rapids Democrat*, April 5, 1895.
24. *DFP*, April 15, 1895; *AET*, April 15, 1895.
25. *Grand Rapids Democrat*, April 14, 1895.
26. *AET*, April 15, 1895.
27. *AET*, April 16, 1895.
28. *Ibid.*
29. *Grand Rapids Democrat*, April 16, 1895; *AET*, April 16, 1895.
30. *Grand Rapids Democrat*, April 17, 1895; *AET*, April 17, 1895.
31. *ADTE*, April 12, 1894; *AET*, April 16, 1895.
32. *AET*, April 17, 1895.
33. *Ibid.*
34. *ADTE*, April 18, 1895.
35. *AET*, April 17, 1895.
36. *AET*, April 17, 1895; *Chicago Inter Ocean*, April 18, 1895.
37. *AET*, April 18, 1895; *ADTE*, April 18, 1895.
38. *AET*, April 17, 1895.
39. *ADTE*, April 19, 1895; *TSN*, April 27, 1895; Baseball Reference.
40. *SL*, May 4, 1895.
41. *TSN*, April 27, May 4, 1895.
42. *St. Paul Daily Globe*, April 20, 1895.
43. *SL*, March 30, 1895.
44. *SL*, March 30, 1895; *AET*, March 20, 1895.
45. *AET*, March 20, 1895.
46. *SL*, Feb. 29, 1895.
47. *St. Paul Daily Globe*, April 20, 1895.
48. *ADTE*, April 22, 1895.
49. *St. Paul Daily Globe*, April 21, 1895.
50. *Ibid.*
51. *St. Paul Daily Globe*, April 22, 1895.
52. *St. Paul Daily Globe*, April 28, 1895.
53. Baseball Reference.
54. *St. Paul Daily Globe*, April 23, 1895.
55. *St. Paul Daily Globe*, April 24, 1895.
56. *Ibid.*
57. *ADTE*, April 24, 1895.
58. *AET*, April 24, 1895.
59. *ADTE*, April 25, 1895; *St. Paul Daily Globe*, April 25, 1895.
60. *St. Paul Daily Globe*, April 25, 1895.
61. *Ibid.*
62. *St. Paul Daily Globe*, April 26, 1895.
63. *AET*, April 25, 1895.
64. *Ibid.*
65. *TSN*, May 25, 1895; *SL*, March 30, 1895.
66. *AET*, April 25, 1895.
67. *AET*, April 29, 1895.
68. *AET*, May 1, 1895.
69. *ADTE*, April 29, 1895.

70. *AET*, May 1, 1895.
71. *St. Paul Daily Globe*, April 27, 1895.
72. *Ibid.*
73. *Ibid.*

Chapter 8

1. *AET*, March 27, 1895.
2. *Ibid.*
3. *ADTE*, March 15, 1895.
4. *AET*, March 27, 1895.
5. *AET*, April 17, 1895.
6. *AET*, March 27, 1895.
7. *AET*, March 20, 1895.
8. *Kalamazoo Daily Telegraph*, May 10, 1895; *ADTE*, April 10, 1895; *TSN*, May 25, 1895.
9. *Kalamazoo Daily Telegraph*, May 10, 1895.
10. *TSN*, May 25, 1895; *DFP* May 19, 1895.
11. *AET*, March 27, 1895.
12. *ADDTE*, May 11, 1895.
13. *AET*, April 24, 1895.
14. *ADTE*, April 29, 1895; May 20, 1895.
15. *ADTE*, May 20, 1895.
16. *AET*, March 20, 1895.
17. *AET*, March 27, 1895.
18. *AET*, April 17, 1895, May 1, 1895; Paul Kraft Death Certificate. State of Michigan.
19. *SABR*, John R. Husman on 1883 Fleetwood Walker games; SABR, David Fleitz on Cap Anson.
20. National Baseball Hall of Fame.
21. National Baseball Hall of Fame; Baseball Reference.
22. *DFP*, Feb. 15, 1898; Federal Census.
23. *AET*, April 17, 1895.
24. *Baseball-Almanac*; Peter Morris, *Game of Inches* (Chicago: Ivan R. Dee, 2006), 29.
25. *Baseball-Almanac*.
26. *Grand Rapids Democrat*, April 13, 1895.
27. *TSN*, May 25, 1895; *ADTE*, May 8, 1895.
28. *TSN*, May 25, 1895.
29. *ADTE*, April 29, 1895.
30. *AET*, May 2, 1895.
31. *AET*, May 3, 1895.
32. *AET*, May 3; *ADTE*, May 4, 1895.
33. *AET*, May 4, 1895.
34. *AET*, May 3, 1895.
35. *AET*, May 6, 1895.
36. *ADTE*, May 6, 7, 1895.
37. *Rock ISLand Argus*, May 8, 1895.
38. *Rock ISLand Argus*, May 9, 1895.
39. *AET*, May 15, 1895.

40. *Rock ISLand Argus*, May 9, 1895.
41. *AET*, May 13, 1895; *ADTE*, May 13, 1895.
42. *AET*, May 13, 1895.
43. *ADTE*, May 13, 1895.
44. *AET*, May 15, 1895.
45. *ADTE*, May 15, 1895.
46. Baseball Reference.
47. *Kalamazoo Daily Telegraph*, May 15, 1895.
48. *Kalamazoo Daily Telegraph*, May 16, 1895.
49. *Ibid.*
50. *Ibid.*
51. Baseball Reference; *AET*, May 17, 1895.
52. *Kalamazoo Daily Telegraph*, May 17, 1895.
53. *Ibid.*
54. *Kalamazoo Daily Telegraph*, May 18, 1895.
55. *Ibid.*
56. *AET*, May 18, 1895.
57. *AET*, May 15, 1895.
58. *ADTE*, May 16, 1895.
59. *ADTE*, May 20, 1895.
60. Federal Census, 1880, 1900; 1863 Special Federal Tax Assessment.
61. *ADTE*, May 21, 1895.
62. *AET*, May 21, 1895.
63. *AET*, May 15, 1895.
64. *ADTE*, May 22, 1895.
65. *AET*, May 23, 1895.
66. *Ibid.*

Chapter 9

1. *Fort Wayne News*, May 20, 1895.
2. *Fort Wayne Journal Gazette*, May 23, 1895.
3. *Fort Wayne News*, May 20, 1895.
4. *Fort Wayne News*, May 22, 1895; *Fort Wayne Journal Gazette*, May 24, 1895.
5. *ADTE*, May 27, 1895; *AET*, May 29, 1895.
6. Baseball Reference.
7. *Fort Wayne Journal Gazette*, May 23, 1895; *ADTE*, May 24, 1895.
8. *Fort Wayne Journal Gazette*, May 23, 1895.
9. *Ibid.*
10. *Ibid.*
11. Baseball Reference.
12. *Fort Wayne News*, May 24, 1895.
13. *ADTE*, May 24, 1895.
14. *AET*, May 25, 1895.
15. *AET*, May 29, 1895; *ADTE*, May 28, 1895.
16. *ADTE*, May 27; *ADTE*, May 28, 1895.

17. *Cincinnati Enquirer*, May 29, 1895.
18. *Cincinnati Enquirer*, May 30, 1895.
19. *ADTE*, May 31, 1895.
20. *Cincinnati Enquirer*, May 31, 1895.
21. *ADTE*, June 3, 1895.
22. *AET*, June 3, 1895.
23. *ADTE*, June 3, 1895.
24. *AET*, June 3, 1895.
25. *Morning Republican*, June 6, 1895.
26. *Findlay Daily Courier*, June 6, 1895.
27. *ADTE*, June 6, 1895.
28. *AET*, May 29, 1895.
29. *ADTE*, June 4, 1895; *AET*, June 4, 1895.
30. John Holway, *The Complete Book of Baseball's Negro Leagues: The Other Half of Baseball History*, (Fern Park, FL: Hastings House, 2001), 30.
31. Sol White, *Sol White's History of Colored Baseball, with other Documents on the Early Black Game, 1886–1936*, compiled by Jerry Malloy, (Lincoln: Nebraska University Press, 1995), 146.
32. *ADTE*, June 4, 1895; *AET*, June 4, 1895.
33. *AET*, June 4, 1895; *ADTE*, June 4, 6, 1895.
34. *Battle Creek Enquirer*, Sept. 11, 2015.
35. *Ibid.*
36. *ADTE*, June 6, 1895.
37. *AET*, June 6, 1895.
38. *AET*, May 22, 1895.
39. *AET*, May 24, 1895.
40. *ADTE*, May 31, 1895.
41. *Lansing Republican*, May 28, 1895.
42. *AET*, May 29, 1895.
43. *ADTE*, May 31, 1895.
44. *AET*, May 30, 1895.
45. *ADTE*, May 31, 1895.
46. *Ibid.*
47. *Ibid.*
48. *DFP*, April 21, 1895.
49. *ADTE*, May 31, June 13; *DFP*, June 13, 1895.
50. *ADTE*, May 31, 1895.
51. *Ibid.*
52. *DFP*, April 1, 1895.
53. *ADTE*, June 4, 1895.
54. *Lansing Republican*, June 7, 1895.
55. *ADTE*, June 3, 1895.
56. *AET*, June 7, 1895.
57. Arthur Oram Passport Application; Snyder, 403; Federal Census 1900; *Adrian Telegram*, April 2, 1960.
58. *AET*, June 8, 1895.
59. *AET*, June 10, 1895.
60. *Ibid.*

61. *ADTE*, June 10, 1895.
62. *AET*, June 10, 1895.
63. *ADTE*, June 10, 1895.
64. *Ibid.*
65. *Ibid.*
66. *ADTE*, June 10, 1895; *AET*, June 10, 1895.
67. *AET*, June 10, 1895.
68. *ADTE*, June 10, 1895.
69. *Ibid.*
70. *Adrian Weekly Press*, June 4, 1895.
71. *ADTE*, June 10, 1895.
72. *AET*, June 10, 1895.

Chapter 10

1. *ADTE*, June 10, 1895.
2. *Monroe Democrat*, June 13, 1895; *AET*, June 13, 14, 1895.
3. *AET*, June 13, 1895.
4. *ADTE*, June 14, 1895.
5. *AET*, June 14, 1895.
6. *AET*, June 19, 1895.
7. *AET*, June 15, 1895.
8. *Hastings Banner*, June 20, 1895.
9. *Ibid.*
10. *Ibid.*
11. *Ibid.*
12. *AET*, June 17, 1895.
13. *DFP*, June 16, 1895; Baseball Reference.
14. *Hastings Banner*, June 20, 1895.
15. *ADTE*, June 17, 1895; *Hastings Banner*, June 20, 1895.
16. *Hastings Banner*, June 20, 1895.
17. *Ibid.*
18. *AET*, June 17, 1895.
19. *AET*, June 17, 1895; *Hastings Banner*, June 20, 1895.
20. *AET*, April 16, 1895.
21. *AET*, June 17, 1895.
22. *Hastings Banner*, June 20, 1895.
23. *ADTE*, June 17, 1895; Riley, p. 113.
24. *Hastings Banner*, June 20, 1895.
25. *AET*, June 17, 1895.
26. Find-A-Grave, SABR Negro League Grave Marker Project.
27. *Hastings Banner*, June 20, 1895.
28. *Ibid.*
29. *TSN*, June 29, 1895.
30. *ADTE*, June 22, 1895.
31. *ADTE*, June 18, 1895, 20; *Owosso Evening Argus*, June 19, 1895.
32. *Owosso Evening Argus*, June 18, 1895.
33. *The Michigan Alumnus*, Vol. 8, (Ann Arbor: University of Michigan Press, 1902), 42–43; UM Bentley Historical Library, Ann Arbor,

MI, 1895 Baseball Team Photo, on-line; Baseball Reference.
34. *Owosso Evening Argus*, June 18, 1895; *ADTE*, June 18, 1895.
35. *Owosso Evening Argus*, June 19, 1895; *DFP*, June 19; *DFP* June 21, 1895.
36. *ADTE*, June 20, 1895.
37. *Owosso Evening Argus*, June 20, 1895.
38. *Ibid*.
39. *Ibid*.
40. *ADTE*, June 21, 1895.
41. *AET*, June 21, 1895; *ADTE*, June 21, 1895.
42. *AET*, June 21, 1895.
43. *Kalamazoo Daily Telegraph*, June 22, 1895.
44. *ADTE*, June 22, 1895; *Kalamazoo Daily Telegraph*, June 22, 1895.
45. *Kalamazoo Daily Telegraph*, June 24, 1895.
46. *AET*, June 24, 1895; *ADTE*, June 16, 1895.
47. *AET*, June 29, 1895.
48. Riley, 109, 202.
49. *AET*, June 26, 1895.
50. *AET*, July 2, 1895.
51. *ADTE*, June 25, 1895; *The Nashville News*, June 28, 1895, MJC.
52. *The Nashville News*, June 28, 1895, MJC.
53. *AET*, June 16, July 1, 1895; *ADTE*, June 28, 1895.
54. *ADTE*, June 25, 1895.
55. *DFP*, July 2, 1895; *Lansing Republican*, July 2, 1895.
56. *AET*, July 2, 1895; *Lansing Republican*, July 13, 1895.
57. *ADTE*, May 31, 1895.
58. *AET*, July 8, 1895.
59. *AET*, July 5, 1895.
60. *AET*, July 10, 1895.
61. *AET*, July 12, 1895.
62. *Ibid*.
63. *ADTE*, June 29, 1895; *Hudson Post*, July 12, 1895.
64. *Hudson Gazette*, July 12, 1895; *Hudson Post*, July 12, 1895.
65. *Hudson Post*, July 12, 1895.
66. *Hudson Gazette*, July 19, 1895.
67. *AET*, July 11, 12, 13, 15, 1895.
68. *AET*, July 15, 1895.
69. *AET*, July 16, 1895; *ADTE*, July 16, 1895.
70. *Ibid*.
71. *Hudson Post*, July 19, 1895.
72. *Hudson Gazette*, July 19, 1895.
73. *AET*, July 16, 1895; *ADTE*, July 16, 1895; *Hudson Gazette*, July 19, 1895.
74. *Hudson Gazette*, July 19, 1895.
75. *AET*, July 16, 1895; *Hudson Post*, July 19, 1895; *Hudson Gazette*, July 19, 1895.

76. *Hudson Post*, July 19, 1895.
77. *Hudson Gazette*, July 19, 1895.
78. *AET*, July 16, 1895; *Hudson Post*, July 19, 1895.
79. *ADTE*, July 16, 1895.
80. *AET*, July 16, 1895.
81. *ADTE*, July 16, 1895.
82. *AET*, July 16; July 17, 1895.
83. *SL*, July 20, 1895.

Chapter 11

1. *ADTE*, July 18, 1895
2. *Ibid*.
3. *AET*, July 29, 1895.
4. *AET*, July 24, 1895.
5. *AET*, July 23, 1895.
6. *AET*, July 20, 1895.
7. *AET*, July 19, 20, 1895; *The Weekly Press*, July 26, 1895.
8. *SL*, July 20, 1895.
9. *Ibid*.
10. *TSN*, Aug. 3, 1895.
11. *TSN*, Aug. 10, 1895.
12. *AET*, July 20, 1895.
13. *AET*, July 26, 27, 1895.
14. *AET*, July 25, 1895.
15. *Hudson Post*, July 19, 1895.
16. *Findlay Daily Courier*, July 23, 1895; *Morning Republican*, July 23, 1895.
17. *Findlay Daily Courier*, July 24, 1895.
18. *ADTE*, July 25, 1895.
19. *AET*, July 27, 1895.
20. *ADTE*, July 27, 1895.
21. *AET*, July 29, 1895.
22. *ADTE*, July 20, 1895.
23. *ADTE*, July 20, 1895; *AET*, July 30, 1895.
24. *ADTE*, July 30, 1895; *The Weekly Press*, Aug. 2, 1895.
25. *Ibid*.
26. *AET*, July 30, 1895.
27. *Ibid*.
28. *St. Paul Daily Globe*, July 30, 1895.
29. *AET*, July 31, 1895; *ADTE*, July 31, 1895.
30. *ADTE*, July 31, 1895.
31. *AET*, July 31, 1895; *ADTE*, July 31, 1895.
32. *AET*, July 31, 1895.
33. *AET*, July 31, 1895; *ADTE*, July 31, 1895.
34. *Ibid*.
35. *ADTE*, July 31, 1895.
36. *AET*, Aug. 1, 1895.
37. *ADTE*, Aug. 1, 1895.
38. *Ibid*.
39. *AET*, Aug. 1, 1895; *ADTE*, Aug. 1, Aug. 5, 1895.
40. *AET*, Aug. 9, 1895; Riley, 673, 412, 847.
41. *AET*, Aug. 1, 1895.

Chapter 12

1. *AET*, Aug. 2, 1895; *ADTE*, Aug. 2, 1895.
2. *AET*, Aug. 2, 1895.
3. *Muskegon Morning News*, Aug. 6, 1895.
4. Baseball Reference.
5. *Muskegon Morning News*, Aug. 6, 1895.
6. *Muskegon Morning News*, Aug. 4, Aug. 6; *AET*, Aug. 6, 1895.
7. *ADTE*, Aug. 5, 1895.
8. *ADTE*, June 25, 1895.
9. *ADTE*, Aug. 20, 1895
10. *AET*, Aug. 7, 10, 1895.
11. *AET*, Aug. 14, 1895.
12. *ADTE*, Aug. 21, 1895.
13. *ADTE*, Aug. 21, 1895; *AET*, Aug. 21, 1895.
14. *ADTE*, Aug. 22, 1895; *AET*, Aug. 22, 1895.
15. *AET*, Aug. 22, 1895.
16. *AET*, Aug. 12, 13, 14, 16, 19, 21, 1895; *ADTE*, Aug. 8, 20, 1895; *Charlevoix Sentinel*, Aug. 21, 1895.
17. *DFP*, Aug. 21, 1895.
18. *DFP*, Aug. 22, 1895.
19. *Reed City Weekly Clarion*, Aug. 21, 1895.
20. *Reed City Weekly Clarion*, Aug. 28, 1895.
21. *AET*, Aug. 26, 27, 1895; *ADTE*, Aug. 27, 28, 1895; *DFP*, Aug. 28, 1895.
22. *AET*, Aug. 29, 1895; *ADTE*, Aug. 29, 1895; *Owosso Times*, Aug. 30, 1895.
23. *ADTE*, Aug. 30, 1895, *DFP*, Aug. 30, 1895.
24. *Alma Record*, Aug. 30, 1895.
25. *Gratiot Journal*, Aug. 30, 1895.
26. *Gratiot County Herald*, Sept. 5, 1895.
27. *Gratiot County Herald*, Sept. 5, 1895, *Alma Record*, Sept. 6, 1895.
28. *ADTE*, Aug. 31, 1895; *Gratiot County Herald*, Sept. 5, 1895.
29. *AET*, Sept. 2, 1895.
30. *AET*, Sept. 2, 1895; *ADTE*, Sept. 2, 1895.
31. *ADTE*, Aug. 29, 1895.
32. *AET*, Sept. 3, 1895; *ADTE*, Sept. 3, 1895.
33. *Ibid*.
34. *AET*, Aug. 26, 1895; *ADTE*, Sept. 3, 1895.
35. *ADTE*, Sept. 4, 1895, Essex, Ontario, Marriage Records, 1896; Baseball Reference.
36. *ADTE*, Sept. 4, 1895; Baseball Reference.
37. *ADTE*, Sept. 4, 1895.
38. *Ibid*.
39. *AET*, Aug. 26, 1895.
40. *AET*, Aug. 30, 1895.
41. *AET*, Sept. 7, 1895; *ADTE*, Sept. 7, 1895.

42. *AET*, Sept. 14, 1895.
43. *ADTE*, Sept. 5, 1895.
44. *ADTE*, Sept. 7, 1895; *AET*, Sept. 7, 1895.
45. *AET*, Sept. 7, 1895.
46. *ADTE*, Sept. 14, 1895; *AET*, Sept. 14, 1895.
47. *AET*, Sept. 14, 16, 1895; *ADTE*, Sept. 16, 1895.
48. *ADTE*, Sept. 16, 1895.
49. *ADTE*, Sept. 17, 1895.
50. *ADTE*, Sept. 17, 1895; *AET*, Sept. 17, 1895; Baseball Reference.
51. *ADTE*, Sept. 17, 1895; *AET*, Sept. 17, 1895.
52. *ADTE*, Sept. 17, 1895.
53. *ADTE*, Sept. 17, 1895; *AET*, Sept. 16, 17, 1895.
54. *ADTE*, Sept. 18, 1895.
55. *AET*. Sept. 19, 1895.
56. *Ibid.*
57. *AET*, Sept. 19, 1895; *ADTE*, Sept. 19, 1895.
58. *AET*, Sept. 20, 23, 1895; *ADTE*, Sept. 23, 1895.
59. *ADTE*, Sept. 23, 1895; *TSWN*, Oct. 5, 1895.
60. *AET*, Sept. 16, 17, 1895; *Homer Index*, Sept. 18, 1895.
61. *Ingham County News*, Sept. 19, 1895.
62. *Fowlerville Review*, Sept. 12, 27, 1895.
63. *ADTE*, Sept. 21, 1895.
64. *Ibid.*
65. *ADTE*, Sept. 23, 1895.
66. *Ibid.*
67. *ADTE*, Sept. 24, 1895.
68. *AET*, Sept. 25, 1895; *ADTE*, Sept. 25, 1895; *Pontiac Daily Gazette*, Sept. 25, 1895.
69. *ADTE*, Sept. 24, 1895.
70. DEP, Sept. 26, 1895.
71. *ADTE*, Sept. 24, 1895.
72. *ADTE*, Sept. 26, 1895; *AET*, Sept. 26, 1895.
73. *AET*, Sept. 26, 1895; *ADTE*, Sept. 27, 1895.
74. *AET*, Sept. 28, 1895; *ADTE*, Sept. 30, 1895.
75. *ADTE*, Sept. 30, 1895.
76. *AET*, Oct. 1, 1895; *ADTE*, Oct. 1, 2, 1895; *Steuben Republican*, Oct. 2, 1895.
77. *AET*, Oct. 2, 1895.
78. *ADTE*, Oct. 2, 3, 1895; *AET*, Oct. 3, 1895.
79. *ADTE*, Oct. 4, 1895.
80. *ADTE*, Oct. 4, 1895; *AET*, Oct. 4, 1895.
81. *Ibid.*
82. *ADTE*, Oct. 7, 1895; *AET*, Oct. 7, 1895.
83. *ADTE*, Oct. 7, 1895; *AET*, Oct. 18, 1895.
84. *AET*, Oct. 7, 1895.
85. *ADTE*, Oct. 1, 1895.
86. *AET*, Oct. 4, 1895.

87. *ADTE*, Oct. 7, 1895; *AET*, Oct. 7, 1895; *DFP*, Sept. 22, 24, 1895; Baseball Reference.
88. *ADTE*, Oct. 8, 1895.
89. *AET*, Oct. 8, 1895; *ADTEA*, Oct. 8, 1895; *Indianapolis Journal*, Oct. 8, 1895.
90. *ADTE*, Oct. 8, 1895; *DFP*, Oct. 8, 1895; Riley, 873.
91. *AET*, Oct. 7, 1895.
92. *Ibid.*
93. *ADTE*, Oct. 8, 1895.
94. *AET*, Oct. 8, 1895; *DFP*, Oct. 8, 1895.
95. *DFP*, Oct. 9, 1895.
96. *AET*, Oct. 10, 1895; *AET*, Oct. 10, 1895; *DFP*, Oct. 10, 1895.
97. *AET*, Oct. 11, 1895.
98. *AET*, Oct. 11, 1895; *AET*, Oct. 11, 1895.
99. *ADTE*, Oct. 11, 1895.
100. *AET*, Oct. 12, 1895.
101. *AET*, Oct. 14, 15, 1895.
102. *AET*, Oct. 14, 1895.
103. *ADTE*, Oct. 18, 1895; *DFP*, March 17, 1901.
104. *AET*, Oct. 18, 1895.
105. *AET*, Oct. 17, 1895; *ADTE*, Oct. 22, 1895.
106. *ADTE*, Nov. 13, 1895.
107. *ADTE*, Nov. 12, 1895.

Chapter 13

1. *ADTE*, Jan. 18, 23, 1896.
2. *ADTE*, Jan. 23, 1896.
3. *ADTE*, Feb. 5, 6, 8, 1896.
4. *ADTE*, Feb. 8, 1896.
5. *ADTE*, Feb. 11, 1896.
6. *ADTE*, Feb. 15, 1896.
7. *ADTE*, Feb. 21, 1896.
8. *ADTE*, Feb. 19, 1896.
9. *ADTE*, March 16, 1896.
10. *ADTE*, March 20, 1896.
11. *ADTE*, March 26, 1896.
12. *ADTE*, March 28, 1896.
13. *AET*, Feb. 28, 1896.
14. *ADTE*, March 11, 1896.
15. *ADTE*, March 28, 1896.
16. *Chicago Daily Tribune*, Aug. 20, 1895.
17. *TSN*, Nov. 14, 1896.
18. *ADTE*, March 28, 1896; *AET*, March 30, 1896.
19. *ADTE*, March 28, 1896.
20. *AET*, March 21, 1896.
21. *AET*, March 30, 1896.
22. *ADTE*, March 11, 1896.
23. *AET*, March 30, 1896.
24. *ADTE*, March 28, 1896; *AET*, March 30, 1896; *TSN*, April 11, 1896.
25. *AET*, March 30, 1896.
26. *The Daily Herald*, March 23, 1896.
27. *AET*, April 4, 1896.
28. Baseball Reference.

29. *Chicago Daily Tribune*, April 5, 1896; *AET*, April 6, 1896; *ADTE*, April 6, 1896.
30. *AET*, April 6, 1896; *ADTE*, April 6, 1896; *TSB*, April 11, 1896.
31. *Indianapolis News*, April 4, 1896.
32. Baseball Reference.
33. *Indianapolis News*, April 7, 1896.
34. *Indianapolis News*, April 7, 1896; *AET*, April 7, 1896; *SL*, April 18, 1896; Baseball Reference.
35. *AET*, April 8, 1896.
36. *ADTE*, April 2, 1896.
37. *ADTE*, April 22, 1896.
38. *DFP*, April 22, 1896.
39. *ADTE*, April 22, 1896.
40. *ADTE*, April 23, 1896.
41. *TSN*, March 28, 1896, April 11, 1896.
42. *TSN*, March 28, 1896, April 11, 1896; *AET*, April 17, 1896.
43. *DFP*, April 12, 1895; Baseball Reference.
44. *DFP*, April 13, 1896; *TSN*, April 18, 1896.
45. *AET*, April 15, 1896.
46. *Ibid.*
47. *AET*, April 18, 1896.
48. *AET*, April 16, 1896; *DFP*, April 16, 1896; *AET*, May 13, 1896; Baseball Reference.
49. *The News*, April 23, 1896.
50. *SL*, April 18, 1896; *Chicago Daily Tribune*, April 20, 1896.
51. Baseball Reference.
52. *St. Paul Daily Globe*, April 28, 1896.
53. *St. Paul Daily Globe*, May 2, 1896.
54. *ADTE*, May 5, 1896.
55. *AET*, May 11, 1896.
56. *Ibid.*
57. *Ibid.*
58. *ADTE*, May 19, 1896.
59. *AET*, May 13, 1896.
60. *Logansport Reporter*, May 26, 1896.
61. *Copper Country Evening News*, May 20, 1896.
62. *Logansport Reporter*, May 26, 1896.
63. *AET*, May 12, 13, 14, 21, 22, 1896.
64. *AET*, May 26, 27, 1896.
65. *Logansport Reporter*, May 26, 1896.
66. *Logansport Reporter*, May 26, 1896; *Logansport Pharos-Tribune*, May 26, 1896.
67. *Logansport Reporter*, May 26, 1896; *AET*, May 27, 1896; *Indianapolis Journal*, May 27, 1896.
68. *Indianapolis Journal*, May 28, 1896.
69. *AET*, May 27, 1896.
70. *AET*, June 1, 1896.

Chapter 14

1. *AET*, June 1, 1896.
2. Riley, 563.
3. *AET*, June 1, 1896.
4. *AET*, June 1, 1896; Riley, 405.
5. *St. Paul Daily Globe*, June 2, 1896.
6. *AET*, June 3, 1896.
7. *Ibid.*
8. *AET*, June 5, 1896.
9. *AET*, June 10, 1896; *Democratic Northwest and Henry County News*, June 11, 1896.
10. *AET*, June 11, 1896.
11. *AET*, June 10, 1896.
12. *Ibid.*
13. *AET*, June 11, 1896.
14. *DFP*, June 11, 1896.
15. *AET*, June 11, 1896.
16. *AET*, June 12, 1896.
17. *ADTE*, June 12, 1896.
18. *AET*, June 13, 1896.
19. *DFP*, June 14, 1896.
20. *ADTE*, June 15, 16, 1895; *AET*, June 16, 1895.
21. *AET*, June 17, 1896; *ADTE*, June 16, 17, 1896.
22. *ADTE*, June 19, 1806; *AET*, June 19, 20, 1896.
23. *AET*, June 25, 26, 1896.
24. *AET*, June 22, 1896; Federal Census 1880, Frank Waters WWI Draft Registration; Frank Waters death certificate.
25. *AET*, June 27, 1896.
26. *AET*, June 25, 1896.
27. *ADTE*, June 29, 1896.
28. *DFP*, June 28, 1896.
29. *Daily Republican*, June 25, 1896.
30. *Daily Republican*, June 29, 1896.
31. *Daily Republican*, June 30, 1896; *AET*, June 30, 1896; *ADTE*, June 30, 1896.
32. *AET*, June 30, 1896.
33. *ADTE*, June 30, July 1, 1896.
34. *AET*, July 2, 1896; *ADTE*, July 2, 1896.
35. *ADTE*, July 1, 1896.
36. *ADTE*, July 2, 1896.
37. *AET*, July 2, 1896.
38. *AET*, July 2, 1896; *ADTE*, July 2, 1896.
39. *ADTE*, July 2, 1896.
40. *ADTE*, July 2, 1896.
41. *AET*, July 3, 1896; *ADTE*, July 3, 1896.
42. *ADTE*, July 3, 1896.
43. *Ibid.*
44. *AET*, June 19, 1896.

Chapter 15

1. *Ourdocuments.gov* on Plessy v. Ferguson.
2. *Ourdocuments.gov* on Plessy v. Ferguson; (New Orleans) *Times-Picayune*, April 12, 1896.
3. *Ourdocuments.gov* on Plessy v. Ferguson.
4. *Ibid.*
5. *Biography.com* on Henry Brown; *Britannica.com* on Plessy v. Ferguson, Henry Brown.
6. *Ourdocuments.com* on Plessy v. Ferguson.
7. *Ibid.*
8. *DFP*. May 19, 1896.
9. *Chicago Tribune*, May 19, 1896.
10. *Inter Ocean*, May 19, 1896.
11. *Wall Street Journal*, May 18, 1896.
12. *The Boston Post*, May 19, 1896.
13. *Hopkinsville Kentuckian*, May 26, 1896.
14. *The Roanoke Times*, May 19, 1896.
15. *New Orleans Times-Picayune*, April 12, 1896.
16. *Louisiana Democrat*, May 27, 1896.
17. *New Orleans Times-Picayune*, May 19, 1896.
18. *Richmond Planet*, May 23, 1896; Library of Congress.
19. *AET*, May 18–25, 1896; *ADTE*, May 18–25, 1896.
20. *ADTE*, July 3, 1896.
21. *DFP*, July 4, 1896.
22. Baseball Reference.
23. *DFP*, July 6, 1896; *AET*, July 6, 1896.
24. *ADTE*, July 6, 1896.
25. *DFP*, July 11, 1896; *AET*, July 11, 1896.
26. *ADTE*, July 10, 11, 1896.
27. *ADTE*, July 13, 1896; *AET*, July 13, 1896.
28. *ADTE*, July 14, 15, 1896.
29. *AET*, July 14, 1896.
30. *AET*, July 14, 1896.
31. *ADTE*, July 16, 1896; *AET*, July 16, 1896.
32. *AET*, July 17, 1896.
33. *Ibid.*; Baseball Reference.
34. *AET*, July 20, 1896.
35. *AET*, July 17, 1896.
36. *Marysville Journal-Tribune*, July 23, 1896.
37. *AET*, July 17, 1896.
38. *AET*, July 18, 1896.
39. *Ibid.*
40. *AET*, July 20, 1896.

Chapter 16

1. Romig, 155.
2. *DFP*, July 19, 1896; *AET*, July 20, 1896.
3. *AET*, July 28, 1896.
4. *Ibid.*
5. *Ibid.*
6. *TSN*, June 27, 1896; SABR Bio on Charlie Ferguson by Mitch Lutzke.
7. *AET*, July 28, 30, 1896.
8. George B. Caldwell, *1893 Atlas of Lenawee County Plat Book* (George B. Caldwell and Company, 1893).
9. *ADTE*, July 31, 1896; *AET*, July 31, 1896.
10. *AET*, July 31, 1896.
11. *ADTE*, July 31, 1896.
12. *ADTE*, July 31, 1896; *AET*, July 31, 1896.
13. *ADTE*, July 31, 1896.
14. *AET*, July 31, 1896.
15. *Brittanic.com*; *Medical-dictionary.com*; *TheFreeDictionary.com*.
16. *Daily Republican*, July 31, 1896.
17. *AET*, Aug. 1, 1896.
18. *ADTE*, Aug. 1, 1896; *AET*, Aug. 1, 1896.
19. *AET*, Aug. 3, 1896; *ADTE*, Aug. 3, 1896.
20. *AET*, Aug. 1, 1896.
21. *ADTE*, Aug. 4, 1896.
22. *ADTE*, Aug. 5, 1896; *AET*, Aug. 7, 1896.
23. Maude Taylor death certificate.
24. *ADTE*, Aug. 18, 19, 1896; *AET*, Aug. 19, 1896.
25. *ADTE*, Aug. 19, 1896; *DFP*, Aug. 19, 1896.
26. *ADTE*, Aug. 19, 1896.
27. *AET*, Aug. 20, 1896.
28. *ADTE*, Aug. 19, 1896.
29. *AET*. Aug. 21, 1896.
30. *ADTE*, Aug. 21, 1896.
31. *AET*, Aug. 21, 1896.
32. *AET*, Aug. 21, 1896; *ADTE*, July 29, 1896.
33. *AET*, Aug. 22, 1896.
34. *AET*, Aug. 26, 1896.
35. *The True Northerner*, Aug. 26, 1896.
36. *Williamston Enterprise*, Aug. 26, 1896.
37. *AET*, Aug. 26, 1896.
38. *AET*, Aug. 29, 1896.
39. *AET*, Aug. 29, 1896; *ADTE*, Aug. 29, 1896; *Saginaw Courier Herald*, Aug. 29, 1896.
40. *AET*, Aug. 29, 1896; *ADTE*, Aug. 29, 1896.
41. *Saginaw Courier Herald*, Aug. 29, 1896.
42. *Saginaw Courier Herald*, Aug. 30, 1896.
43. *Ibid.*
44. *Saginaw Courier Herald*, Sept. 1, 1896.
45. *Ibid.*
46. *Ibid.*

Chapter 17

1. *DFP*, Sept. 1, 1896.
2. *The True Northerner*, Sept. 2, 1896.
3. Williamston Enterprise, Aug. 26, 1896.
4. Williamston Enterprise, Sept. 2, 1896; Leon Webb Diary, Sept. 1, 1896.
5. *DFP*, Sept. 3, 1896.
6. *DFP*, Sept. 5, 1896.
7. *The Yale Expositor*, Sept. 4, 1896.
8. *DFP*, Sept. 7, 1896.
9. *DFP*, Sept. 8, 1896.
10. *Baseball-Alamanac.com*; *HistoricDetroit.com*.
11. *ADTE*, Aug. 31, 1896.
12. *DFP*, Sept. 9, 1896.
13. *AET*, Sept. 9, 1896.
14. *AET*, Sept. 11, 1896.
15. *TSN*, Sept. 19, 1896.
16. *AET*, Sept. 12, 1896.
17. *New York Sun*, Sept. 14, 1896.
18. Michael Lomax, *Black Baseball Entrepreneurs, 1860–1901*, (Syracuse, NY: Syracuse University Press, 2003), 145–46.
19. *TSN*, Oct. 3, 1896.
20. Lomax, 148.
21. *TSN*, Oct. 3, 1896.
22. *TSN*, Sept. 26, 1896.
23. *Ibid.*
24. *Democratic Northwest and Henry County News*, Sept. 10, 1896.
25. *TSN*, Sept. 26, 1896.
26. *AET*, Sept. 14, 1896.
27. *Hudson Gazette*, Sept. 15, 1896; *Hudson Republican*, Sept. 16, 1896.
28. *Hudson Gazette*, Sept. 15, 1896.
29. *Ibid.*
30. *AET*, Sept. 16, 1896.
31. *Hudson Gazette*, Sept. 16, 1896; *TSN*, Sept. 26, 1896.
32. *Hudson Post*, Sept. 18, 1896.
33. *Hudson Republican*, Sept. 16, 1896.
34. *Hudson Gazette*, Sept. 16, 1896.
35. *ADTE*, Sept. 17, 1896.
36. *TSN*, Sept. 26, 1896.
37. *AET*, Sept. 18, 1896.
38. *ADTE*, Sept. 19, 1896; *TSN*, Sept. 26, 1896.
39. *SL*, Nov. 14, 1896.
40. *ADTE*, Sept. 21, 1896.
41. *AET*, Sept. 21, 1896.
42. *ADTE*, Sept. 21, 1896.
43. *The True Northerner*, Sept. 16, 1896.
44. *The True Northerner*, Sept. 23, 1896.
45. *Ibid.*
46. *ADTE*, Sept. 23, 1896.
47. *TSN*, Oct. 3, 1896; *SL*, Oct. 31, Nov. 14, 1896.
48. *AET*, Sept. 18, 1896.
49. *ADTE*, Sept. 23, 1896.
50. *AET*, Sept. 24, 1896.
51. *ADTE*, Sept. 24, 1896.
52. *AET*, Sept. 24, 1896.
53. *ADTE*, Sept. 24, 1896.
54. *AET*, Sept. 26, 1896.
55. *AET*, Sept. 25, 1896.
56. *Ibid.*
57. *Ibid.*
58. *AET*, Sept. 19, 25, 1896.
59. *AET*, Sept. 25, 1896.
60. *AET*, Sept. 19, 1896.
61. *AET*, Sept. 25, 1896.
62. *Ibid.*
63. *ADTE*, Sept. 26, 1896.
64. *AET*, Sept. 26, 1896.
65. *Ibid.*
66. *Ibid.*
67. *SL*, Oct. 31, 1896.
68. *Ibid.*; White 43.
69. *ADTE*, Oct. 2, 1896.
70. *ADTE*, Oct. 3, 1896; *AET*, Oct. 3, 1896.
71. *AET*, Oct. 2, 1896.
72. *ADTE*, Oct. 2, 1896.
73. *ADTE*, Oct. 3, 1896; *AET*, Oct. 3, 1896.
74. *AET*, Oct. 3, 1896.
75. *The Daily Herald*, Oct. 5, 7, 1896.
76. *SL*, Nov. 14, 1896.
77. *The Daily Herald*, Oct. 9, 1896.
78. *AET*, Oct. 10, 1896.
79. *Marysville Journal-Tribune*, Oct. 8, 1896.
80. *SL*, Oct. 31, 1896.
81. *SL*, Nov. 14, 1896.
82. *Ibid.*
83. *SL*, Nov. 21, 1896.

Chapter 18

1. *ADTE*, Dec. 6, 1895.
2. Bonner, 442.
3. *ADTE*, Oct. 26, 1894.
4. *ADTE*, Nov. 4, 1895.
5. *ADTE*, Nov. 6, 1895.
6. *ADTE*, Feb. 10, 1895.
7. *ADTE*, Feb. 14, 1895.
8. *ADTE*, Feb. 13, 1895.
9. *ADTE*, Feb. 13, 17, 1895.
10. *ADTE*, Feb. 21, 27, 1896.
11. *ADTE*, Nov. 13, 1896.
12. *AET*, Oct. 12, 1896.
13. *Ibid.*
14. Lomax, 145, 148, 153.
15. *SL*, Jan. 16, 1897.
16. *SL*, Jan. 30, 1897.
17. *TSN*, Feb. 6, 1897.
18. *ADTE*, March 8, 9, 1897.
19. *AET*, March 8, 1897.
20. *TSN*, March 6, 1897.
21. *AET*, March 8, 1897.
22. *SL*, Jan. 16, 1897.
23. *TSN*, Feb. 6, 1897.
24. *TSN*, March 30, 1897.
25. *TSN*, Feb. 13, 1897.
26. *SL*, April 17, 1897.
27. *AET*, March 16, 1897; *ADTE*, March 16, 1897.
28. *ADTE*, March 19, 1897.
29. *ADTE*, March 16, 1897; *AET*, March 16, 1897.
30. *AET*, April 30, 1897.
31. *SL*, Jan. 30, 1897.
32. *SL*, April 3, 1897.
33. *AET*, April 1, 1897.
34. *AET*, March 29, 1897.
35. *AET*, April 2, 1897.
36. *AET*, April 1, 1897.
37. *AET*, March 29, 1897.
38. *AET*, April 5, 1897.
39. *ADTE*, April 5, 1897.
40. *ADTE*, April 5, 1897; *Chicago Daily Tribune*, April 6, 1897; *AET*, April 7, 1897.
41. *AET*, April 6, 1897.
42. *AET*, April 7, 1897.
43. *Chicago Daily Tribune*, April 7, 1897.
44. *TSN*, April 10, 1897.
45. *Chicago Daily Tribune*, April 7, 1897.
46. *TSN*, April 10, 1897.
47. *AET*, April 8, 1897.

Chapter 19

1. *TSN*, April 10, 1897.
2. *AET*, April 17, 1897.
3. *TSN*, May 1, 1897.
4. *Chicago Daily Tribune*, April 22, 1897.
5. *TSN*, May 1, 1897.
6. *The Des Moines Leader*, April 24, 1897.
7. *Ibid.*
8. *Iowa State Bystander*, April 23, 1897.
9. *Iowa State Bystander*, April 30, 1897.
10. *The Iowa State Register*, April 25, 1897.
11. *The Iowa State Register*, April 27, 1897.
12. *AET*, May 1, 1897.
13. *AET*, April 27, 1897.
14. *AET*, May 1, 1897.
15. *AET*, April 30, 1897.
16. *Chicago Daily Tribune*, April 26, 1897.
17. *Ibid.*
18. *Ibid.*
19. *Chicago Daily Tribune*, May 9, 1897.
20. *AET*, May 10, 1897.
21. *Chicago Daily Tribune*, May 9, 1897.
22. *AET*, May 10, 1897.

23. *Chicago Daily Tribune*, May 10, 1897.
24. *Logansport Reporter*, May 11, 1897.
25. *Ionia Daily Standard*, May 10, 1897.
26. *Ibid.*
27. *Ionia Daily Standard*, May 11, 1897.
28. *Ibid.*
29. *ADTE*, May 12, 1897.
30. *Ionia Daily Standard*, May 12, 1897.
31. *AET*, May 21, 24, 1897.
32. *AET*, May 10, 1897.
33. *ADTE*, May 24, 1897.
34. *ADTE*, May 17, 24, 1897; *AET*, May 22, 1897.
35. *ADTE*, May 17, 1897.
36. ASTE, May 18, 1897.
37. *TSN*, May 29, 1897; Baseball Reference.
38. *DFP*, May 20, 1897.
39. *DFP*, May 23, 1897.
40. *AET*, May 24, 1897.
41. *AET*, May 26, 1897.
42. *AET*, May 29, 1897.
43. *ADTE*, May 24, 1897.
44. *The Defiance Democrat*, May 27, 1897.
45. *Democrat Northwest and Henry County News*, May 27, 1897.
46. *AET*, May 31, 1897.
47. *ADTE*, May 31, 1897.
48. *AET*, May 29, 1897.
49. *The Daily Crescent*, June 1, 1897.
50. *The Daily Crescent*, June 1, 1897; *Daily Republican*, June 1, 1897; *AET*, May 31, 1897; *ADTE*, May 31, 1897.
51. *ADTE*, May 31, 1897; *AET*, May 31, 1897.
52. *The Daily Crescent*, June 1, 1897.
53. *Ibid.*
54. *The Daily Crescent*, June 1, 1897; *Daily Republican*, June 1, 1897.
55. *The Daily Crescent*, June 1, 1897.
56. *AET*, June 3, 1897; Baseball Reference.
57. *AET*, June 9, 1897.
58. *Ibid.*
59. *AET*, June 11, 1897.
60. *AET*, June 9, 1897.

Chapter 20

1. *Chicago Daily Tribune*, June 6, 1897; *AET*, June 8, 1897.
2. *AET*, June 19, 1897.
3. *AET*, June 12, 14, 1897.
4. *AET*, June 17, 1897.
5. *Ibid.*
6. *DFP*, June 22, 1897.

7. *AET*, June 25, 1897.
8. *Inter Ocean*, June 29, 1897.
9. *DFP*, June 28, 1897.
10. *AET*, June 29, 1897.
11. *DFP*, June 30, 1897.
12. *Ionia Daily Standard*, June 24, 1897.
13. *DFP*, June 30, 1897.
14. *ADTE*, June 30, 1897.
15. *Ionia Daily Standard*, July 2, 1897.
16. *DFP*, June 30, 1897.
17. *The Times*, June 13, 1897.
18. *Green Bay Gazette*, June 26, 1897.
19. *AET*, July 14, 1897.
20. *AET*, July 15, 1897.
21. *AET*, July 21, 1897.
22. *AET*, July 27, 1897; *ADTE*, July 28, 1897.
23. *AET*, July 21, 1897.
24. *ADTE*, July 28, 1897.
25. *Ibid.*
26. *ADTE*, Aug. 10, 1897.
27. *Dixon Evening Telegraph*, July 23, 1897.
28. *Ibid.*
29. *Dixon Evening Telegraph*, July 24, 1897.
30. *Green Bay Press Gazette*, Aug. 2, 1897.
31. *Ibid.*
32. *Green Bay Press Gazette*, Aug. 2, 1897; *AET*, Aug. 3, 1897.
33. *AET*, Aug. 6, 1897.
34. *Oshkosh Daily Northwestern*, March 28, 1898.
35. *Oshkosh Daily Northwestern*, Aug. 3, 1897.
36. *Green Bay Press Gazette*, Aug. 9, 1897.
37. *AET*, Aug. 6, 7, 10, 1897.
38. *AET*, Aug. 10, 12, 1897.
39. *AET*, Aug. 13, 1897.
40. *AET*, Aug. 16, 1897.
41. *Ibid.*
42. *Oshkosh Daily Northwestern*, Aug. 17, 1897.
43. *Oshkosh Daily Northwestern*, Aug. 18, 1897.
44. *Manistee Daily News*, Aug. 6, 20, 1897.
45. *Manistee Daily News*, Aug. 8, 1897.
46. *Manistee Daily News*, Aug. 17, 1897.
47. *Manistee Daily News*, Aug. 23, 1897.
48. *Ibid.*
49. *Manistee Daily Advocate*, Aug. 23, 1897; *Manistee Daily News*, Aug. 23, 1897.
50. *Manistee Daily Advocate*, Aug. 20, 1897; *ADTE*, Aug. 21, 1897.
51. *Manistee Daily Advocate*, Aug. 23, 1897.
52. *ADTE*, Aug. 23, 1897.
53. *AET*, Aug. 24, 1897.

54. *Manistee Daily News*, Aug. 23, 1897.
55. *Manistee Daily Advocate*, Aug. 23, 1897.
56. *Ibid.*
57. *Manistee Daily News*, Aug. 23, 1897.
58. Traverse City Record Eagle, Aug. 21, 22, 1897.
59. *Manistee Daily News*, Aug. 23, 1897.
60. *Manistee Daily Advocate*, Aug. 24, 1897; *AET*, Aug. 24, 1897.
61. *Traverse City Record Eagle*, Aug. 25, 1897.
62. *Michigan State 1898 Gazetteer*, Polk, p. 1590.
63. *Traverse City Record Eagle*, Aug. 24, 25, 1897.
64. *ADTE*, Aug. 26, 1897.
65. *Clinton Republican*, Aug. 26, 1897; *St. Johns News*, Aug. 26, 1897.
66. *AET*, Aug. 21, 1897.
67. *AET*, Aug. 30, 1897; *Battle Creek Journal*, Aug. 30, 1897.
68. *Battle Creek Daily Journal*, Aug. 30, 1897.
69. *Battle Creek Daily Journal*, Aug. 28, 1897.
70. *Battle Creek Daily Journal*, Aug. 26, 1897.
71. *ADTE*, Aug. 26, 1897.
72. *AET*, Sept. 1, 1897.

Chapter 21

1. *AET*, Sept. 6, 1896.
2. *Ibid.*
3. *Ibid.*
4. *AET*, Sept. 7, 1897.
5. *Oshkosh Daily Northwestern*, Sept. 13, 1897.
6. *Ibid.*
7. *Ibid.*
8. *Steuben Republican*, Sept. 8, 1897.
9. *AET*, Sept. 14, 1897.
10. *AET*, Sept. 7, 1897.
11. *AET*, Sept. 13, 1897; *ADTE*, Sept. 13, 1897.
12. *AET*, Sept. 8, 1897.
13. *AET*, Sept. 14, 1897.
14. Hudson Street Fair Booklet, Hudson, Michigan, September 1897.
15. *DFP*, Sept. 10, 1897.
16. *AET*, Sept. 11, 1897.
17. *DFP*, Sept. 19, 1897.
18. *Hudson Gazette*, Sept. 14, 1897.
19. Hudson Michigan Historical Museum photo.
20. *Hudson Gazette*, Sept. 14, 1897.
21. *AET*, Sept. 14, 1897.
22. *Hudson Gazette*, Sept. 14, 1897; *AET*, Sept. 14, 1897.
23. *AET*, Sept. 15, 1897.

24. *Hudson Gazette*, Sept. 16, 1897.
25. *AET*, Sept. 16, 1897.
26. *AET*, Sept. 17, 1897.
27. *Hudson Gazette*, Sept. 16, 1897.
28. *Battle Creek Daily Journal*, Sept. 15, 1897.
29. *AET*, Sept. 16, 1897.
30. *Hudson Gazette*, Sept. 17, 1897.
31. *AET*, Sept. 17, 18, 1897.
32. *AET*, Sept. 18, 1897.
33. *AET*, Sept. 15, 1897.
34. *AET*, Sept. 17, 18, 1897.
35. *ADTE*, Sept. 23, 1897.
36. *AET*, Sept. 24, 1897.
37. *Daily Herald*, Sept. 29, 1897; *Steuben Republican*, Oct. 6, 1897.
38. *DFP*, Sept. 25, 1897.
39. *Battle Creek Daily Journal*, Sept. 23, 1897.
40. *Battle Creek Daily Journal*, Sept. 27, 1897.
41. *ADTE*, Sept. 27, 1897.
42. *Battle Creek Daily Journal*, Sept. 27, 1897.
43. *Battle Creek Daily Journal*, Oct. 6, 1897.
44. Michigan Marriage Records, 1867–1952.
45. *Iowa State Reporter*, Aug. 3, 1903, MJ Collection.
46. *Battle Creek Daily Journal*, Oct. 4, 1897.
47. *The True Northerner*, Oct. 6, 1897.
48. *Battle Creek Daily Journal*, Oct. 9, 11, 1897.
49. *AET*, Oct. 16, 1897.
50. SET, Sept. 25, 1897.
51. *TSN*, Oct. 30, 1897.
52. *DFP*, Nov. 1, 1897.

Chapter 22

1. *SL*, Oct. 16, 1897.
2. *TSN*, Nov. 13, 1897.
3. *Ibid*.
4. *Ibid*.
5. *Ibid*.
6. *TSN*, March 5, 1897; *ADTE*, Oct. 4, 1897.
7. *TSN*, Nov. 13, 1898.
8. *TSN*, Oct. 23, 1897.
9. *Ibid*.
10. *DFP*, Feb. 18, 1898.
11. *AET*, March 19, 30, 1898.
12. *AET*, Oct. 16, 1897; April 2, 1898.
13. *TSN*, March 5, 1898.
14. *ADTE*, March 31, 1898.
15. *AET*, April 2, 1898.
16. *Navysource.org*, Feb. 15, 1898.
17. *ADTE*, April 25, 1898.
18. *DFP*, May 5, 1898.
19. *DFP*, May 14, 18, 1898.

20. *AET*, April 20, May 10, May 24, 1898.
21. *ADTE*, April 24, 1894.
22. *Cgocouncil.org*
23. *DFP*, Jan. 17, 1898.
24. *ADTE*, April 14, 22, 1898; *SL*, Jan. 15, March 5, 26, April 2, 30, 1898; *TSN* Jan. 29, April 23, 1898.
25. *AET*, April 11, 1898.
26. *ADTE*, April 14, 1898.
27. *ADTE*, April 14, 1898; *TSN*, April 16, 1898.
28. *AET*, April 16, 1898; Baseball Reference.
29. *AET*, April 18, 1898.
30. *DFP*, April 18, 1898; *SL*, April 30, 1898.
31. *DFP*, April 18, 1898; *AET*, April 18, 1898; Baseball Reference.
32. *SL*, April 30, 1898.
33. *ADTE*, April 22, 1898.
34. *Cincinnati Enquirer*, April 22, 1898.
35. *AET*, April 22, 1898.
36. *AET*, April 25, 1898.
37. *AET*, April 29, May 2, 1898; *DFP*, May 1, 1898.
38. *AET*, May 2, 1898.
39. *ADTE*, April 26, 1898.
40. *DFP*, May 26, 1898.
41. *Pittsburgh Daily Post*, May 1898; *The Democratic Standard*, May 6, 1898; *AET*, May 11, 1898; *Massillon Item*, May 11, 12, 1898.
42. *Massillon Item*, May 12, 1898.
43. *Ibid*.
44. *AET*, May 6, 7, 1898.
45. *AET*, May 20, 1898.
46. *AET*, May 7, 1898.
47. *AET*, May 24, 28, 1898.
48. *AET*, May 10, 1898.
49. *AET*, May 24, 1898.
50. *AET*, May 20, 1898.
51. *DFP*, May 12, 1898; *Detroit historical.org* on DAC.
52. *DFP*, May 14, 1898.
53. *Ibid*.
54. *DFP*, May 15, 1898.
55. *AET*, May 17, 1898.
56. *AET*, May 26, 1898.
57. *DFP*, May 26, 1898; Baseball Reference.

Chapter 23

1. *DFP*, May 26, 1898.
2. *DFP*, May 14, 15, 1898.
3. *DRP*, May 25, 1898.
4. *ADTE*, June 10, 1898.
5. *DFP*, June 3, 1898.
6. *SABR Bio*, Rube Waddell by Dan O'Brien.
7. *DFP*, June 3, 1898.
8. *AET*, June 4, 1898.
9. *DFP*, June 5, 1898.
10. *DFP*, June 6, 1898.

11. *Daily News-Democrat*, June 8, 11, 1898.
12. *Mattoon Gazette*, June 17, 1898.
13. *The Daily Review*, June 18, 1898.
14. *ADTE*, June 22, 1898; *AET*, June 23, 1898.
15. *ADTE*, July 5, 1898; *AET*, July 5, 1898.
16. *ADTE*, July 11, 1898.
17. *AET*, June 29, 1898.
18. *ADTE*, July 19, Aug. 5, 1898.
19. *ADTE*, July 11, 1898; *The KOTM/dubsarhouse.com*.
20. *ADTE*, Aug. 9, 1898.
21. *ADT*, Aug. 8, 1898. (*The Adrian Evening Telegram* became the *Adrian Daily Telegram* on Aug. 8, 1898).
22. *ADTE*, July 19, Aug. 12, 1898.
23. *ADTE*, July 11, 1898.
24. *ADTE*, Aug. 10, 1898.
25. *Ibid*.
26. *ADT*, Aug. 8, 1898.
27. *DFP*, July 2, 1898.
28. *DFP*, July 4, 1898.
29. *Oshkosh Daily Northwestern*, July 14, 1898.
30. *Oshkosh Daily Northwestern*, July 15, 1898.
31. *Ibid*.
32. *Ibid*.
33. *Oshkosh Daily Northwestern*, July 16, 1898.
34. *Ibid*.
35. *Ibid*.
36. *Oshkosh Daily Northwestern*, July 18, 1898.
37. *Ibid*.
38. Green Bay Press Gazette, July 21, 1898.
39. *Ibid*.
40. *Green Bay Press Gazette*, July 22, 1898.
41. *Oshkosh Daily Northwestern*, July 22, 1898.
42. *ADT*, Aug. 8, 1898; *DFP*, Aug. 9, 1898.
43. *ADTE*, July 27, 1898.
44. *AET*, Aug. 6, 1898.
45. *ADT*, Aug. 12, 1898.
46. *ADT*, Aug. 13, 1898.
47. *ADT*, Aug. 17, 1898.
48. *DFP*, Aug. 17, 1898.
49. *ADT*, Aug. 17, 1898.
50. *ADT*, Aug. 18, 1898.
51. Baseball Reference.
52. *ADT*, Aug. 18, 1898.
53. *Ibid*.
54. *Ibid*.
55. *DFP*, Aug. 19, 1898.
56. *ADTE*, Aug. 19, 1898.
57. *ADT*, Aug. 18, 1898; *ADTE*, Aug. 19, 1898.
58. *ADTE*, Aug. 19, 1898.
59. *ADT*, Aug. 20, 1898.

Chapter 24

1. *Chicago Daily Tribune*, Aug. 20, 1898.
2. *The Baltimore Sun*, Sept. 10, 1898.
3. *Cincinnati Enquirer*, Oct. 16, 1898.
4. *ADTE*, Oct. 29, 1898.
5. *ADTE*, Aug. 29, 1897.
6. *ADTE*, Oct. 21, 1897.
7. *ADTE*, Dec. 3, 9, 1897.
8. *ADTE*, Jan. 10, Feb. 14, 1898.
9. *ADT*, Sept. 8, 1898.
10. *ADT*, Sept. 2, 1898.
11. *DFP*, Aug. 20, 1898.
12. *Chicago Daily Tribune*, Sep. 12, 1898.
13. *ADT*, Sept. 20, 1898.
14. *DFP*, Sept. 23, 1898.
15. *DFP*, Sept. 29, 1898; *Owosso Times*, Sept. 20, 1898.
16. *Chicago Daily Tribune*, Oct. 2, 1898.
17. *TSN*, Nov. 12, 1898.
18. *TSN*, Dec. 31, 1898.
19. *SL*, Feb. 4, 1899.
20. *SL*, Jan. 19, Feb. 4, 1899.
21. *SL*, Feb. 4, 1899.
22. *SL*, March 25, 1899, April 11, 1899.
23. *ADT*, March 4, 1899.
24. *ADTE*, March 21, 1899.
25. The *Daily Republican*, Feb. 16, 1899.
26. *DFP*, Feb. 16, 1898.
27. *ADT*, March 7, 1899.
28. *Ibid.*
29. *Ibid.*
30. *TSN*, Feb. 4, 1899.
31. *ADT*, March 6, 1899.
32. *Ibid.*
33. Baseball Reference.
34. *Green Bay Gazette*, March 6, 1899.
35. *Fort Wayne Journal Gazette*, March 14, 1899; *Steuben Republican*, May 15, 1899.
36. *SL*, March 4, 1899.
37. *ADTE*, March 15, 1899.
38. *ADT*, March 18, 1899.
39. *ADT*, April 1, 1899.
40. *ADT*, March 27, 1899.
41. *ADTE*, March 15, 1899.
42. *Ibid.*
43. *Fort Wayne News*, April 11, 1899.
44. *TSN*, April 15, 1899.
45. *DFP*, May 12, 1899.
46. *ADT*, May 20, 1899.
47. *ADT*, May 18, 1899.
48. *ADT*, April 20, 1899.
49. *Ibid.*
50. *DFP*, Sept. 12, 1899.
51. *The Lima News*, May 23, 1899.
52. *Cincinnati Enquirer*, May 22, 1899.
53. *The Lima News*, May 24, 1899.
54. *Oshkosh Daily Northwestern*, July 15, 1898; *ADTE*, Sept. 21, 1894.

Bibliography

Books

Bianculli, Anthony. *Trains and Technology: The American Railroad in the 19th Century.* vol. 2. Newark, NJ: University of Delaware Press, 2002.

Bonner, Richard Illenden. *Memoirs of Lenawee County, Michigan, from the earliest historical times down to the present, including a genealogical and biographical record of representative families in Lenawee County.* vol. I and II, Madison, WI: Western Historical Association, 1909.

Brown, Charles Exera. *Brown's City Directory of Adrian, Michigan.* Adrian, MI: Adrian Times and Expositor Printing Office, 1870.

Brunson, James. *The Early Image of Black Baseball.* Jefferson, NC: McFarland, 2009.

Cadell, George B. *Atlas of Lenawee County Plat Book. 1893.* MI: George B. Cadwell & Co., 1893.

Chapin, Henry H. *Adrian City Directory, 1885–1886.* Adrian, MI: Henry H. Chapin, 1885.

Chapman Brothers. *Portrait and Biographical Album of Lenawee County, Michigan.* Chicago, IL: Chapman Brothers Books, 1888.

Corson, Rosel, ed. *Early Adrian.* Adrian, MI: American Association of University Women, 1965.

Dixon, Phil, and Patrick J. Hannigan. *The Negro Baseball Leagues, A Photographic History.* Mattituck, New York: Ameron Ltd., 1992.

DuBois, W.E.B. *The Souls of Black Folk.* New York: Bantam Classic, 1989.

Gay, Hoig L. *A Capsule History of Adrian, Michigan and the State of Michigan, Adrian Area Chamber of Commerce.* Adrian, MI: Swenk-Tuttle Press, 1964.

Haviland, Laura S. and S. B. Shaw. *A Woman's Life Work.* 5th ed. Grand Rapids, MI: Shaw, 1881.

Heaphy, Leslie. "The Page Fence Giants, Nineteenth Century Champions." *Black Ball 4/2,* Fall 2011.

Holway, John. *The Complete Book of Baseball's Negro Leagues: The Other Half of Baseball History.* Fern Park, FL: Hastings House Publisher, 2001.

Hudson Free Street Fair Booklet 1897. MI: Business Men of Hudson, Michigan, 1897.

Knapp, John I., and R. I. Bonner. *Illustrated History and Biographical Record of Lenawee County, Michigan.* Adrian, MI: The Times Printing Company, 1903.

Laing, Jeffrey Michael, and Bud Fowler. *Baseball's First Black Professional.* Jefferson, NC: McFarland, 2013.

Lindquist, Charles. *Adrian: The City That Worked, A History of Adrian, Michigan, 1825–2000.* Adrian, MI: Lenawee County Historical Society, 2004.

Lomax, Michael. *Black Baseball Entrepreneurs, 1860–1901.* New York: Syracuse University Press, 2003.

Morris, Peter. *A Game of Inches.* Chicago, IL: Ivan R. Dee Publishers, 2006.

Morris, Peter. *Baseball Fever, Early Baseball in Michigan.* Ann Arbor, MI: University of Michigan Press, 2006.

Morris, Peter. *Catcher, How the Man Behind the Plate Became an American Folk Hero.* Chicago, IL: Ivan R. Dee, 2009.

Mudge, Charles E. *Reproduction of Mudge's Directory of Lansing City, with an Introduction by David R. Caterino and a Directory of Business and Occupations, Street Directory and Index of Miscellaneous Information.* Lansing, MI: Historical Society of Greater Lansing, 1991.

Peterson, Robert. *Only the Ball Was White.* New York: Oxford University Press, 1992.

Peterson, Todd. *Early Black Baseball in Minnesota.* Jefferson, NC: McFarland, 2010.

Polk, R. L. *Michigan State Gazetteer and Business Directory, 1897.* Detroit, MI: R.L. Polk and Company, 1897.

Richardi, Jan. *Fencing the World, Adrian's Page in History.* Adrian, MI: Lenawee County Historical Society, 1999.

Riley, James A. *The Biographical Encyclopedia of the Negro Baseball League.* New York: Carroll and Graf, 2002.

Romig, Walter. *Michigan Place Names.* Detroit, MI: Wayne State University Press, 1986.

Sanborn Fire Insurance Maps, 1888, 1893, 1899. New York: Sanborn Map Company.

Snyder, H. M. *Business and Professional Directory of Detroit and Surrounding Towns*. Detroit, MI: H. M. Snyder, 1899.

Swanson, Ryan. *When Baseball Went White*. Lincoln, Nebraska: University of Nebraska Press, 2014.

University of Michigan. *The Michigan Alumnus*. vol. 8. Ann Arbor, MI, 1902.

Webb, Leon. *1896 personal diary of Leon Webb (unpublished)*. Williamston, MI: Possession of the Williamston Depot Museum.

White, Sol. *Sol White's History of Colored Base Ball, with other Documents on the Early Black Game, 1886–1936, compiled by Jerry Malloy*. Lincoln, NE: Nebraska University Press, 1995.

White, Sol. *Sol White's Official Base Ball Guide by Gary Ashwill*. South Orange, NJ: Summer Game Books, 2014.

Whitney, W.A. *History and Biographical Record of Lenawee County, Michigan*. Adrian, MI: W.A. Whitney, W. Stearns & Co., 1879–80.

Wilkerson, Isabel. *The Warmth of Other Suns, The Epic Story of America's Great Migration*. New York: Vintage Books, 2010.

Wilson, D. Barrett, and W. Wendell Gaskin, W. Wendell. *African American Journal of Adrian*. Adrian, MI, 1895 (portions on-line at www.migenweb.net/Lenawee; Mary Teeter, 2005–2017).

Magazines

Powers, Thomas E. "Adrian and Her Page Fence Giants." *Chronicle, Historical Society of Michigan, Lansing, Michigan*, Spring 1983.

Sporting Life, Philadelphia, Pennsylvania

The Sporting News, St. Louis, Missouri

Newspapers (published in Michigan, unless otherwise noted)

Adrian Daily Times and Expositor

Adrian Evening Telegram/Adrian Daily Telegram

Adrian Telegram

Adrian Weekly Messenger

Adrian Weekly Press

Adrian Weekly Times and Expositor

Allegan Journal

Alma Record

The Baltimore Sun (Maryland)

Battle Creek Daily Journal

The Boston Post (Massachusetts)

Charlevoix Sentinel

Chicago Daily Tribune (Illinois)

Chicago Tribune (Illinois)

Cincinnati Enquirer (Ohio)

Cincinnati Gazette (Ohio)

Clinton Republican

The Coiled Spring Hustler (Page Fence Factory newspaper)

Copper Country Evening News

The Daily Crescent (Defiance, Ohio)

The Daily Herald (Delphos, Ohio)

The Daily News Democrat (Huntingdon, Penn)

Daily Northwestern (Oshkosh, Wisconsin)

The Daily Review (Decatur, Illinois)

The Daily Republican (Monongahela, Penn)

Des Moines Leader (Iowa)

Defiance Daily Republican (Ohio)

The Defiance Democrat (Ohio)

Democrat Northwest and Henry County News (Napoleon, Ohio)

The Democrat Standard (Coshocton, Ohio)

Detroit Free Press

Dixon Evening Telegraph (Illinois)

Findlay Daily Courier (Ohio)

The Findlay Union (Ohio)

The Findlay Weekly Jeffersonian (Ohio)

The Fort Wayne Journal Gazette (Indiana)

Fort Wayne News (Indiana)

Fowlerville Review

Grand Rapids Democrat

Grand Rapids Evening Press

Gratiot County Herald

Gratiot Journal

Green Bay Press Gazette (Wisconsin)

Hancock Courier (Ohio)

Hastings Banner

Homer Index

Hudson Post

Hudson Gazette

Hudson Republican

Hopkinsville Kentuckian (Kentucky)

Indianapolis Journal (Indiana)

Indianapolis News (Indiana)

Ingham County News

Inter Ocean (Chicago, Illinois)

The Ionia Daily Standard

Iowa State Bystander (Des Moines)

The Iowa State Register (Des Moines)

Kalamazoo Daily Telegraph

Lansing State Republican

The Lima News (Ohio)

Logansport Pharos-Tribune (Indiana)

Logansport Reporter (Indiana)

The Louisiana Democrat (Alexandria, Louisiana)

Manistee Daily Advocate

Manistee Daily News
Marion Chronicle (Indiana)
Mattoon Gazette (Illinois)
The Marysville Journal-Tribune (Ohio)
Massillon Item (Ohio)
The Morning Republican (Findlay, Ohio)
Monroe Democrat
Muskegon Morning News
Nashville News
The News (Frederick, Maryland)
The New York Times (New York)
Owosso Evening Argus
Owosso Times
Pittsburgh Daily Post (Pennsylvania)
Pontiac Daily Gazette

Reed City Weekly Clarion
Richmond Planet (Virginia)
Roanoke Times (Virginia)
Rock Island Argus (Illinois)
Saginaw Courier Herald
St. Johns News
St. Paul Daily Globe (Minnesota)
The Steuben Republican (Indiana)
The Times (Philadelphia)
The Times-Picayune (New Orleans)
Traverse City Record Eagle
The True Northerner (Paw Paw, Michigan)
The Wall Street Journal (New York)
Williamston Enterprise
The Yale Expositor

Collections

Adrian Public Library, Adrian, Michigan; Shirley Ennis
Hudson Museum, Hudson, Michigan; Mike Roys
Mike Johnson's miscellaneous newspaper clippings and game scores about the Page Fence Giants. (Private collection)
Lenawee County Historical Museum; Jan Richardi
National Baseball Hall of Fame, Player Files, Bud Fowler and Grant Johnson.

Correspondence

Noelle Keller, M.Ed., M.L.S., Shipman Library, Adrian, Michigan, January 4, 2017.

Websites

Ancestry.com
Baseball almanac.com
Baseball-reference.com
Biography.com
Britannica.com
Cgocouncil.org (Council of Georgist Organizations)
Daughters of the American Revolution applications via Ancestry.com
Detroithistorical.org (Detroit Athletic Club by Brett Maynard, 2015)
Federal United States Census Returns
Find-A-Grave.com
TheFreedictionary.com
Google Earth
HistoricDetroit.org by Dan Austin.
Knights of the Maccabees/dubsarhouse.com
Lenawee.migeneb.net census returns transcribed by Janice McCaughan
Lenawee.migenweb.net Afro-American Directory 1895, scanned by Mary Teeter
Library of Congress
Medical-dictionary.com
Michigan Marriage Records, 1867–1952, Michigan Dept. of Community Health via Ancestry.com
National Baseball Hall of Fame
Navysource.org
Newspapers.com
Ourdocuments.gov
SABR (Society of American Baseball Research); Player Biographies: Cap Anson by John R. Husman; Charlie Ferguson by Mitch Lutzke; Rube Waddell by Dan O'Brien.
SABR Game Stories; 1883 Fleetwood Walker by David Fleitz.
Seamheads.com
University of Michigan Bentley Historical Library

Index

Numbers in **_bold italics_** indicate pages with illustrations